CU09646230

N.F.S. Grundtvig

For all my Danish friends
and especially for J.K.H. and N.K.R.

vor død til trods
opliv du os

A.M. Allchin

N.F.S. GRUNDTVIG

An Introduction to his Life and Work

with an Afterword by Nicholas Lossky

DARTON, LONGMAN AND TODD

First published in Great Britain in 1997 by
Darton, Longman and Todd Ltd
1 Spencer Court
140-142 Wandsworth High Street
London SW18 4JJ

© 1997 Aarhus University Press

This edition published in 1997 by arrangement with
Aarhus University Press
Building 170, University of Aarhus, DK-8000 Aarhus C, Denmark

ISBN 0-232-52260-X

A catalogue record for this book is available
from the British Library

Word-processed by Elisabeth Glenthøj
and Flemming Hedegaard Rasmussen
Printed in England by the Alden Press, Oxford

Preface

This book, as its subtitle suggests, is intended to be an introduction to Grundtvig's life and work; its function is a preliminary one, opening a door onto a field which has hitherto been inaccessible to English-speaking readers who have no knowledge of the Danish language and of the tradition which that language conveys. The book is full, some will think over-full, of quotations from Grundtvig and his contemporaries. Wherever possible I have wanted to let the Danish sources speak for themselves. Since very little of what Grundtvig wrote has been hitherto put into English, the translations which the book contains are almost all new.

Although the book's primary purpose was, from the beginning, to present Grundtvig to the English-speaking world, I have become aware as time has gone by that such an enterprise may also be of interest to Danish readers. Whatever the imperfections of the work, it is, so far as I know, the first time that someone neither Danish nor Scandinavian has attempted to make an extended presentation of Grundtvig's life and work. Necessarily things are seen in a different perspective when they are seen from further away. It may be useful for those whose acquaintance with Grundtvig is much closer, to catch a glimpse of his figure as seen from a greater distance.

The book is divided into three parts. The first gives a series of glimpses into Grundtvig's long and varied life. I have not aimed at completeness or balance here. Rather I have concentrated on a few crucial moments of development and discovery, allowing them to appear in some detail, particularly when they seem to throw light on Grundtvig's growth towards inner unity and greater confidence. One of the special difficulties in trying to give an account of Grundtvig's life lies in the fact that there has been no full scale biography in Danish since the last of Frederik Rønning's four volumes was published in 1913. Fascinating though his work is, no-one could say that it gives either a complete or fully balanced picture of its subject.

The second part of the book looks at a number of basic themes in Grundtvig's writing. Here it becomes clear that the focal point of the present work is to be found in Grundtvig's presentation of the Christian faith. Grundtvig's writing is so many-sided that it could reasonably be presented in a great variety of ways. Here the focus is intentionally, though not exclusively, theological. Starting from the fact of the historic life of the one Church of Christ, it comes at its centre to Grundtvig's understanding of God as trinity of persons and of humankind and the world as made in God's image. From that central point it broadens out to enquire how that understanding of God has consequences for the whole of human life, social as well as personal.

The third and longest part of the book goes on to present the doctrines of the Christian faith as we find them articulated by Grundtvig in his sermons and hymns for the Christian year. Here above all I have wanted Grundtvig's voice to be heard. His exposition of the Christian faith, his theology, is at once old yet new, necessarily western in its form, yet constantly coloured by insights characteristic of the Christian East. This is a theology of praise and proclamation, a doxological and kerygmatic presentation of the faith, with ecumenical implications which need to be explored.

An earlier and slighter version of this book was being planned in 1960. I had the conviction that Grundtvig needed to be presented to the English-speaking world and I hoped to help on the process. The book then planned was never written, though some of the work done all those years ago has found its way into these pages. From amongst my Danish friends who encouraged that first attempt at a Grundtvig book two must be mentioned in particular; Poul Exner, at that time pastor on the island of Anholt, and the late Niels Krogh Rasmussen, then a student at Blackfriars in Oxford.

For a great variety of reasons that first project came to nothing, though the hope of writing something about Grundtvig was never altogether abandoned. My hopes were renewed by the publication, in 1977, of a notable book of essays on Grundtvig's hymns and sermons edited by Professor Christian Thodberg. It was a book which rekindled my interest and enthusiasm. Invitations to take part in the celebration of the bi-centenary of Grundtvig's birth in 1983 provided further stimulus to a new study. Then, in 1989, the Centre for Grundtvig Studies in the University of Aarhus was founded and I have been closely involved with its work ever since.

Without the support and encouragement of the three founders of that Centre, Christian Thodberg, Anders Pontoppidan Thyssen and Jens Holger Schjørring, it is certain that this book could not have been written. To Jens Holger Schjørring I owe more than I can say for his unfailing help. It goes without saying that the views presented in this book are my own and do not implicate the Centre as such. Amongst other friends in the University of Aarhus I think in particular of Professor Jakob Balling and of the two se-cretaries of the Centre, first Susanne Gregersen and then Kim Arne Pedersen. I am specially indebted to Elisabeth Albinus Glenthøj not only for her detailed collaboration in correcting my translations, but also for much patient and skilful work in preparing the text for publication. Amongst friends in England two must be specially mentioned, S.A.J. Bradley of the University of York and Kenneth Stevenson, Bishop of Portsmouth, who not only shares my enthusiasm for Grundtvig but also unites in himself the peoples of Denmark and England. I must also thank Jenny Hollis for all her indefatigable work with the computer.

Bringing to a conclusion a work which has been too long in the making,

I am vividly aware of two things. The first is my indebtedness to a host of friends in Denmark who have helped me to come to some understanding of their country. To know Grundtvig it is necessary to know Denmark and therefore all one's friends are of help towards that end; and yet, one will not get far in a study of Denmark without making the acquaintance of Grundtvig. The two in the end are inseparable.

Secondly, I am aware of the many inadequacies which this book contains. If, as I believe, Grundtvig is a man who deserves to be known across the world, then I can only hope that this work will indeed act as an introduction to him, opening a door through which others will find their way into the study of this man, who still has important things to say to us about the future of the human enterprise.

April 1997   *Arthur Macdonald Allchin*

A Note on Terminology

In the Scandinavian languages, Danish, Norwegian and Swedish, the term Scandinavia, strictly speaking, refers to those three countries alone. Grundtvig regularly uses the term *Norden*, which I have translated *the North*. This term includes Finland to the east and Iceland to the west. In Grundtvig's use of it, it can also sometimes include England.

Contents

Contents

Frequently Quoted Works

Den Danske Salmebog (Danish Hymnal Book).

Grundtvigs Erindringer og Erindringer om Grundtvig. Edited by Steen Johansen and Henning Høirup, Copenhagen 1948.

Grundtvig-Studier. Published in Copenhagen by The Grundtvig Society of 8th September 1947. The annual publication of the Grundtvig Society from 1948 onwards.

Heritage and Prophecy: 'Grundtvig and the English-speaking World'. Edited by A.M. Allchin, D. Jasper, J.H. Schjørring, and K. Stevenson, Aarhus 1993.

N.F.S. Grundtvigs *Poetiske Skrifter*. Vols. I-VII edited by Svend Grundtvig, Copenhagen 1880-89; vols. VIII-IX edited by Georg Christensen, Copenhagen 1929-30.

N.F.S. *Grundtvigs Sang-Værk* til den danske kirke, vols. I-V, reprinted Copenhagen 1982-84. (Grundtvig's Song Work).

N.F.S. Grundtvig, Tradition and Renewal: 'Grundtvig's Vision of Man and People, Education and the Church, in Relation to World Issues Today'. Translated by Edward Broadbridge. Edited by Christian Thodberg and Anders Pontoppidan Thyssen, Copenhagen 1983.

N.F.S. Grundtvig, *Værker i Udvalg*, vols. I-X. Edited by Georg Christensen and Hal Koch, Copenhagen 1940-49.

N.F.S. Grundtvig, *Udvalgte Skrifter*, vols. I-X. Edited by Holger Begtrup, Copenhagen 1904-9.

Quotations from Grundtvig's sermons are taken from the following editions:

N.F.S. *Grundtvigs Præstø Prædikener*, 1821-22, vols. 1-2. Edited by Christian Thodberg, Copenhagen 1988.

N.F.S. *Grundtvigs Prædikener*, 1822-26 and 1832-39, vols. 1-12. Edited by Christian Thodberg, Copenhagen 1983-86.

N.F.S. *Grundtvigs Christelige Prædikener eller Søndags-Bog*, vols. 1-3, Copenhagen 1827-30. (Christian sermons or Sunday Book).

N.F.S. *Grundtvigs Vartovs-Prædikener*, 1839-60. Selected sermons edited by Holger Begtrup, Copenhagen 1924.

N.F.S. *Grundtvigs Kors-Prædikener*, 1839-60. Selected sermons edited by N. Clausen-Bagge, Copenhagen 1925.

N.F.S. *Grundtvigs Sidste Prædikener*, 1861-72, vols. 1-2. Selected sermons edited by C.J. Brandt, Copenhagen 1880. (Last sermons).

Grundtvig and Denmark

I

How are we to begin to introduce Grundtvig to a world in which his name is not even known? An old tourist brochure picked up in Copenhagen airport some forty years ago might seem an unlikely place to begin, but at least it gives us a start. It is a brochure which is intended to introduce the first-time visitor to Denmark to some aspects of Danish life. It insists much on the quality of Danish agricultural produce and its importance for the Danish export trade, at that time particularly notable. It includes a picture of the 'streamlined Danish bacon pig'. But at the outset of its account of modern Denmark, it declares directly

Grundtvig, the clergyman and poet has meant more to Danish trade than has Rockefeller to that of the United States. Rockefeller bored for oil. Grundtvig bored in the depths of the people and discovered unsuspected sources of power. From the spiritual and national awakening created by him a good hundred years ago modern Denmark arose.

This spiritual and national awakening, we are told, was nothing theoretical or abstract. It had immediate repercussions in everyday life,

and a particularly effective result of the chain reaction he engendered was the co-operative movement. At the end of the century cooperative dairies shot up all over the country, and later slaughter houses and other activities also.

My immediate reaction to those sentences forty years ago was, there can be few nineteenth century theologians whose teaching had such a direct effect on the working lives of their contemporaries. Here evidently was a theologian who managed to be truly incarnational in his teaching. And now forty years later, however limited I recognise this vision of Grundtvig to be, it still tells us something vital about how Danish people feel about this unexpected clergyman and poet. It tells us that he dug down into the depths of people's lives and released sources of energy that have had a greater power of transformation in them than the springs which we dig from oil wells.

An account of the importance of Grundtvig for the contemporary world of an altogether more penetrating and sophisticated kind can be found in a radio broadcast made in 1980 by a distinguished Danish poet and critic, Poul

Borum. His remarks place Grundtvig in his nineteenth century literary context and show us, a little, how he is estimated in the Danish cultural tradition. They give us an idea of the way in which people in Denmark today see him, and how difficult he is for them to grasp, because of the sheer volume and variety of his writing. They also hint at the way in which his works may be difficult to fit into the customary categories of European literature and thought:

It is strange to think that Denmark's greatest contributors to world literature, Grundtvig, Hans Christian Andersen and Kierkegaard were all active in Copenhagen in the 1840's producing works that lie outside the three main genres — drama, the novel, poetry — that are dominant in the European literature of the time. Grundtvig wrote hymns, Andersen fairytales and Kierkegaard philosophical writings which often approach intellectual novels and the poetry of ideas — in the great wide world Kierkegaard is known and respected as a philosopher not as a poet, Andersen is 'merely' a writer of children's stories, and Grundtvig is unknown.
    Yet Grundtvig is not really known within Denmark either. We read Andersen as children and take him with us through life; some of us discover Kierkegaard and plunge into him from a giddy height; but Grundtvig is so enormous and formidable and mysterious and remote, and seems to be reserved as it were to two strange races called 'Grundtvigians' and 'Grundtvig-scholars'. Even so there is of course a Grundtvig for the people; many of us have been connected with the Folk High Schools he inspired, and we are all influenced indirectly in our upbringing by his educational ideas. Then there are the hymns which we have all met at Church and at school and cannot help remembering bits of, bits that turn up at the most impossible moments.[1]

Here we begin to get some idea of Grundtvig's all encompassing influence on Danish life in the last one hundred and forty years, not only on industrial and agricultural developments, but much more on the growth of educational and social ideas and movements. The Folk High Schools, the centres of popular adult education, still very much alive, are one of the most lasting signs of that influence, and the only part of Grundtvig's work that has become at all widely known internationally. In educational circles, not only in Europe and America, but also in the third world, there are places where the prophetic nature of Grundtvig's thinking about education is recognised.
    In Denmark itself, there are some who claim direct descendance from his immediate friends and followers, and who thus form a not very clearly defined group of 'Grundtvigians'; there are others who in the last fifty years have made a massive and systematic attempt to study and interpret the great forest of his writings; these are the 'Grundtvig-scholars'. Everyone in Denmark however, consciously or unconsciously, will have felt the effects of his teaching. 'Education for life', education centred on personal growth and development in which technical instruction and the examination system play a very secondary part, this is something which has become characteristic of Danish life as a whole.

For those of us who look on from outside Denmark, while Poul Borum is helpful in enabling us to place Grundtvig in relationship to other, better known, Danish writers, we have to admit that he introduces us into a landscape which has unfamiliar features. We are at grips with a language, in which like German, the word which we translate as poetry, *digtning*, includes many forms of imaginative writing in prose, as well as writings in verse. Much of Grundtvig's work, particularly in the great body of his sermons, comes under this heading. From an English point of view it is perhaps more disconcerting to learn that here is a poet, and Borum does not hesitate to say 'our greatest poet', though that would not be everyone's judgement, whose best known work is an extensive body of hymns. Here is a literary tradition in which hymns have a central and honoured place, recognised as literary masterworks by believers and unbelievers alike. The literary and artistic traditions of Denmark have been marked by Christian ideas and values to a remarkable degree. In ways which are sometimes familiar to us, and sometimes strangely unfamiliar, faith and culture have been intertwined through the centuries. To think of Grundtvig's work explicitly in terms of Christian humanism is not very common in Denmark. But it is a way of approach which is likely to suggest itself at once to the outsider.

One of the Danish scholars who does think in these terms is Jakob L. Balling, a church historian of great distinction who is particularly expert in the history of ideas, and who has made a special study of the theological poets of the old European Christendom. In Grundtvig he declares,

the old Europe and the new, tradition and the contemporary world ... come together with an unparalleled closeness. This is in part due to the fact that his way of formulating things, whether he writes in prose or in verse, is poetry.[2]

Like the great theological poets of earlier centuries — Balling cites Dante and Milton — Grundtvig expresses himself in the language of images rather than that of concepts. This enables him to hold together views and attitudes which are usually considered to be inconsistent with one another.

Thus we might say that Grundtvig's view of the Church is both Catholic and democratic; his view of the possibilities of human life both Lutheran and humanist; pessimistic in its recognition of human limitations and the reality of death, optimistic in its openness to the possibilities of change and new development, optimistic above all through its sense of the nearness of God's kingdom to human life. In this way Grundtvig's theology comes, in some ways, astonishingly close to the tradition of the early centuries, and we may add, to the insights of the Christian East, yet it is open to the future in a way which is constantly surprising and which reflects something of the richness of his own long life, of which the first part was mostly turned inwards towards reflection, scholarship and the past, and the second part outward towards involvement in the contemporary life of his church and people.

II

It will already be clear from what has been said that Grundtvig was a man whose life was inextricably involved in the life of his people and in a great variety of ways. It is this identification of Grundtvig with Denmark and all that is Danish, which has undoubtedly constituted one of the major obstacles to the 'translation' of his views into a wider international world of discourse. For, if Grundtvig is not widely known, so too knowledge of Denmark in the English-speaking world is sparse and superficial. Yet, as has already been suggested, there are elements in his life and teaching which have universal human significance, not least for today. It is true that he is rooted, earthed, in the time and place to which he belonged, but he must not be imprisoned there. There are, it may be, aspects of his achievement which will only be appreciated as he is seen in a broader context both in space and in time.

But before we come to consider the course of his long life let us for a moment pause to look at some of those factors which make him difficult of access for those who come from outside Denmark, and in particular his ineradicable identification with his own country, its land, its people, its language, its destiny. Here there are questions which are so simple that they can be easily overlooked. What difference does it make for a great man to be part of a numerically small nation? What difference does it make to speak a language which is known, in global terms, to relatively few people? To be a member of a small nation — Denmark, Estonia, Ireland, Greece — is very different from being a member of a nation whose population is ten, twenty, fifty times larger. In the small nation there is a necessary awareness of national identity, an awareness which becomes particularly acute when that identity is threatened by pressures from outside.

More than once in Grundtvig's lifetime Denmark felt threatened in its identity and being by its great southern neighbour Germany, and in Grundtvig's youth it was common enough for the language of administration and culture to be in large part German. Where the small nation is characterised by its own particular language, there will tend to be a heightened sense of the importance of that language as the vehicle of its tradition and experience. The very fragility of its situation makes it more consciously valued. Furthermore the different levels of language, formal and informal, erudite and colloquial, tend to remain in closer touch with one another than in the case of a language with greater geographical extension where the dangers of fragmentation and dispersion are great. It is not by chance that in Britain it is in Wales, rather than in England that Grundtvig's thought about people and language has been appreciated and influential, particularly through the work of the early Welsh nationalist, D.J. Davies.[3]

Such factors must not be neglected in the study of Grundtvig, a member of a small nation where, for better or for worse, everyone knew everyone else. In the course of his lifetime he was brought into direct contact with a great variety of people with different viewpoints and different gifts, in a way which might not have happened for a man of his capacity in France or Germany or England. He could be involved in so many sides of his nation's life, because the nation itself was still a surprisingly unified whole.

If we want an image of that small, united country we may think for instance, of Johan Vilhelm Gertner's painting of the coronation of King Christian VIII in 1840, the canvas crowded with figures, some famous, most now forgotten, Henrik Nicolai Clausen and Hans Lassen Martensen, Hans Christian Andersen, Adam Oehlenschläger, Grundtvig himself and at the centre Bishop Jacob Peter Mynster reaching out his hand to anoint the King.[4] It is a last vivid image of the old tightly knit society of Denmark before the changes of 1848 which introduced a constitutional monarchy and parliamentary democracy. It was a society in which sacred and secular were intermingled in surprising and to us unfamiliar ways. It was from some points of view a stiflingly narrow world, on the point of explosion. But it was still a coherent whole, centred on a royal house which was neither remote nor foreign. In studying Grundtvig's life we shall discover the closeness of his relationship with certain members of that family and the part which those contacts played in his career.

To speak of the royal house of Denmark brings forward another image which must strike any visitor to Denmark from abroad as a powerful symbol of the continuity of national life through the centuries; the series of royal tombs in the Cathedral of Roskilde. Can there be anywhere else in Europe quite such an uninterrupted series of royal monuments? These things speak to us of a nation whose life shows in a very particular way a tradition which is constantly renewed, a capacity to change in such a way as to preserve the heritage of the past, a capacity to be loyal to the past without imprisoning the future. Grundtvig is typical of that society. He is above all a rooted man. If we want an image of him it must surely be that of a great tree which puts down its roots deep into the soil, so that its branches may spread high and wide. He was a man rooted in the history of his people, in their songs and proverbs, their myths and legends. His conscious life put down its roots deep into his own unconscious instincts and affections. At times these powerful feelings almost overthrew him; his inner makeup was tempestuous and volcanic; but more often those feelings opened up in the course of his long life a constantly renewed source of energy and vision, an unfailing power both to love and to know.

But for a thousand years the life of the Danish people has been rooted in another and greater tradition, that of the universal church of Christ, and of that fact Grundtvig was also very conscious. If we want symbols of the continuity of Danish history through all the changes of the centuries, where can we find them better than in the seventeen hundred pre-Reformation parish churches, those wonderful yet humble buildings, which everywhere in this land speak both of tradition and renewal, of continuity through time, and of the meeting of the timeless with time? Those churches, with their constantly sounding bells,[5] were central in the whole of Grundtvig's life and experience, not primarily as buildings, but rather as places where, through the ages, God's people had been gathered around the living Word, the singing and speaking Spirit.

III

For Grundtvig the experience and the act of Christian worship was never a nostalgic thing, simply turning back to the past. It was a present realisation of the healing power and presence of God now. How can it be that in the mid-nineteenth century Grundtvig had such a vivid understanding of the nature of liturgical time, a sense that the Church's anamnesis is not a psychological act turned towards the past, but a sacramental act which fills the present with the riches of eternity? How is it that in his sermons, and still more in his hymns, he could realise so strongly the presence of the risen Christ, making himself known in the power of the Spirit?

To answer these questions, one of the most vital clues is to be found in his own experience of worship Sunday by Sunday, in the years of his childhood and early adolescence. We must go to Udby and to Thyregod to find the sources of his inspiration. We must open the pages of the old seventeenth century Thomas Kingo hymn book and see what he found there, that old hymn book which Grundtvig treasured so highly, whose replacement by the book of 1798 he so violently resented. There we find that the Sunday morning service was a vernacular adaptation of the eucharistic liturgy of the Western Church, a liturgy which had its roots in a period long before the schism of East and West, let alone the crises of the Reformation. There we find, in the readings, the prayers and above all in the hymns, the expression of that liturgical realism, that celebration of the living Christ in the midst of his people, which was to find such marvellous new expression both in Grundtvig's preaching and hymnody.

From Easter to Whitsun, Sunday by Sunday, the congregation sang in Danish as the gradual, one of the most ancient of Latin sequences,

Tell us now Mary, whom did you see on the way? I saw the glory of him that is risen. I saw God's angels and the grave clothes which bear witness; Christ our hope is truly risen and he shall meet you in Galilee.

From Christmas to Candlemas they sang in Luther's words,

Praise be to you Lord Jesus Christ, for that you have become man, born of a virgin pure and fair. Therefore all the Angel host rejoice. Kyrie eleis.

In his sermon for Christmas day in 1823 Grundtvig remarks specifically of these very verses,

I remember how uplifting it was for me during my childhood days that from Christmas to Candlemas, every holy day we sang, 'Praise be to you, Lord Jesus Christ'.

These experiences of the power of the liturgy were not open to many Christian children at the end of the eighteenth century. In the Anglican world, matins had replaced the eucharist as the principle Sunday morning service, and it was sung without any congregational hymns. In the Roman Catholic Church, the liturgy remained in Latin, and so was inaccessible to the people; such vernacular hymns as there were lacked the power and content of the hymns of the early centuries. In the Churches of the Genevan Reformation the basic structures of the liturgy had been abandoned and the whole experience of worship as a present participation in Christ's death and resurrection had been obscured. Only in the East, in Greece or Russia, in Egypt or Romania, would this same experience of eternity have been conveyed through the singing and symbolism of the divine liturgy, through the richness and elaboration of its Eastern forms. And in both cases, both in East and West there were singing and action which spoke to the whole person, to the very old and the very young, to the stupid and sleepy as well as to the intelligent and attentive. What moved Grundtvig so deeply not only in his childhood but throughout his life, was a way of worship which expressed the faith of the whole Christian people, which touched the heart and the will and the imagination no less than the mind, a way of worship which was full of the experience of Christ, risen and triumphant over death.

> Sunday morning from the dead
> Jesus rose triumphant.
> Every Sunday's dawn
> Now brings healing in place of death
> And wonderfully recalls
> All the days of the Lord's life.
>
> Thousand-tongued the Lord's words
> Are now reborn throughout the land,
> Wake now from sleep and sloth
> Every ear that can hear.
> Arise soul from the dead
> And greet the dawn of Easter.
>
> Every Sunday death shudders
> Darkness trembles beneath the earth,
> For with glory then Christ gives light,

> The word of life has giant tones
> And victoriously does battle
> With the prince of death and the kingdom of darkness.[6]

This magnificent hymn occurs in Grundtvig's great collection of hymns, the *Sang-Værk*, in the middle of translations from the Greek and Latin. In it we see a meeting of the spirit of the ancient liturgy, both of East and West, with the faith and experience of a nineteenth century Lutheran. In the first verse we find the theme of anamnesis. All the days of the Lord's life are wonderfully recalled, made present in the power of the resurrection. In the second verse, the work of the Holy Spirit is celebrated, the Spirit who as well as uniting multiplies, diversifies, enriches, enlivens. But in the final verse we can hear the anguish of the conflict with death, which is characteristic of a man who is quite near to our own time, a man who has the searching experiences of the Reformation in his flesh and in his bones.

It is important to recognise that the triumphantly corporate nature of Grundtvig's hymns does not in any way take away from their deeply personal quality. The Church is never an impersonal collectivity, it is always a communion of persons made free in the Holy Spirit. So Grundtvig can see the spirit of the liturgy, the spirit of the Church, made present in the old serving woman, Malene, who acted as his nurse, who had lived for so long in his parents' house as to have become a fixture there. Malene had been an orphan; she is described as a cripple, one who is physically disabled, yet her speech was full of the proverbs and sayings of the people, so rich and strong that Grundtvig, in later years, would speak of her as his language teacher. It was she who sang to him as a child the hymns and songs which he came to love, singing with the whole of her body, as folk-singers sometimes do.

> With her heart on her tongue,
> With her book on her lap,
> With a longing to sing
> As the words led her,
> With the aching of her body,
> In the band of weakness,
> With fluttering hands,
> In the spirit of the Fathers,
> Magdalene sang out in full pure tones
> With tears, the so beautiful hymns.[7]

Grundtvig's work as a preacher and hymn writer centres on an amazed and amazing affirmation of the potential of every human life to become God-bearing, pregnant with a meaning and a joy which are fully and entirely human and yet have their origins beyond what is merely human. This affirmation involves a wonderful exchange or reciprocity, an interaction, *veksel-virkning* of what is human and what is divine, of what is old and what is new, of what is learned and esteemed, the thought of the great scholar and preacher, with what is simple and disregarded, the faith and the song of the old serving woman in the country vicarage. Perhaps it is not by chance that Grundtvig was born on September 8th. Before the Reformation that was the feast day of the nativity of the Blessed Virgin Mary, the one who celebrates the putting down of the mighty from their seats and the exaltation of the humble and meek.

IV

In the course of this book a great deal of space will be given to the content of Grundtvig's preaching. The reasons for this concentration on the sermons will have already begun to become clear. A large part of Grundtvig's prose writing is occasional and frequently controversial. To read it with any understanding demands a detailed knowledge of the social and intellectual history of the nineteenth century in Denmark. Who, we ask, is he arguing against? Why does he feel so strongly about it? As Johannes Knudsen remarked forty years ago, in the preface to his book intended to introduce Grundtvig to American readers

Grundtvig was a warrior. Practically all his prose writings, even to some extent his world histories, are polemical. He is always battling for something and therefore always battling against something. As a result he pressed his ideas so strongly that they became one-sided in their emphasis.

And Knudsen goes on to point us towards Grundtvig's tendency to 'doctrinalize' his ideas. Hypotheses became dogmas, dogmas for which he would fight to the death.[8]

The one area of Grundtvig's prose of which this is not true, or at least only very partially true, is the body of his sermons. It is significant that only a relatively small selection of these sermons were in print at the time when Knudsen was writing. The publication, in the last fifteen years, of the sermons for the 1820s and 30s, fourteen volumes in all, has made a fundamental change possible in the study of Grundtvig, enlarging and deepening our understanding of his vision of the Christian faith. It is not that the sermons are without their occasional elements of polemic, certainly not that they are without reference to the changing circumstances in which they were preached. At their heart however they contain a theology of praise and proclamation, a doxological and kerygmatic theology, which while it is rooted in its own time and place, is not bound and limited by these things in the way in which the polemical writings inevitably are.

It has been the great contribution of Professor Christian Thodberg, the general editor of the newly published sermons, to have done two things; first to have insisted on the importance of the sermons for any full understanding

Portrait of Grundtvig by C.A. Jensen, 1843. Oil on canvas, 664x552mm.
The Hirschsprung Collection, Copenhagen.

of Grundtvig's life and work; secondly, in a series of detailed and brilliant studies to have shown how the sermons are linked to the hymns and the hymns to the sermons. There is a constant interaction between them.

Preaching is Grundtvig's theological workshop. In the sermons Grundtvig writes himself into clarity — and to put it briefly, this is the clarity we find in the hymns. It is the background, the premises, which are to be found in the sermons.[9]

In this book we shall not attempt the close comparison of hymns and sermons which Thodberg has practiced in a number of studies. For one thing that presupposes a detailed knowledge of the shades of meaning and idiom in Danish. We shall however presuppose the general interaction of the two bodies of material, prose and verse, which together make up the core of Grundtvig's literary production.

Here, at the outset, let us quote some paragraphs from a sermon preached in 1850, published in one of the older selections of Grundtvig's sermons, which will introduce us to some of his most characteristic themes, above all the subject of joy, the joy which comes from humanity's fulfilment in God. It is a sermon preached on the second Sunday after Epiphany, and its theme is the marriage at Cana in Galilee. We may perhaps recall that the preacher is in his sixty-eighth year.

There was a wedding in Cana of Galilee where both Jesus' mother and the Lord himself, with his disciples, were among the wedding guests — so begins the gospel for today, and this beginning, when it is preached with life, has always stirred up joy and wonder in all those who have ears to hear ... Yet, Christian friends, the heavenly Father has taken every conceivable care that the gospel of his Son, our Lord Jesus Christ, should come to the children of men, as the most joyful possible news that their ears could hear and their tongues could frame ... Not only did he let his only begotten Son be a guest at an earthly wedding, and with a creative act increase and glorify the wedding's joy, so that we should know that he who created us in his own image and likeness, loves all our human gladness, and will in no way disturb it, but will purify and hallow and transfigure it, but finally he has taken the joy of a wedding, the highest joy which we know and can name in our ordinary life, and used it as a parable of the perfect eternal joy, which in his house and paradise, he has prepared for all who believe in his Son, our Lord Jesus Christ, and love him as he first loved us, and love one another as he loves us ...

Here at the outset Grundtvig introduces us to this theme of joy, a theme which he is never tired of treating, and he speaks of the way in which human joy is not destroyed by heavenly joy but only deepened and confirmed by it. This joy is something which has its origin in the very life of God, and it makes us participant in the very life and being of God, as he goes on to declare.

The eternal joy which the Father has prepared for us in his kingdom, and which shall be revealed when his Son comes again visibly, to be glorious in his saints and wonderful in all his faithful, is likened to a wedding where the Only Begotten is himself the bridegroom, his Church the bride, all God's angels the guests, and both heaven and earth echo and re-echo with the song of rejoicing.

That this is only a parable is self-evident, and the Lord has moreover told us straight out, that the meaning is that he will be one with us in the Spirit, as he is one with his Father, he in us and we in him, by means of love which is the bond of perfectness. However this may be, this word of God is just as joyful, that the

Lord will rejoice over us, as a bridegroom over his bride, and that we shall enter into all our Lord's gladness and glory, as a queen into that of her royal bridegroom.

It is perhaps worth noting here even at the outset, not only that we are to be one with Christ in the Spirit, as he is one with the Father, but also that God rejoices over his people and over every member of that people as a bridegroom rejoices over a bride. We enter into his joy as his bride and his beloved.

Grundtvig goes on to speak of another realisation of this joy, the joy of Christian worship, in the presence of the risen Christ; this is also a marriage, as he sees it, a marriage between the light of Sunday which is known in Church and the life of everyday, which we find all around us.

Yes, my friends, we know the light of Sunday, the reflection of the light of God's countenance, and the rays of his glory which we always see on the Lord's days in his house, where he is depicted for us, as he was and went about, lived and talked, spoke the word of eternal life, and did his deeds of love, suffered patiently, died peacefully and arose gloriously in this world, and where in his, our Lord Jesus Christ's name, the great mystery of godliness is preached, that as he was and is, so all his faithful can and shall be, both here and hereafter, so that in them also God is revealed in flesh, and we also with him are taken up into glory. And it follows naturally, that this light does not shine in the Lord's house as an idle glitter, or as a theatrical show, but in order that it may shine through, enlighten and transfigure the everyday life of Christians, so that their life becomes more and more like the Lord's life, till the countenance of his Church, like his own upon the mountain, shines as the sun and its clothing becomes white as the light.'[10]

In this passage we see something of Grundtvig's understanding of Christian worship and of its relationship to the life of the world. On the one side he declares, in worship, above all in the eucharist, we have a real beginning of eternal life, an anticipation of the world which is to come. In the power of the Spirit, all the days of the Lord are wonderfully recalled, the events of the Gospel become real and present for us. The words of the Lord are heard, his presence is revealed. There is here a real participation in the life of God, a foretaste of that final union of human and divine in which we shall evermore dwell in God and God in us.

And then on the other side he goes on in a magnificent image to declare that all this inner life of worship is not something which exists as an end in itself. It is not a manifestation of 'religion' in that sense. The light of Sunday, the uncreated healing light of God, is to shine out through the words and deeds of Christians in their everyday existence, so that the countenance of the Church shall be transfigured, as was that of the Lord on Mount Tabor. The presence of Christ in the Church is not a static presence to be adored, it is an active, loving, suffering presence in the power of the life-giving Spirit, the Spirit who joins together visible and invisible, earth and heaven, humankind and God. The transfiguration of Christ on the Holy Mount implies the transfiguration of the whole of creation.

It is this experience of the presence of the Lord at the heart of the Church's worship which gives such power to Grundtvig's preaching and his hymnody, and which we shall suggest is the heart of his teaching. It is the perception that this inner reality must shine out into the stuff of everyday existence which acts as the motive power behind all the multiplicity of his public actions in the service of the life of his people. We see in such a passage already the intimate and inseparable connection between the inner and outer aspects of Grundtvig's life and work. Grundtvig indeed dug down deep into the hearts and minds of his people, but before that he dug down deep into his own heart and mind. New powers of life were released which effected the transformation not only of individuals but of a whole society. Through his words and deeds a whole people found a new sense of direction and the liberation of hitherto unexpected powers of life.

Part I

Glimpses of a Life

CHAPTER ONE

Childhood to Ordination
1783–1811

I

Grundtvig was born on the 8th of September 1783, in the South Zealand village of Udby, where his father had been priest since 1778. The child was baptised at home on the following day and was given the names Nicolai Frederik Severin. He was received into the Church publicly on October 8th. The youngest of five children, Grundtvig's only sister, Ulrikke Eleonore was nearest to him in age. His three elder brothers were respectively eleven, eight and six years older than he was. As the last child of elderly parents Grundtvig seems to have had a somewhat lonely childhood. At least he gives us a picture of himself as a child who, as soon as he could read, lost himself in books.

Grundtvig's father, Johan, was already in his fiftieth year when his youngest son was born. Johan Ottosen Grundtvig (1734-1813) seems to have been a conscientious country pastor, a man of the old school of theology, very little touched by the dominant rationalism of his time. One has the impression of a man of deep but unobtrusive piety, content to stay in his parish until the day of his death in 1813. One may perhaps think, in English terms, of a man like the elder John Keble at Fairford, father of a son much more brilliant than himself, who yet influenced that son throughout his life as a kind of embodiment of the tradition of the Church. In one of his poems Grundtvig writes about his father as a man who lived his faith rather than talked about it,

> My father, may God gladden
> His soul in his choir,
> Let no-one cry out
> For bread at his table.
> It was not dead morals
> He gave to his offspring
> But words of life;
> When the cripple with the stick,
> When the lads on the bench,
> When the dog on its chain,
> He himself generously remembered.[1]

Johan's living words were deeds, providing for the disabled, for the workers, for the dog in the yard outside. His was a large and varied household, not only human. The fact that Grundtvig calls his acts of practical concern, living *words* is particularly important. Throughout his life Grundtvig was to speak of the role of the living word, and for him that always meant an embodied word, a word which had become deed.

We have a rather clearer picture of Grundtvig's mother, Cathrine Marie Bang Grundtvig (1748-1822). Unlike her husband she came from an old and distinguished family with wide reaching connections. She was a high-spirited and determined woman and of her is told the first story in Grundtvig's life. It is rather nice that like a medieval saint, our first notice of him should be when he was still in his mother's womb! In the months before his birth there was a gathering of clergy in the vicarage to meet the newly appointed Bishop, Nicolaj Edinger Balle. Balle's first wife had been Johan Grundtvig's sister, and although she had died in 1781, the connection between the two men was never broken. At table that day, one of those present had said, half in jest, that he supposed if the expected child were a boy they would hardly be able to afford an academic education for him. After all there were already three elder brothers to be looked after. Grundtvig himself tells us,

> Mother you yourself confess it
> You became heated and angry...
> Across the table you at once replied
> Bold in faith, and a little proud too
> 'Even if all my clothes go to rags,
> The boy shall be kept at his books'.[2]

It was she who first taught Grundtvig to read, an art which at first he found surprisingly difficult. Also, as we have already seen, the old serving woman Malene, was a part of the family, and she too had a great influence on the young Grundtvig, an influence which lasted all his life. Never was he to neglect or despise the contribution of the *almue*, the common people, the peasants.

In a poem called *Udby Have,* Udby Garden, Grundtvig gives us an idyllic picture of his early years.[3] The garden round the vicarage with its tall trees and winding paths was a kind of paradise to the boy. He lay there in the grass, looking up into the sky, watching the clouds pass by and wondering how God could walk on such thin and insubstantial things. Once he had learned to read, reading became his great delight. There in the long summer days he immersed himself in old seventeenth and eighteenth century chronicles and universal histories. He read the stories and the myths of classical Greece and Rome, he lived through the stories of the Old Testament; now he was David, now he was Themistocles. Throughout his life he had a great capacity to enter into writings which he found congenial, making them his own. Throughout his life he was seeking to write a new universal history, which would encompass the whole significant story of the human race.

But if there were books which took him out into the history of the world as it was known then, there were also books, some of them so weighty that he could hardly carry them, which took him, in much greater detail, into the history of his own people and showed him the descent of the Danish royal house,

> Springing from its deep root
> In the midst of Adam's paradise.

Again he learnt to find himself in the stories of his ancestors and learnt what it was to become proud of the people to whom he belonged. Again, all through his life, particularly in his historical poems and ballads, Grundtvig was seeking to make the ancient history of his own country familiar to his fellow Danes.

From national history Grundtvig turned to the history of the Church. A new world began to open up for him. Here he read about martyrs and Church fathers and the stories of the Reformation. Then one day there came a great discovery. It never occurred to him that any single person might have a whole book to himself. But now his father brought out of his study a life of Martin Luther. The boy was fascinated as never before. He sat in the living room 'at the brown table', lost in the book. They had to drive him off to meals, 'but my soul was with Luther... old doctor Martin Luther! I was then eight years old...'

All his life Grundtvig was to be occupied with the history of the Church, and all his life he was to be negotiating with Luther, certainly both a hero and a model and yet also at times someone of whom he could be critical.

II

Grundtvig was growing up in a decade of great events in Europe. Naturally enough news of the revolution in Paris came to the village and was the source of heated discussion. More surprisingly, he tells us how excited he was one day in 1788 when the village school master announced, after reading the newspaper, that the Russian troops were advancing along the Black Sea and hoped to be in Constantinople for Easter. It was not so much the thought of the Russians and their military campaign which excited the five year old, but, as he tells us, the combination of Easter with Constantinople. That seemed like new life from the dead. Already he seems to have acquired that fascination for all things Greek which remained with him through his life.[4]

At the age of nine Grundtvig was sent away to school; in one sense it was a great break. It meant leaving the family home, it meant leaving the gentle, welcoming landscapes of Zealand and venturing out into the wilder, bleaker landscape of mid-Jutland. How wild those Jutland heaths appeared to an Englishman more than fifty years after this, we shall discover later on. But if much was unfamiliar, much remained the same. The school to which he was sent was another country vicarage where the pastor Lauritz Feld took pupils into his home. Feld was an unmarried man, an old friend of Grundtvig's father, like him an old fashioned believer. He was evidently a good scholar and one who encouraged his pupils to read widely, and not to be afraid of new ideas.

Throughout his life Grundtvig was suspicious of large and impersonal educational institutions. The ideal of an extended family as the context for learning seems to have stuck with him. At least at the beginning the Folk High Schools were small and had something of this character to them. Here, at Thyregod, he was still a member of such an extended family, still living next door to a village church in which, every Sunday, he could enter more deeply into that way of worship which we know, from his sermons, impressed him so much.

The years in which Grundtvig was growing up in Udby and Thyregod were also highly significant years in the development of Denmark. Until almost the end of the eighteenth century the organisation of Danish agriculture remained largely in the hands of a small number of large and wealthy landowners. The majority of those who lived on the land were tenant farmers, who were not only obliged to pay rent but also had to render labour services to the landlord. Although the tenant farmers were not strictly speaking serfs, their lives were at many points directly subject to the will of the landowners, who at times exercised their rights in highly oppressive ways.

In the eighteenth century more and more of the landowners were becoming unhappy with this inherited and largely feudal system. It was not particularly efficient; still more it was blatantly unjust and was felt to be so. In the years 1786-88 a series of land reforms were initiated. These improved and clarified the legal situation of the tenant farmers, strictly delimiting their obligations to render services. What was more, they allowed them actually to buy their farms as freeholds at highly advantageous terms. Within two generations the situation of the peasant farmers had been transformed and by the middle of the nineteenth century the vast majority of them owned their own land. It was this class of small independent farmers who were to provide the central stabilising element in Danish society for more than a century.[5]

It is difficult to know how quickly the effects of the reforms were felt in particular districts, but it is evident that throughout Denmark the fact of the land reform of the 1780s was something which was everywhere recognised and acknowledged. It was, as one modern commentator has called it 'a revolution without violence', a very notable example of the best kind of eighteenth century enlightened despotism.[6] It is impossible to suppose that a small boy, as intelligent and perceptive as the young Grundtvig was, could have been unaware of these changes. Surely they provided a vital element within his extremely positive memory of his years of childhood and early adolescence.

III

The years of childhood ended finally in 1798. In the autumn of that year Grundtvig went to the Cathedral School in Aarhus, the so-called Latin-school, a Danish equivalent to a Grammar school in England. Looking back on these years in later life, Grundtvig felt profoundly dissatisfied with them. He felt that the educational system into which he had been introduced was altogether wrong-headed; too formal, too bookish, too authoritarian, too abstract. He felt that its influence on himself had been almost wholly harmful. He had become lazy and undisciplined, he had wasted his time and lost any sense of purpose. When the records which document his two years in the school at Aarhus are examined it is evident that things were not nearly so black as he remembered them to have been. The school was not all that bad as schools go. It gave a good classical education, it helped Grundtvig to become a sound scholar in both Latin and Greek. It is clear that the pupil himself was by no means idle. His teachers recognised in him a student of outstanding promise.

But it is clear that in these years a new period in his life began which was to continue into the first four or five years of the next century. This was the period in which, from 1800 to 1803 Grundtvig completed his university education and in the autumn of 1805, at the age of twenty two, took his first full time employment as tutor in the family of a manor house on Langeland, Egeløkke. They were years of inner conflict and disillusionment. The secure base of his childhood had dissolved. He thought of himself as a Voltairean sceptic. His thoughts went in one direction — he told himself he was cold-hearted and cynical — his feelings went in another direction.

In 1802-3, for instance, the brilliant young literary scholar Henrik Steffens, as it happens a distant cousin of Grundtvig's, gave a series of outstanding lectures at the university on the nascent romantic movement in Germany. These lectures marked an epoch in Denmark's own involvement in European Romanticism. Grundtvig, at the time, could feel nothing but puzzlement and incomprehension for them. He attended the lectures but could not respond to them. It was only some years later, after his own inner life had been turned upside down, that he remembered their content and realised their importance.

In understanding Grundtvig's lack of a strong sense of direction during these years, the example of his three elder brothers is perhaps significant. All three had followed in their father's footsteps and been ordained. Did the parents take it for granted that Frederik would take the same path and if they did what must Frederik have thought about that? The careers of the three brothers went in very different directions. Otto, the eldest, who was eleven years Frederik's senior, was ordained in 1795 when Frederik was still in

Thyregod. In 1798 he became a parish priest in Roskilde; in 1800 he moved to another living and was in it for the next twenty-three years. Otto Grundtvig seems to have been a kind, friendly man, of no particular distinction, but one who faithfully supported his brilliant younger brother from time to time, particularly at moments of crisis.

The destiny of the next two brothers, Jacob Ulrik Hansen Grundtvig (1775-1801) and Niels Christian Bang Grundtvig (1777-1803), was very different. First the one and then the other was ordained as chaplain to the Danish colony on the coast of Guinea in West Africa, and both died of tropical fever within a few months of arriving there. In itself this was not something totally unexpected for Europeans going to West Africa in the early nineteenth century. But there were facts of a more unsettling kind in the case of the second of the two brothers. Whereas Jakob Ulrich seems to have acquitted himself in his brief ministry in Africa in a thoroughly respectable way, Niels Christian, in the few months that he was there, seems for much of the time to have been at the centre of a kind of uproar; for four days he was under house arrest, he was suspended from his duties for five weeks, he was accused of having an African woman into his quarters at night. The eyewitness accounts of the rage and self righteousness with which the young man defended himself would be comic if they were not also tragic. At least they testify to the actions of a person who had little or no understanding of himself, still less ability to control himself.[7]

There is no evidence that our Grundtvig was ever particularly close to these two elder brothers. They were already away at school at the time when he was growing up. But he cannot have been altogether uninfluenced by them, and it is difficult not to think that the example of the two chaplains in Africa must have contributed something to his sense of disenchantment with the religion of his childhood in his university years, and must have given him unquiet thoughts about his own future role in the ministry if he were ordained himself. The fate of Niels Christian must have taught him too that there was a streak of wildness in the family character which he needed to be aware of.

The stay as tutor to the little boy at Egeløkke, which began in 1805, developed in a way which was not difficult to foresee. Grundtvig fell wildly in love with the lady of the manor, Constance de Leth, an attractive young woman of twenty-eight. She was a person of much greater sophistication and social assurance than her young tutor and everything suggests that she handled the situation tactfully and without undue alarm. But Grundtvig was thrown into a deep inner turmoil which he recorded in his copious diaries. He was in love for the first time, and forced to recognise that he was a deeply feeling human being. His passionate nature could no longer be suppressed. He went through a typical romantic awakening. He began to read furiously, Schiller, Fichte, Goethe, Shakespeare. The content of Steffens' lectures came back to him. Now he understood what before had been dark. Above all he

found himself attracted by the philosophy of F.W.J. Schelling, with its tendency towards an idealistic pantheism, which brought all things together
through a dialectical process into a resolution in the Absolute. For a time at
least such an insubstantial but fashionable philosophy of life seemed to him
to be adequate.

At the same time his childhood interest in history reawakened and was
joined by a new enthusiasm for the mythology of the North. Not for the last
time in his life, Grundtvig found that the inner upheaval occasioned by
falling deeply in love began to give his whole life a new sense of shape and
direction. His calling as a poet, his concern for the life and history of his
fatherland, his deep interest in the mythology of the North, all these things,
which were to be with him for the whole of his life, began to take hold of
him now. His first major book *Nordens Mythologi* was published in 1808. By
this time he was back in Copenhagen, teaching in a fashionable private
school, hoping to make his way as a poet and a man of letters. By this time
too, his childhood faith in God was beginning to return.

In a poem written in 1807, in which he reflects on his experience at Egeløkke, he finds that he can thank God for the pain that he had felt there
because it was pain which had showed him that he was a being with a heart,
capable of feeling, a being who could not be satisfied with cold cleverness
and scorn.

> The spirit within him looked out
> He saw himself on the edge of the abyss,
> He looked hard and long
> For salvation and found,
> Found wherever he looked,
> God over all;
> Found him in the poet's song,
> Found him in the word of the sage,
> Found him in the myths of the North,
> Found him in the passage of time,
> Clearest and surest of all,
> Found him in the book of books.[8]

For Grundtvig both inwardly and outwardly things were beginning to come
together again at a new depth.

IV

Before they could come together in a more permanent and fully satisfying
way however, there were more precipices to be crossed.

In the spring of 1810, to his considerable dismay, he received, first from his
father, and then more insistently from his mother, letters requesting him to

be ordained and to come back to Udby as his father's curate. The old man, who was now seventy-six, needed assistance through the last years of his ministry. The request threw Grundtvig into a quandary; part of him felt that he ought to go, a large part of him knew that he did not want to go. Why should he leave an independent life in the capital city where he was beginning to be known as a poet, a critic and a freelance writer, and return to a village where he had grown up, to act as his father's assistant in a parish community where everyone would have known him as a child, and where all the old ladies would have had their favourite stories about his escapades as a four year old?

Academically his degree in theology was quite enough to enable him to seek ordination, so in principle he could agree to his father's request, if he decided to, and though he felt reluctant about it, he went on to fulfill a number of minor requirements for ordination, including, the preparation of a trial sermon which he preached on the 17th of March in 1810.

The sermon was called 'Why has the Lord's word disappeared from his house?' It is a passionate denunciation of the clergy of Copenhagen for their inability to present the word of God in its true strength and effectiveness. It shows us a young man who fancies himself as a prophet and who has lost neither the cold intelligence, nor the scorn, which he had discovered in himself in his rationalistic days. The sermon was preached under examination conditions, i.e. in the presence of a single auditor, a Professor in the University, who thinking it a good sermon, marked it *Egregie*, excellent. What he did not know was that Grundtvig intended to publish it and did so a few weeks later, without the permission of the University. Naturally the sermon as published caused a storm, and it won Grundtvig the hostility of many of the clergy of Copenhagen. They did not soon forget it.[9]

Meanwhile in Udby, the situation had changed. The Bishop had decided that if there was to be a curate it must be a clergyman of the diocese already ordained, who was without a living. Grundtvig's father was unwilling to accept this arrangement and the young Grundtvig felt that perhaps he had been let off. He threw himself with new fury into intellectual activity. At the same time the thought that perhaps he was called to be a reformer of the Church kept coming back to him. But the more he thought about it the more he began to wonder whether he had any right to seek to reform the Church when he hardly knew whether he was a Christian himself.

All the buried feelings of guilt inside him, particularly those occasioned by his reluctance to agree to his father's request for help, boiled up within him. As the year drew to an end his friends became more and more worried about him, as they saw him overworking in an attempt to escape his inner conflicts. But the feelings of guilt and anxiety at times seemed overwhelming, and there were rapid swings of mood, from manic to depressive, from arrogant assertiveness to helpless feelings of dependence. He was weighed down by the questions 'Are you yourself a Christian?', 'Have you the forgiveness of your sins?' Now perhaps he was going to have to return to Udby, not to help, but to be helped. Perhaps there he might find refuge.

Shortly before Christmas in 1810 he set out for Udby accompanied by his friend Frederik Christian Sibbern, who had been almost commissioned by Grundtvig's other friends to see him safely home. On the way there they stopped the night at a wayside inn, Vindbyholt Kro. They shared a room. Sibbern was anxious in case Grundtvig's loud and insistent prayers in the middle of the night should wake up the other guests. Next morning, he records, as they travelled on, 'Grundtvig told me, that he had felt the devil like a snake, physically wind himself round his body.' When eventually they got to Udby and Sibbern told the old pastor about his son's condition he was again astonished at how simply and in what a matter of fact way the old man took it. 'My son has *anfægtelser*', he said and knew at once where he was and what to do.[10]

At this moment Grundtvig had indeed come home, to the house in which he was born and baptised, and the village in which he had grown up; he had come home to something which lies at the heart of the Lutheran tradition within Christianity, that experience of *Anfechtung*, as it is called in German, those *anfægtelser*, for which we have no exact equivalent in English, a term which speaks of the inner place of conflict, guilt and near despair, in which through the cross of Christ the soul in the end discovers light in the darkness, hope against all hope, new life in the place of death.

As we shall see there are disagreements among Grundtvig scholars about which is *the* turning point in Grundtvig's life. There are a number of candidates. But that this is *a* turning point, no one can deny. For myself I think it is *the* turning point. 1825, 1832, these were vital moments of new vision, of liberation, of new directions. But this black moment at Christmas 1810, was the moment of deepest darkness, the turning point from which all could begin again. In a sermon preached many years later Grundtvig speaks of 'the sorrow, the anguish, the fear, which presses out of us a great cry and a heartfelt sigh, that is something born only at night when darkness appals us, in winter when the cold oppresses and shakes us,' that is something which God gives us precisely so that the hard crust of the heart may be broken up and the earth prepared to receive the dew and the rain, the light and warmth from above; 'thus we can easily understand why the seed grows most at night and in winter, though it is only in the light of day and in high summer, only towards harvest that we see it.'[11]

So Grundtvig came home at Christmas 1810. Early in the New Year the application for permission for him to be his father's curate was renewed. This time the authorities consented. There were other formalities to be completed, ending with an examination by Bishop Friedrich Chr. Münter on Friday 24th of May. The following Wednesday, May 29th, Grundtvig was ordained by the bishop in the Church of the Holy Trinity in Copenhagen.

In a poem addressed to his friend Sibbern a few weeks later, Grundtvig writes,

> The apostles on the holy feast of Pentecost
> Were clothed with power from on high.
> In the week of Pentecost it came to pass
> That I was ordained to be the Lord's priest.
> The gifts of grace are varied
> Yet all bestowed by the same Spirit.
> When the brethren reached out their hands
> To ask the Lord to grant that
> The Spirit of love and power and truth
> Should mercifully descend on me
> *Then* the well of tears in the heart was opened,
> Then the soul burst its prison chains,
> And when I heard the brethren together
> Say Amen in the name of Jesus Christ,
> Then that echoed in my heart
> And I felt myself atoned with God.[12]

It is very striking and altogether characteristic of Grundtvig, that a crisis which is at its heart an inner crisis of guilt and sorrow for sin, of repentance and renewal of life, is worked out in and through a reconciliation with his parents and all the necessary outward formalities which bring him to the moment of ordination. The outward and the inward are not separate, they work together to a wholeness in which God is made known through his creation. We discover God's love in recognising the love of our friends.

This point is made in a remarkable way in the same poem to Sibbern. It is a poem of farewell, since Sibbern has just ended his doctoral thesis in the University and is about to take a long journey through the philosophy departments of the universities of Germany. He has chosen one way to go forward, Grundtvig has chosen another. In the poem Grundtvig expresses the deepest point of his gratitude by affirming explicitly that it was in Sibbern and in his other friends that God was present and at work. He speaks of the time

> When God taught me through doubt and conflict
> To *feel* sorrow and to *feel* joy,
> To feel, after long sighing,
> How hard it is not *to be able* to weep.
> I thank God, and him in you, my friend
> And in the other dear friends of youth
> In whose company I became a child again,
> And learnt to know the evil of my pride...[13]

And in another revised version of the same poem Grundtvig adds lines which emphasise the point yet again,

> I thank God and I thank him in you
> For all your friendship in the heavy days,
> You went about, you suffered, you prayed with me
> You were not tired by my cries of distress.[14]

It was in his friends that God's grace had come to him; through them that he had come to know the importance of the human heart and will when sustained by God's gift and grace; through them no less than in countless other ways, that he had come to know Christ as his redeemer.

CHAPTER 2

Conflict and Vision
1811–29

I

As was to be expected Grundtvig threw himself wholeheartedly into the work of the parish at Udby. He was particularly successful in his work with the young, with children and with those being prepared for confirmation, a service which in Denmark is conducted not by the Bishop but by the priest who has himself taught the young people. He visited the poor, the sick and he sat with the dying and found that there too there were possibilities of human contact and exchange which he had hardly expected.

Needless to say he preached regularly and fervently. In one particular sermon for Whitsun Monday we hear the first announcement of a theme which he is to develop and deepen for the next sixty years, the inner relation of the three great feasts of the Christian year with one another, and the way in which they correspond to the changing seasons of the natural year. It seems, he says, as if they were fore-ordained for our benefit and in accordance with the situation of the land in which we live and work.

Under the heart of winter, when all is withered, when the earth lies dead in the bonds of the cold, there comes Christmas ... and everything bids us praise him, the spiritual sun of the world, who brought life and light to the dark, famished earth.

When we keep Easter and remember the first fruits of the resurrection, that blessed morning hour in which the believing human race rose up from its dark dwelling, transfigured in and with the Saviour, when the angel's song from the grave proclaimed the victory of light over darkness, of life over death, see, then the earth in our fields also awakes from its winter sleep and the sun and the morning lark proclaim the coming of spring and the rebirth of life.

Finally, when the wood grows green, and the beech tree is crowned by joyful May, and all the small birds build their nests in it ... when the lily blossoms in the meadow, more splendidly clothed than Solomon in all his glory, in that delightful hour, when all the deep longings in the human heart awake, when the eye becomes clear and everything breathes joy, then comes Whitsun to us and says, all the sights and feelings which so sweetly move and delight your hearts are only a shadow and a likeness for the senses, of the holy springtime in which I was born, of that great hour when God let his holy Spirit descend in order to fuse humankind together with himself in love, ... and when the tabernacle of Christ's Church was raised up on earth, a shelter and a cooling shade for his children of dust.[1]

It is impossible not to note how already here Grundtvig sees Easter as both a cosmic and corporate reality, involving the whole believing human race, and thus sees as the end and fulfilment of human history nothing less than a fusing together of human and divine, a fusing together of heaven and earth in the love which the indwelling Spirit brings.

The years at Udby were quiet but not uneventful. In 1811 Grundtvig became engaged to Elisabeth (Lise) Christine Margrethe Blicher (1787-1851), the daughter of a neighbouring pastor. Grundtvig had known the family since his student days. Indeed, in 1803, he had thought himself in love with Lise's elder sister Marie. But he had been too shy to declare his feelings, and she married someone else. Now he again came into touch with the same friendly family circle and this time he felt sure that it was Lise he was in love with. He proposed to her in September 1811; their engagement was to last until 1818, when Grundtvig at last came into a financial situation which allowed him to think of establishing a family.[2]

The time at Udby was short. Two years after his son's arrival as his assistant the old pastor was dead; and since Grundtvig's appointment was as his father's personal curate his appointment too came to an end with his father's death. It seemed as if, for some years at least, he was not going to be able to find another living in the Church.

II

Grundtvig returned to Copenhagen in a Denmark now in the last years of the Napoleonic wars, in which the quixotic loyalty of King Frederik VI to the French alliance made Denmark, in the end, the only ally that France had left. It was a period of considerable political and economic upheaval, when the country experienced a painful time of national bankruptcy.

Once again Grundtvig plunged into literary projects. For a time he seems to have wanted, at all costs, to impress himself on the public. These were the years in which his critics speak of his fanaticism, his bigotry, his determination at all costs to proclaim his newly discovered Lutheran orthodoxy, in all its Bible-based clarity and strictness. William Michelsen remarks,

Grundtvig's writings in these years changed his status in Danish literature completely. He became an extremely controversial man. One of his closest friends, the historian Molbech, publicly repudiated him; the physicist, H.C. Ørsted, attacked in particular Grundtvig's judgement on the natural philosopher, Schelling ... .[3]

Only gradually Grundtvig seems to have become aware that these tactics were hardly succeeding. Indeed they were closing to him the possibilities of any place in the university, either in Copenhagen itself, or in the newly founded university at Christiania (Oslo) in Norway. In both places his applications for professorships were unsuccessful.

But if outwardly his plans were frustrated, in terms of his writing these were very active and productive years. He pursued three main lines of research, one primarily historical, another philosophical and a third and perhaps the most important of all, a line involving the work of translation.

On the first line of action, the distinguished Norwegian scholar, Sigurd Aarnes remarks,

even for Grundtvig with his incredible work capacity the *World Chronicles* of 1812, 1814 and 1817 are an outstanding achievement. Three times in the course of five years the young Lutheran minister sets out to give a unified presentation of European history (at that time regarded as 'world history').[4]

Grundtvig's attitude towards history, particularly at this time in his life, is remarkably pre-modern. He thinks of the story of the human race as the field in which God is at work, and is seen to be at work. It is the historian's task to unveil the divine purposes latent in human affairs. It is true that he sees a distinction to be made between the biblical history and history in general.

Grundtvig distinguishes between a truth for salvation, which God's revelation in the Bible alone is the bearer of, and a truth for 'the transfiguration of life' which history gives us access to. The first is for Grundtvig the area of pure theology, the second of natural theology.[5]

But in Grundtvig's mind both ways work towards the same end, the salvation of sinful man, though following different paths.

The First World Chronicle, of 1812, was particularly provocative in its way of presentation. It ended with 'an open, ideological criticism of prominent people in Danish society, mentioned by name.' Not surprisingly it sold well, but it greatly strengthened the hands of Grundtvig's critics, both in the Church and in the university. The nomination committee for the post of Professor of History in Copenhagen in 1817 wrote of Grundtvig's historical work,

as well as revealing an ignorance of and indifference to every art of history and genuine scientific treatment, it contains so many warped judgements and ignoble expressions that it must be regarded as fortunate for the fatherland that the person from whose hand such products come is not allowed to present himself as a public teacher at any scientific institute.[6]

The second, more philosophical line of inquiry which Grundtvig followed at this time is embodied in the numbers of a periodical called *Dannevirke*[7], which Grundtvig began to publish in July 1816 and which ran until January 1819. It was a very Grundtvigian publication since the editor wrote all of it himself. The numbers of *Dannevirke* contain some of Grundtvig's most interesting reflections on the relation of reason to revelation, on the nature of human knowledge, on the role of the imagination in poetry and the arts, as well as on more social questions connected with the characteristics of different nations, and the respective roles of Church, state and school in human life. Needless to say Grundtvig's presentation of his ideas is not strictly systematic; indeed Grundtvig was profoundly suspicious of any philosophy which thought to present itself as a total system. To do that the philosopher would have to stand outside time, and that precisely was what he could not do. We find in these pages the first full formulation of Grundtvig's poetic-historic view of human life and destiny.

Through the various articles in *Dannevirke* there runs a kind of tension between Grundtvig's rediscovered sense of the absolute claims of God's revelation of himself in Christ, on the one side, and his own earlier and never repudiated sense that God is present and at work in the whole of creation and in the whole of history. God reveals himself in Christ as the God three-in-one. Yet traces of that same triune pattern are to be seen throughout human experience, written into the very nature of things. The doctrine of the Trinity is thus not only a revealed doctrine, it has a created analogue. As always Grundtvig insists on making a correlation between human and divine, between grace and nature, between creation and redemption. If, on the one side he will not try to construct an all inclusive system, on the other side he seeks to avoid too easy a setting of one thing against another, an exclusion of one thing at the expense of another. His intention is, in the end, to gather things into one.

In the essays in *Dannevirke*, Grundtvig is of course constantly in conversation, sometimes explicitly, more often implicitly, with the German philosophical and theological thinking of his time. It is perhaps in this area, that a comparison with the work of S.T. Coleridge would be particularly fruitful. It is certainly an area of Grundtvig's work where even in Denmark scholars sense that there is more to be done.

The third strand in Grundtvig's activity in these years, between 1815 and 1821, is the strand of translation. This may well seem the least important at first sight, yet, in the end, and with this writer, it may turn out to be most important. Grundtvig, as a scholar, had a remarkable gift for entering into, and making his own, pieces of writing from far away in space and time. He approaches such works with both the power of his imagination and the weight of his scholarly expertise. In this case he had three major texts in view; *Beowulf, The Chronicles of Denmark*, of Saxo Grammaticus, and *The Chronicles of the Kings of Norway* by Snorri Sturluson, three vital texts for the understanding of the early medieval history of the North.

In his fine article on the way in which Grundtvig undertook this work, Andreas Haarder writes,

translation means several things. Every single element in the linking together of a large body of material has to be treated. It is relatively easy to read a text if one has a reasonable command of the language, but to deal with every single element, control it, and find a fitting garment for it, is a laborious journey. And the areas Grundtvig had to traverse were gigantic ... In this particular instance the originals are in Old English, Old Icelandic and Medieval Latin, respectively, and it is the common man whom Grundtvig is addressing.[8]

There is something more that needs to be said here, to underline the importance of Grundtvig's gift as a poet for his work as a translator. Vernon Watkins, a Welsh poet of this century who wrote in English, was very much aware of the problems and possibilities of translation from one language to another; he writes,

the approach of scholarship appears to stop short at the original poet's written text, but the translator, who is a poet, is concerned with the whole orbit of the poet's thought during the period of composition, the written text is the track of a secret and more elaborate movement to which he alone, through an affinity of mind, has the key.[9]

Even if there is an element of exaggeration here, for not all translators are necessarily poets, there is nonetheless an important element of truth. The tools of historical and philological scholarship are certainly necessary but they are not in the end altogether adequate. The translator who is himself a poet may well find himself in a more intimate and inward relationship with the original poet. It is this fact which, as we shall see in the following chapter, gives Grundtvig's translations their special quality and which makes the work of translation of such particular importance to him.

In these works, which necessarily occupied him for a number of years, Grundtvig felt as if he were burrowing down into the past, becoming, as he says, a bookworm, attempting to digest the dusty, unexplored riches of the history of the North. He goes down into a buried world, the world of the early Middle Ages, and seeks to bring up from it a treasure which can renew life. This work was not in the end altogether unrecognised by the king. In 1818 he was awarded an annual stipend as a reward for his efforts as a translator. This meant that in 1818, at last, he was able to marry Lise Blicher to whom he had been engaged for seven years. At last they were able to set up house together.

These efforts of translation were of course directly related to the cultural and spiritual heritage of the North and of Denmark in particular, and were part of Grundtvig's great lifelong project of making this history accessible to his contemporaries. Seeing them in the context of Grundtvig's life, we can see them first as a preparation for the great breakthrough into a moment of extraordinary creativity which occurs in 1823-25, years which produced one of his greatest poems, *New Year's Morning*, one of his greatest hymns, *The Land of The Living*, and some of his finest and most inspired preaching. But in a larger perspective it is difficult not to see them also as a preparation for another and more universal work of translation which he was to carry out in the following decade, the work which resulted in the *Sang-Værk* of 1837. This was a work intended to provide the Danish Church with a body of hymns which would reflect the fullness of the Christian tradition through the ages. It was a work touching not just the North, but Palestine and Greece, Rome, England and Germany. As we shall see in the following chapter, in that enterprise Grundtvig revealed an even greater capacity to resonate to the old and to transmute it into something new.

III

We have spoken of Grundtvig's comparative isolation at this time, of his feeling that he was shutting himself away in his study; but we should not exaggerate this state of affairs. In 1818, for instance, he was actively involved in a major literary controversy which was fought out around the reputation of two of the outstanding Danish poets of the time, Jens Baggesen and Adam Oehlenschläger. In 1820, amongst many other things he produced a patriotic song, which remains, after almost two centuries, remarkably popular and alive as a statement of Denmark's understanding of itself and which can give us a glimpse into another whole dimension of his work.

It is a song of praise for the motherland, but full, at every turn, of a wonderful irony, a gentle mocking of ideal pretensions. Each verse begins with a concession to the outsider. Those foreigners, he allows, certainly have countries which are bigger, stronger, richer, more famous, more powerful than ours, and yet ... I do not attempt a translation of the whole song, I simply paraphrase and abbreviate some of the verses.

Far higher mountains have others than us, our mountain is only a hill. We are not made for pomp and display, to be with the earth suits us best.

Others may well have far finer districts. We are content here at home with our beech woods by the shore. It suits us best to live out our life in our flowering fields, set amidst the waves of the sea.

Far greater exploits may be found elsewhere, perhaps, both for honour and gain. We at least will stick to our guns, our flag and our shield. We won't give up our identity.

Far cleverer people I suppose, may be found than here at home, but we have a bit of reason and good sense. We don't screw ourselves up into being gods and time will show that with a passion for truth and justice we didn't think so badly after all.

There are, it may be, far nobler, finer languages, on foreigners' lips. Yet we Danes too can speak and sing of excellence and delight, if only we are true to our mother tongue.

Far more of metal, both white and red, have others, in mines and in exchanges. But among Danes daily bread is to be found in the hovels of the poor. And we have found true riches indeed in our land when few have too much and fewer too little.

Perhaps one day finer kings may be found, fathers of their land, but it will take much to equal our royal house. May they flourish and prosper.

Others may praise their kings more extravagantly; but do they really mean what they say? Here, in Denmark, we sing truly, May our Frederik's time be praised as Fredegod's of old.[10]

The poem was written in 1820 for a dinner party given in honour of a civil servant going out to work in the administration of the Danish colonies in the West Indies. It was an occasional piece of light verse of a kind still frequently composed in Denmark. It has lived for one hundred and seventy seven years and surely it will live much longer. There can be few pieces more quintessentially Danish and Grundtvigian than this. It demands a little more consideration.

Let us start at the end, with the two verses addressed to the king. These are now usually left out; this is understandable but a pity. The Danish royal family had a remarkable place in Danish society before the changes in 1848. The king was, in theory, an absolute monarch. In practice things didn't work quite like that. There were informal checks and balances in the political system, which moderated the power of the monarchy. What is more, Denmark was a small enough country and Copenhagen a small enough city, for people to feel they knew the monarch personally and that they had personal access to him.

Frederik VI behaved more like the landlord of a large estate than like a monarch conceived on an imperial scale. Grundtvig himself, for all his stress on all that is *folkelig*[11], had a close link with the royal family. It was the king who would finance his study tours to England; it was the king who got him his place at Vartov; it was the king who at last gave him at least the title of bishop. Perhaps at the end of our second millennium we have reached a point in time when it is possible to see that a royal family can play a vital part in creating the memory of a people, and in ways which are difficult to quantify, play its role in maintaining a sense of national identity.

But it is the verse immediately before the two royal verses which contains the most remarkable of all the affirmations of the poem. Denmark is a country which is truly rich because it is a country where few have too much and fewer have too little. The formulation here has in fact behind it a distant reference to the law of the jubilee in the Old Testament, the law which involved a periodical liquidation of debts, intended to prevent the disparity between rich and poor becoming too great within the people of Israel. But in nineteenth century terms Grundtvig's formulation strongly contrasts with the utopian and in the end often destructive statements of an ideal and absolute equality, such as those made by the French Revolution.

Here the vision is more modest, more practical, perhaps less clearly defined. It is not said that all must have precisely the same. The aim is defined, in a negative way, as the avoidance of excess. But for all its lack of clear definition, the goal which it presents is real and a matter of life and death. Those who have lived in societies, whether in Europe or North America, where a few have far too much and many have far too little, and in which that disparity is growing, know that that kind of economic injustice can be deeply destructive of any true human sense of society and community. *Folkelighed* does not imply total equality. It does imply a conscious sense of solidarity and interdependence, of mutual responsibility and accountability between the different groups which make up a people or a nation. It is this verse which in some sense contains the heart of the song, and which certainly speaks most eloquently to English and American readers who discover it. But of course each of the earlier verses adds its own distinctive element to the whole picture.

Throughout the poem there is a quiet mockery of the ideals of the great and the proud, perhaps primarily the Germans, but also the French and not forgetting the English. Precisely because the Danes, by reason of the smallness of their numbers, have to accept limitation as part of the nature of things, they are able to get further than those who aim too high and then fall back into cynicism and despair. We do not try to make ourselves into gods; we do not take ourselves too seriously; there, he seems to say, is our true strength.

That attitude of self depreciation can also become a snare, as many Danish people are very much aware. But it is a snare which people can learn to avoid.

IV

Grundtvig's period in the wilderness came to an end early in 1821 when he was suddenly and unexpectedly appointed to the parish of Præstø in South Zealand. Præstø is a market town on the east coast of the island, not far from Udby; it was the place where Grundtvig's mother was living in retirement in her old age. He accepted the offer of the parish with alacrity and at once entered with fresh enthusiasm into the calling of a preacher and a pastor. Here the first of his children, a boy called Johan was born, in April 1822. At the end of that year, something more unexpected happened. He was at last called to a church in the capital, and at the beginning of Advent that year preached his first sermon as assistant pastor at the Church of Our Saviour.

The years that followed were a time of great creativity for Grundtvig, but they were not at all untroubled years. Sometimes Grundtvig felt lifted up and able to speak a prophetic word to his generation, at other times he felt cast down by the apparent lack of response to his message. The outburst which occurred in 1825 after the publication of his highly controversial work, *The Church's Rejoinder*, was in some ways the climax of this period. The court case which followed, and which Grundtvig lost, did not and could not look at the substance of the questions the book was intended to raise, but it revealed the degree to which, in these years, Grundtvig had been caught up in his own thoughts, his own experiences, his own vision, and was out of touch with his society. He believed himself to have a word to speak both to Denmark and to the universal Church which he felt to be a prophetic word of life, a word of resurrection from the dead. It was a word, which like the prophets of old, he found his contemporaries could not or would not hear.

Let us look for a moment at the greatest poem from this period, *New Year's Morning*. It has always been found a difficult poem; difficult to construe and difficult to expound, yet even a first reading of its opening stanzas with their repeated invocations of God's peace over the land, God's peace and good morrow, gives a strong sense that a new time, a new age is beginning, a world emerging into light out of darkness, into life out of death. The central episode of the poem takes up precisely this theme of resurrection into new life. As Jakob Balling remarks,

Looking back at his struggle to revivify national history and make it meaningful to his fellow countrymen, the poet gives expression to his experience by means of a modified retelling in the first person singular of the ancient tale — transmitted around the year 1200 by Saxo Grammaticus in his *Gesta Danorum* — of King Hadding's descent to the underworld ...[12]

In the poem the poet himself goes down into the place of the dead as the ancient king had done, he seeks to recall for his countrymen the forgotten riches of the life of their past. A female figure leads him down into the darkness, a woman who shows him the wall that divides the land of the dead from the land of the living. She gives him the sign of the crossing of the wall; 'She takes a cock, wrings its neck, throws its head over the wall — and it crows on the other side.'

Here indeed is a strange image of resurrection; new life proclaimed by the cock-crow, new life, not for one alone, but for all, a new life which not only creates community between the present and the past, but which also creates community between human beings now.

All this is seen as the experience which makes a true community with fellow men possible; the bearer of the experience, the prophetic voice of the poet, is the chosen instrument of proclamation and appeal to fellows and brethren.[13]

This sense, that he is called to bring new life to his people, is inevitably seen by Grundtvig in terms of his Christian vocation. He is not afraid to see a genuine parallel between his own calling as 'delver into the past, translator and historian' and the journey of Christ himself into the place of the dead, and his destruction there of all the powers of death. We shall see in many places how vital for Grundtvig is the doctrine of the descent into hell. We begin to see here already something of the reason why this should be so.

No less significant for this period is one of the greatest of Grundtvig's hymns, *The Land of the Living*; this too is a work which, like *New Year's Morning*, is impossible to translate adequately. The difficulty here lies in the text of the work itself. It raises for us, in an acute form, the question of where a poem ends and a hymn begins. In this case Grundtvig himself seems to have been aware of a difficulty, since the work exists in a number of different versions. Grundtvig could not refrain from making revisions and the revisions tend to increase the theological explicitness of the poem. As Grundtvig goes on working on it, it becomes more and more a hymn, but perhaps at the expense of something of its original freshness and beauty as a personal expression of faith.

The poem centres on the human longing for the land of perfect joy, of true fulfilment. This land is seen as lying beyond the sea of this life, sometimes visible to us but ultimately unattainable. Grundtvig had already described the human situation in this way in one of his earliest essays, 'On Religion and Liturgy', published in 1807. It is a striking example of how sometimes his deepest and most lasting thoughts are formulated very early. He speaks of the human situation as placed 'in a valley hemmed in by an immense stormy sea.' We feel 'dimly that on the other side of the sea there must be a land where more beautiful things grow and where the air is purer — our original home'. We have two messengers to send, poetry and philosophy. 'Poetry strikes out over the sea and is lost in the clouds'. Philosophy 'comes to within a stone's throw of the land before being halted by the raging waves which mount up to the clouds'.[14]

This idea of our longing for the paradise which is lost, is of course one of the favourite themes of European romanticism as a whole. It is very striking that a Swedish poet Erik Johann Stagnelius (1793-1823), published a poem in 1818 called 'The Island of Blessedness' whose opening verses parallel the opening verses of Grundtvig's poem very closely. Both writers express the same longing for eternity; but whereas the Swedish poet cannot go further than this and has to acknowledge that the longing is in vain, Grundtvig, as we shall see, goes on to say much more.[15]

Grundtvig takes up this theme with great skill. In the earlier verses he uses all his ability to describe that land for us, where time and eternity meet,

> Where autumn embraces the blossoming spring,
> Where evening and morning go always in dance
> In the light of midday.

This vision is above all the vision of childhood, and the first three verses describe it in an entirely positive way. The following three verses express the sense of growing disappointment and disillusionment which the experience of life can bring. The poet's work is in the end in vain, because he can only paint an image of the true land, and the closer the likeness is the more painful is the sense that the reality is not accessible to us.

Then comes the turning point in the poem. What human power cannot achieve, that God's grace will give to us. So the seventh verse begins with an invocation of the Spirit of love who reaches down from heaven to earth and opens our eyes to the reality of our true home. The following verse calls on

the heavenly name; we follow with Grundtvig on a Trinitarian path from the
Spirit through the Son, to the Father. There follow verses which speak of the
work of faith, hope and love in building the bridge across the stormy sea,
bringing us home through baptism and the eucharist to the land of the living.

> Oh likeness to Christ!
> You grant to our hearts what the world never knows.
> What we only glimpse feebly while our sight is so weak,
> *That* lives in our hearts, as we very well feel,
> My land, says Life, is heaven and earth
> Where love makes its home.[16]

Love, the love of God the Father who is love, who gives himself to us in his
Son and through his Spirit, the Son of his love and the Spirit of love, already
now binds heaven and earth into one and gives us a foretaste of that ultimate
fulfilment which will be at the end when God is all and in all. The vision is
eschatological; it looks to a fulfilment beyond this world. But it is also
present, known here and now; the eschatology is realised, anticipated, as in
the Johannine writings of the New Testament. Already in this world of space
and time, with all its imperfection, the eternal is made known, because the
reality of God's love is truly present and at work through the reality of
human love.

V

The content of Grundtvig's work *The Church's Rejoinder*, which was published
in 1825, is discussed in chapter 1 of the second section of this book and the
final outcome of the controversy which it raised is there recorded. Suffice it
to say here that Grundtvig himself felt that this was a moment of
'unparalleled discovery', when he discovered anew the original truth about
the nature of the Church of Christ and the place of the Bible within it. But
with Grundtvig's resignation in 1826, there came a six year break in the
sequence of his preaching. Not till 1832 did he have the opportunity to preach
regularly again. But of course his literary production did not slacken during
this period. The years from 1826 to 1829 were very productive, particularly
in works of a theological tendency. For instance in 1826-27 two closely related
studies appeared called *On True Christianity* and on *The Truth of Christianity*.
Then, between 1827 and 1830, he produced three volumes of his sermons
from the first half of the decade, with the title *Christian Sermons or The Sunday
Book*. The printed sermons are based on the sermons actually preached, but
in fact are entirely rewritten, expanded and made more explicitly theological
and often more exuberantly poetic.

In these years too, Grundtvig, for the first time, found himself working in
close collaboration with others, in particular with Jacob Christian Lindberg,
a churchman who had a gift for the publication and circulation of ideas, and

who tried to make a link between Grundtvig and the meetings of the godly, the revival meetings which were spreading through Denmark at this time. Grundtvig supported these groups of lay people against all attempts on the part of the authorities to suppress them. But he himself remained for long very cautious of them and of their particular kind of non-sacramental, enthusiastic piety.

Then, in the winter of 1827, a royal intervention made possible a decisive and unexpected change of direction. Grundtvig had a meeting with King Frederik VI, who had always retained a friendly attitude towards him, through all the vicissitudes of the previous years. Grundtvig tells us that the king asked him what work he had on hand.

'Nothing, your majesty', I replied, 'nor do I know what I should do, unless your majesty should send me to England to study the Anglo-Saxon manuscripts which can be of importance also for us in Denmark'. Against all expectations, the king took me at my word, and only regretted that the public travel allowances for the current year had all been taken up, so that I must wait for the coming year. To this I replied that there was no great hurry, since at my age (he was 45!) I was not all that keen on journeys abroad.[17]

So the matter was decided, and in the summers of 1829, 1830 and 1831 Grundtvig made extended visits to England, journeys which marked a turning point in his life and had a remarkable influence on all that was to come.

CHAPTER 3

New Directions Inner and Outer
1829–39

I

1832 and the years which followed formed a major turning point in Grundtvig's life. In that year he was nearly fifty and though he could not have known this, he had forty years of active life before him. During this latter period his position in Danish society was to change radically. In his earlier years he had always, it is true, been well-known. His was a personality which could not be hidden. But for much of the time he had been a rather solitary figure, often in opposition to the leading tendencies of his day, often feeling himself to be misunderstood. His projects and initiatives had frequently been, to all appearances, a failure. In the course of the thirties this situation began to change. By the end of the decade he was coming to be recognised as a national institution. One did not necessarily agree with him; no-one could deny that he was there.

If we ask what it was that ushered in this change, we shall have to acknowledge that the three English journeys of 1829, 1830 and 1831 had not a little to do with it. In a quite unforeseen way they resulted in a major change in Grundtvig's attitude to the world in which he was living, which was to affect the whole of the latter part of his life. Hans Henningsen puts it like this, 'In England Grundtvig made one of his most important discoveries, namely the discovery of the present. Admittedly, he still insisted that history is above all the source for the enlightenment of man, but his attention to history now turned to the present, as well as to the future — to the possibilities and tasks that lay ahead. Grundtvig had become conscious of himself as a modern man'.[1]

But in England something else also happened, something immediately caught up with the primary purpose of his journey, the study of the Anglo-Saxon manuscripts. This again took him into the study of the past and involved changes which were less immediately evident but which deeply strengthened his awareness of himself as a sacred poet called to give voice to the Church's praise. There was an inward as well as an outward strengthening of his sense of vocation.

It is important to recall at the outset that these journeys, together with his visit to England in 1843, were, apart from a brief visit to Norway, Grundtvig's only journeys outside his native land. In the course of his long life he travelled remarkably little. It is also important to remember to what a degree Grundtvig's mind was responsive and receptive to impressions coming from outside. Often his inner creativity was set in motion by things he had seen or heard, by people he had met, events he had been involved in. Seen in this perspective it is not perhaps surprising that these English journeys should have had such an important role in determining the overall shape of his later life. Thus it is vital to recognise both the inner and the outer aspects of Grundtvig's English impressions; the inner aspects, relating to his work in the archives, the outer to his contact with the world around him in a foreign country. It is this latter aspect which we shall consider first.

Grundtvig came to London in the summer of 1829. His first weeks in the capital were difficult. He did not like his first experience of being abroad; he found more difficulty both in speaking and in understanding the English language than he had expected. Lecturing in Copenhagen in 1838 he recalled that first meeting with England,

Gentlemen, in my experience England is a boring country to be in if one has no house or home there or daily business to satisfy one. For everybody there, from the Prime Minister to the pickpockets, is so terribly busy with his own occupation, and the inns are so cheerless and the private houses so enclosed and fortified in every way that a stranger is either left entirely to his own devices ... or he at once gets tired of seeing what an effort it takes and what a sacrifice it is for an Englishman to devote half an hour to him, let alone a whole hour. I have therefore never been closer to despair than when I arrived in England for the first time, which to some extent was undoubtedly due to the fact that I was already getting on in years when I first ventured out into the world, so to speak, and that I arrived, somewhat precipitately, having gone out of the Customs House here on to a Danish ship to disembark just like that at the Customs House in London, which could not help but seem to me like arriving like a perfect stranger in another world.'[2]

Gradually however Grundtvig began to make contacts. He found himself in touch, almost by chance, with a circle of professional men, mostly younger than himself, lawyers, journalists, writers, on the edge of the political world, radical in their social views and mostly Unitarian by religion. This was a new kind of society for Grundtvig to be involved in. He found their religion and theology not particularly interesting, but he was fascinated by the openness of their attitudes to political and social issues and the freedom with which they expressed their views on all kinds of questions.[3]

These were the years leading up to the Reform Bill of 1832, years of great political ferment in Britain. It was a time in which measures of reform which had been postponed for half a century, on account of the revolution in France and the subsequent conflict, were at last being seen to be unavoidable. Grundtvig found himself in a society in which freedom of speech and debate was taken for granted in a way which was still unthinkable in the smaller, more static world of Denmark. It was a world very different from that which he knew at home and he found many things in it most attractive.

It was not only a world of free speech, it was also a world of great practical and commercial activity. England was in the midst of the early stages of the Industrial Revolution. Everybody seemed so busy in the London of 1829 and people kept asking him, 'But what is it that you *do*?' He found it increasingly difficult to answer them. He faced new questions inside himself. Had he shut himself away too much in his study? Had he allowed himself to become too entirely an intellectual? Did he have a duty to his contemporaries which he had perhaps neglected? In a way which no-one had intended he found these months in England were altering his attitude to the world around him.

If Grundtvig's encounter with the ferment of English society proved un-expectedly stimulating, the same cannot be said of his first contacts with the Church of England. Grundtvig was visiting England in the years immediately before the revival of Church life which began in Oxford in 1833, and which was to transform the Church of England in a variety of ways. It was a time when many aspects of the Church's life, administrative, scholarly, liturgical were at a low ebb. If Grundtvig found Anglican worship cold and formal — he must have been painfully struck by the lack of congregational hymn-singing — so, it must be said, did many Anglicans at that time. The movement which began in the 1830's brought long overdue changes to the worship of the Church, architecturally in the reintroduction of visual imagery into the building and the reinstatement of the altar at the heart of the sanctuary, more inwardly by the development of new congregational music. The Book of Common Prayer had never since the Reformation made provision for congregational hymn-singing; the metrical psalms only partly filled the gap. Now in the space of twenty-five years there was a great activity of literary and musical composition, so that already in 1861 the Church of England was provided with its first full hymn-book, *Hymns Ancient and Modern*.

This collection was at once an outstanding success. It is tantalising to think that if things had taken a different turn in Grundtvig's relations with the leaders of the Oxford Movement, the book could have contained translations from the Danish of N.F.S. Grundtvig. As it was, it was only during his third visit in the summer of 1831 when Grundtvig stayed for a time at Trinity College, Cambridge, that he made real contact with Anglican theologians and clerics, who seem to have enjoyed his company as he enjoyed theirs. His impressions of the old Oxford and Cambridge college system were remarkably positive and contributed much to his later conviction that the Folk High Schools in Denmark must be communities of learning, where teachers and taught shared a common life. But of genuine theological exchange, there seems to have been very little.

II

But, of course, all this was in one sense only incidental in relation to the stated purpose of his journey. He had come with a scholarship from the king in order to study the Anglo-Saxon literary manuscripts. He was a highly conscientious scholar, determined to profit from this opportunity to the utmost. What is more, his work on the manuscripts was far more than a matter of duty. For more than twenty years he had been fascinated by the poetry of the Anglo-Saxons. Now he had the chance to make a first-hand contact with the original texts. Grundtvig was a scholar of very considerable philological and palaeographical skill. He fell on the manuscripts in the British Museum, in the libraries of Oxford and Cambridge and in the Cathedral Library at Exeter with a passionate intensity of intelligence and desire. S.A.J. Bradley, in his detailed study of the transcripts which Grundtvig made during these summers has shown how hard he worked.

Of course what he was discovering in these days in England was, in one sense, what he had always known was there. Already, twenty years or more before, he had glimpsed the greatness of the poetry of Anglo-Saxon England. He had already understood the importance of *Beowulf*, as an early heroic poem which in a remarkable way combined Christian and pre-Christian values and insights. He had already begun to form in his own mind, his vision of the crucial role of the Church in early Northumbria, the Church of Cuthbert and Bede, in the universal history of Christendom. This was the place where Christianity ceased to be a religion geographically locked around the shores of the Mediterranean and became a religion freed to travel north and west throughout Europe and to the world beyond.

Already, in a poem of 1817, *Ragnaroke*, he had caught sight of the figure of Cædmon, the legendary poet who offers his gift to God, placing it wholly at the service of the Word, who wills to become manifest in him and through him. All this he had already seen or begun to see. Now he could test it out in earnest, in the laborious work of transcribing texts, verifying readings, making lists of crucial terms, puzzling over mistakes and blunders in manuscripts a thousand years old.

For Grundtvig this work of transcription was not a purely academic exercise. He had other and larger intentions than the simple production of new and better editions of ancient texts. For him, the materials with which he was dealing were witnesses to a tradition of life and understanding which demanded to be heard anew. This was a tradition which was coming to life under his hands. Voices were crying out to be heard again. He was involved in a renewal of communication, a restoration of communion, between two parts of the same body,

an act of rehabilitation, of deliberate reestablishment of near-disrupted continuity, a demonstration in practice of the concept of the unity of truth between civilised religious community in the ancient past and civilised religious community in the present,

as Bradley puts it.[4]

This whole activity, for him, became focused in the figure of Cædmon, whom he saw as

the first Christian poet of the English language — and therefore, in Grundtvig's view of history, the first Northern Christian poet, and, as such, an archetype, a patriarch, indeed the founding father, among Christian poets of any subsequent age working within the languages and poetic traditions of the North.[5]

In his poem of 1817, Grundtvig had already felt himself in solidarity with the spirit of Cædmon, as Cædmon, in the poem in question, found himself identified with David the royal poet of Israel. It is Cædmon who speaks,

I dreamed, I dreamed that I saw King David: he gave into my hands his harp so fair. The golden strings I struck with might. In middle-earth still my song is recalled. I bent my ear to the ancient Book; its speech found tone and tongue found voice. Pictures sublime my gaze discovered, cheerfully I spent my talent on the text. *Great duty is ours, that we praise with words the heavens' Keeper, the Glory-King.* Notes such as these, I well dare hope, never would sink in Time's foaming waves. My ear I lent also to olden-day legend, I wove them in garlands, I bound them with art, like swaying branches one gathers and binds and fashions an arbour in forest wild. *Lo! we have heard of the majesty of the people's kings of the Spear-Danes in days of yore;* and still, I trust, Hrothgar and Beowulf recite in the hall the warriors' praise. Thus on the harp I exalted true legend, ennobled to epic olden-day poesy; fragments once fractious I deftly conjoined, truth took on beauty and fable truth.[6]

In these lines, Grundtvig, with great skill, has incorporated two passages from Anglo-Saxon poetry, the opening lines of *Genesis* and the opening lines of *Beowulf.* He has joined together, as only he could, what is called the sacred and what is called the secular; for him, in differing ways, both are sacred. Then he goes on to recall David directly;

To David belong all those harps whose strings are made to resound in church; therefore I come and with justification call upon the harp which is fashioned, David's and mine.[7]

Bradley remarks that Grundtvig, as the disciple of Luther, who also features in this poem, might perhaps be expected to show some hesitation in such an endorsement of 'the monkish Cædmon', as well as in such a conjunction of *Beowulf* and *Genesis.* Grundtvig is not unaware of these problems, but in the perspective of the Spirit's work, both in the inspired poet and in the tradition which he hands on, these problems are transcended.

There is therefore no conflict conceded between what Cædmon says he has taken from Scripture (represented by the quotation of the opening of the Old English *Genesis*) and what he has taken from the ancient Northern secular tradition of legend and of poetic form (represented by the quotation of the opening of *Beowulf*). There is no conflict conceded between Cædmon as monk and Cædmon as the great vision-inspired Christian poet of the North. There is, by implication, a simplicity, a directness of inspirational relationship between God and his mouthpiece, the poet-seer, speaking to the congregation of God's people, just as there ever has been back to the days of David.[8]

In such a passage we already begin to see how for Grundtvig the practice of God's praise, and the tools which make possible that practice, can be handed on from Jerusalem in the tenth century BC to seventh century Northumbria and nineteenth century Denmark. Through Cædmon and all that he represents Grundtvig finds a new possibility of appropriating the universal tradition of the first Christian millennium in a way which at once affirms its universal qualities as well as the human and cultural experiences of the peoples of the North.

If we ask what is the content of this vision, as we find it in these Old English texts, we find it to be at once universally Christian and at the same time particular in its way of articulation.

The sequence of poems taken as a whole presents an optimistic, buoyant reading of Christian history. Despite the fall of man, in each poem the principal figures retain through generation upon generation something of the image of God in which they were created. This is manifest not least in their inward capacity to recognise and to mirror that truth of which God himself is the embodiment and the never-faltering example: they are *soðhfæst* ('steadfast in truth, righteous') towards a God who is himself defined as *soðhfæst*. Meanwhile, their adversaries equally manifestly partake in the subversive purposes of Satan and are repeatedly defeated — until, in the final poem, the perfectly *soðhfæst* man, the Christ and the consummation of all the preceding images of righteousness and steadfastness and truth, ultimately renders vain and worthless all Satan's purposes and deeds. The poem *Genesis* and the poem *Christ and Satan*, which open and close the sequence, have the relationship that Creation and Incarnation have in St John's Gospel: the benevolence and the light-bringing, life-willing fiat of the Creator God is manifest again in the coming of the Son into the world in order to put death and the darkness of sin to rout. In the cycle of poems in this codex, creation theology and redemption theology are perceived in a unity.[9]

I have quoted this carefully considered summary of the doctrinal vision of the Anglo-Saxon poets at some length, since it seems worthwhile to notice at how many points it brings confirmation and illumination to Grundtvig's own settled convictions. There is, in this early poetry, no slightest tendency to evade or obscure the element of conflict in the Christian vision of things; light and darkness, truth and the lie, Christ and Satan, stand in opposition to one another. This vision of the conflict between the powers of good and evil, is as we know central to Grundtvig's own understanding of the course of human history. With his love for the mythology of the North, how could it be otherwise? There is nothing that he rejects more firmly than the type of monistic philosophy which is characteristic of the early Schelling. It had attracted him for a moment in his youth and ever afterwards he regarded it as a snare. There is, for him, no dialectical resolution, however skilfully worked out, of the conflict between life and death, truth and the lie.

But having acknowledged this necessary and essential element of conflict in the Christian scheme of things, Grundtvig can and does go on to affirm a final resolution of all things in the will of God, through his affirmation of the final triumph of life over death. This is something which altogether eludes our attempts at a systematic all-inclusive statement; yet it follows on naturally from a vision of things in which the good will of God, though thwarted and baffled is always present and never in the end defeated. Hence we have the buoyant reading of the human story which Bradley finds in the poetry of the Anglo-Saxons; absolutely not a superficial optimism but a deeply felt conviction about the triumph of good. Hence the insistence, against a certain strain in pietism, on the continuing signs of God's image and likeness in fallen humankind, seen above all in the human capacity to respond with faithfulness to the faithfulness of God.

It is in this light that we are to understand Grundtvig's strongly expressed preference for the theology of Irenaeus, with its insistence on the underlying unity of the old and the new covenant and its ultimately optimistic confidence in the triumph of the good. It is in this light too that we can see the constantly Johannine emphasis in Grundtvig's presentation of the central teachings of the Christian faith. The Pauline strand in the New Testament is neither denied nor neglected. It could not possibly be so in one who was deeply influenced by the teaching of Luther. But in the end it is the great Johannine affirmations which sound out above all in Grundtvig's teaching, as one of the most distinguished Danish New Testament scholars of our time, Bent Noack, who is also a translator of Anglo-Saxon poetry, has observed. Thus we find both in his sermons and his hymns this remarkable conjunction of creation theology with redemption theology, not the one or the other, but the two held together in constant interaction.[10]

III

What we have been seeing here is something of the way in which Grundtvig responded to the poetry of Anglo-Saxon England and the way in which he felt inwardly impelled to approach it so as to bring it into the present, to let it come to life again in a different time and for different people. It can hardly be by chance that this appreciative appropriation of the Anglo-Saxon past came at the beginning of the decade in which he was to undertake a more universal work of translation and transposition from the distant past into the present. In the 1830s he was to construct his *Sang-Værk*, his great and intentionally catholic collection of hymns, intended for the use of the Danish Church.

Here again, particularly in his translations from Latin and from Greek, we shall find a phenomenon we have already recognised. Grundtvig takes hold of new things which to some extent he already knows. He finds in the text he is translating, things which he had already discovered within his own heart and mind. But now he can express such things with greater strength and assurance because of this remarkable coinherence or exchange between one age and another, between one language and another, between one poet and another.

Something of this process as regards the Greek sources we shall see in the hymns and sermons considered in the chapter on Easter in part III of this book. Here we shall look briefly at the quality of Grundtvig's translations from the medieval Latin, and in particular from the works of the writers of the first generation of the Cistercian Reform. We are coming here into a very different world from that of *Beowulf* and *The Dream of the Rood*. It is a sign of the manifold character of Grundtvig's genius that he seems so much at home with both. Here again we shall spend some time seeing what it is in a particular area of tradition, that attracts him most strongly. Here too we shall ask what this attraction can tell us about his own inner way of development and growth.

In the case of the translations from the Latin we have the advantage both of a pioneering study by Jørgen Elbek published in *Grundtvig-Studier* in 1959, and also of two more recent articles from the pen of Jørgen Pedersen, two remarkably substantial and penetrating discussions of Grundtvig's indebtedness to the hymns of the Latin Middle Ages.[11] Both writers see the experience and understanding of the fusion of love with knowledge which is found in the Latin hymns, to be something of crucial importance in Grundtvig's attraction to them.

This is a fusion which takes place both at the level of grace and at the level of nature, and which at both levels is essential for the growth of any true life. Speaking of the Latin hymns Elbek declares that true life means fellowship with God. The prayer of the hymns is in the same breath for the love of God and for the knowledge of God.

In the world which the prayer opens out onto, thought and feeling have the same root, and tend to the same goal. Love is knowledge, knowledge is love. Grundtvig found this insight preserved in the hymns, and he appropriated it with delight. While in the hymns this insight is seldom expressed in so many words, since there it is a self-evident pre-supposition, it is proclaimed in the translations.[12]

So, in his translation of the famous early Cistercian hymn, *Jesu dulcis memoria*, Grundtvig writes of the memory of Jesus,

> Thus is born the heart's love
> To you, who suffered death for us;
> Thus is born a knowledge eternally true
> Of the light of life and the land of life ...
>
> Only he who loves, knows God
> And you, his true messenger ...[13]

This union of love and knowledge has, as we shall see, far reaching consequences. The God who is discovered when thought and love come together into one, is not only the God within, found in the depths of the human heart, but also the God without, present and at work in his whole creation and in all human history. Elbek continues,

As for the Middle Ages there is a harmony between loving and thinking, so there is harmony between all the themes they include; indeed, at the deepest level they are seen to be one. Wherever thought turns in time and space, in the world around and in pre-Christian history, it meets the divine. So the hymns give their translator an opportunity at times to draw nature, at times to draw the Old Testament into his hymns.[14]

To come to know and love God truly in the depths of the heart, is also to come to know and love God truly in all that he has made and in all that he does.

Jørgen Pedersen develops this thought of the coming together of love and knowledge into one by looking much further into the biblical and traditional notion of wisdom, *sapientia*, and what is implied in it. It is a word which for the medieval writers is linked with the word *sapere*, to taste, 'Oh taste and see how gracious the Lord is'. It speaks of an experience of God and it thus can provide a background to Grundtvig's constant use of the word 'feeling', a word which otherwise might be understood in an entirely subjective and romantic way. It is also a concept which is of great importance for the understanding of Grundtvig's way of seeing the relation of the heart to the head and of both to the mouth and the hand. In the growth of wisdom, knowledge and clarity are fused together with love and feeling, in a gift which is at once human and divine.

If we look back into the wisdom literature of the Old Testament, we find that this gift begins in the very practical discipline of learning how to live well; 'The fear of the Lord is the beginning of wisdom'. The gift grows in the understanding heart of Solomon, and is there seen to involve both a knowledge of the natural world and of all living things, and also a penetrating insight into human motivation and action; true understanding of the world of nature, true judgement in the world of human history are both facets of this gift of wisdom. But this gift, which at the horizontal level spreads out to encompass all creation, also leads upwards on a way which takes us beyond the creation towards the knowledge and the love of God. The fear of the Lord grows into awe, awe grows into wonder and amazement, wonder and amazement into praise and thanksgiving.

For this human gift of wisdom, which we have been considering, is a gift from God, a reflection at the human level of that divine wisdom, that divine *sapientia* by which all things were made. And this gift of God in creation 'in which the human turns itself to its maker and is enlightened by his truth', is met by God's gift of himself to humankind in the person of Christ, in whom the divine Wisdom is incarnate, and in the coming of the Holy Spirit, 'a gift of grace in which God himself is present' crowning his gifts in creation. It is in this union of love and knowledge that the human person becomes apt to receive that gift of the Holy Spirit, that gift in which God himself becomes gift, in which human and divine are fused into one.[15]

This wisdom, given both in creation and redemption, is of course seen throughout Scripture and tradition as at once one and many, multiple, pluriform, specifically sevenfold. It speaks of the diversity and richness of creation as we experience it in the world around us, and as we experience it in the world within, with all its own richness and diversity. All this, inward and outward, is gathered together in one in the coming of the Spirit, in whom nothing of the diversity of things is lost, but a new unity shines out in the clarity of God's gift, in the transfiguring splendour of grace.

In this growth into wisdom, men and women learn to see God present in the whole creation, and to know and love him in and through all things. But that discovery of the presence and activity of God around us is rooted in the inner and immediate perception of the presence of God at the heart of human existence, in that unity of the spirit in which we become one Spirit with Him (1 Corinthians 6:17) as Bernard, and still more William of St. Thierry, loved to insist. In this perception we know because we love, we love because we know, not with the mind alone but with the whole power of the human person gathered together into a single point, in a love and knowledge that grow together in a constantly developing interaction and exchange.

It is not difficult to see that the discovery of this fusion was a matter of the greatest personal importance to Grundtvig. It was for him the key to discovering how to become a whole and integrated person. In this fusion the gifts of the imagination themselves might become unified and unifying, esemplastic in Coleridge's term, as the human spirit responds to the gift of the divine Spirit. In this fusion inner activity and outer activity are not in competition with one another; they support and complement one another. The turning to the world which is such a notable feature of the 1830s is not made at the expense of the life within. Grundtvig the translator of Cistercian hymns and Grundtvig the promoter of new forms of adult education is one and the same person.[16]

As Pedersen points out, this understanding of human life, in which love and thought grow together in the way of wisdom, is characteristic of the theology of the pre-scholastic period in the Latin West. In a different context we can see traces of it in Grundtvig, colouring not only his Christianity but his whole understanding of human existence. We can see its effects, for instance, in his thoughts about human growth and education. Hans Henningsen's remark 'all true enlightenment is gentle and soft so that it pleases our heart'[17], is an affirmation which reflects, in our late twentieth century world, something of this much earlier experience and understanding of the constantly necessary interchange between love and knowledge for the development and understanding of any true human life, personal or social.

Thus formulas worked out in one situation can grow and live and acquire new meaning and resonance in another. The teaching methods of the eighteenth century Latin school, as Grundtvig had known it as an adolescent, were, in his experience, something which divorced heart from head, which left the mind turning and turning again in a barren, cold desert, and which left the heart lost and undirected, a prey to its own powerful but blind impulses. It was a way of division and it led towards death.

To put the two things together, however, to let them come together into a living unity is the work of a lifetime, a work which can be undertaken only on the presupposition that before it is a task it is a gift, a gift of the Spirit who unites the two powers in a single movement of lucid and delighted contemplation and creation. For Grundtvig, as everything we know about him tells us, was a man with a frightening power of active intelligence and at the same time a frightening power of loving desire. It was through bringing the two sides of his tempestuous nature together, that, we may surmise, he found the secret of the extraordinary capacity for new creation which accompanied him throughout his life.

It seems that here we have an aspect of Grundtvig's work which needs further exploration. Is the sapiential quality of early Latin theology, as we see it from Gregory the Great to William of St. Thierry, something which could shed light on his characteristic ways of thinking? Would the Eastern Orthodox tradition, with its rather different way of approach to the figure of Holy Wisdom, represented in this century in the sophiology of Father Sergei Bulgakov, provide further insight into his vision of the world as created with an active potential of response to the initiatives of God? It seems there are paths which could be followed with profit here.

We touch here on one of the most crucial factors which gives to Grundtvig his particular quality and character. He was not only a man who combined loving and knowing to an exceptional degree, he was a man who could combine them in a way which is not at all common in the modern world which began in the eighteenth century and which seems just now to be coming to an end. Is this why he so constantly eludes our categories? Is he a scholar or a poet? An intellectual or a man of action? A man of the past or a man of the future? A God-centred man or a man wholly centred on humanity, or is he even a man wholly centred on himself? He refuses to accept our dichotomies. He finds himself by transcending them. Perhaps it is this fact which arouses in him such a deep and passionate resonance to earlier periods in human history, to ages in which this fusion of apparent opposites could be taken more for granted than it was in his own time or than it is in ours.

Perhaps he had a deep personal need to draw on the wisdom and insight of earlier ages, on the qualities which he finds in the sacred poetry of the Anglo-Saxons, in the liturgical hymns of the Byzantine Church, in the monastic theology of the early medieval West. He needs these resources for his own life, and he is able to transpose them into his world of the nineteenth century, which if it is no longer our world is yet a world in which we can still feel at home. He can be for us a vital link, a point of connection with these older worlds whose riches he had deciphered and transcribed with such love and labour.

The whole project and achievement of the *Sang-Værk* was intended to open to the congregations of the Danish Church something of the fullness and catholicity of the Christian tradition of love and knowledge, of praise and thanksgiving. The work which was accomplished outwardly was one which had first to be carried out inside its author's own heart and mind. It had to be accomplished there. There had to be an inner catholicity and fullness of the heart before that inner fullness could be shared and imparted to a whole people. This it was that Grundtvig prayed for in one of the greatest of his verses.

> You who have given me yourself
> Let me love life in you,
> So that the heart beats only for you,
> So that you alone in all my thoughts
> Are the deep coherence.[18]

IV

To Danish readers of this book it will probably seem simply perverse that in a chapter on Grundtvig in the 1830s so much has been said about his translations from ancient languages and his inner discovery of himself as called to be a poet in the tradition of David and Cædmon. As we noticed at the beginning of this chapter the most obvious result of Grundtvig's visits to England was a turning towards the world, a turning not towards the past but towards the present, not to ancient hymnody but towards pragmatic social and political concerns. Indeed, for one of the most weighty and influential of Grundtvig scholars in the years since the second world war, Kaj Thaning, the year 1832 was without any question *the* turning point in Grundtvig's life. It was for him the moment when he turned his back on the old, inward-looking, penitential religion of Lutheran orthodoxy and pietism, and discovered the true meaning of his life and calling in a prophetic intuition of a world-affirming secular Christianity, a Christianity whose watchword was the aphorism 'first human — then Christian'.

This view of Grundtvig has been of great influence in Denmark in the last quarter of a century. There is certainly truth in it, particularly in all that it says about Grundtvig's newly found capacity to write about human and social issues and to involve himself, in a variety of ways, in the public life of his time. There was, in the thirties, a liberation of new forces in his life, after a long period in which, at the outward level, he had frequently found himself disappointed and frustrated. He found that he could and that he should work with others, even when they were not in complete agreement with him, nor he with them.

But, I would suggest, that to see this change as an about turn is mistaken. It came about not because he had turned his back on the theological concerns which had stirred him in the previous decade, but because he had carried them further. Let us briefly consider some of the principal signs of Grundtvig's new concern for human and contemporary matters. In 1832, he published a wholly new study of the *Mythology of the North*, in which, for the first time, he advanced his conviction, that traditional Christians, amongst whom he numbered himself, should be ready to work with all who in a general way would accept the Judaeo-Christian tradition. These people he called 'naturalists'; the position he thinks of them holding has a good deal in common with that of the Unitarians whose acquaintance he had made in England, people who could still respect the structures of Christian morality, who still held a belief in a personal God, but who found it impossible to accept the traditional view of man's salvation through Christ. This certainly was, from Grundtvig's point of view, a new opening to the world outside his own circle, though in twentieth century terms it seems a rather limited one. The change was not all that drastic.[19]

In the years following 1833 he published three volumes of an entirely reworked *Universal History*, a handbook to world history. Here again, in contrast to his earlier historical writings, he gave much greater emphasis to purely human factors; he spent much more time producing and discussing the source material on which his history was based. He was writing, he said, for the school and not for the Church. But the theological purposes which had been so evident in his earlier historical writing, though they were now more in the background, had not entirely disappeared. William Michelsen, who has written perhaps more than anyone on Grundtvig's view of history, maintains that his view here is basically still the same as it had been twenty years before, 'but his opinion as to how far it could be scientifically realised has changed from one book to another.'[20] Here there is certainly a strong change of emphasis, but perhaps no ultimate change of direction.

Then, in 1836, there came one of the first of Grundtvig's educational writings, *The Danish Four-Leafed Clover*. Here he placed new stress on the need for truly popular education, for education that would be adapted to the needs and situations of people of the nineteenth century. The possibility of establishing consultative assemblies as part of a process of growing towards democracy was being discussed in these years, and thus the first moves towards a parliamentary regime were being made. Grundtvig saw that for such assemblies to be really useful, the ordinary working people of Denmark would need new and more appropriate forms of education. He himself was venturing into new fields in encouraging such developments, but he was not departing from his earlier convictions.

This was then a decade of remarkable outward activity, but it was also a decade of some of Grundtvig's finest preaching and his most outstanding productivity as a hymn writer. The inner and the outer developments went hand in hand.

V

We have an exceptionally interesting impression of Grundtvig during these years in the memoirs of Hans Lassen Martensen (1808-84) who first met Grundtvig in 1836. At this time Martensen was still a young man. In the course of a brilliant career he was to become one of the most distinguished of Danish churchmen, Bishop of Copenhagen, a theologian of European and more than European renown. At a time when the names of Søren Kierkegaard and Grundtvig were scarcely known outside Denmark Martensen was being studied in Europe and America. In his own life-time his *Dogmatics* and his *Ethics* were translated into English and were highly regarded by his contemporaries. In church political matters Martensen came to be totally opposed to Grundtvig and in later years relationships between them were difficult. Nonetheless as a young man, Martensen had quite a lot of contact with Grundtvig and had been surprised to find that there was more in common between them than he had expected.

The occasion of their meeting was the celebration of the third centenary of the Danish Reformation in 1836. Martensen accompanied the eminent German theologian P.K. Marheineke (1780-1846), who was in Copenhagen for the occasion, to visit Grundtvig and it was on this occasion that Grundtvig uttered one of the most famous of his aphorisms. The German professor who was much influenced in his theology by the work of Hegel, asked Grundtvig for his views on speculative theology and dialectic. Grundtvig replied that he was frightened to enter into such topics. 'Why are you frightened?' said Marheineke? Grundtvig replied 'I am frightened for myself. For me the chief contradiction is between life and death.'

It is clear that the German visitor neither sympathised with nor altogether understood this reply. Martensen tells us that he himself was deeply impressed by Grundtvig's remark, even though his own inclination at the time was towards speculative theology. He recognised that in his opposition of life and death there was something very striking ... By it he meant that the oppositions which are most important for us, and which determine both our duties and our problems, are much more than logical or intellectual oppositions; they are what are called existential oppositions ... In later life I have often thought back to the flash of light which shone out in this conversation when Grundtvig said, 'Mein Gegensatz ist Leben und Tod.' With the passing of the years, with growing experience, this word, which is also Scripture's word, has gained for me new and deeper power.[21]

From this time onwards the young Martensen came to visit Grundtvig quite frequently and evidently enjoyed drawing him out on a great variety of topics.

In his daily conversation he had an admirable eloquence, which was often mixed with wit and humour. I talked with him on many of the most interesting topics. I got him to talk about Danish poetry, about Oehlenschläger, Baggesen, Ingemann, sometimes also his own poetry; it was always fascinating and instructive. I heard him talk about mythology and revelation, about the popular and the Christian, subjects which I already knew from his writings. In history we often went back to the Middle Ages, and we talked many times about Anskar and his dreams. Grundtvig had a special preference for the Middle Ages and declared that even in our day there are some people who are most at home in the Middle Ages; I sometimes had the impression that he thought of himself as a medieval character.[22]

Martensen was surprised that Grundtvig had so little interest in academic theology. For Grundtvig the hymns took the place of dogmatics; 'In the hymns he found and expressed his teaching of the faith.' But there was one particular point of theology in which Martensen found himself in full and wholehearted agreement with him,

in his conception of bodiliness. Although the spirit was for him the first, indeed the only truly real, yet he could not think of the spirit without bodiliness, and a spirit in which nature and the bodily was excluded, was for him an abstract spirit, the spirit of the rationalists with which he would have nothing to do. Thus he had in his viewpoint a higher, spiritual realism, which is also found in Lutheranism, particularly in the teaching about the sacraments. Here I was in complete agreement, and thereby also in the great importance he gave to image language, which for him had a greater truth and reality than abstract concepts and whose highest form he found partly in Holy Scripture, in the utterances of the prophets and in the sayings of Christ, partly in the myths and the symbolic language of the North. There was to be no playing with image language, and he often said that true poets were serious in their use of such language and that through it they expressed the *truth* in their view of life.'[23]

This convergence of view on the part of two such men is particularly interesting. It suggests that in nineteenth century Denmark Grundtvig was not always so isolated theologically as he sometimes thought himself to be. Martensen and he shared strong convictions about the bodily nature of life in the Spirit, and about the embodied character of Christian worship as expressed in the sacraments. Martensen was willing to follow him too in his conviction that the poetic image can be the vehicle of divine truth and is not merely a product of the human imagination.

It was in Grundtvig's view of the Church, as it developed after 1825, that Martensen found himself most at variance with him. From his point of view Grundtvig seemed to have broken with the basic principles of Luther and the Reformation. He recognised that this was not Grundtvig's intention but nonetheless it was what he seemed to have done.

In the best and most favourable case he could only take me to the ancient Catholic Church of the second and third centuries with Irenaeus and Tertullian, while for me the Reformation Church was something much deeper and higher.[24]

In the light of what has been written earlier in this chapter, about Grundtvig's use of the poetry of the Anglo-Saxons and the hymns of the Latin Middle Ages, we can recognise the full significance of what Martensen says about Grundtvig's feeling of being at home in the Middle Ages. The reference to Anskar, and in particular to the vision of Christ described in his Life, a thing which we shall find Grundtvig mentions in one of his Pentecost sermons, is particularly interesting. A nineteenth century Protestant theologian who is willing to take with full seriousness the description of a dream-vision, found in the life of a dark age saint, is certainly a man who is not bound by the characteristic prejudices of his own time.

Martensen gives us a picture of Grundtvig as seen by an exceptionally intelligent and well read Danish contemporary. We also have from these years a slighter but also revealing portrait from a young Anglican priest, who was acting as chaplain in the 1830s to the British community at Elsinore. Nugent Wade, who came to Denmark in 1833, was in fact an Irishman; he had been born in Dublin and ordained in Kilmore. He was not unaware of his Irish roots; he brought with him, in his baggage, an Irish dictionary and a request from friends at Trinity College Dublin to enquire after the possibility of there being Irish manuscripts in the Royal Library at Copenhagen.

Quite soon after his arrival in Denmark he made the acquaintance of Grundtvig and was altogether fascinated by him. He records in his diary, in November 1834,

— had a most delightful & useful interview with Pastor Gruntvig: he is decidedly a man of genius & of a first rate order, I don't know that I ever met with so comprehensive a mind, he seems to sweep the whole world history at a glance & philosophise upon it & that soundly & with *one* scope God & his dealing with man for his Redemption.[25]

Wade shows from the outset a genuine insight into Grundtvig's understanding of history. His words reveal how clearly, in 1834, the religious intention was still a dominant motive behind Grundtvig's historical writings. But if Wade was impressed by the scope of Grundtvig's vision of things, there were elements in his outlook which he found puzzling and disconcerting. Grundtvig did not share the common enthusiasm of the time for overseas missionary activity; Wade notes that he did not think that the time for missions had arrived. Still more surprising for Wade were his doubts about the value of the work of the Bible Societies, something unquestioned in Britain and Ireland; he 'looked upon the circulation of the Scriptures in heathen lands without a previous preaching as quite *absurd*.'[26]

Wade was much impressed by the openness and liberality of Grundtvig's theological views;

his ideas of *the Extent of the benefits of Christs death* are liberal indeed & wide — that in whomsoever God may see the *desire* for truth & seeking after it — tho they may not have had the opportunity of Knowing Christ, thro his death they shall yet be saved.

But he was even more impressed by the depth and quality of the man he was meeting. 'I was greatly affected by the earnestness of his manner — his own deep conviction — his evident personal feeling — his Holiness.'[27] This last term is one which would not come easily in the writing of a Dane, still less of a Lutheran; it is interesting to find it here.

We have tantalisingly brief notes of a conversation which took place something over a year later in February 1836,

a long evening Intellectual feast with *Gruntvig* — on a great variety of subjects — Irish manuscripts — Northern languages — History of the very Northern nations particularly of Iceland ...[28]

Is it possible that even then Grundtvig was speculating about the nature of the Irish presence in Iceland before the arrival of the Vikings?

Martensen and Wade, in their different ways, give a picture of Grundtvig at the height of his powers, discoursing effortlessly on a great variety of topics; we shall find this impression again in later witnesses. Here we feel the presence of a man who is now sure of himself, who is certainly still a fighter, but who no longer needs to assert himself with quite the same violence that he had shown in the previous decade. It is, we may surmise, a picture of a man in whom outer and inner interests and concerns have come together in unity. The preacher and the hymn writer was growing simultaneously with the man who could immerse himself in the current affairs of the Danish people.

CHAPTER 4

Unexpected Fulfilment
1839–58

I

We have seen in the previous chapter how the 1830s were a time when Grundtvig's position in Danish life became more generally recognised. The end of the decade saw this process carried further. One of the things which helped to make him better known was his new friendship with the Crown Prince, Prince Christian Frederik. The old King Frederik VI was visibly failing; it could not be long before there was a change of monarch. Prince Christian was attracted by Grundtvig's blend of liberal and conservative ideas on political questions and the two men found they had much in common. Grundtvig also met the Crown Princess Caroline Amalie, and this was the beginning of a long lasting friendship. The Princess became one of his most faithful admirers. In the spring of 1839 she invited him to come and give lectures on Danish history to the ladies of the court. This was a new kind of audience for Grundtvig, an audience which he said hardly understood Danish, and was certainly unfamiliar with such a thorough-going Danish presentation of affairs as his was.

This new royal contact was almost certainly of great influence in another development which took place in 1839. Throughout the 1830s Grundtvig had been allowed to preach at the evening service in one of the Copenhagen churches, but this arrangement had been by special permission. He had no security of tenure, and also no stipend. Now he applied for the position of Chaplain at Vartov, a set of alms houses, (perhaps 'sheltered accomodation', would be a better description) in Copenhagen, and despite the lack of support from the bishop he was given the post. It was certainly not an eminent position to hold, but it meant that at last he had an official position in the Church which he was to hold for the rest of his life. It gave him a place in Copenhagen where he could preach and build up a congregation; it also gave him an assured salary.

Looking from outside Denmark people have sometimes wondered how it was that Grundtvig, all his life, managed to keep within the established Church and never founded a denomination of his own. Certainly there were those who thought, and maybe sometimes hoped, that he would do so. He remained stubbornly opposed to the idea of creating a schism. But in the course of time his view of the Church itself altered. Whereas in 1825 he had hoped to carry the Church as a whole with him into his new and prophetic vision of its nature, by the 1830s it was becoming clear that he and his sympathisers were only a minority within a Church much wider than themselves. In face of this situation Grundtvig gradually worked out a new theory, which saw the institution of the Church at the national and diocesan level as providing a framework, a civil structure of no religious significance in itself, in which the true Church, in the shape of believing, worshipping congregations, could find a place to shelter. The institutional Church was like a tree and the congregations like birds which came and made their nests in its branches.

Perhaps inevitably the tendency of Grundtvig to 'doctrinalise' his ideas got to work here. What had started out as a way of making a certain amount of sense of an anomalous situation came to be taken as a theology of the Church. Curiously enough it still has this status, at least amongst some of those who are called Grundtvigians in the Church of Denmark. This is one of the primary reasons why at the present time attempts to strengthen the life of the Church as an institution, for instance by the establishment of a national synod, are strenuously resisted by powerful elements within the Church. One of the major inconveniences of this understanding of the Church is that, when carried through consistently, which happily is not always done, it tends to cut the Danish Church off from the rest of the Christian world, for the Danish situation is in many ways without parallel. Where else, at the end of the twentieth century, is there a Church which is willing that a large part of its administration should be carried on by a government department? Where else is there a state which is still willing to take so much responsibility for the administration of the Church's life? More importantly this view is one of the primary reasons why some of the basic implications of Grundtvig's own earlier ecclesial view have not yet been worked out in the life of the Danish Church.

The success which had marked Grundtvig's open lectures on the subject of modern history in 1838 came again for another series which was given in the winter of 1843-44. Their subject was Greek and Norse mythology and on this occasion women also were welcomed to be a part of the audience, a move which seemed revolutionary at the time. In these same years, Grundtvig's educational ideas were beginning to have active repercussions in the world outside Copenhagen. It was in this decade that the first Folk High Schools were founded.

Then came 1848, the year of revolution in Europe. In Denmark as before, the revolution occurred without violence. The King agreed to the establishment of a Constitutional Assembly. The old order of the absolute monarchy which had existed since 1660, came to an end. Denmark became a constitutional monarchy with a parliament elected by a reasonably wide suffrage amongst male voters.

It was by this time unthinkable that Grundtvig should not be a member of the Assembly. After it had completed its work he was elected a member of the *Folketing*, the lower house of parliament, and remained there for the next ten years. The course of Grundtvig's parliamentary activities is one of the aspects of his life which we are not able to follow up here, but an extract from a speech made to the Constitutional Assembly on the subject of religious liberty will at least give us a flavour of his interventions, and of the way in which they could be received,

According to all that I know either of Christianity itself or of its history, it is so far from wishing in any way to limit the freedom of religious belief that it much rather establishes it in the strongest possible way; I am fully convinced that it is never the original, genuine Christianity, but always merely a false and merely a self-made Christianity which tries to obtain a kingdom of this world. (Hear! Hear!) It is always the case that anyone who knows that Christians in all ages have themselves demanded full freedom for their faith and worship of God must also be able to see that if Christianity were to deny the same freedom to others, it would both forfeit its own freedom and at the same time impair the element of freedom in which alone it can breathe and live and thrive. (Spoken like a Christian! Hear! Hear!) ... the whole of world history teaches us that where this freedom is lacking, no civic freedom can rightly strike root or bear fruit; therefore, if not for its own sake, yet for the sake of all civic and human freedom, one should strive to have it as completely as possible; and if people try to frighten us out of this freedom by enumerating the many dangers which it might bring with it, we should behave as we would if someone tried to frighten the life out of us by enumerating and depicting all the dangers to which human life is undeniably exposed from the cradle to the grave: just as in that case we never ought to give any other answer than: 'Life is good for everything, and death for nothing; therefore we will keep life and try to avoid and get through its dangers as well as we can', so we shall answer here: 'Freedom is good for all that is good. Slavery is no good for anything that is good in the world of the spirit, therefore we will have freedom with all its dangers.

Grundtvig left the speaker's rostrum, greeted with shouts of 'Bravo!'.[1]

We should remember that these sentiments were being uttered at the end of two centuries of monarchical rule during which the practice of one religion alone, the Lutheran religion, had been not only safeguarded but at times actually enforced by the power of the law. Even in the 1830s there were cases of the children of Baptist parents being forcibly taken from their parents in order to be baptised in the national Danish Church.

We are not surprised to discover that when, in 1850, a small book called *Clara Raphael* was published, speaking, for the first time ever in Danish, on behalf of the rights of women, Grundtvig was one of the few public figures to welcome it, and to give his active support to its anonymous and then unknown author, Mathilde Fibiger, at that time just twenty years old. In the following year, when she published a second and even more controversial book, with much of which Grundtvig himself disagreed, he felt moved to support her even more strongly, inviting her to stay for a time with him and his newly married second wife.

II

Grundtvig was, as we have seen, a man of great natural energy. All through his life he was undertaking new projects, entering into new controversies. Nowhere is this overflowing energy of life more fully revealed than at the beginning of the eighteen fifties, the time of his second marriage; one of the strangest, most characteristic and in the end perhaps most beautiful incidents in his long and varied existence. It was certainly the moment which brought him the greatest earthly happiness. As he approached his seventieth year he found his youth renewed in a way which no-one could have expected.

This second marriage however was not without its grief and pain. It was ushered in with pain, not only on account of the death of his first wife, Lise Blicher, but still more on account of the gradual breakdown of his relationship with her in the years which preceded her decease. And then the happiness which came to him in 1851 was not to last; it was ended after three brief years by the premature death of his second wife.

We must not underestimate the importance or the strength of Grundtvig's first marriage to Lise Blicher. It was a marriage which was prepared by a seven year engagement and it lasted for thirty years. In its earlier stages it seems in many ways to have been a very good marriage; to the end it remained an honourable relationship. But in its latter years it had become clear both to Grundtvig and to Lise that they were no longer able to support or really understand one another. He had travelled too far beyond the man that she had married, his inner life had been altogether too demanding for her to be able to follow him.

Lise was a woman of courage who did not hesitate to support her husband at moments, as in 1826, when he felt the necessity of escaping the bonds of his clerical profession. At such a time she accepted the financial and social insecurity of the family with great generosity. She brought up his children and she did her best to accompany him. But how impossible it was to keep up with him! By nature she was too quiet, too gentle a person to be able to respond fully to the demands of a partner so inexhaustible and unpredictable. The more one knows of Grundtvig the more one sees how impossibly difficult he must have been to live with day by day.

In the last years of her life she became more and more aware of her inability to respond to Grundtvig's needs. She knew times of illness and depression; worst of all she knew that Grundtvig was strongly attracted to another, younger woman, a woman of very different character and background, Fru Marie Toft.

Ane Marie Elisa Carlsen (1813-1854) was born in an aristocratic family which traced its history back to the Middle Ages. She was first married in 1840, to a landowner, Harald Toft; within little more than a year her husband was dead. She was left in possession of a handsome manor house in western Zealand, Rønnebæksholm, and two months after her husband's death she became the mother of a daughter Haralda. Marie Toft first came into touch with Grundtvig because of a perceived disagreement with him. As a young and active landowner she took a great interest in the life of the district where she lived and had a strong sense of responsibility towards her tenants. She found herself more and more involved in the religious revival meetings which were stirring up the peasantry of Zealand and Funen at this time and anxious to encourage them. Amongst the clergy who supported these meetings some were friends of Grundtvig. He himself however remained firmly fixed in his decision not to identify himself with such enthusiastic gatherings which he felt might easily become sectarian in character.

Marie came to see him first in the spring of 1845 to try and convince him that he should be more forthcoming in his attitude towards the revival. She found he was not at home; this did not deter her. She came again later in the year and they met and had a quite stormy discussion in which neither party was afraid to express their point of view. What Grundtvig said remained with her. She wanted to pursue the differences between them further. Above all she saw that here was a man to whom she could bring her deepest questions about faith and life; a man who would not give her correct clerical answers but would speak from the heart, a heart which was also a centre of intelligence and reflection.

So she came again and again. There is something very eloquent in the way in which their relationship began with points of conflict and disagreement. One of the reasons why there was something unique in Marie Toft's relationship with Grundtvig was rooted in the fact that she was never afraid of him. All through his life he had been looking for someone who would be able to respond to him on a level of equality. He had found plenty of opponents and, as time went by, he also found plenty of admirers and disciples. There were few, however, who could meet him as an equal and who could respond to him with the whole of their being. In Marie he had found someone who could do just that, who loved life and lived it with an intensity and a joy which equalled his own.

Grundtvig himself describes her as 'a strong, magnanimous, *folkelig*, noble-woman'. The conjunction of the last two words tells us that she was at once conscious of the long history of her family and at the same time open and eager to have contact with people of every class. Her largeness of spirit, Grundtvig adds, did not lead her into pride, nor did her strength turn into aggression. This he believed was due to her fear of God; from her respect for God flowed a respect for all her fellow creatures.

In 1845 it was she who had come to visit him. In the following year he was invited to speak at a meeting at Næstved, a place in the immediate vicinity of Rønnebæksholm. So he came with friends and stayed the night there. From this time onwards it became clear to those who knew them both that there was a deep and growing attraction between them.

Five years later, in January 1851, Lise Blicher died. At her funeral Grundtvig began his sermon with the words,

I stand here today as an old man, who takes a considerable step towards his own grave, as he buries the mother of his children, the bride of his youth, who for forty years, already seven years before she vowed it at the altar, lovingly shared both good times and bad times with me, and more often the second than the first.[2]

But his friends could not help noticing that throughout the sermon he failed to say anything about his own feelings for the one who had been the wife of his youth and the mother of his children, as he had so clearly put it at the beginning of his address.

If part of him felt the approach of death in the death of his first wife, there was a larger part of him which felt an unpredictable renewal of life in the new love which was engulfing him. Only nine months later in the October of the same year he was married to Fru Marie.

As Rønning puts it in his biography, a book written only forty years after Grundtvig's death, when nineteenth century feelings and attitudes were still well understood, many even of Grundtvig's friends felt uneasy about this marriage.

That one of the partners was a priest of almost seventy years, and that he who never made room between his innermost heart and his outer being for any kind of hypocrisy, was in this case behaving more like a youth of twenty than an old man, was certainly painful enough, people thought; but even worse, in the view of many, was the fact that there was only a six month period between the moment when he stood by Lise's coffin in the Church of Our Saviour and the moment when he gave his first kiss to Fru Marie in Skytteskoven.'[3]

Amongst those who found the whole situation particularly painful and difficult were, as one might expect, Grundtvig's children.

For him, however, the over-riding factor was that he knew himself to be in love as he had never been before. Out of the wholeness of his feelings there flowed poems, which in their directness and simplicity have no equal in his abundant production. Here above all one needs a poet as translator, but even without one, something of the quality of these lines may come through; their simplicity, their humour, their irony, their total truthfulness.

> Take me whole and entire
> As I stand before you
> As a poet, as a clod

With ash-grey hair,
As a priest, as a firebrand,
As a member of parliament.
I take you just as you are.

As a flower in the grass
As a song in the wood,
As lady of the manor
With rights and with dues
Like the goddess with her riddles,
As a woman with moods,
I take you just as you are.

What is it my Marie
That makes it that we two
Whether we talk or keep silent,
Whether we walk or we sit,
Feel vowed to one another
As the Church is to its Amen
As the priest is to his people?

It is that we shall be
To each other, as we are,
It is that we can bear
Each other as we are;
It is, that our lips
Whether we wake or sleep
Meet in a kiss.

Therefore we bind ourselves
In faith and so in love
With the conqueror of death,
Who came down to us,
Who to God the Father's glory
Will carry our dust homeward
In the embrace of the Spirit.[4]

Or, in another verse, more explicitly religious in its formulation,

Dear Mary, faithful friend,
Helpmate to the poet as heart is to mind,
Strong as a man, yet gentle as a woman,
Thanks for your heart and thanks for your hand,
May He, in whose name you have placed your hands in mine,
May He, with his voice of love, bless them forever.[5]

The lyrics Grundtvig wrote at this time were not all so intimately personal. In another poem from this period he celebrates the places in Zealand which he had known as a boy and which he now felt were being given back to him, through the discovery of Marie. The poem is called *Syd-Sælland*. It recalls the years of his childhood, his adolescence and his young manhood. It is a poem in praise of the places and the people whom he had known fifty or sixty years before, full of the interaction of the different dimensions of life and experience, of past and present.[6]

It is the interpenetration of person and place that runs through it all. He remembers places because he remembers the people who lived there, and he remembers the people as if embodied in the places. The interpenetration of present and past is also central to the poem, for it is his new relationship with Fru Marie of Rønnebæksholm which has brought the past to life. He is present now as he was present then and his joy and his song transcend the barriers of time. Behind it all there is an interpenetration of heaven and earth, of visible and invisible, of this world and another world, something brought about by love, however exactly that interpenetration is experienced or understood.

The poem begins from this very point. Now almost seventy years old, the poet can still hear his nursemaid saying, when he was very small, 'Fladsaa with the tall elms', but because she spoke with a South Zealand accent what the boy heard or understood was 'Fladsaa with the tall elves' and that was something much more magical and mysterious. To us late twentieth century people, unless we have been influenced by New Age thinking, the idea of spirit presences in particular localities is so strange that we find it difficult to take it seriously when we meet it in a writer of a century and a half ago. But Grundtvig is not alone in the early nineteenth century in this sense that there are spirits, angels, heavenly presences, in us and around us. One can find very similar expressions in some of Newman's early letters and diaries.

What was said was 'Fladsaa with the tall elms', but what was heard by the child was 'Fladsaa with the tall elves'. One of the points which the poem makes is that although the elms are now felled the spirits have not departed. The poet who rejoiced in these things two generations ago, is now, with his unforeseeable good fortune, here still, still declaring his undeserved joy.

The poem proceeds, as such a poem should, with a very precise naming of people and places. They are not for the most part famous places, nor very grand ones. There are hospitable manor houses, there are friendly vicarages, there are villages, each with their own story. Each place has its own history, its own character; each house has its own family, which often takes its name from the house where it lives. Udby church is where we begin, with the wooded slope of Ambjerg to one side, and Valdemar's tower just in front. Then there is Iselinge, a little manor house nearby, with its quiet dark wood and its quiet shining happiness; with its plough which is always at work, with the small and the great, with their friendly blue eyes. Here too there are greetings and welcome.

There is Praestø bay and Praestø town; a place of sunset, for there his mother died, a place of midsummer sunrise, for there he set out for his work in Copenhagen. Nysø with the old hedges, now famous because of Thorvaldsen's time there. There is Ulse Olstrup with its tidy vicarage, with its choir of nightingales, with its golden-haired wood, where Grundtvig had met his first wife, Lise Blicher, daughter of the pastor there. So he goes on,

> As an old man well on in years,
> Now I see you all again,
> Now I come back to you, with song
> Like a friend of youth who had departed ...
>
> Here it was long ago,
> That light first dawned for me
> Light about life, light about time,
> What is and what was,
> Where every leaf reminds me
> Of the kiss of youth and the song of youth,
> Of the words and deeds of manhood.[7]

Yet the poet does not remember all these things simply as shades of the departed. The people and places come to meet him still vividly alive. Old memories and old joys bid him welcome home.

> Praise my soul your poet's fortune,
> Such as seldom is or was.[8]

The poem reaches its climax with verses of praise for the lady of Rønnebæksholm. Grundtvig records her generosity, her courage, her openness and her care for the 'awakened', the religious circles of country people whom Fru Marie had supported so strongly and of whom he had been so suspicious. The poet celebrates their coming together, both in their different ways so concerned for the life and well-being for the common people of their land. As he celebrates again these places and their history, he becomes aware that they are threatened, threatened as Denmark constantly felt itself to be, in the nineteenth century, by the overwhelming weight and power of Germany.

The apparently idyllic poem, with its memories of quiet country families and vicarages, with its feeling of Jane Austen, ends on a note of patriotic affirmation and patriotic defiance of the German threat. As always in Grundtvig, personal and public cannot be kept apart. They interpenetrate and support each other. The poem ends with an exhortation to the men of Zealand to defend their motherland, their mothertongue and their womenfolk. His newfound personal happiness had renewed his commitment to the places where he grew up and to the land of his ancestors.

III

Grundtvig's friends in Copenhagen were not the only people to be surprised by his second marriage. By a curious coincidence we have the reactions to it of a notable Anglican writer of this time who happened to be visiting Denmark in the summer of 1852. While none of the original leaders of the Oxford Movement ever visited Grundtvig in his own country, J.M. Neale, the outstanding figure in the Catholic revival in the Church of England to have come from Cambridge, had his only meeting with Grundtvig in Copenhagen. This chance encounter gives us an opportunity of seeing another view, not only of Grundtvig, but of Denmark, in the middle of the nineteenth century.

Neale was a man of a younger generation, almost twenty years younger than Pusey and Newman, more than thirty years younger than Grundtvig. He was a man of a very different temperament from the Oxford leaders, an artist with words, a man of vivid and creative imagination no less than a scholar with a brilliant flair for languages. As the premier translator of medieval hymns in nineteenth century England he has inevitably been compared with Grundtvig, especially since he, like Grundtvig, was greatly attracted by the hymns of Eastern Christendom. It is striking that in one of the recent studies of Neale's work there should be an extended comparison between these two men as translators.[9]

Neale's life was a very active one, but it was from early on overshadowed by the threat of TB. He died a little before his forty-ninth birthday, in 1866. However, being a man of great intellectual energy he left behind him a mass of writings, liturgical, historical, and polemical. He also left a group of historical novels on explicitly Christian themes, which were very popular in the nineteenth century and were translated into many languages, Russian and Danish as well as French and German.

Neale's original enthusiasm as a student at Cambridge had been for the study of medieval church architecture. He was one of the founders of the Cambridge Camden Society, an association which played an important part in the revival of Gothic architecture as the principal style used in church building in nineteenth century England, and which was itself a manifestation of the general fascination in the Europe of the time, with the art of the Middle Ages, something which, in a different way, had moved Grundtvig so deeply.

Throughout Neale's life he delighted to travel in order to 'take' notable churches, visiting them and making copious notes on their particular features. This method of surveying medieval church buildings had been one of the first activities promoted by the Society in its early years in the 1840s. It contributed much to a more accurate and detailed knowledge of the wealth of medieval church building in the British Isles. Neale did not confine his attention to Britain. He made numerous tours on the continent to study the varieties of church architecture in Portugal and Spain, in Germany, Austria and in Dalmatia and in 1852 in Denmark.

Neale reports on this architectural visit to Denmark in a lengthy letter to his friend and associate Benjamin Webb. It is a letter which gives us a vivid picture of how foreign Denmark could seem at this time, even to someone who had travelled widely. Having first visited Lund, Neale returned to Copenhagen and set off by rail across Zealand. First he comes to Roskilde. 'This church, you know, was quasi-Primatial of Denmark, wonderfully stern Romanesque and has very interesting monuments'. The next day he went on across Zealand by train.

Wednesday, through Zealand. A very lovely island; Ringsted Church grand Romanesque, and all the village churches of the same date and excellently worth seeing. At the Academy of Soröe, and at Slagelse I had introductions; and everywhere met with the greatest kindness. It was lucky for me that I had read a good deal of German in the course of the last year, so as to be able to converse in it. Every educated Dane speaks German but scarcely anyone French.[10]

It had been a long day, for although the distances were not great Neale had seen many interesting things. Next day he crossed Funen, visiting Odense and the following day he crossed the Little Belt, and began the Jutland part of his tour. Here the tone of the narrative changes. We get a very sharp impression of the extent to which Jutland was still, in the mid-nineteenth century, a world of its own. We have seen how Grundtvig as a boy had felt this difference when he left the familiar, fertile pastures of South Zealand for the barren heathlands of Jutland; he seemed to be entering another world. For Neale necessarily the sense of strangeness was even greater, and no railway had yet penetrated here.

At Copenhagen, everyone stared when I spoke of going to Jutland; said that nobody ever went, that there were no roads, that the people were absolute savages. The Secretary of Legation told me that, though he could speak Dansk like a native, he would not trust himself there alone.

This was the kind of adventure which Neale really enjoyed.

I was there three days; and certainly I never saw nor could conceive such wildness. I travelled on foot or on a basket wagon almost night and day — for here you can 'take' churches from 3 am until 10 pm easily, and the people seem always up. The churches are all Romanesque and all brick; the cathedrals of Ribe, Viborg and Aarhus, are glorious (Aalborg I did not see). The roads they did not exaggerate at Copenhagen, generally there are none. You can almost always see from church to church and you walk right across the heath.[11]

All along the way he was in villages and small country towns, where nothing was spoken except Danish and in many places it was Danish spoken with a powerful Jutish accent.

Here German is no use and the *patois* so excessive that even Danes find it difficult. I was almost reduced to pantomime. Nothing to eat but sour black bread and a kind of smoked cheese. The last day, I confess, I was nearly worn out (and you know it takes a good deal to do that to me). However, I bagged churches right and left.

Finally he was reduced to hiring a basket wagon himself,

and though I and my knapsack are no great weight and we were on the best road in Jutland, three horses were absolutely necessary. When we were not going over the heath the wheels were often up to the axles in sand. On Whitsunday I came to Aarøsund on the east coast and thence a steamer took me to Kiel and so to Hamburg again.[12]

It is good to be reminded, by such a letter, how different the different parts of Europe were in the days before steam trains had brought distant regions together and promoted a new kind of uniformity. It is good too to see how bare and poor large parts of Jutland seemed to a foreigner, even to one who had travelled widely and was accustomed to different kinds of scenery. Denmark in the twentieth century is such a prosperous country that we forget how different things were in the first half of the nineteenth century.

Neale's impressions could be confirmed from the writings of Danish authors of this time. H.C. Andersen for instance, was much impressed by the bareness of the western parts of Jutland, with its barren heathland and its long white sand dunes. Steven M. Borish comments,

These features rendered much of the windswept peninsula of Jutland bleak and almost uninhabitable. Although some of the farmland in East Jutland was of excellent quality, the heath country found in much of West Jutland made the practice of agriculture difficult and onerous in those places.[13]

It was an impoverished Denmark which Neale saw, before the development of improved agricultural methods which followed in the latter half of the century, a world far from the sophistication of Copenhagen and the comfortable farmland of Zealand. It was in this milieu that the Folk High Schools were to take root and to do some of their most important work.

Now having described his architectural tour, Neale comes to the main purpose of his visit to Denmark. He had evidently heard that in Denmark there was some sort of a Catholic movement going on. In England the departure of a second group of converts to Rome in 1851, notable among them H.E. Manning, had made some Anglicans look with new interest towards the Lutheran churches of Scandinavia. Neale was clearly doubtful about the situation and wanted to know at first hand what this movement really involved.

We have two letters from Nugent Wade addressed to Grundtvig from March and April of this year, which help us to understand the background to Neale's visit. Wade had told Grundtvig of Neale's project and explained that he knew of him though he did not know him personally. It seems likely that it was Wade who provided Neale with his introductions. He asked Grundtvig whether there existed in Denmark an interest towards England at all comparable to the English interest in things Danish.

I want very much to know how Church matters are going on with you. I hear you have got 'religious Liberty' fuldstændig. What does this mean and is it true, would this for instance allow you if so disposed to get the link of Apostolic Succession restored by receiving consecration from us? ... is there any strong feeling amongst you — 'your high-Churchmen' at least — of a desire for the succession and for closer communion accordingly with the Church in England, there seems to be a yearning for Unity spreading in many parts of Christendom.[14]

And then he refers to a letter which he had received from a Danish pastor (Ludvig D. Hass) who was evidently interested in this project.
    In a second letter Wade refers to this possibility again, and again asks

what prospect there might be of our being linked together through this bond, by the restoration of Apostolic succession in the Episcopate to you. I remember what *your* feeling was on this subject how desirable could it be effected without however denying what you have received through the presbyterian line, how far does this feeling prevail with others likeminded with yourself in respect of Catholic truth?[15]

It is very clear from this letter that Wade had little or no idea of the way in which Grundtvig's mind had been moving in the previous years, and how much less favourable he was towards the idea of a possible restoration of unbroken episcopal succession in the Danish Church. Wade was evidently thinking back to their conversations in the 1830s. By the 1850s Grundtvig's attitude had altered profoundly.
    Neale at any rate was soon to be under no illusions.

As to the Danish movement, it is all humbug; there is none. There are about ten men of influence who are dissatisfied with the state of things, and wish for something better, though they are not agreed what. They, of course, have their followers; Grundtwig is the best, and in his way (but what a way!) learned. Rudelbach, I think, comes next. But these men defend Presbyterian Ordination tooth and nail. Grundtwig says that *nothing* could make him doubt his own orders.[16]

But this is only the beginning, there is worse to come.

Now as to G. At the age of sixty-nine he lost his wife. Within nine months he married again — a widow — on the avowed principle that he was so much in love he could not help it! And *that* for the leader of the movement! I don't want to be hard on the man, but what sort of being must he be?

There is something wonderfully revealing about Neale's reaction to Grundt-vig's second marriage.[17] Like all the Tractarians, Neale had a very high ap-preciation of celibacy; one of the most important works of his life was the foundation of a community of Sisters, the Society of St. Margaret. But being himself a happily married man he could hardly object to clerical marriage in itself. However, like some of Grundtvig's Danish contemporaries, he was astonished and dismayed at the youthful enthusiasm of the seventy year old patriarch. If only Grundtvig had quietly married his housekeeper while no-one was looking, things would, he seems to say, have been somewhat better.

Neale goes on to speak of the provision for private confession in the Da-nish Prayerbook and comments on the fact that there seemed little or no desire to restore its use.

In fact, it comes to this, what we call Christian they call Catholic. They do wish to be *Christians*, they do believe in the Incarnation and in the Trinity, and in the Real Presence — and that is about the amount of what they mean ... I have now quite made up my mind about the Danes, and will fight against them to the knife.

Once again the contact with England had broken down over the question of apostolic succession.[18]

IV

J.M. Neale, as we have said, was more deeply influenced by the Christian East than any other of the leaders of the Anglican revival. The full tragedy of the lack of understanding which made real contact between him and Grundtvig, between England and Denmark, impossible at that time, becomes plain when we see just how deeply Grundtvig too was influenced by his meeting with the Christian East. Jakob Knudsen, an outstanding re-presentative of the Grundtvigian world in the early years of this century, makes this clear in two passages which take us back to his childhood, i.e. to the years of the 60s in which Grundtvig was still alive, and which show us how surely Grundtvig's influence was received into a Danish family of the time. We see how, in some sense, Grundtvig's presence was felt throughout the country.

Jakob Knudsen tells us that in the course of their religious teaching he had the impression that his mother hesitated about how to tell her children the story of the crucifixion. Perhaps she felt uneasy with the detailed meditation on the incidents of the passion, which had been so prevalent both in Catholic and Protestant devotion. Anyhow she decided to take another way.

So it was one afternoon while mother sat and nursed the smallest of us, that she told us she was going to sing a song for us. But first she would tell us something, and that was the story of how Jesus at the end was taken to prison, accused by his enemies, condemned by Pontius Pilate and crucified as a criminal. She told us all this quite briefly. But after they had killed him, she said, he rose up again and overcame death even in the midst of its kingdom and lead its prisoners out to life. And that is what I am going to sing about,

> Last night there came a knocking at the gates of hell,
> It sounded like the threatening roll of thunder,
> The herald was strong, his message full of power,
> And everything beneath the earth gave heed.

She sang about Jesus' triumphant journey from Good Friday evening until Easter morning, and we could see that this was a victory such as none of the old Norse heroes had ever won. They could defend themselves against their enemies. But Jesus did not do that; he let events come over him, he let them bind him by the chains of death. It was thus that he rose, breaking the bonds, conquering death forever.

> So on the third day in glory
> Our Saviour arose who though innocent was crucified;
> And this is now on earth a matter of salvation,
> ·That God's Son has visited the depths of hell.

This was something much greater than anything about Thor and the other gods. And then it was *real*. Mother did not say anything special about that but one could see it in her. Yes, that is the way children come to believe, that is the way they receive the reality of heaven.[19]

There cannot have been many children in Western Christendom in the second half of the nineteenth century, who were introduced to the central elements of the Christian story in this way. For most, one may assume, the story of Good Friday would have predominated, and it would have been told in a strictly realistic way. Easter would have been added as a kind of sequel, however it was described. The harrowing of hell would scarcely have been mentioned.

Here Grundtvig had taken the mystery of Christ's conquest over death and made use of imagery inspired by the poetry of Anglo-Saxon England and by the theology of the Greek fathers, as he had found it in the Byzantine liturgical texts. His genius lies in his capacity to make this into something which it was possible for a mother to sing to her children in an entirely domestic setting. Grundtvig's desire to make the deepest mysteries of the Christian faith available to everyone, to children and those without any formal education, seems here to have been triumphantly fulfilled. It is a remarkable testimony to the power of the poetic image to convey a message to people of very different capacities.

If the doctrine of the descent into hell, so central in the faith of Eastern Orthodoxy, has a surprisingly central place in the theology of Grundtvig, so too does the mystery of the transfiguration which he sees as having a universal significance. This also is an aspect of Christian faith particularly developed in the Orthodox East. In another essay, Knudsen tells us about this too, in speaking of the impact made by the Christmas tree with its burning candles as seen by a child on Christmas Eve. It is an impact which speaks not just about Christmas but about the triumph of life and the final transformation of all things.

'When we are raised from the dead at the last day ... our bodies will be *transfigured*', Knudsen writes,

It is, I suppose, Our Lord's transfiguration on the mountain that we think of when we use this word. But that transfiguration was only seen by the three disciples who were with him on Tabor; we did not see it. But we do know from our childhood experience of Christmas Eve what transfiguration means.

And then Knudsen goes on to speak of the Christmas tree with its lights and gifts suddenly revealed to the children as they come in from outside.

Although everything was the same as we saw it every day ... yet is was not at all the same that evening, because it belonged to quite a different world from the ordinary one. The Christmas tree stood there and welcomed us when we came in out of the dark hallway ... and it created its own world in which everything was transfigured, the furniture, the stove, the peat box, the meagre Christmas presents, because they all belonged to the world of the Christmas tree.[20]

Knudsen sees this concept of transfiguration as applying to the whole created order. The transfiguration of Christ on the mountain of Tabor implies the potential transfiguration of the whole world. The light of eternity penetrates into the world of time, the light of the Godhead shines out not only in the face of the Lord but even in his clothing. The implications of all this for the material world were not neglected by the theologians of Byzantium. Now all things are changed through the presence of the dark tree which is full of light. A pre-Christian, natural, and indeed pagan element in the Christmas celebration, has become for him the way into the heart of the mystery of Christ.

For each one of us, Knudsen says, there is a journey to be made from the Christmas joy of childhood, through the doubts and pains of early adult life, in which we come to realise the meaning of our baptism, a dying and rising with Christ, on into the fullness of the life of faith, its ripening and interiorisation. This is, for each one of us, our own appropriation of Pentecost.

It is not just the Christian life from the cradle to the grave, taken as a whole, which is marked by the trinity of Christmas, Easter and Whitsun. As one often sees all the bricks of a particular building marked with the trade mark of the brickyard where they were made, so every little section of a Christian's life is marked by the triple sign of Christmas, Easter and Whitsun. One can call it the particular underlying movement, the beat and rhythm of Christian life. Just as every wave in the sea has its swell, its trough, its crest, so every event in Christian life unfolds under the sign of Christmas, Easter, and Whitsun.[21]

The personal, the ecclesial, the universal dimensions of existence are fused together into a unity which yet preserves the distinct characteristics of each particular element within the whole. In a remarkably dynamic way Knudsen has restated the Greek patristic vision of the one Logos as active and present in the logoi, hidden within things.

There can be no doubt how it is that Knudsen came to realise this vision. It was, as he would have been the first to declare, through the gift of Grundtvig's hymns and songs, that this remarkable fusion of different elements of life and thought had taken place. Something deeply characteristic of Eastern Orthodoxy had come to life in the experience of a nineteenth century Danish family. It makes the failure of J.M. Neale to see beyond the surface of disagreement all the more tragic.

CHAPTER 5

Last Impressions
1858–72

I

The death of his second wife, after so short a period of married life, left Grundtvig, for a time, deeply bereft. But his energy for life and work continued unabated, despite the fact that he was coming into his mid-seventies. Till 1858 he remained a member of the *Folketing*, the lower house of parliament, and was actively involved in the preparation of measures for the reform of aspects of Church law. From 1855 onwards successive instalments of his lectures on Christian faith appeared as articles which were finally gathered together and published as *Den Christelige Børnelærdom*, *Elementary Christian Doctrine*.

In 1860 a further long poem *Christenhedens Syvstjerne*, The Seven Stars of Christendom, was published. This poem is an account of the history of the Church as Grundtvig saw it, an extended meditation on the account of the seven Churches of the Apocalypse, as described in the last book of the Bible. This passage, Grundtvig saw as revealing the underlying pattern which worked itself out in the subsequent history of the Church. There had been, he believed, six great Churches. The Jewish, the Greek, the Latin, the English, the German, the Northern. The seventh was yet to be, and he peered into the future in an effort to discern its outline. The same basic pattern of thought underlay his last great series of public lectures, which were given from 1861 to 1863, lectures on the history of the Church, which were subsequently published with the title *Kirke-Spejl*, The Mirror of The Church.

We have, as it happens, a vivid description of these lectures from the pen of a Norwegian theological student who was studying in Copenhagen at the time, Otto Arvesen.

Grundtvig sat in his big armchair, in front of his work-table and gave his lecture. This usually lasted one hour and as we could see, it had been worked out beforehand. He had a heap of hand-written quarto in front of him, and he would occasionally glance down at his manuscript with his big magnifying glass. But the lectures were quite free and gave not the slightest impression of being tied to the notes.

They gave an overview of the Church's life from the first glowing days of the Hebrew Church, from the strong religious philosophical tendencies of the Greek Church, from the powerful administrative centuries of the Roman Church and so on. He pointed out the nature and character of the peoples which conditioned the nature of the reception which Christianity received and indeed had to receive, in the seven different groups of Churches through which Christianity made its victorious way ...[1]

The lectures were given to a mixed audience, men and women, clerical and lay, professional and non-professional. Amongst them, not infrequently, was the Queen Mother, Queen Caroline Amalie. Questions would come from any part of the audience afterwards and Grundtvig was always glad to respond. One question inevitably touched the Pauline injunction that women should be silent in Church. Grundtvig's answer was short.

We should follow Paul and the other biblical writers respectfully but freely. What Paul says about women suited that time and corresponded to the feelings of the people.

When, on another occasion he was asked whether there shouldn't be more restriction of freedom in matters of faith, whether compulsion wasn't sometimes necessary, Grundtvig's answer was even shorter.

Anyone who can seriously talk about compulsion in matters of faith cannot possibly have understood what faith is.[2]

Arvesen tells us that Grundtvig sat in his old arm-chair, and that alerts us to the fact that these lectures were given at home in the main room in Grundtvig's last, and perhaps most hospitable, dwelling. For in April 1858, almost three years after the death of his second wife, Grundtvig married again. His new wife, Asta Reedtz (1826-90), was, as his second wife had been, a young widow and again from an aristocratic family. She had been born Countess Asta Tugendreich Adelheid Krag-Juel-Vind-Frijs. At the time of their marriage she was thirty-one and already had three small children from her previous marriage. Grundtvig was her senior by some forty-three years.

There has been a tendency to treat Grundtvig's third wife as something of a nonentity, a simple uncomplicated person who nursed the old man dutifully through his last days. Such an assessment of her is, I think, mistaken. She was a courageous and enterprising woman who took charge of a large and complicated family and household and evidently managed it with some success. It was a family with the three small children from her first marriage and Grundtvig's younger son, Frederik Lange, the child of Marie. To them there was added the daughter born to her and Grundtvig in 1859, and named, after his three wives, Asta Marie Elisabeth. It was also a family which still included Grundtvig's children from his first marriage, some of whom were older than she was. There was not only the family to look after. There was a constant flow of visitors of many and various kinds. Asta was a woman of some wealth and the Grundtvigs could now live in a spacious house, which became a centre for many kinds of meeting, political and cultural as well as religious; among them the lectures on Church history.

II

We have from these later years some very interesting memories of the impression Grundtvig made on his visitors.

One of his notable characteristics was his lack of small talk. It was difficult to get him going. Ernst Trier (1837-93) tells us about this particular trait as he encountered it on a first visit to Grundtvig in 1859.

I had been told, that he himself never began the conversation with his visitors, and that things only got going when his visitor came with questions to put before him. It was good that I had been warned of this because it is just what happened. He received me kindly, invited me to sit down with him, but otherwise said nothing to get the conversation going. But since I was prepared for this I had taken care beforehand to have my questions ready about things on which I wanted to have his opinion, and so I produced them one by one. But this didn't succeed in getting him going on any of them. He answered quite kindly, but only with a 'yes' or a 'no' or a 'well …' or something similar, and when after half an hour I saw that my supply of questions was almost used up I began to feel embarrassed and sad, thinking I would soon have to leave without having got anything out of my visit.

Then it happened, I don't quite know how, that I mentioned the 'Latin School', and how resentful I was over the education which was given us there. Then he began to listen properly; now *he* took the word and went on for two and a half hours. (In the course of this time his wife came in and invited us into the next room to the coffee table; there he continued the subject and afterwards he invited me back into his study and went on). Now it was practically he alone who was talking; he set out the contrasts between the 'Latin School's form of education and that which he favoured, and he described his own view of genuine enlightenment. I cannot describe how amazed and fascinated I was by the richness of his talk as it came welling out, the clarity which he gave me about the matter, the certainty of conviction which was revealed, the greatness which I had encountered.[3]

Apart from the matter of the difficulty of getting Grundtvig going, there is the delight of seeing his immediate reaction when one of his favourite themes has been brought up; the Latin School which he so much hated, the antithesis of everything which he believed education should be. We are made aware of the flow of his language once it has got going, which rushes on unabated for two and a half hours. Certainly there could be temporary interruptions. Asta could come in and invite them to the coffee table; a coffee time, which, like an old fashioned tea-time for us, would certainly have included sandwiches, cakes and pastries. But this could not halt the flow. It becomes a mere incident in the course of Grundtvig's exposition of his theme.

Another very interesting glimpse which we have of the older Grundtvig in his personal relations with younger men comes in the memoirs of Frederik Barfod (1811-96), journalist, historian, politician. In these particular memories it is interesting to notice Grundtvig's extreme discretion in raising religious issues with someone who is clearly passing through a period of agnosticism. It is even more interesting to note what it was in Grundtvig's attitude and in his teaching which particularly attracted the younger man. Grundtvig's confidence in the power of truth, his lack of anxiety about the question of conversion impressed Barfod deeply, and this in his mind was clearly related to Grundtvig's teaching about Christ's descent into hell. This was a matter in which Grundtvig's understanding of the faith differed radically from that of much nineteenth century Protestantism, and enabled him to see questions about salvation in a much larger and more open way than did many of his contemporaries.

I was very much at home with the Grundtvigs. I would come there at all times of the day and was always welcome. We talked about everything possible, though not so often on religious matters. He himself never brought them up either with me or with anyone else, but he always gladly discussed them whenever we brought them up with him. It was in such a conversation … that he once said to me, 'Barfod, you are no Christian and perhaps it will be a long time before you are, but I have no anxiety about you, for you are a person who loves the truth and you will find the truth, either here or beyond.' It was this warm, kindly expression 'here or *beyond*', which made such a powerful impression on me. I had on one occasion heard it developed further by him in a sermon preached at Vartov. At home I had felt myself greatly taken with his hymn, 'Last night there came a knocking at the gates of hell'. It was his teaching about the possibility of a conversion *after* death which before anything else won *me* for Christianity. The thought that all those dear people whom I had known, both from history and in life, should be damned forever, because they had not learned to know and accept the faith, *here below* in this brief span of life, had outraged my feelings as a flagrant injustice. Now I saw that there was another possibility and I was glad, I can certainly say, glad both for their sake and for Our Lord's. However, several years were to pass before I could finally accept Christianity. Then Grundtvig found support in my Emily [his wife].[4]

Barfod goes on to tell us more of the way in which he returned to the practice of communion, and it gives us an interesting insight into Grundtvig's attitude as a priest and a pastor.

I had thought of going to communion, before I brought my bride home. And a month before, I sat on a sofa with Grundtvig and told him of my intention. He was not altogether unwilling to accept my wish, but he asked me to delay it until I was more sure that it was really the Lord's true body and blood that he would give me. When the time came, I should come to him again and he would rejoice to do it. So by mutual agreement I postponed it until next spring, when I came to him together with my wife.[5]

Here we see something of the way in which Grundtvig would prepare people for the sacraments. Again there was no sense of hurry, but rather that all should be carefully thought through and that everyone's freedom should be respected. But here we see his insistence on the reality of the gift in the sacrament and his evident dislike of anything which resembled formalism. In view of his constant stress on the importance of the sacraments in his theological teaching it is particularly interesting to have a glimpse of his way of bringing an individual back to the Lord's table.

It was in this domestic setting that some of the great festivities of Grundtvig's latter years took place. There was, for instance, the celebration of the golden jubilee of his ordination to the priesthood in May 1861. In the morning there had been a service at Vartov and later there was a gathering at home, where Grundtvig was presented with a seven-branched candlestick, a gift from friends in Denmark, Norway and Sweden, and where, as the climax, the Minister of Church Affairs arrived to announce that the King had been pleased to confer on Grundtvig the rank and title of Bishop. In 1863 it was his eightieth birthday which was celebrated; from then onwards nearly every year, at the beginning of September, 'meetings of friends' were held in Copenhagen, great gatherings of those who recognised in the old man a leader, a teacher, a prophet of the North.

It would be foolish to deny that a kind of cult grew up around Grundtvig in his last years. It was scarcely possible that it should not. The old man had after all lived so long that he had become a legend in his own lifetime. And so the house was full, not only of children, but of admirers, and not least of women admirers. Asta seems, very sensibly, to have cultivated the friendship of one or two of her contemporaries and to have invited them from time to time to stay with her and to help in the management of this large household. Letters of hers which have only recently come to light give the impression of a woman who was more independent in her thoughts and ways than has sometimes been imagined. Certainly as the years went by, her political and ecclesiastical sympathies moved more and more to the left.[6]

In the middle of it all Grundtvig sat in his old arm-chair, reading, writing, listening, talking, presiding over the household. There are memories of the family prayers with which the day began and it may be worthwhile to transcribe the invocation which Grundtvig used at the beginning of them. As we shall see in a later chapter, in part III, the sign of the cross remained for him a thing of great importance. This is a text which seems to have been written down from memory by one or two of those who were there and there are slight variants in the different versions,

The sign of the Holy Cross, both before our face and our breast, traced in holy baptism in the name of Jesus Christ for a full and clear separation between us and the Evil One, and for an eternal witness that we belong to you, our crucified yet risen Lord Jesus Christ, our divine saviour and redeemer from sin, from death and from the kingdom of Satan, not with silver and gold, but with your holy and precious blood, which you shed for us in the garden of Gethsemane and on the tree of the cross, for the forgiveness of sins and for the redemption of a people for your own possession, born of God, true and active in all good works. Amen.[7]

III

It would however be altogether untrue to suggest that these last years were without anxieties and disturbance. One incident is so extraordinary, yet in a way so characteristic, that it is necessary to look at it in some detail.

As we have had reason to see on a number of occasions, Grundtvig was a man of strong and tempestuous feelings and of sometimes violent swings of mood. At least three times during his long life he seemed on the point of a complete psychological breakdown. One such occasion was in 1810-11 at the time when he returned to Udby and agreed to become his father's curate. Another similar moment occurred in 1844 when his mood of depression became so strong that he had for a while to take a time of complete rest and allow himself to be nursed back to health. However the most extraordinary and public occasion of this kind occurred in 1867 when Grundtvig was 83; here was a case not of depression but of manic euphoria which reached a high point in the Sunday service in Vartov, on Palm Sunday, April 14th of that year. We have a number of eye-witness accounts of the event and although they vary in detail the general outline of what happened seems clear.

The days before the Sunday had already been marked by unusual happenings in the Grundtvig household. Grundtvig found that the sore places on his legs were healed; that he could walk without a stick; that he no longer had to use the special reading glasses which he had had made, but could read with his old spectacles which he had not used for many years. As often happened there were many visitors.

In the evening [of the Friday] Hulda and Charlotte were there and he still talked with a youthfulness, a liveliness and a power which they had never seen before. When the visitors were leaving, he said that he would kiss them on the eyes, so that they would become sighted, they would then be able to see God's wisdom and grace, and he would kiss them on the hands so as to lead them to Christ. This he did with each one. He also said that there would soon be a battle in the sound outside Copenhagen, and that our Lord would give us the victory.[8]

Already two of the motifs which recur in the following days are present; Grundtvig's expectation of a German attack by sea, and his tendency to want to kiss everyone who comes to see him. The sexual element in his fantasies is clearly evident, but it is striking that at this early stage he kisses people on the eyes and on the hands. The former gesture is a necessarily gentle one which had originated in a dream of his wife's. She had dreamt that she kissed a blind man on the eyes and that his sight was restored. Grundtvig insisted that she kiss him on the eyes, and attributed the improvement of his sight to that act. Already it is clear that things were not as normal. His wife Asta, who in general went along with his wishes, and at a later stage was very reluctant to recognise his delusions, became anxious and worried. She told him that he must stop kissing his friends in this way since it would cause scandal. The old man was much upset by this suggestion. On Saturday there seems to have been a reaction to the excitement and activity of Friday, Grundtvig felt unwell and rested a good deal. It was perhaps a wise preparation for Sunday.

It was usual in Denmark at that time that the main Sunday service, the *Højmesse*, should be preceded by a brief penitential rite. The celebrant gave an exhortation to confession, a general confession was said, and then anyone who wished was invited to come to the altar rails where the celebrant would say a formula of absolution over each one, together with a laying on of hands. From the very beginning of the service on this Sunday it became clear that something unusual was happening. Grundtvig came in without his stick, walking like a man of sixty rather than eighty. With great insistence he invited all to come to the altar, and said that those who did not would not be welcome to receive communion later in the service.

Gradually more and more people began to come up to the altar-rails. The church was crowded and the giving of absolution to row after row of penitents took time. After a while

Grundtvig stood to his full height and strength and addressed the Queen Mother [Queen Caroline Amalie] who was sitting in her usual place; 'where is the Queen of Denmark, will she not come, lo, the Queen of the South came to hear the wisdom of Solomon, and a greater than Solomon is here.' Then the Queen Mother came up to the altar and kneeled down. Grundtvig laid his hand on her head and said with a voice which rang through the whole church, 'And to you is granted the merciful forgiveness of all your sins, in the name of the Father and of the Son and of the Holy Ghost; and thus all Denmark's sins are forgiven.' Then he continued in a lower voice, 'Now then, let the King of Prussia come!'[9]

For a time things seemed to become quieter, Grundtvig went into the pulpit and began the service in the usual way. Before reading the Gospel, however, one of those who were present that day, Frederik Helveg (1816-1901), tells us he began expounding the first three petitions of the Lord's prayer and stressing how seriously they were to be taken. He said that he had been shown for the first time the meaning of the Lord's words about going into our inner room and closing the door. We are to enter into our heart, taking the Lord with us, and there shut the door against the devil. Here he folded his hands together and clasped them against his breast, to show how we are to close the door of the heart. Here Frederik Helveg tells us he asked, 'Isn't that good teaching?' to which quite a few voices gave a quiet 'Yes.'[10]

Here we have a first example of the way in which on this occasion Grundtvig develops ideas which have been with him throughout his life; the importance of the Lord's prayer, and the conjunction of heart and hand in receiving God's word.

Grundtvig then proceeded to the sermon. Another of those who were present and who was to take a central part in the service was Frederik Hammerich (1809-77). He describes the sermon as an extraordinary mixture of inspired thought and madness. In it Grundtvig spoke about the restlessness of the human heart and the age old longing to square the circle. He spoke of the things that had hindered the coming of the Lord and said that now they were taken away. The Lord had placed the human soul in the east but the human heart in Denmark, and now they had come together. Now the Jordan had flowed into the Sound. The circle could now be squared, because the living circle of the world of time had arrived at the kingdom of eternity, at the four-square city of the New Jerusalem. The Lord was now about to ride into Jerusalem; the ass's colt had been growing up in Denmark. Grundtvig himself had loosed it that day.[11] It is not surprising that people in the congregation were already greatly perplexed. For some of the less critical Grundtvig was simply inspired. For others he was simply mad. Perhaps at this stage the majority were somewhere in the middle, feeling that although there was something impressive about the old man there was something surely wrong.

We have already met two of the principal witnesses to the events of the day, Frederik Hammerich and Frederik Helveg. Hammerich had known Grundtvig since he was a student thirty years before and had stayed with Pusey in Oxford in 1836. He was now professor of church history in Copenhagen, the first of the Grundtvigians to make a breakthrough into the academic world. Helveg was at this time without a parish and indeed without regular employment. He had not known Grundtvig so long as Hammerich but he had been closely associated with him as a periodical writer and editor. He was a man of much and varied reading, and he had the distinction of being perhaps the only one of those close to Grundtvig who had read Kierkegaard with real understanding and appreciation.

At this stage in the service Grundtvig himself sent to Hammerich and asked him to help with the communion which must now follow. Hammerich was in some perplexity and sent the verger to fetch Helveg whom he had seen in the congregation. I quote his own account;

While the congregation was singing, Grundtvig sent a message and asked me to help at communion. It was a painful moment for me, but wasn't it a duty to accept? There was no time for reflection, I had to act according to my immediate feelings, and they did not deceive me. And yet I could not be alone with Grundtvig at the altar. I turned first to Chaplain Køster [Grundtvig's personal assistant] who replied as if he did not know what to do, and then to my friend Pastor F. Helveg. 'Things are really getting out of hand', I said, 'what shall we do now? Do you dare take part in the communion, and do I?' 'At least', answered Helveg, 'nothing has so far been said which conflicts with our faith. For my part I have always been prepared for Grundtvig's departure from this world to have, despite all the differences, some likeness to that of Søren Kierkegaard's'. 'So then', I said, 'let the two of us go together in God's name'. And so we did, and went to the vestry and put on our cassocks.[12]

We shall consider later the full significance of Helveg's remarkable words about Kierkegaard. Let us for the moment simply notice that both men must have been deeply concerned at the plight of an old and venerated friend and worried that he might do or say something scandalous or even blasphemous at the most holy part of the service. They were also aware of something which we might not have suspected, which is that there might be serious legal consequences for them as well as for Grundtvig if Grundtvig were to do anything too irregular.

'Meanwhile', I continue with Hammerich's account,

Grundtvig had conducted a baptism in which he had chatted with the baby and on the whole behaved strangely. He came back to his chair and said to us, 'I don't know at one moment what I will do the next; everything is given me on the spot. I think I shall have to offer my resignation, and that we shall all have to do, for in this way we cannot be priests in the state church.' I asked him whether he would use the words of institution and the Lord's prayer at the communion. 'Yes, of course', he replied, 'but with a free address'. The altar service began, and I stood beside him with the intention of breaking off the service if anything unseemly should happen. Helveg did the same.[13]

The fact that two well-known and respected men such as Hammerich and Helveg stood with Grundtvig at the altar, must have made the congregation feel more secure.

In fact the service now proceeded fairly normally, except that there was an unusually large number of communicants. Grundtvig, Hammerich, Helveg and Køster took turns in distributing the sacrament to those who came to the altar rails. What was most astonishing to contemporaries was that at least some who had not yet been confirmed were received to communion. Amongst them were a few young people whom Grundtvig was preparing for confirmation and Grundtvig's young son Frederik, aged thirteen. After communion another totally unexpected event took place. Grundtvig embraced and kissed his fellow clergy and then went and kissed the Queen Mother and told her that next February she would give birth to Holger Danske, [as it might be in an English context King Arthur]. After that the service concluded normally enough with the blessing and the final hymn. By now it was half past two.

News of these events soon spread through the city. For some it was simply a cause of mockery and scorn, the most painful and laughable incident in the life of an old man, who not this time only, but throughout his days, had been 'getting out of hand'. For others, at the other extreme, it was still difficult to believe that Grundtvig was not divinely inspired. Certainly during the earlier part of the service there had been many who had still been thinking in that way. But as the service had continued and as the days that followed were to confirm, in the end it became clear for everyone that the old man was seriously ill, suffering from a great variety of delusions; amongst others awaiting the arrival of the Prussian fleet and sitting up all night to do it, and announcing that he was the angel Gabriel and that all the women he kissed would bear sinless children in nine months' time.

Grundtvig himself was quite unaware that he was ill and resented fiercely any such suggestion. At first there was no-one in the household who could check his euphoric mood. When his son Svend tried to calm him down his father was highly indignant. During the course of the week Grundtvig announced his intention of resigning the ministry and preaching a farewell sermon on Good Friday. At this point members of the congregation, Hammerich among them, decided that they had to act. In conjunction with the church authorities they managed to prevent Grundtvig from preaching again and eventually persuaded him that he had to accept the supervision of a doctor, a man who interestingly enough was a member of the Vartov congregation.

It is clear that it was not only Helveg who thought that this incident would be the end of Grundtvig's life. Hans Peter Birkedal Barfod who as a young man was there, gives us a long and excited account of the day, and clearly expected that Grundtvig would die within the next twenty-four hours. This seems to have been a common expectation. Even if he did survive no one expected him to recover. One of the most extraordinary aspects of the whole affair is that of course he did. After some months of enforced rest in the countryside during which he was discouraged from receiving visitors, with medical assistance the delusions gradually subsided. He still had five years of active life before him. Throughout the whole episode his wife never ceased to support him and at the same time to look after the family.

What are we to make of the incident? Some have been inclined to minimise its importance. It was, to say the least, for those who revered and admired him, a deeply embarrassing moment, difficult to explain and difficult to forget. More recently some have tended to give it more significance, and to see in Grundtvig's words and actions during these days, clues to understanding the whole course of his life. This is perhaps to go to another extreme. But in his sermon and in his conversation, themes keep emerging, sometimes in bizarre forms, with which we are familiar from his poetry and his preaching; the reconciliation of heart and soul, the coming together of East and West, the culmination of human history in the revelation of the Heavenly Jerusalem in Denmark and the fruitful contact of spirit and flesh, of man and woman, through the medium of a kiss. S.A.J. Bradley has suggested that many of the images which occurred in the sermon derive from the theological poetry of the Anglo-Saxons which Grundtvig had studied so closely. It is possible that a hint that at one stage in the sermon Grundtvig spoke in tongues, might have been due to the preacher quoting at length in Anglo-Saxon. However we interpret the whole incident, to minimise its significance would be to fail to recognise something important in the complexity of Grundtvig's psychological and spiritual make-up.

Perhaps the most impressive and thought-provoking remarks of the day are Helveg's, and in particular his comparison between Grundtvig's situation and Kierkegaard's. 'I had always thought that there would be something similar in their departure despite all their differences.' In the last fifty years Kierkegaard's thought has become known internationally, his work translated and discussed in many languages and in many contexts. In the nineteenth century the situation was very different. Even in Denmark at this time his thought was not widely studied, its general shape and tendency little enough understood. Helveg was one of the few who took Kierkegaard seriously as a thinker and who wrote long and considered appreciations of his thought. He was certainly one of the very few Danes of that time who would have thought of the two men together, perhaps the only person present at the service in Vartov that day whose mind went to the tragic last months of Kierkegaard's life twelve years before.

What did he see in common between them? I think the answer may lie in some words which he wrote in his report to the Church Minister about the whole incident.

Is what is happening and has happened straightforward mental illness, or is it an act of the Lord which in the end has become too strong for Grundtvig to be able to bear without breaking on one or other less essential point?[14]

Certainly Helveg is here making the best of a very difficult situation and perhaps minimising its paradox. What he is saying, however, is that Grundtvig was not entirely mad but that the pressure of the divine upon him was for the moment too great for him to bear. In certain less essential points he had simply broken down. We remember his reply to Hammerich, in his own words from his report, 'I have no misgivings. I have heard nothing which is against our faith and hope.'

Grundtvig's mind was indeed thrown off balance, but it was not totally destroyed. This, Helveg suggests, was what had been seen in the last months of Kierkegaard's life. Here again, in his judgement, there was no madness even though, under the extreme pressure of his convictions, Kierkegaard's last publications became more and more violent, so that it became evident that his mind too had become unbalanced on some less essential points. However we understand Helveg's remarks, it is the judgement of a very rare mind in nineteenth century Denmark, a mind which can see through all the manifest differences between Kierkegaard and Grundtvig, and recognise in both a common desire to bear witness to the truth and mystery of God, and beyond that an experience of the impact of God on the soul so strong that at times it could overthrow its normal balance.

Helveg was never a man who achieved any notable place in either the ecclesiastical or academic establishment. The last years of his life were spent as a vicar in the parish of Købelev on Lolland. In 1867 he was in a particularly vulnerable position, without regular employment in Copenhagen, seeking a living in the country. In helping Grundtvig at this moment at the altar, he and Hammerich knew that they exposed themselves to the wrath of Martensen as Bishop of Copenhagen. In fact, it became clear that Martensen indeed wished to take legal action against them for breaking the law in giving communion to the unconfirmed. Fortunately the Church Ministry refused to pursue the matter any further; maybe also the king made his mind known. But if the incident reveals an unexpected greatness in the unknown Frederik Helveg, it shows up the highly successful primate of the Danish Church in his least attractive aspect.

III

Grundtvig recovered from the breakdown of Easter 1867. By the end of the year he was back at home in Copenhagen, receiving friends and visitors, reading and writing in his accustomed way. At the height of his illness he had offered his resignation from his position at Vartov, but now, at the unanimous wish of the congregation he received permission to withdraw his resignation. A little before Christmas he resumed his regular Sunday preaching, a practice which he kept up till the last days of his life.

By a curious chance it happens that the fullest and most vivid description of Grundtvig which we have from any English observer dates from those very last weeks. In an entertaining and delightful book, *Two Visits To Denmark*, Edmund Gosse gives us a lively account of the Copenhagen of 1872 and 1874, a city which he had discovered as a young man deeply interested in Scandinavian literature and staying abroad for the first time. Gosse's book was first published in 1911 and it is based on the diaries he kept forty years earlier. In the section from 1872 he tells us how, one summer Sunday morning, he remarked to his hosts, 'How I wish I had come to Denmark during the lifetime of Grundtvig!', and goes on, 'There was a shout from everyone, 'But he *is* alive, and he still preaches every Sunday morning in the Workhouse Church!' 'This is Sunday morning — I *must* listen to a poet who was born five years before Byron, and who recollects the execution of Louis XVI. Where is this Workhouse Church?'.[15]

The visit to Vartov — the translation Workhouse is hardly illuminating — proved to be more complicated than Gosse had realised it would be. He was staying with one of the most eminent clergymen of the city, Bruun Juul Fog, the Dean of Holmens Kirke, a historic church in the centre of Copenhagen.

Fog was an intimate friend and assistant of Bishop Martensen, indeed he was to be his successor. In these later years Grundtvig's relationship with the bishop had not been at all easy. The Dean's sister, who presided over her brother's household, began to explain to Gosse that it was not to be thought that any one of the family could accompany him to hear such a dangerous schismatic. To her intense astonishment her brother suddenly thought otherwise, 'I declare I feel tempted to accompany our young friend to the Vartou myself!' So the two sallied forth on that Sunday morning in July.[16]

Before he comes to his description of the impression Grundtvig made on him, Gosse gives us a brief account of who he was. It is evident that he had little enough understanding of Grundtvig's theological or ecclesiastical position, though he had evidently gathered that to many of the clergy of the established church he had seemed an impossible and dangerous figure. What is perhaps more surprising is that Gosse shows very little understanding of Grundtvig as a writer, despite the fact that he already had a considerable knowledge of Danish literature and was to become in later life one of the outstanding literary critics of his time.

The writings of Grundtvig, whether in prose or verse, have never been attractive to me. They are so exclusively national as to be scarcely intelligible to a foreigner; they lie, if I may say so, outside the European tradition', he declares.[17]

It is, if I may say so, one of those judgements which tells us as much or more about the one who makes it as about the one of whom it is made. Here perhaps is one of the roots of the commonly received opinion about the unintelligibility of Grundtvig. But here too is a revelation of the limitations of a critic like Gosse when confronted with the genius and variety of Grundtvig's work. For Grundtvig European literature is rooted, not only in the classical world of Greece and Rome, but also in Israel and in the pre-Christian myths of the North. It is a literature which can encompass the middle ages as well as the renaissance and which can include the popular world of ballads and hymns as well as the cultivated literature of the court. This vision was something altogether too large, too varied and too openly religious for Gosse to comprehend. In Grundtvig he had met a writer who could not be fitted into his categories.

This being so, we shall read his description of the old man with a certain caution as well as with anticipation. There is no question but that it is a highly perceptive picture. But it is a picture drawn by someone who does not see far beyond the surface, and indeed seems at times to have misunderstood what he saw.

We arrived … so far as seeing the great man was concerned, in most ample time at the little Workhouse Church, opposite the trees and still waters of the western ramparts. We found seats with difficulty, the chapel being crowded with communicants, doubtless attracted by a rumour that this would be the last time that the aged prophet would address his disciples. After sitting more than half an hour, surrounded by strange, fanatic faces, and women who swung themselves backward and forward in silent prayer, the word was passed round that the Bishop would probably be unable to come. The congregation began to sing hymns of his composition in a loud, quick, staccato manner invented by the poet, which was very little like the slow singing in the State churches. Suddenly, and when we had given up all hope, there entered from the vestry and walked rapidly to the altar a personage who seemed to me the oldest human being I had ever seen. Instantly an absolute silence prevailed throughout the church, and then there rose a sound as though some one was talking in the cellar below our feet. It was the Bishop praying aloud at the altar, and then he turned and addressed the communicants in the same dull, veiled voice. He wandered down among the ecstatic worshippers, and stood close at my side for a moment, while he laid his hands on a girl's head, so that I saw his face to perfection. For a man of ninety, he could not be called infirm; his gestures were rapid and his step steady. But the attention was riveted on his appearance of excessive age. He looked like a troll from some cave in Norway; he might have been centuries old.

From the vast orb of his bald head, very long strings of silky hair fell over his shoulders and mingled with a long and loose white beard. His eyes flamed under very beetling brows, and they were the only part of his face which seemed alive, for he spoke without moving his lips. His features were still shapely, but colourless and dry, and as the draught from an open door caught them, the silken hairs were blown across his face like a thin curtain. While he perambulated the church with these stiff gestures and ventriloquist murmurings, his disciples fell on their knees behind him, stroking the skirts of his robe, touching the heels of his shoes. Finally, he ascended the pulpit and began to preach; in his dead voice he warned us to beware of false spirits, and to try every spirit whether it be of God. He laboured extremely with his speech, becoming slower and huskier, with longer pauses between the words like a clock that is running down. He looked supernatural, but hardly Christian. If, in the body of the church, he had reminded me of a troll, in the pulpit he looked more like some belated Druid, who had survived from Mona and could not die. It was an occasion of great interest to me. Had I missed hearing and seeing Grundtvig then, I should never have heard or seen him, for he took to his bed a few days later, and in a month the magnificent old fighting man was dead.[18]

Danish commentators on this passage have been struck on the one hand by the accuracy of the descriptions of Grundtvig's appearance. We have photographs of him taken at this very time and the face they reveal is as strange as that in Gosse's description. On the other hand, some have suspected that Gosse must have imagined at least some elements of the behaviour of the 'ecstatic worshippers'. It is true that Grundtvig's disciples at the end of his life had an almost superstitious reverence for him; but the desire to touch his clothes and his shoes seems distinctly un-Danish, not to speak of un-Lutheran! It is important to remember that in this book Gosse is writing up his diaries after an interval of almost forty years. More than once on reading it one feels that the anecdotes with which it abounds have grown in the telling. On one point he is certainly inaccurate. This was not the last sermon that Grundtvig preached. He had still over a month of life before him, and he was active to the last.

Gosse sees Grundtvig altogether from the outside and regards him as some strange Nordic or Celtic apparition. This perception though perhaps superficial is by no means unintelligent. The Christianity which Grundtvig represented was something much more deeply earthed in the world of the pre-Christian North than anything with which Gosse would have become acquainted among the Plymouth Brethren of his upbringing. But when he gives us the impression that the old man was already dissociated from the things of this world, and already nearly dead, he is very far off the mark. Grundtvig was not only intellectually active to the end, he retained a vivid interest in current affairs and political events.

What is perhaps even more impressive is the capacity to recall names and facts from the remote past which he reveals in one of the last accounts that we have of a conversation with him. While Gosse gives us the most vivid English picture of Grundtvig that we have, one of the latest Danish impressions of the old man reveals how present England and English history was to his mind, even in the summer of 1872. Frederik Hammerich, we have already met. As a student he had stayed with Pusey at Christ Church in Oxford in the 1830s and had acted as a go-between between the two scholars. Much later in life he had become the first of Grundtvig's close associates to attain a professorship in the university. He was, as we have seen, one of the two priests who supported Grundtvig at the altar on Palm Sunday in 1867. In his memoirs he also gives us a vivid picture of his last meetings with the old man,

In his last years Grundtvig came round to visit more than he had done before; he usually took a turn after his midday meal and went to see now one, now another, of his friends. So I had the pleasure of seeing him regularly in our house in Strandvejen, where he used to sit in a summer house with the Sound immediately in front of him, where he lit his pipe and stayed for an hour or so. This year he often came once a week, and since I was busy on a book on the earliest ecclesiastical literature of the Gothic people, we often talked of such topics.

Grundtvig had, as is well known, a long established love for the Anglo-Saxons. He was thoroughly at home in their writings. He had translated *Beowulf* and parts of *Cædmon*, he had published and translated *The Phoenix*. On his English journeys he had studied and copied out their manuscripts, and put out plans, in English, for an edition of them, and by doing so had stirred up the English themselves finally to pay attention to their rich inheritance from the early centuries. The last time he was with me, the Wednesday (28\08\1872), five days before he died, he had recently been sent a little English essay about an Anglo-Saxon poem, *An ancient saxon poem*, by J. Earle. There was no-one in his immediate family who could read it for him; his son, Professor S. Grundtvig was away, and Professor Stephens was not at home when he called. He told me all this. Otherwise all was well; he sat by the Sound till darkness fell. He had come that day rather late to us.

The following Friday, three days before his death, I went off to Tuborg, in order to see the little book and tell him what it contained. He had not been very well after his visit to us, but now he felt better and intended to preach the next Sunday, which he did. I went through the book, told him its main points and read something of it to him. There was nothing new in it, except the suggestion that the ruined city which the poem so vividly describes could possibly be Bath. Grundtvig said that he knew the poem well from Hickes' Thesaurus.[19]

Hammerich read Grundtvig the opening passage of the poem which speaks of the roofs and towers of the ruined city.

> Roofs have caved in, towers collapsed,
> Barred gates are broken, hoarfrost clings to mortar,
> Houses are gaping, tottering and fallen,
> Undermined by age.

'Yes', said Grundtvig, 'there is something of that majestic quality in which the English have always had their strength. Inevitably, on hearing those lines, one finds oneself thinking of the whole of Anglo-Saxon literature, for that itself is a very proud ruin and so can be well compared with the ruined city of which the old skjald sang.' We talked more about the Anglo-Saxons and he gave me the poem; so I left him and never thought it was the last time I should see him in this life.[20]

There is something very moving in this description of Grundtvig as he approaches his eighty-ninth birthday. There is the old man's determination, he wants to know what is in the book. Svend is away, no-one at home knows English, so he goes first to Stephens and finding him out he goes on to Hammerich. It was quite an expedition for him, even though presumably he was taken in his carriage. We are not surprised that he came home somewhat exhausted by it. There is his physical frailty and the failure of his eyesight, but at the same time there is the accuracy of his memory. This takes him back to Hickes' early eighteenth century collection of Old Norse and Anglo-Saxon texts, the George Hickes who beyond his pioneering work on Northern philology, had been Dean of Worcester, and then for twenty years or more, the leading figure among the English non-jurors. Grundtvig remembers the poem and at once he sees it not as a work on its own but as a work set in a whole context, a work which can stand for the corpus of Old English literature, a majestic ruin, still proud and eloquent in decay.

We see here the amazing tenacity of the old man's interests, perhaps it would be better to say the faithfulness of his loves. He had loved the literature of the Anglo-Saxons with an abiding passion for more than sixty years. It was a love which had taken him very far into the study and elucidation of that large and often difficult body of writing which he had received and appreciated with imagination and accuracy. It was a love which was with him to the end. To Gosse he may have looked and sounded half dead; behind the strange deeply lined features of the face there was a man still fully alive.

That was on Friday 28th August. On the following Sunday Grundtvig preached and after the service entertained to lunch a group of leading left-wing politicians. He had a long and animated conversation with them which shows him to have been fully aware of the latest developments in parliament. The following day he listened for a while while someone read to him from a study of Swedish history, the work of an eminent Swedish historian, Erik Gustav Geijer, whose thought had been in many respects parallel to Grundtvig's. There had been much talk the previous day about the relations between Denmark and Norway and Sweden and how important it was that, despite their differences, they should stand together and support one another. After a while he felt tired and asked that the reading should stop. A little later he went to sleep and died sitting in the large old chair in which many of his latter days had been spent.

Part II

Five Major Themes

Introduction

In this second section of the book we shall look at five major areas in Grundtvig's thought which will help us to get a better view of its shape as a whole. We begin straightaway in the year 1825, when Grundtvig was in his early forties and already had a significant history of intellectual development behind him. This year was certainly, in his own estimation, one of the decisive turning points in his life, the year of the *mageløse opdagelse*, the unparalleled discovery.

Ever since his return to the religion of his fathers in 1810-11, Grundtvig had described himself as a Bible-Christian. But his intense historical and poetic sense, coupled with his awareness of the critical questions raised by the scientific study of the biblical text made him more and more unsatisfied with such a designation. Through his preaching in the first years of this decade a new clarity began to form in him, a clarity which reached its fullness in the discovery of 1825. He saw that we cannot found the Church on the Bible, we must take the Bible and lay it open on the altar of the Church. Prior to the written text is the living Word, Christ himself, risen from the dead, present in the midst of the congregation through the sacraments of baptism and eucharist.

1825 is not the only turning-point in Grundtvig's life. An influential school of Grundtvig scholars has seen in 1832, and in the turning to the world which began at that time, a still more important and crucial revolution in his thinking. But that second move would not have been possible without the former one, and if we are looking at Grundtvig in terms of the history of Christian theology, we can hardly fail to see in 1825 a moment of decisive significance which can be paralleled in other places in the Christian world at the time.

In the period of the 1820s, 30s, and 40s, in a number of different places in the Christian world, people became aware in a new way of the history of the Church as an organic whole and began to think of the possibility that the divisions between Christians might find some resolution in the future. In Orthodox Russia, it was Alexei Khomiakov, in Catholic Germany it was Johann Adam Möhler, in England, it was the leaders of the movement which was to start in Oxford in 1833, Keble, Pusey and Newman. These were Grundtvig's contemporaries, and in the years that followed 1833 he became very much aware of the developments going on in England.

Something of the questions raised by that rediscovery of the centrality of the Church as a historic sacramental reality, is examined in the first two chapters of this section. The problems about the apostolic ministry which articulates the life of this historic Church are considered in some detail. This is a question where Grundtvig and his English interlocutors could find no way to agreement; in the end no way even to a common language. It is a question which has been taken up again in the last two decades between Anglicans and Lutherans, not only in Europe but in North America, with a new hopefulness of mutual understanding.

These two chapters are followed by a third in which we come to the doctrine of God the Holy Trinity. This chapter is not only the central chapter of this section, but to some extent the central chapter of the book. The trinitarian pattern which sees persons in relationship gives us not only a way into Grundtvig's understanding of the ultimate meaning of faith in God, but also into his understanding of human nature and the nature of human society. Like his contemporaries, Khomiakov in Russia and F.D. Maurice in England, he sees the doctrine of the three persons united but not confused, distinct but not separate, as a pattern for all true human community.

There follow on from this central chapter two further chapters which look in greater detail at Grundtvig's understanding of the nature of this world created in God's image and likeness. He takes this phrase, usually confined in Christian thinking to the human family and designating its particular openness to the divine, and he applies it to the earth and all that grows in it. Creation itself is made in God's image and likeness, made, that is to say, with a hidden, unrealised aptitude for God. By their bodily nature, human beings are in solidarity with all creation; by their bodily nature they are in solidarity with Christ, members of his body, and through them all creation is, in some way, called to share, in his resurrection, the conquest over death by death.

In particular Grundtvig's ideas about the potential capacities of human nature begin to be worked out in practice in the foundation of the first Folk High Schools. These schools, and the movement which they represent, have more and more caught the attention of people in some of the developing countries of Asia and Africa. The Grundtvigian vision of personal and national rebirth, and the place of adult education within it, has spread in unexpected ways and in unexpected places.

In these two chapters we see something of the all-inclusive intention of the apparently narrow affirmations of the earlier chapters about the Church and the sacraments of the Church. There is in Grundtvig's later life a distinct element of turning to the world as he becomes more directly involved in the social and political life of his country, a member of the Constitutional Assembly in 1849, for instance. For any complete appreciation of his life and thought it would be essential to examine these areas more closely than can be done here.

But in these very same years he reaches the highest point of his work as a hymn writer and makes his most significant contribution to the tradition of Christian liturgy and praise. We need to recognise the validity of both movements, held together within his complex, all-inclusive personality, in a life which is at once centred on God yet deeply human, deeply human and yet centred upon God.

CHAPTER 6

Discovering the Church

The years 1824 to 1825 were, as we have seen in the first part of this book, a time of particular importance in Grundtvig's life, leading up to what he himself called his *mageløse opdagelse*, the *unparalleled discovery*. At its heart there was a new vision of the unity of the Church in space and time, which found expression in a pamphlet, *Kirkens Gienmæle*, The Church's Rejoinder, which appeared in the autumn of 1825. This work is in itself so remarkable and so important to any understanding of Grundtvig's later theological position that it is necessary to quote it at some length.

It is, as its title suggests, a reply written by Grundtvig in the name of the Church, to a learned work on the doctrines, rites and constitutions of Protestantism and Catholicism, published by H.N. Clausen, one of the professors at the University in Copenhagen. Clausen had studied in Germany and was considerably influenced by the theology of Schleiermacher. He argued that the Bible was the foundation principle of Christianity, but in itself an inadequate expression of the full meaning of Christian faith. It was the task of theology,

by philological learning and philosophical criticism to supplement its vagueness and to bring about a higher unity between the different types of doctrine and their methods of presentation.

In doing this the laity must acknowledge the authority of the theologian who is the expert and specialist in this matter. The proper sphere of the laity was in the organisation and management of the Church, and in Clausen's book the Church is described as a 'community for the purpose of advancing general religiousness.'[1]

The appearance of this work suddenly sparked off in Grundtvig an enormous outburst of energy. The convictions, the ideas which had been forming in his mind during the previous years, suddenly came together, and within a few days his reply, or as he called it The Church's Rejoinder, appeared. It is a pamphlet written at a white heat of passionate conviction, and is in parts of an unprecedentedly violent nature. In it Grundtvig denounced Clausen as an anti-Christian teacher and demanded either that he abjure his un-Christian doctrines or else resign his living and renounce the name of Christian. The attack was so personal that it directly impugned Clausen's professional integrity. As a result he was able to have recourse to the courts and to initiate a libel action which, as we shall see, he won.

But this personal element in the work is of importance only as demonstrating the intensity of conviction which lay behind Grundtvig's defence and restatement of what he believed to be the Christian faith. In the introduction he writes,

> I know that the step I am now taking is unusual in our days; for many it will seem laughable and to many irresponsible, but it is nonetheless premeditated and entirely necessary, unless with my present understanding of things I am to be a traitor to the Church in which I have received the hope of salvation and in which I have the calling to dispense and to defend the great Gospel, which is entrusted to me to preach.[2]

Grundtvig feels himself to be writing not simply as one scholar in criticism of another, he is speaking on behalf of the truth of the gospel as it is revealed in the Church.

Later in the introduction he writes,

> I know very well that people will cry 'Woe and Alas' at my heresy hunting as they call every protest which the Church makes against its false friends; but I also know that they will have to admit that they have not seen this type of heresy hunting recently, indeed not since the book was written from which I have learnt it, that is to say the blessed book of Irenaeus on the Church's defence, which is now for the first time to be understood and used.[3]

The introduction is dated *Irenæi Dag, 1825*. However surprising it may seem, the whole work, in Grundtvig's mind, is seen as a renewal and continuation of Irenaeus' treatise *Adversus Haereses*.

I

What then is its basic idea? It is that Christianity is not a theory to be derived from the Bible and then elaborated by professors. Christianity is a fact of history which cannot be denied, a divine-human fact which stands firm in its own integrity. On the title page of the pamphlet Grundtvig places a quotation from Article VII of the Augsburg Confession, *Una Sancta Ecclesia perpetuo mansura sit*. The one Church exists; it is grounded in the apostolic confession of faith and in the sacraments of the gospel; these are the unshakeable foundation of the Church. From this great historic fact we learn what Christianity is and how the Bible is to be understood. We cannot build the Church on the Bible alone, still less on the interpretation of individual experts. It is in the life of the Church and in the sacraments of the Church, in which God is present and at work, that we hear God's word addressed to us and discover what true Christianity is.

Two consequences follow at once from this initial point. First, the great gulf between the present and the past, between the nineteenth century and the apostolic age, which the critical historical study of the Bible and the sceptical philosophy of the time had opened up, is bridged by the historic reality of the Church. The Church here is understood as a community of faith and life in which the risen Christ makes himself known through the power of the Spirit. Second, it is clear that though Christianity may well have a profoundly personal and interior dimension, it can never be understood in terms of the individual taken alone. Christianity is revealed as being profoundly corporate and relational. The individual grows into the life of Christ precisely as he is incorporated into the household of faith.

It is important to notice how this fundamental intuition about the nature of the Church and Christian life fits in with and complements Grundtvig's views about human life and knowledge as a whole. In his essays in the previous decade Grundtvig had developed what he called his 'historical view' of human life as opposed to what he called a purely 'intellectual view'. The individual does not exist in isolation. We live within the stream of history and we arrive at the truth by way of that history of which we are a part. The mind itself, in such a view of things, does not act in isolation but always in relation to other minds. As Alasdair MacIntyre remarks in a slightly different context,

the intellect is not to be thought of as either a Cartesian mind or a materialist brain, but as that through which thinking individuals relate themselves to each other and to natural and social objects as these present themselves to them.[4]

Sigurd Aarnes, writing on Grundtvig's work as an historian, sums up the matter like this,

While the 'intellectual view' isolates the individual with his inadequate intellect outside the living stream of history, the 'historical view' creates an empowering contact with all the great men and the great events of the past, and in the last resort with 'the power from on high' which works in and through it all. Because the 'intellectual view' is always the work of a single individual it is for Grundtvig fragmentary and haphazard, whereas the 'historical view' establishes contact with the collective and ongoing cognitive process which fulfils itself in the history of mankind.[5]

What is true in a general way about the whole process of human history, is true in a special way within the life and history of the one Church of Christ. We come to know and understand its meaning not as individuals, nor just as theologians or exegetes, but as living members of an historic communion in which all who are initiated have a vital part to play. How is this communion to be recognised?

'This characteristic quality', Grundtvig writes,

upon which the earliest Christian Church built, and by which it was recognisable, not only to its enemies but especially to its friends, must undeniably be found in every Church which can rightly be called Christian; and I maintain that it is found in our own Church and everywhere, where the apostolic confession of faith (i.e. the apostles' creed) is made the exclusive condition for incorporation into the fellowship, and where the means of grace, baptism and the Supper, are granted to have a power which corresponds to the confession of faith, that is a saving power. And this I maintain, not just as a theologian, not just as an ecclesiastical scholar but principally as a believing member of the great universal Christian Church, which by the apostolic confession of faith and the means of grace, not only differentiates itself from Jews, Turks and heathens, but still more secures to its believing members the forgiveness of sins and salvation in the name of Jesus Christ; and this claim of the Church, Professor Clausen and every such Protestant is obliged to refute historically, when he wishes to deprive our Church of the name of the one, true, universal Christian. Thus we meet Professor Clausen and all those who will give out their own fantasies as the Christian revelation, their own brain-children as Christianity, with the unshakeable fact that there has been and is a Christendom on earth, recognisable from all else by its unique confession of faith, with which, in all its languages and in all its surprising forms, it has proclaimed and proclaims faith in Jesus Christ, crucified and risen again, as the sure, the only way to salvation for sinners, as a way which leads through baptism and the Supper to God's kingdom and the land of the living.[6]

In such a perspective the question of the union and universality of the Church of God, the question of its catholicity, certainly becomes a matter of urgent importance. It is vital for Grundtvig to insist that this one Church exists in and through the divided Churches which actually confront us in the world we know. In some ways it was easier for him, in 1825, to make this affirmation than it would be today. Christendom, in its European form, Eastern and Western, stood unshaken. In the Denmark of his day, in effect, only one Church existed. This is the Church to which he always makes appeal, the local embodiment of the universal Christian congregation in which his whole life had been lived and which formed his vision of all things in heaven and on earth. But on the other hand the divisions between Catholic and Protestant, between Eastern and Western, seemed permanent and immovable. Suddenly for him the question of rediscovering Christian unity became a matter of life and death.

For him the one Church with its apostolic faith and its divinely instituted sacraments not only shows us what Christian life is but actually initiates us into it. Here, in the community of faith, there is forgiveness of sins and salvation in the name of Jesus Christ. Salvation is found to be not only a personal matter but also an intensely communal one. It is a reality of shared life in a community of faith which for nineteen hundred years has lived and grown in the midst of the history of the nations. It has taken many forms and spoken in many languages but it has been united in the life which it has lived. The ideas and intuitions of particular teachers, even the greatest, are altogether secondary when seen in relation to this fact. The Church exists in and through the faith and worship of all its members and it is the task of those who teach and learn to make that faith and worship articulate on behalf of the whole community. A whole new vision of the Church is coming before him.

Grundtvig at once goes on to concede that it is possible not to share in this faith, not to enter into the communion of life which is offered here. No-one is forced to be a Christian. What for him it is not possible to deny is that this is in fact what Christianity is.

Whether or not this is true, whether this dark secret way really does lead to communion with God who is light without any darkness, and who alone has true immortality, eternal life, this is something which can be disputed and without evident self-contradiction, denied. But what one cannot doubt unless one does not believe one's own eyes, what one cannot deny unless one is a desperate liar, is that this way is exclusively for Christians, and that the confession of faith which forms the narrow Church door is the unchangeable, we believe, unshakeable foundation both for faith and learning in the Christian Church. This is a truth as clear as the sun. One wonders how this principle will be contested, that the sacraments with the corresponding confession of faith, which is the one thing which all Christians, in all situations, in all Churches, in all times, have had in common, which has both made the Church recognisable to friends and foes, and bound together the community, which has thus undeniably been both the outward characteristic and the bond of union, that this is the foundation which has up till now answered to the value which the Lord put on the rock, which despite the gates of hell and the powers of death, should bear up his Church all the days until the end of the world.

One cannot deny a *fact* by *reason,* which even the divine, omniscient and al-mighty reason can only explain but never overthrow, or without self-contradiction contest. No-one can deny by the New Testament that which the New Testament itself in every way presupposes, rests and builds upon, as it is undeniably simply the witness of the Christian Church which makes of this book the light of the Church, and as the Scripture is explicitly addressed to the communion of those who already believe and are baptised and is not meant to teach them something new but only to strengthen and confirm them in their Christian faith ...[7]

This insistence on the Church's priority over the Bible is of course one of the most striking characteristics of what Grundtvig is saying. It does not, he will insist, deny the vital importance of Scripture in the life of the Church, though it certainly seems to place a question mark against the appeal to Scripture alone of the sixteenth century Reformation. For Grundtvig, however, this vision of the Church situates the Scriptures in the context where alone they can be rightly understood. From his insistence on the priority of the confession of faith made by the whole Christian people and on the power of God working in the sacraments in which all share, there follow crucial consequences as regards the place of theology within the life of the Christian people. The work of theology, what Grundtvig often calls 'the School' has to be seen as grounded in the life of 'the Church'. The preservation of Christian truth is seen as the work of the whole worshipping community.

The activity of the theologian, of the Christian scholar needs to be free, but it needs to be exercised within this context and not to contradict this basic rule of faith. When this rule of faith is denied, then the denier, 'the Protestant' by his own action, excludes himself from the community of faith and life in which alone the Christian faith can be understood and truly interpreted. We shall see shortly more of what Grundtvig understands by this relationship between 'the Church' and 'the School'. For the moment let us see how he goes on to expound more fully what it means for the life of the Church itself.

It is indeed high time that all of us who will, in Spirit and in truth, be Christians, should unite ourselves so as to build only on the rock, which through the course of time has defied the raging storms and the battering waves, should confine ourselves as the community of faith, as the Church, to the crib at Bethlehem, which history teaches can triumphantly defend itself against all the powers of the world and hell, that we should so to speak turn back to the sanctuary and hold out our hands to one another, and to all the faithful who sleep in the Lord, over the font, and exchange the kiss of peace before the altar, and should in the one Bread and the one Cup, as brethren let all disputes over doubtful questions drop, and when we are strong, not misuse our power to weigh down the weak, but rather to bear with their weaknesses.

Yes, Christians, wherever you are, it is time that we unite again on that which is Christian, on that which both lay and learned, and those Christian teachers, coming from such different worlds of ideas, such as Justin Martyr, and Irenaeus, Anskar and Luther, Reinhard and Balle had in common, and which undeniably is basically Christian, unite on that, tolerating in one another all theological differences compatible with it, but deviating from it never a hair's breadth, either for open enemies or for false friends, and solemnly separating ourselves from those who by rejecting the Church's original confession and divine means of grace, have themselves separated from us, and who only retain the name of Christian in order to mislead the congregation under the guise of friendship and steal the glory of the Church's great witness, which they do not want to believe.[8]

This passage with its long excited sentences surely deserves to be reckoned as one of the great prophetic texts of the twentieth century ecumenical movement. We notice the way in which Grundtvig makes the Church's historic confession of faith vivid and concrete by using the image of the crib at Bethlehem; all is founded in the incarnation, the Word made flesh. We notice too how the unity of the Church is described in liturgical and sa-cramental terms. We are, he says, to turn back to the sanctuary. It is there that our unity of faith and life will be found, in the joining of hands over the font, and the kiss of peace at the altar. This unity includes 'all the faithful who sleep in the Lord'. The Church's life is not a thing which exists in this world alone, it includes the Church triumphant in heaven. The idea of the communion of saints is a vital aspect of this mysterious reality. In the formula often used by George Florovsky there is an ecumenism in time which is no less vital than the ecumenism in space.

This recognition of our fathers in the faith, as part of the living history to which we belong is vital also for Grundtvig. Unity of faith must be established not only across the divisions which divide Christians from one another now but across the divisions which the centuries make between the past and the present. The line of witnesses whom Grundtvig cites, three from before the Reformation and three from after it, may be unfamiliar to Christians who are not Lutherans and who are not Danish. To Grundtvig they are of vital significance, stretching from apostolic times to the Bishop of Copenhagen who was his father's own diocesan.

Sometimes he enlarges the list giving greater weight to the earlier period, and filling out the tradition of the Western Church, 'Polycarp and Irenaeus, Augustine and Benedict, Anskar and Bernard, Luther and numberless others'.[9] The intention is always the same. In and through the differences of time and space, 'the different worlds of ideas', in which the Christian faith has expressed itself through history, there is a life-giving, a saving unity. His list of witnesses represents a tradition of faith and teaching to which he feels himself to belong. He knows in his own experience that he has been brought by baptism into the fellowship of the one Church. He is anxious to acknowledge and celebrate its great historic representatives, who all, in their different ways, point to the heart and meaning of the whole. It is the one Christ, making himself known in the power of the life-giving Spirit, who is present and at work at the font and at the altar.

As we shall see, we have here one of the basic motivations for Grundtvig's immense work as a writer and translator of hymns. In the congregation's response of praise and thanksgiving, this unity of life across the differences of time is again affirmed and celebrated. Here too is the root of his constant concern for the study of Church history; the historic dimension of the Church's existence is for him of vital importance.

II

Grundtvig goes on to look in greater detail at what this will mean in relation to the intellectual life of the Church, the work of theology and Christian teaching. We see here the sharpness of his polemic against a position which seemed to him to have turned the proper order of things on its head, which had put the individual before the community, ideas before the given reality of history, the cleverness of man before the wisdom of God. As we shall see in this context, Grundtvig is not worried about abandoning the name of Protestant. He has more scruples about seeming to give up the claim to reason. But it is his treatment of the name Lutheran which is particularly fascinating. He will not relinquish the right to be called Lutheran 'in the School', for he is sure that as a theologian he follows in the footsteps of

Luther. But 'in the Church' he will gladly give up the name. How could there be such a thing as a 'Lutheran Church'? Does not the Augsburg Confession itself bring all the followers of Luther to 'the one true, historic-Christian, unchangeable, catholic Church'?

The Church's original confession of faith, in the words of the apostles' creed as used in baptism, is always for Grundtvig the one essential thing. It is to this that the whole Church through the ages bears witness, for God himself bears witness to it through the Apostles.

For the Church Fathers this original confession had the divine witness so truly that they did not witness falsely but sealed their witness with their blood; for us the confession of faith has this divine witness in the apostolic Scriptures and in the Church's whole wonderful history; but no rule of interpretation except that the Scripture should be understood by the confession of faith and that it cannot be understood except by the faithful through the Holy Spirit, no rule of interpretation apart from that has the divine and human witness of the Apostolic Church and of history. To this the Church must hold fast, and for the rest allow the School to be free, let the theologians and exegetes discuss, and if they really want to, dispute with one another, so long only as they allow that the Holy Scripture is enlightening and edifying for all Christians according to the measure of wisdom and faith which the Lord gives, and so long only as they do not try to make a division between the Scripture and the Church's confession of faith, by doing which naturally they exclude themselves both from the Church and from the Church-School. Indeed in this way, we applaud all the spiritual universalism, all the scientific freedom that the Church as a unity of faith can allow itself, without, with an evident self-contradiction, proclaiming itself a community in truth-abolished, a false and lying community.

Those both learned and lay who cannot confine themselves within this necessary restriction, thus will not by any manner of means be Christians, they must also lay aside the name of Christian, in place of which we grant them any other, even the most glittering, they choose to give themselves. Will they be called Protestants! Well then indeed they may, and we renounce any claim to that name which undeniably suits them best, who have nothing else definite in common but to protest against the Christian Church and against every community of faith which will confess its faith and stand by its confession. Will they be called rationalists! Well then, we certainly cannot renounce reason, either as it is in God or as it is in his image in us, but we have nothing to boast of and therefore willingly grant to our opponents this arrogant name, just as the Fathers of the Church without committing themselves to stupidity, conceded the name of Gnostics to their opponents. Will they finally, with unbelievable humility, be called Lutherans! Well then, in the Church, we will not dispute it with them, for we are not baptised into Luther's name, and our Fathers taught us, not that Luther, but that Christ was crucified for us; but in the School we must defend this our father in Christ and demonstrate that all Protestants against the historic Christian Church who appeal for his support, either stagger in a dreadful historical darkness, or else associate with falsehood, and in either case dishonour the blessed memory of that wonderful man, and in either case misuse his name, rightly famous throughout Christendom, to adorn what he detested from the bottom of his heart.

For it is certain that whatever the Reformers and Martin Luther, their great leader, in their struggle with the papacy, maintained as *theologians* about the Scripture as the rule of faith, yet as *priests*, that is teachers in the Church, they presupposed both Church and faith constantly, and were united on the fact that Scripture could not be rightly understood except with the aid of the Holy Spirit, that is by believing Christians, who could not possible derive faith from Scripture before they understood it. It is also certain that our Communion in the Augsburg Confession, which Luther and Melanchthon certainly did not protest against, bound its teachers to the Apostolic confession of faith, (Article III), and to the one, true, historic-Christian, unchangeable, catholic Church (Articles VII and XXI).[10]

It need hardly be said that Professor H.N. Clausen did not see things in this light. He was indeed the very type of the liberal establishment theologian; young, brilliant and of an impeccable ecclesiastical ancestry. His father was Archdeacon of Copenhagen and had already been involved in tussles with Grundtvig. Here, he must have thought, was this madman, undeniably learned, but in such a strange and impossible way, demanding that on account of his supposedly heretical teaching he should be deprived of both his ministry and his professorship. He had at once to defend himself. He clearly decided that it was impossible to argue with Grundtvig, and in this, at a certain level, he was probably right. Instead he decided to go to law and instituted a case for libel against Grundtvig, a law case which in the following year he won. Grundtvig was fined a considerable sum, and all his published writings from now on were subject to official censorship, a requirement which remained in force until the end of the next decade. But already, before the case was concluded, Grundtvig had decided to resign his position in the Church. Again he found himself in the wilderness, a freelance literary and theological writer.

What has been quoted from *The Church's Rejoinder* will be sufficient to show something of the interest and importance of this fascinating document. It certainly marked a vital stage in the development of what in Danish is known as Grundtvig's *kirkelige anskuelse*, his *ecclesial view*. In his rejection of a biblicist or individualist conception of Christian faith and life, Grundtvig is clearly at one with the leaders of the Oxford Movement, as he is also in his appeal to the historic life and witness of the Church of the early centuries. In his affirmation that the Church is to be known and recognised through the apostles' creed and the sacraments, there are interesting parallels with the thought of F.D. Maurice. For Maurice indeed the sacraments of the Church seemed to have a self-authenticating quality. While the clergy and the theologians were darkening counsel in the pulpit, God himself, he held, was proclaiming the truth of the Gospel at the font and the altar. However differently Grundtvig's thought was to develop from that of the Tractarians and his other English contemporaries it is important to recognise their common starting points. It is also surely impossible not to regret that in his own lifetime it was not possible for Grundtvig to establish a more constructive dialogue with his English contemporaries.

In terms of his own development it becomes apparent in the light of the leading ideas of this document why, in the subsequent years, the writing of hymns became of such great importance for Grundtvig. If the Church becomes itself, or rather is created by God, through the sacraments and the liturgical confession of faith, then it at once becomes necessary that the congregation should have hymns in which to express this faith, hymns to use in the celebration of the sacraments. For this purpose the individualistic piety and the moralism of the Danish hymn book produced at the end of the eighteenth century which Grundtvig had always detested was clearly altogether inadequate. Grundtvig began to think about how a new hymn book might be prepared. At first he seems to have thought principally of adapting the classical Lutheran hymns of the sixteenth and seventeenth centuries, both German and Danish. But gradually he found himself embarked on a wider task, and in the spirit of *The Church's Rejoinder* he set about the attempt of gathering up into one, extracts from the whole course of Christian hymnody and making them available to the Danish public.

All this was to come to fruition more than a decade later. Writing in 1837, to his friend Bernhard Severin Ingemann, in a letter accompanying a copy of his *Sang-Værk*, he says,

What specially pleases me about it is the fusing together of notes from all the chief passages of the universal Church, which in the preparation came to my ears and moved my heart; and though I know well enough that the different notes have lost a great deal of their own character in passing through me, yet I dare to hope, that there is a trace still there, which will bring joy to faithful hearts, as a foretaste of the new song with which all tribes and tongues shall praise him, of whom and by whom and for whom all things are.[11]

Rooted in history, and in its historic confession of faith, the Church in its prayer and praise looks forward to God's coming kingdom. In all its diversity it is a sign of the presence of that kingdom already being made known in the world of space and time.

CHAPTER 7

The historic Ministry

I

As we have seen, an important element of the 'unparalleled discovery' of 1825 was the vision of the one Church of Christ as an historical reality continuous through the centuries, sustained and identified by the celebration of the sacraments of baptism and the eucharist and by the confession of the apostolic faith. The words from the Augsburg Confession which Grundtvig had put on the title page of the *Church's Rejoinder*, '*una sancta ecclesia semper mansura sit*' acquired new meaning for him. What was involved in this view of the historical nature of the Church, what role if any did the ordained ministry and in particular the episcopate have in maintaining its unity and continuity in time? Knowing Grundtvig's admiration for the writings of Ignatius of Antioch and above all for Irenaeus, we can hardly imagine that the early Christian emphasis on the role of the bishop as a centre of unity within the local church and as a link between later Christian generations and the apostles of the Lord would altogether escape him.

But of course he faced a difficulty here. The Church of Denmark had maintained the episcopal office at the time of the Reformation. The bishops occupied, and occupy today, the same episcopal sees as their pre-Reformation predecessors. But whereas in England as in Sweden the first Reformation bishops had been consecrated by men who were themselves bishops, in Denmark the first Reformation bishops had been consecrated by Johannes Bugenhagen, a colleague of Luther's who was only a priest. Did this mean that the Danish Church had lost the 'apostolic succession'? It was commonly thought so. When in 1783 Samuel Seabury came to England from the newly independent American states to seek episcopal orders, and found that for reasons of civil law the bishops in England were unable to consecrate him, he wondered where he should turn. 'Don't go to Denmark', advised Dr. Routh, the learned high church president of Magdalen College, Oxford. So Seabury turned and went to Scotland. It is, however, interesting that Denmark had obviously been discussed as a possible place for him to go. The Danish Church was known as a sister-church on the continent of Europe, which in the eighteenth century had actively participated in the missionary work of the SPG (The Society for the Propagation of the Gospel) in South India.

As is well known, the view that the whole validity of the Church's ministry depends on a valid episcopate and that a valid episcopate depends

on an unbroken succession of consecrations from the apostles' days until
now, became extremely important in the Anglican world from the time of the
Oxford Movement onwards. In a somewhat uncritical way the Tractarians
placed more and more emphasis on this doctrine. But this renewed emphasis
— I say renewed because it can be found in some seventeenth century
theologians and particularly among the eighteenth century non-jurors — only
began to make itself felt in England after 1833. It is clear that Grundtvig was
thinking about these questions well before that and certainly before his visits
to England in 1829, 1830 and 1831.

In 1826-27 for instance he already makes clear his interest in the question
of ordination,

I make no secret of it that in my theological judgement there is no Christian
teaching order without ordination with the laying on of hands, and that where
episcopal ordination is not continued unbroken, there are, from an ecclesial
viewpoint, no bishops, but a great lack of bishops, whereof there could and should
be a remedy, since God has taken care that episcopal ordination has continued in
the rightly believing English Church; but on that account I neither may nor will in
any way make heretics of theologians who are of another view, or maintain that
Christianity stands and falls with this understanding of the teaching order, which,
from the witness of Church history, is the early Christian and according to my
conviction, the only one which fully accords with Scripture and answers to the well-
being of the Church.[1]

During the visits to England which he made from 1829 onwards, his contacts
were more with literary scholars than theologians and more with non-
conformists than with Anglicans. It was not in England that his views on
episcopacy developed. The question, as we have seen, was occupying his
mind already in the late 1820s. Indeed it may have been one of the reasons
which made him anxious to see England at first hand. In a tract published in
1830, 'Shall the Lutheran Reformation really be advanced?', we see something
more of his thoughts on the subject. In a passage, at the end of that work,
where he is concerned with the relationship between theology and the
theologian on the one side and the common faith of the Church on the other,
he writes of the love which should bind people together into one, and of the
Spirit who is sent out from the one Father of all, as the source of that love.

As an image of this in the beginning the bishop stood at the Lord's Table with the
bread and the cup, the staff and the key and around him there knelt in the Saviour's
name, both learned and lay and forgot all worldly differences in the word, 'we are
all one body for we are all partakers of the one bread which came down from
heaven, and we have all been granted one Spirit, just as there is one Lord, one faith,
one baptism, one God and Father of all, over, with and in us all'. And receiving the
Lord's blessing they went each to his secular calling and his earthly concerns, with
heaven in their hearts and eternity before their eyes.[2]

However curious and anachronistic the details of Grundtvig's picture of the second century bishop may be, the bishop with his staff and cope, the communicants kneeling around him at the altar rail, one cannot but admire the theological intuition that had so quickly seized the essentially liturgical and pastoral nature of the bishop's office, the bishop seen as president of the eucharist, pastor of the flock, holding the keys of absolution. There is something of St. Ignatius of Antioch in this vision of the bishop in the midst of the people, the sign and symbol of God's reconciling love, bringing together into one the many different callings of humankind, and sending them out again with the Father's blessing to live eternity in the world of time. One might ask how many of the Anglican writers of this period who from 1833 onwards were to lay new stress on the importance of the episcopal office had so clearly grasped its essential nature?

This was the image and now we have only a shadow of it in the letters of the apostles, where both Peter and Paul however high they fly and however deep they go, yet kneeling and in silence and in concord, seek life and blessing in that love which melted John's heart and which proceeds from his lips in a living stream, in the divine love which passes all understanding and which will outlive all prophecy and learning and eventually render even faith and hope as superfluous as are sun and moon in the new Jerusalem where the Lord himself shines in all his glory.[3]

Here again we must recognise the richness of Grundtvig's thought. We have here one of his typical three-fold structures. Peter stands for faith, Paul for hope and John for love, and all three are essential for the life of the Church, but here it is John who is presiding over the other two. For Grundtvig the only ultimate source of authority in the Church is the divine love. We recall how for Ignatius of Antioch the Church of Rome is 'the Church which presides in love'. We also see how for Grundtvig the eucharist which is set at the heart of the Church's life is always seen in its eschatological context. It is the meal of the fulfilment of love, a foretaste of that coming kingdom in which God shall be all in all. Thus it would seem that the innermost reality of the Church even now, its heart and core, is not so much to be found in the preaching of Paul or in the pastoral authority of Peter as in the hidden witness of a life in which faith and hope are already being fulfilled in love, in a life of prayer and adoration. It is striking to find in the thought of one whose own life was so full of every kind of external activity, a life indeed of Peter and Paul, this witness to the priority of the contemplative element within the Church.

But Grundtvig goes on rather sadly,

The image cannot be reborn from the shadow, but it both can and shall remind us of what we lack; and where, as in Denmark, we have never belittled episcopal consecration, though since the Reformation we have felt the lack of it, the Lord will surely grant it to us with the fullness of blessing.

At this point he adds a footnote to this effect,

> Though the episcopal Church in England at present does not greatly do honour to
> its name, yet it is a rightly-believing church with real (not self-made) bishops and
> I know now by my own experience that it has a different weight when a bishop,
> rather than one of us, blesses in the Lord's name.[4]

This seems to refer to an occasion in the cathedral at Exeter in 1829 when the
bishop was presiding at the service.

   This restoration of a living episcopal office he regards as part of the fulfilment of the Lutheran Reformation, for he goes on,

> When it happens that the priests stand at the font as Sion's watchmen in the power
> of the Spirit, and the bishop stands at the altar truly representing the good shepherd
> who lays down his life for the sheep, while the congregation gladly let their light
> shine in good works, and the learned keep vigil over the Book with their lamps lit
> from the flame on the altar, and take care that the church has open doors so that
> men may go out and come in, then all is in its Christian order and then the
> Lutheran Reformation is completed. But the wreath can naturally only be placed on
> the building when it has its right form[5] and not like a triple crown on the bishop's
> head before his lifetime is ended, and Christ our Head who is now hidden behind
> the clouds is revealed. Here below none of us, whether he be bishop or theologian,
> priest or prophet, can wear any wreath but a martyr's crown, indeed the crown of
> thorns which the crucified has left to us and which the ascended Lord will there
> redeem with a crown of eternal flowers, the crown of life and glory which he has
> promised only to those which will be faithful to death, those who for his crown will
> drain his cup, and in order to share in his glory will share in his suffering.[6]

We have here a very interesting statement about episcopacy as well as about
the Church as a community made up of a variety of different orders and
vocations. Although we do not have a clearly worked out doctrine, we have
the raw material out of which a doctrine can be built. The office of the bishop
as a servant of the Church's unity centred in his liturgical functions as
president of the eucharistic assembly is clearly indicated. He is the one who
holds together and co-ordinates the varied ministries lay and ordained which
go to make up the Church's life.

   It is interesting to see how Grundtvig's sense of the interaction and reciprocity of the different callings within the Church can be paralleled in the
thought of his Russian contemporary, the eminent Orthodox lay theologian,
Alexei Khomiakov.

> It is the whole Church which produced the Holy Scriptures; it is the Church which
> makes them living in tradition; or rather, the two manifestations of the same Spirit
> are but one; for the Scripture is the tradition written down, and tradition is the
> living scripture.

Khomiakov goes on to argue for a reciprocity between the laity and the ordained ministry precisely in the teaching office of the Church, in which it might seem that the learned and the ordained had an absolute priority.

Every word inspired by a feeling of true Christian love, of living faith and hope is a teaching; every act marked by the Spirit of God is a lesson; every Christian life is a model and an example. The martyr dying for the truth, the judge who grants justice not for man's sake but for God's, the workman whose insignificant labour is accompanied by the constant lifting up of his thought to his Creator, live and die and give a lofty teaching to their brethren. When occasion comes, the divine Spirit will put into their mouths words of wisdom which the scholar and the theologian would not be able to find. 'The bishop is at once the teacher and the disciple of his flock', as the contemporary apostle of the Aleutians, Bishop Innocent has said. Everyman, however highly placed he may be in the ladder of the hierarchy, or however hidden he may be in the obscurity of the most humble situation, in turn teaches and receives teaching; for God distributes the gifts of his wisdom to whom he pleases, without favour of functions or persons. It is not only the word that teaches, but the whole life. To admit no teaching other than that of the logical word would be rationalism.[7]

Here, in the tradition of Eastern Christendom, there is a strongly communitarian dimension to the life of the Church.

There is within the Church an interaction and exchange over which the Spirit presides, which defies our attempts to confine the teaching office to any one ministry or order within the body. The oldest may learn from the youngest, the most learned from the most apparently simple. As in the New Testament, all must bow before the insight given to the most childlike and simple of heart. To develop such insights need not lead us to abandon the traditional hierarchy of the Church, it may enable us to see it in its true perspective and meaning.

II

It is important at once to say that later in his life Grundtvig altogether changed his mind on the subject of episcopacy. In the *Elementary Christian Doctrine* published in 1868 he speaks for instance, of the 'arrogant episcopal Church with its black spiritual poverty' and of his own surprise at finding

that the so-called apostolic episcopal consecration in unbroken succession which the high church people swagger about with and from which they derive their unparalleled glory, is the emptiest of all illusions.[8]

This change of attitude towards episcopacy is linked with a whole change of attitude towards the Church, as a visible institution, in part occasioned by the difficulty of his own relations with the state Church in Denmark and by the way in which the struggle for liberty in the Church had developed. But it is clear enough from the terms in which he speaks about it that one at least of the decisive factors in bringing it about was the unfortunate impression he had received in Oxford.

It is one of the ironies of nineteenth century church history that Grundtvig only made personal contact with the leaders of the Oxford Movement at a time when it was scarcely possible that they should understand one another. His second and crucial visit to Oxford took place in 1843 when Newman had already lost all confidence in the Church of England and Pusey had just been prohibited from preaching in the University. Had he come some ten or even five years earlier when their views were less set and their fortunes more flourishing it might have been possible that some genuine contact could have been established. As it was, the inevitable happened. Grundtvig's orders could not be recognised, and in terms of the theology of the period that was the end of the matter. 'What I said with respect to yourself', wrote William Palmer of Magdalen,

> was *not* that you were or were not a fellow member of the visible Church, not that you were or were not in some sense a servant or 'Minister' of Christ working among your fellow men for good ... but *this* is what I *did* and *do* say, that you cannot (in my judgment) be recognized as a 'Clerk' a 'Presbyter' 'Priest' 'Sacerdos' or 'ἱερεύς' in the Ecclesiastical and Canonical sense of these words.[9]

But this naturally enough was exactly what Grundtvig could not accept. Judging by the experience of the mystery of Christ which was evidently his and his insight into the nature of baptism and the eucharist which was expressed in his preaching, we can hardly be surprised at the firmness of his convictions.

As this question of Grundtvig's relation to the Oxford Movement is of some importance in the context of Grundtvig's relation to the English-speaking world, and to the more Catholic strands of the Christian tradition as a whole, it demands to be considered in more detail. In the Grundtvig archive there are two drafts of a letter to Pusey written either in 1836 or 1837. It is not clear whether in the end this letter was ever sent but it is clear from its contents that at this time Grundtvig was still longing to make contact with the Oxford Movement despite the evident difficulties of the situation. He could not help feeling that on many things he and they were at one and he could not but be excited by the evident power and enthusiasm with which they were propagating their ideas. We see in these two drafts more than anywhere else, the strength of his desire to break out from the isolation of his position in Denmark. The new power of this movement in the university of Oxford to reassert the historic Catholic nature of the Church which he had looked for in vain on his first three visits to England had come to him as an almost unhoped-for source of hope and encouragement, 'as cold water to a thirsty soul so is good news from a far country'. He was no longer alone, he found he had unexpected allies across the sea, in that island kingdom which so much fascinated him. Here were priests and theologians in another Church which like his own had passed through the experience of the Reformation seeking, as he was, 'to cut their way through the Protestant wilderness in order to find a city to dwell in'. He knew there were obstacles in the way of mutual understanding but he felt it must not be now as it was at Babel. Then together as allies they might sound the trumpet 'for the primitive, true Catholick Church, the Mother of us all'. The first draft reads as follows,

Dear Sir
Nearly for thirty years I have been cutting my way thro' the Protestant wilderness in order to find 'a city to dwell in' and though The Lord wonderfully has strength-ened me like 'an iron pillar and brasen walls against the whole land', yet I was very sorry for it, that from nowhere else I heard the trumpet sound for the primitive, true Catholick Church, the Mother of us all, and even by my visits to England [1829-31] where it was most likely, that her 'servants should take pleasure in her stones and favour the dust thereof', in this respect I was disappointed. But at last I heard you were awakened from a long and deep slumber, and tho' the reports were vague, yet I begged my friend Mr Hammerich, who had been favored with your acquaintance, to tell you what was going on with us, and from your answer to him I see, you look with serious interest also upon this small corner of 'the great Palace', tho' my friend's statement may have been rather obscure to you. During this [time] also from 'The British Critic' and from some of your tracts I have got more authentic information of your views than I had before, and tho' I dare not say that upon all points we agree, still by the restoration of The Holy Catholic Church it must not be the same case as by the erecting of the tower of Babel, when they did not understand one another's speech, and therefore I will try, how far it may be possible by 'pen and ink' to make myself understood and how far we may agree, for 'as cold water to a thirsty soul so is good news from a far country', and very 'pleasant it is for brethren to dwell together in unity'. But here I stumbled on the great question between you and us, whether you believe you may have 'brethren in the Lord' or not, where there has been no uninterrupted succession of Bishops, for I don't speak of those, who despise the Episcopal order and succession, never the case in Denmark, where the Superintendents always have been named and consecrated Bishops, only not with due respect to the uninterrupted succession. No doubt, that we ought to desire the Consecration with you, but the question is, whether or not you would recognize not only our Baptism but also our ordination of Presbyters as valid, tho' our first Ordinators after the Reformation have only been Presbyters, not Bishops themselves. I am quite sure, you ought to do so, for the Lord has blessed my own ordination to such a degree, that I might as well slighten my Baptism as my Ordination, and could do neither without the most barefaced ingratitude, and still I doubt, whether your extravagant notions of Episcopacy would allow you to recognize me as a Presbyter. The fact is, as far as I am able to understand, that you, like the *Neophyte* Bishop Cyprian, would make Episcopacy the very foundation and fundamental of the Church, which has been the root of all Popery, the oneheaded as well as the manyheaded, alike detestable to me.[10]

And then, aware that he is getting angry, he breaks off and tries again another day.

The second draft begins with a paragraph in which he says that he fears that Hammerich had given a very imperfect account of the situation in Denmark. In the second paragraph he gives Pusey an account of the change of his own views in 1825 which he says was twelve years ago.

For almost 30 years I have preached the Gospel under a hard struggle with the infidels, who at the beginning of this century had got almost full possession of our establishment and were about to abrogate even the Baptismal Covenant. For a long time I certainly would prove all from the Bible as I was taught, but finding it impossible, I very earnestly sought for a clearer and surer testimony, of which [*sic*] I felt truth divine must carry along with it, and twelve years ago I found it out or rather I stumbled upon it, as it is laid open to our eyes, tho' we did not see with eyes nor hear with ears. From that moment the 'Holy Catholic Church' stands unmoveable before me upon its rock: the word of His mouth, who is the Word himself, and all the State-Establishments, from that of Constantin to the last, that may be, sunk down as human fabricks and platforms, christian only so far as they kept the essentials or fundamentals of the primitive, Apostolical, Catholic Church. Under these circumstances I must be quite a stranger to church history if I could overlook the Bishops, or that gross mistake of ours by which they have been not despised but neglected, and upon that score I have always admired your Establishment, the only Protestant one, where the Bishop really has been kept, for in Sweden they have kept appearances only.

He goes on as in the previous draft to express his fear that they will not be able to agree on the question of his orders. But he argues that on the principle *qvod semper, ubique et ab omnibus* they ought to prefer the testimony of Polycarp or Irenaeus, of St. Paul, St. Peter and St. John, over that of Cyprian or the bishops of the Council of Nicaea. From them

we shall hear, that not the Clergy, but only the Creed and the Baptism are 'the one needful thing', tho' among the many things, that pertain to 'life and godliness', the Clergy and especially the Bishops certainly belong to the principal ones.[11]

Here we see how his own view of the Church was at this time developing in a way which made the question of ordination secondary though not unimportant. It is interesting to note that in both drafts though Grundtvig is adamant on the question of his orders, he is not only willing but apparently anxious to envisage the possibility of rectifying 'that gross mistake of ours' by which the episcopal office had come to be 'not despised but neglected'.

III

A further insight into Grundtvig's attitude to events in Oxford is to be found in an article which he published in 1842, one year before his final visit to

England, in *Nordisk Tidskrift for Christelig Theologi*.[12] This is a substantial article of almost thirty pages. Much of it is concerned with Newman's Tract XC. The writer, one feels, is fascinated, baffled and in the end made angry by what he is discussing, and yet at the same time still deeply involved in it. Certainly there is criticism, but it is not altogether unfriendly. One feels even now a certain critical solidarity with the movement, despite those elements in its development which he clearly cannot follow.

From the first it must be said that though Grundtvig's interest in the movement is unquestionable and, as one might expect, he has some very penetrating insights into it, his knowledge of it is necessarily partial. It could hardly be otherwise. The years 1833-42 had not been leisurely for him. His direct contacts with Oxford were few. His disciple Hammerich had visited Pusey in 1837, Nugent Wade, the Anglican chaplain at Elsinore, had helped him get books and had discussed matters with him. Beyond this he had no direct contacts with the leaders of the movement. It is clear from this article that his information was limited and not always correct. He thinks for instance that Hurrell Froude had been professor of poetry. It is significant and sad that he seems not even to have heard of Keble. It is clear that he had not read many of the fundamental texts of the movement, Pusey on Baptism, Newman on Justification, and Palmer on the Church. It is also evident that there were many aspects of the historical and constitutional position of the Church of England which he found it difficult to grasp. But as he states in the article, since 1837 he had been a regular reader of the *British Critic* and in that way has been able to follow the developing crisis in Tractarian affairs.

On the one side he admires much of what they have written. Many of their essays 'are very serious and have scientific worth'. He is particularly interested in their feeling for poetry and its relation to faith. He comments on an article of October 1841, 'On Rites and Ceremonies', that it is 'lively and well written tho' unsatisfactory'. To have a high view of outward ceremonies does not, he allows, necessarily mean that one is unspiritual.[13] But on the other side, he is riled by the constant tendency to treat Roman Catholics as erring brethren, while putting Lutherans altogether outside in the company of Calvinists and rationalists. What right, he asks, have they to think they are members of the Church and we are not? He finds Tract XC wrong-headed and hair-splitting. Above all the whole group seems fixed on their ideas that episcopal ordination is the foundation sacrament. That for him is the root error.

Still even now he is hopeful that something can be done and he intends himself to do it, to see whether by a visit to Oxford he cannot himself decisively influence the development of the movement. For he still sees the movement as a sign from God, unlooked-for and unexpected, and he does not think God will let it die. He had long hoped that the historic corrective which would put some limit to German 'self-satisfaction' might come from England but he had hardly dared think it possible. Surely this was it, surely this was a sign that the whole Protestant world should attempt to rethink the Reformation as he had tried to do in his writings since 1825. Taken in this perspective the difference might not after all be insuperable.

When now the Oxford men … lay particular weight on the writings of the Church fathers and on universal Church history, which among Protestants have on the whole been neglected, they necessarily stand on the side of reality against the airy speculations which coming from Germany just now begin to afflict both France and England. Although therefore the spirit of man, not to speak of the Great Spirit, must wish the Oxford ferment more poetic strength and more depth of heart than it has shown up till now, yet the Church can congratulate itself on it, both as a good omen and a good weapon in the great strife against the flesh-head [i.e. materialism] and the wind-machines [i.e.idealism] in all countries. In the whole Protestant world, one will now have to remember that like Rome the Church of Christ was not built in a day, and will have to submit both the Reformation of the sixteenth century and its whole consequent style and scientific method, to a new examination and discussion which is greatly needed. And in all the rest of Europe, all that is human will feel itself drawn to a side where one no longer does violence to the heart and to history, but strives only to remove what is evidently false, a side where one no longer fights with shadows and images like the knight of La Mancha, but on the contrary strives carefully to avoid their confusion with realities.[14]

In this paragraph, which is not always easy to interpret, Grundtvig can still affirm his solidarity, even if a strongly critical solidarity, with the basic thrust of the Oxford movement as he understands it. He can still welcome it as a sign of the necessity for a re-examination of the whole Reformation movement and of the relation between the two halves of Western Christendom, Protestant and Catholic. The former, he seems to suggest, needs to re-examine its first principles and to recognise more the importance of Church history and the witness of the early centuries. In the rest of Europe, i.e. the Catholic part of the continent, there need to be corresponding revisions of inherited viewpoints. Three years later, commenting on Newman's conversion, Grundtvig affirms his conviction that the nineteenth century is a time in which all tendencies among Catholics to recognise the truth in Protestantism and among Protestants to recognise the truth in Catholicism, need to be welcomed and supported. It is a time in which the two parties in the sixteenth century quarrel may yet come to recognise the faith and baptism which they still have in common.

As he sees it, there is a need to find a way forward which will avoid idealism on the one side and materialism on the other. A way in which the Spirit will be seen at work in matter, not divorced from it, in what the Tractarians would have called a 'sacramental' way, uniting inner and outer, personal and corporate.

But in the end the 1843 visit came to nothing. Grundtvig came to Oxford at a time when Newman already knew in his heart, though he had not yet announced it openly, that he was going to leave the Church of England. He met Grundtvig twice, and on the second occasion a genuine conversation seemed to be beginning when, to Grundtvig's intense annoyance, they were interrupted. Newman took the opportunity of slipping away. That summer was also a bad time for making contact with Pusey. He was often away from Oxford, unwell, having been overwhelmed by the controversy which had arisen earlier in the year over his sermon on the holy eucharist, and its condemnation by the University. He and Grundtvig certainly met, but apparently briefly. However, Grundtvig had some remarkably friendly, though sometimes stormy meetings with younger representatives of the Oxford school, among them William Palmer, just returned from his first visit to the Orthodox Church in Russia. Grundtvig was so pleased with these contacts that he arranged to come back to Oxford a second time after his visit to Edinburgh; but his hopes of influencing the leaders of the movement were not to be realised.

There was to be no meeting of minds and hearts between England and Denmark, at least not in the nineteenth century. Grundtvig was forced back into a position of isolation. From henceforth he was surrounded by followers and admirers. In the theological realm at least he had no equal collaborators with whom to test out his ideas. As he grew older, certain of the least satisfactory elements in his system, the notion that Jesus had taught the Apostles' Creed to the apostles word for word during the forty days between Easter and Ascension for instance, became fixed and hardened. It became difficult for him to see what was happening around him in Denmark in a larger perspective. The waves of spiritual energy which flowed out from *Vartov* were a sign not only of *a* renewal of Pentecostal fire but of *the* renewal of the Spirit's working. It is a tribute to Grundtvig's greatness that the whole movement which developed around him did not become more sectarian than in fact it did. It always remained in active interaction with the Church and society at large but undoubtedly something was lost.

And of course there was something lost on the Anglican side as well. If Grundtvig could have helped the Tractarians to reformulate their doctrine of apostolic succession in a more balanced and flexible way, the consequences would have been very important. If they had learned to affirm the central importance of the historic episcopate within the ministry of the Church, but to see that ministry as only one among a number of strands, of doctrine, worship, and life which together served to maintain the Church's identity and continuity through time, they would have been in a much freer position in their relationship with Christian traditions other than their own. If they could have learned from him to recognise that the position of the episcopate in a certain Church may be impaired and obscured, as he was willing to admit was the case in Denmark, without being altogether abolished, they would have been spared the folly of supposing, as many Anglicans at the time did, that the Church of Denmark was no Church. More importantly they could have gained through him a more just and positive view of the Lutheran Reformation as a whole, which would have enlarged their freedom of movement in ecumenical affairs and could have affected the course of negotiations towards Church unity in many parts of the world in the last hundred years.

All of this however is speculation and in that sense fruitless, unless it enables us in our very different situation in the late twentieth century, to see Grundtvig's efforts as a pioneering attempt, frustrated in their own time but nonetheless real, to break through one of the strongest barriers which divide Catholic and Protestant and to free the log-jam of the Reformation. If we can see his efforts in that way then the unfinished business of 1843 might still give rise to fruitful consequences one hundred and fifty years later. That would be a matter of some significance for the growth of the Christian faith into the twenty-first century, and not only in England and Denmark.

CHAPTER 8

Trinity in Unity

One of the most striking things about Grundtvig's theology is the place of the Holy Spirit in it. The hymns for Whitsun are as numerous and as fine as those for Easter; indeed one is tempted to say that they are even finer. Here very evidently is a man who has not fallen into the trap of thinking of the Holy Spirit as a functionary subordinate to the other two persons of the Trinity, something which at least in practice if not in theory seems to have happened in large parts of Western Christianity. Grundtvig's vision of God is fully trinitarian, and for him the doctrine of the Trinity is seen not primarily as an abstract structure of thought, but rather as a vital and God-given way of approach to the mystery of the being both of God and of creation, a way in which Christian faith and life can grow.

Hal Koch expressed this beautifully in a book about Grundtvig published more than half a century ago, a book based on public lectures given in Copenhagen in the autumn of 1940, at the beginning of the German occupation. These were lectures which had an extraordinary effect within the Danish society of their time and acted as a kind of rallying cry of opposition to the whole Nazi ideology and a positive affirmation of the authentic Danish tradition.

It cannot be denied that a large number of Grundtvig's finest hymns, and especially of his original hymns, are hymns of the Holy Spirit. It is also quite true historically that while the period of the Enlightenment did not get much further than the first article of faith [belief in God the Father], and the pietist movement concentrated its attention on the second article, Jesus' suffering and death, in the Grundtvigian understanding of the Church, belief in the Spirit, the Word and the Church sprang up into new life. But what is peculiar to Grundtvig is this, that from his belief in the Spirit and the Spirit's activity in the congregation, he went back to the second and to the first articles of faith. Not for nothing had the experience of 1810-11 been the turning point in his life, an experience in which Jesus had been present to him as saviour, he who has authority over those who believe in him. This did not become otherwise after 1824. On the contrary — but he now understood that our Lord Jesus has not concluded a particular covenant with each separate individual but has called them into fellowship and rooted them in his kingdom, where he rules through the Spirit and the Word. But from here Grundtvig went back ... to the first article of faith, belief in God as Lord and Creator. Here we find that he has recaptured the whole of the Enlightenment belief in providence and its happy optimism which praises the world as 'the best of all worlds', but on an entirely new plane. From this, his language about God as creator and providence acquires a quite different power, and blends in a remarkable way with what he says about Jesus as Lord and Saviour ... With all that can be said about Grundtvig's preference and particular ability for writing hymns about the Holy Spirit, I believe, despite everything, that the true greatness of his hymn writing depends on this unique union of all three articles of faith, so that each particular one becomes the chief concern in its place, but always so that the other two are present as background and accompaniment.[1]

In the presence and action of each person of the Trinity the presence and action of the others is always acknowledged. It is as though the doctrine of *perichoresis* had come to life in hymnody and was present in the midst of the congregation.

This living trinitarian quality in the hymns, in which the Holy Spirit plays so vital a role, is one of the places where the theology of Grundtvig is of particular interest at the present time both internationally and ecumenically. The search for a recovery of a vital trinitarian faith and theology is to be found in many and varied places in current theological discussion on both sides of the Atlantic and beyond. It is to be seen in the work of theologians like Jürgen Moltmann and Wolfhart Pannenberg. It has played a considerable part in the work of the Faith and Order Commission of the World Council of Churches in recent years. In Britain an important contribution to the ongoing discussion was made by the collection of studies published in 1991 by the Council of Churches for Britain and Ireland, under the editorship of Professor Alasdair Heron. In his foreword the editor writes,

The path towards a future ecumenical Christianity ... can only be traversed under the banner of a trinitarian and incarnational faith for which the sovereignty of God the Creator, reconciliation and atonement through the life, death and resurrection of Jesus Christ, and the promise and activity of the Holy Spirit as the pledge of our redemption, are the supreme realities which give an identity, confidence and hope in life and in death. God is with us — the triune God, creator, redeemer and saviour. *God* is with us; God is *with* us; God is with *us*. That, in the simplest terms, is the meaning and perennially astonishing import of the doctrine of the divine triunity.[2]

The fact that this same subject has emerged more and more clearly in the development of more recent Grundtvig studies in Denmark, is also significant. Progress in this area during the last fifteen years, has been due above all to the appearance of Grundtvig's hitherto unpublished sermons. The publication of these sermons has made available a great quantity of new material from which to make a study of Grundtvig's theology. The sermons deepen and enlarge our understanding of the hymns with which scholars have always been familiar, and they need to be seen in constant interaction with them, so that while the sermons help us to understand the hymns, the study of the hymns throws light on the interpretation of the sermons. They reveal to us more of the underlying themes which keep returning in varying forms in Grundtvig's preaching from year to year and thus give us a new understanding of the elements of continuity in Grundtvig's thought.

I

As part of the preparation for the publication of these sermons Professor Christian Thodberg in 1977 edited a remarkable collection of essays on different aspects of Grundtvig's theology as revealed in his preaching. The book was called *For Sammenhængens Skyld*, a title which may be translated *For the Sake of Coherence*. These essays were written by a group of younger scholars who had worked with Thodberg in Aarhus on the transcription and preparation of the texts of the sermons. Through all these studies it becomes clear that while in his preaching, Grundtvig's themes are not set out in a strictly systematic way, there is nonetheless a clear and consistent theology to be found in them. Grundtvig is a man of a many-sided and very varied mind. His powerful poetic imagination is constantly at work suggesting new insights into this or that aspect of Christian doctrine. Through it all, however, there is a remarkable coherence, a kind of spontaneous and coherent consistency of view rather than a systematically worked out articulation of doctrine.

This consistent viewpoint is also evident in one of the most important of Grundtvig's later writings, perhaps his only attempt to set out a complete picture of his theological position, *Den Christelige Børnelærdom*. Translated literally the title means *Christianity as taught to children* but perhaps *Elementary Christian Doctrine* would be better. Based on articles which appeared from 1855–61 the book was finally published in 1868. Its title contains a reminiscence of Luther's *Little Catechism* and involves a protest against the pretensions of academic theology. Before the mystery of God we are all children. We need to receive the faith as children and to reflect on it with childlike candour and openness. It may be that this was what Grundtvig intended by the title, but the child revealed in these pages is, one must say, very mature and decidedly complex! He shows a remarkable knowledge of the Bible, a considerable acquaintance with traditional theology and a wide reading in contemporary German thought. It is certainly not by chance that the first of the articles on which the book is based appeared in the year of Kierkegaard's death. Part of Grundtvig's original motivation for writing the book lay in his desire to respond to Kierkegaard's insistence on the absolute distance between the human and the divine. As we shall see, for Grundtvig the idea of the divine image as reflected in human nature and in the whole of creation takes a more and more central place.

In approaching the detail of this subject of the doctrine of the Trinity we are fortunate to have a masterly treatment of it in the form of a substantial essay from the pen of Regin Prenter. Prenter was perhaps the most out-standing Danish systematic theologian of our century, known internationally both through the English translation of his dogmatic theology, *Creation and Redemption,* and of his study of the theology of the Holy Spirit in Luther, *Spiritus Creator.* Prenter was also a lifelong student and lover of Grundtvig. In his essay on Grundtvig's doctrine of the Trinity published in 1983, he makes much use of the work collected in the symposium to which we have already referred. While at times he distances himself from it on this or that point, there is no doubt about his substantial agreement with its viewpoint and approach.

In Thodberg's book, as in the sermons, it becomes abundantly clear that for Grundtvig the doctrine of the Trinity is of vital and crucial importance. It is a doctrine which he understands not at all as an abstract speculation but as the framework in which Christian life and reflection may grow. Looking at the matter in a wider perspective it may be worthwhile to remark at the outset that this way of approach to the doctrine of the Trinity has much in common with that to be found in the sermons of Lancelot Andrewes, as Nicholas Lossky has so decisively shown.[3] A similar approach is to be found in the teaching of John Wesley, described by recent American Wesley scholars in terms of a Christ-centred, Spirit-filled trinitarian vision.[4] It is in this kind of perspective that the full ecumenical significance of Grundtvig's approach is to be found.

If we start with the pattern which emerges from the sermons themselves it becomes clear that in his trinitarian teaching Grundtvig places at least as much weight on the three as on the one. Perhaps the Danish word for Trinity, *tre-enighed,* tri-unity, encourages him to do this. He begins, as the Scriptures do, with the three persons rather than with the one nature. Here at the outset is a place where his approach seems closer to that of the Greek Fathers than to that of the Latin. This is particularly true in the stress which he lays on the idea of the Father as the unique source of deity, basing himself on the Pauline words, 'There is one God the Father of whom are all things …' (1. Cor. 8:6). So in his essay in the symposium of 1977, Morten Mortensen can sum up Grundtvig's teaching thus:

The Father is the only one who exists by and of himself; both the Son and the Spirit have their existence from and by the Father, even though in all else they are equal with him and co-eternal.

In his teaching about the Trinity, it is striking that Grundtvig lays great weight on the names, Father, Son and Spirit;

What becomes evident here is Grundtvig's understanding that heavenly and divine realities and phenomena cannot be expressed in logical discursive language but can only be conveyed in images.[5]

As we have seen in other places, though the role of concepts is vital in theology, more vital and more fundamental is the role of poetic imagery. This is the root of Grundtvig's dislike for the logically constructed trinitarianism both of patristic and scholastic theology, and of his preference for the theological method and viewpoint of for instance Irenaeus in the period before the Council of Nicaea.

For him the Father is the origin of all, the heart or the depth of deity. The Son however is subordinate to the Father only as Son. In all other things he is equal with him. Indeed he must be equal and co-eternal, for only can the Father be Father if he has a Son from all eternity. The Spirit is he who from all eternity proceeds from the Father. On this Grundtvig is perfectly clear. The Spirit who is sent by the Son proceeds from the Father. The language of the double procession, i.e.that the Spirit proceeds from the Father and the Son is not to be found in him. Nor do we find the term *nexus amoris*, so common in Western theology, which speaks of the Holy Spirit as the bond of love between the Father and the Son. It is very striking that for Grundtvig if the word love is to be applied to any one person of the Trinity in particular, and clearly it applies to all, it applies most appropriately to the Father; it is he who is the ultimate source of love as well as of being.

Of course in his theology Grundtvig in no way separates the Spirit from the Son; both in his sermons and in his hymns he uses the Irenaean image of the Son and the Spirit as the two hands of God and he constantly speaks of a reciprocal relationship between the two. But he insists on the real personhood of the Spirit and firmly resists any tendency to consider the Spirit as an impersonal power or to make use of the pronoun *it* instead of *he* in relation to the Spirit.

The surprisingly Irenaean and pre-Nicene nature of Grundtvig's understanding of the Trinity is a constant feature of his work. It is not that in the sermons or even in the *Elementary Christian Doctrine*, there is any direct criticism of the Trinitarian teaching of Augustine and the West. The matter is simply left in silence. Grundtvig follows his own line. Because for him *the* confession of faith is always the apostles' creed, the creed used in baptism and the eucharist, and never the Nicaeno-Constantinopolitan Symbol, the question of the Filioque Clause does not arise directly. But Grundtvig was a minister of an emphatically Western church, a church which in its liturgical and theological formulas had received the Western teaching that the Spirit proceeds from the Father and the Son. He quite serenely abstains from saying anything about the matter. At the heart of Western Christendom he maintains an affirmation of trinitarian faith which is in many ways pre-Augustinian. It is another of his powerful if perhaps unconscious affirmations of the fundamental unity of the Christian tradition in East and West alike.

II

As we shall see, in his sermons Grundtvig suggests that knowledge of the Trinity given to each one of us in our baptism is something which is to deepen and grow through our constant participation in the life of the Church. But what is true of each one is also in some sense true in the life of the Church as a whole; here too there is growth. Grundtvig has a very dynamic view of the history of the Church and of humankind in which God is even now at work unfolding the revelation, given once for all in Christ. If there are fixed points in his vision of things there is also a great and undefined potential for expansion.

We must note that for him all three persons of the Trinity are at work from the first moment of creation to the fulfilment of all things. God the Word, made man for us of the Virgin Mary, his Mother, crucified and risen again, present with us at the font and at the altar, is the same Lord who has created all things in the beginning, in whose image and likeness we are made. The Holy Spirit by whom Jesus was conceived, descending on him in his baptism, in whom he offered himself to the Father, descending on the infant Church at Pentecost is the same Spirit who moved on the waters of the creation, who is everywhere present fulfilling all things, the inspiration of all true love and knowledge in humankind, the life of all that has life throughout creation. Throughout Grundtvig's teaching there is this remarkable stress on the interaction, *vekselvirkning* between creation and redemption, between universal and particular. We should not be able to see God at work everywhere in his world unless we had been called out of death into life by the redeeming work of Christ the saviour, but we should not be able to hear his word unless there was that in us which was created for God, that which, though darkened by the fall, and so wounded as to be almost dead, could yet respond to the action of the Spirit. That humankind is made in God's image and likeness, is as we shall see, for Grundtvig of all the articles of the faith almost the most essential. The heart of humankind is made to receive and respond to the love which comes from the heart of God.

All these themes, articulated in his sermons, are developed again in a more systematic way in the 'Elementary Christian Doctrine'. As he develops the idea of the image of God in humanity, Grundtvig sees an inseparable relationship between heart, mouth, and hand, both at the divine and at the human level. For him heart, mouth and hand come together around the concept of the word. The word, if it is a living word and not mere idle chatter must proceed from the heart, be uttered by the mouth and must result in action, in the work of our hands. In this formula which Grundtvig employs very frequently, he sees a conjunction of feeling, intellect and active will; of love in the heart, truth on the lips, the power of life in the hands. There is also a conjunction of what is hidden within with what is proclaimed outwardly and what is embodied in act. Inner and outer, subjective and objective, personal and corporate, are all involved and are in a state of dynamic interaction in this vision of things, which as so often in his writings, aims to express a *whole* view of human nature and personality.

At the divine level we may say that God the Son, God the Word, is begotten from all eternity from the Father's heart of love, and that the Spirit, creator of life, proceeds from all eternity from the Father and rests upon the Son. In the divine economy of creation and redemption there is a constant reciprocity between the Son and the Spirit. Always the Father's love is made manifest in the Word who speaks, and is again made active in the Spirit who gives life, making the divine love incarnate. Mouth and hand together reveal the secrets of the divine heart. This threefold pattern then shines forth from God and is reflected in humanity. Human persons are created in the image of God precisely because they too have a heart which can speak words of truth, words which find embodiment in their actions. This is what it means to speak of the image of God in man. This divine truth which is communicated to us in the power of the Spirit becomes the 'Christ Life' within us and among us.

In his essay Prenter asks,

What does Grundtvig understand by the 'Christ Life'? It goes without saying that first of all he means the historic life of Jesus Christ. But it is much more than that when it is defined as the true *kristelighed* or likeness to Christ. It is the life of Christ communicated to those who are reborn, as their 'Christian, spiritual, eternal life', as Grundtvig says to describe human life reborn in baptism.[6]

The word spiritual here needs to be taken in a trinitarian sense for it is life in the Spirit of which Grundtvig is speaking, and for him the Holy Spirit is never conceived simply as an immaterial supernatural power but always as God and Lord, one of the Holy Trinity, as the creator and animator of flesh no less than of spirit. Life in the Spirit is therefore always truly embodied life as is life in the Word.

This 'Christ Life' is communicated to us in the form of faith, hope and love. It begins with faith, it grows through hope, it finds its fulfilment in love. Through the action of the Church, the people of God, this life is given us in the Spirit's gift of rebirth as children of God in the waters of baptism, in which receiving the Spirit of adoption we become sons in the Son. It grows through the sharing and receiving of the word of the gospel which is the word of hope, which is heard in its proclamation in the gathering of the Church to worship and which is strengthened in the practice of constant prayer and praise. It finds its fulfilment in the sacrament of the eucharist, celebrated in the power of the Spirit, the sacrament which is the feast of the fullness of the Father's love.

To put the same thing in another way, in a way which lays more emphasis on the personal appropriation by each one of the gift of life, the divine life is born in us through the act of faith which by the Spirit's gift we are able to make in baptism. It grows in hope through the constant use of the Lord's prayer, the prayer which we make in Christ and which Christ makes in us, in which the Holy Spirit gives voice through us to the unutterable longing of all creation. It comes to fulfilment in a love which carries us out beyond ourselves into hymns of praise and thanksgiving, in the sacrifice of praise which is the heart of the Church's eucharistic feast, which is offered in the power of the Spirit through Jesus Christ our Lord and brings us into the kingdom of the Father. It also comes to fulfilment in a love which carries us out beyond ourselves into acts of generosity and service to our fellow human beings and to the created world. This love is an eschatological reality in which, already here and now, in our life in space and time, we are given a foretaste of that life which shall be ours in the feast of the kingdom, the joy which there is in the Father's presence from all eternity to all eternity. Time and again, both in his hymns and in his sermons, Grundtvig gives expression to the overwhelming power of this joy, which can clarify and transform the sorrows and darkness of this world, with its healing and purifying light.

There are many things which might be said about this highly sacramental vision of the 'Christ Life' growing within us. One of its most fascinating features is its view of the Lord's prayer as central to, and characteristic of all Christian prayer. There is ample precedent for this concentration on the words which Jesus gave to his disciples, in the writings of the Fathers, and it is interesting to note that in some of the languages of Christendom, e.g. in Welsh, the word for prayer is simply *pader*. This text, in all its simplicity, provides the pattern and substance of Christian prayer. Beginning with adoration, ending in petition and intercession, rooted in the daily realities of the world of space and time, the sharing of bread and the forgiveness of offences, yet ending in the vision of the coming of the kingdom and of our entering into it through the trials of the last time. Grundtvig does not spell all this out; he seems to presuppose it as something already understood.

If the scheme as a whole seems overwhelmingly liturgical we need to remember that Grundtvig would have insisted that this life given within the gathering of the community of faith must be embodied in the deeds of love in the work of everyday. The light of Sunday is to shine out into all the variety and difference of the six days of the week. The 'Christ Life' itself is reflected in the many simple direct acts of compassion and love which characterise Jesus in the gospels.

We need also to remember that for Grundtvig what is liturgical, acted out visibly in the congregation, is also always intimately personal, acted out in the hidden places of the heart by the power of the Holy Spirit.

When the priest [in baptism] makes the sign of the cross over the child, the fog is lifted from God's creative purposes ... The priest's hand or finger is not a veiled, but a clear image of God's creative purpose which works according to God's word in the commandment to baptise.

But this outward act is made alive and effective inwardly by the hidden work of the Holy Spirit.

The fiery tongue of the Spirit, with the sign of the cross burns the name of Jesus onto the heart, thus the heart encounters the stamp which corresponds to the image of God in the depths of the heart. The sign of the cross is a promise, 'a letter from heaven' about the operations of the new creation; faith, peace, hope and confidence, love and joy. It is at its root a promise of the constant presence of Jesus in the name which is on the heart, whence the Spirit in the word of faith can always journey up to God.[7]

If, on the one side, the action of God's people gathered together in worship, is to shine out on the world, on the other it has its hidden fulfilment in the innermost places of the human heart and mind.

All this divine-human drama and interchange is made possible by the creation of humankind in the image and likeness of God. 'Redemption', Grundtvig writes,

is certainly a deep mystery, but not at all deeper than creation in God's image, and since, despite the fall, humankind at least kept the essential likeness of God, which lies in the word, then not only was a permanent divine revelation for humanity possible, but God's only begotten Son could become a true human being, born of a woman, without therefore being to a lesser extent the Son of God, for the Word of God and the human word, which are originally of the same kind [*ensartede*] only needed to fuse together for God's Son also to become the Son of Man, and the Son of Man the Son of God.[8]

In another passage Grundtvig stresses even more strongly the fact that the body itself participates in the character of image and likeness;

in order that our Lord Jesus Christ, whom we believe and confess, can be the only begotten Son of God the Father, born of the Virgin Mary, it must be that man, as it is written, should be created in God's image and be so created in it, that the divine nature could be united with the human nature, and could, through the human body, reveal the glory of the divinity, and that the living image and likeness, however much it may have been wounded at the fall, yet could not possibly have been wiped out, since the human life of the Son of God was created in the life of Mary his mother, so that he took flesh of her flesh and bone of her bone as Eve did of Adam.[9]

Prenter comments,

Since both the divine and the human word are living expressions of love, truth and the power of life, and these are 'originally of the same kind' [*ensartede*] bearing the mark of the divine Trinity, the possibility of their fusing together is present.

Prenter protests that this fusion together is not to be taken in a monophysite way, by which, as he explains, he means not by the creation of a mixed person, half human and half divine, nor by the creation of a union in which the human is simply swallowed up by the divine. The doctrine of *perichoresis*, of mutual indwelling, so vital for an understanding of the inner nature of the Trinity, applies no less to the relationship of the two natures in Christ. There is a mutual indwelling, a dynamic and total interaction of the two realities human and divine, in which neither is lost, both are preserved. As for instance a person of dual nationality might say, I am not half Spanish and half Indian; I am wholly Spanish and wholly Indian. Prenter goes on,

> This follows from the fact that the humanity of God's Son, Jesus Christ, expresses the divine love, the divine truth and the divine power with a human heart, a human mouth and a human hand. His human heart houses the divine love, his human mouth expresses (in Jesus' mother tongue) the divine truth, his human hand performs the actions of the divine power. Thus Grundtvig expounds finally and incontrovertibly the image language of the Bible which ascribes a heart, a mouth and a hand to God. The humanity of our Lord Jesus Christ gives living expression with heart, mouth and hand to the divine love, truth and power. The trinitarian background to Grundtvig's concept of the incarnation, and with it of Jesus' humanity, must not be overlooked.[10]

Grundtvig goes further and insists that each person of the Trinity is personally active in a particular way in the work of the healing of humankind, of our growth towards the fullness of divine life. In this assertion of the personal presence and activity of each one of the three persons, there is an important qualification to be made however, which assures the unity of the divine action as well as its threefold quality. The divine persons are transparent to one another in a way which we find difficult to envisage. In our fallen state we know human persons only as self centred individuals, not only distinct from one another but also separated from one another, opaque to one another and often at war with one another. This however is not the true nature of personhood, which implies distinction but no separation. The three divine persons are thus at once totally distinct and totally united.

As we shall see in Grundtvig's preaching, the self-emptying of the Son, seen in his incarnation, gives us a glimpse into the self-effacing nature of the love which for all eternity unites the three divine persons in the Godhead. This is the movement of their *perichoresis* or mutual indwelling, of the dance of love in which each one defers to the other, makes way for the other, exchanges places with the other. This is the pattern of divine personhood which we see in God the Holy Trinity, which is revealed in the self-giving love of Christ and which is the true pattern of all human personhood. Our self-centredness which is a distortion and deformation of our true humanity prevents us seeing the true pattern of the divine life. All this we shall find spelt out by Grundtvig in chapter 12, in three remarkable sermons for the beginning of Advent in 1837.

So the 'Christ Life' within us and amongst us calls us to combat self-willedness, self-opinionatedness and self-reliance. Instead we are to grow into the discovery of our true dependence on one another and on God and into true openness and vulnerability to one another and to God. Thus we shall discover our true nature in Christ through one another, and not seek our life in an illusory centring of ourselves upon ourselves, which in the end can only lead to isolation in pride, darkness and death. Our true discovery of ourselves as persons in all the uniqueness of our own existence, the gift of God to each one which no other can share or know, the white stone with a new name on it (Rev. 2:17), is at the very same time the true discovery of our total mutual interrelatedness. The two dimensions of existence, the vertical and the horizontal, the Godward and the intra-human are not in the end two but one, two facets of the one reality, the one mystery which we point to in the word 'person'. To discover this is to recover the true simplicity of childhood on which Grundtvig so often insists and to recover our true humanity, the humanity which was seen in Jesus through whom all the Father's glory shines.

So Grundtvig writes, 'When now again it is the word of faith in baptism through which the Holy Spirit as the divine spokesman and advocate personally creates the corresponding Christian faith, so it must be the Son, who, hidden in the Spirit, personally creates the hope through the word of baptism and his own prayer, Our Father, in the mouth of the congregation, and so it must be the Father, hidden within the Son, in the Spirit, who, through the eucharistic word personally co-creates the beginning and the growth of the divine love; as it is written,

He who loves me will keep my word and my Father will love him and we shall come to him and make our abode with him,

and again,

I bow my knees to the Father of Our Lord Jesus Christ from whom all fatherhood in heaven and on earth is named, that Christ may dwell in your hearts by faith, that you being rooted and grounded in love may be able to comprehend with all the saints what is the length and breadth and depth and height and to know the overflowing knowledge and love of Christ so that you may be fully gathered into the whole fullness of God.[11]

If Grundtvig is typically Western in being unwilling to make use of the term *theosis* he is surely typically Eastern in the substance of what he is saying here. Although he does not use the term deification and does not appeal to the verse from II Peter about our becoming 'partakers of the divine nature', nothing could be clearer than that here he is using the language of St. Paul and St. John to articulate a vision of human salvation in which, in response to God's loving condescension in coming to share the fullness of our human situation in all its finitude, sinfulness and death, men and women are called to grow into the image and likeness of God through the gift of the Spirit. This means to grow from faith through hope into the fullness of love, a fullness which will mean nothing less than our being filled with all the fullness of God.[12]

Especially in his later years Grundtvig will not hesitate to speak of this union in terms of *sammensmeltning*, a union or fusion of human and divine. The simple yet complex knot of doctrines, Trinity, incarnation, *theosis*, which stands at the heart of the faith and theology of the early Christian centuries in the East and West alike, and which never ceases to be clearly characteristic of the Eastern Orthodox tradition, is also central in the mind and heart of Grundtvig in nineteenth century Denmark. In him heart, mouth and hand worked together and were at one. Here is a man who by God's grace is prodigiously gifted both in his thinking and his loving, in his speaking and his singing, in his acting and his willing. There is in him an overflowing fullness, a generosity of personal being which reflects to us some tiny corner of the infinite goodness and generosity of God, God in God's own innermost reality and mystery, Father, Son and Holy Spirit, creator, redeemer, giver of life.

III

In the conclusion of the article which he devotes to his subject, Prenter points to three fundamental features which characterise Grundtvig's theological thinking; indeed, he would maintain, which characterise his thought as a whole. The first is that for Grundtvig all things hold together in one; that there is a deep inner coherence and consistency in his vision of things. This coherence is not a logical unity, an intellectual construct of a Hegelian kind. There are within it fundamental contradictions, as between life and death, truth and the lie, light and darkness. The element of struggle and conflict is ineradicably present in Grundtvig's vision of human life and the reality of things in this world.

But ... everything which ... belongs on the side of life holds together, or in the deepest sense is held together by the Triune God, both in the economy of creation and redemption. This coherence is not a logical unity but the interconnectedness in a divine-human history, and this is something which one can see only in the light of the Triune God and in his revelation.[13]

This coherence cannot be broken up into a number of different provinces or spheres. There is for Grundtvig an interconnectedness and an interaction between all the different aspects of reality and all the different areas of human thought and action. As we have seen, the word interaction is one of the key terms for understanding his mind.

Life, light and truth cannot be divided up into a number of different spheres independent of one another, e.g. Christian life and human life, Church life and national life, however different they may be, are not to be put each into its own sphere. For in both areas life is created by a word, whose nature in human life and Christian life, in Church life and national life is the same trinity of love, truth and power of life.

This is true, Prenter maintains, even in the case of the difference between

human life unredeemed, lived in the situation of the fall, i.e. under the lordship of death, and human life reborn in Christ and raised up to eternal life.[14]

Here too the living word creates an active interaction between human and Christian, sacred and profane.

It is quite true that in his later writings, Grundtvig recognised that there was a greater distinction to be made between divine and human, sacred and profane, than he had recognised before. For him, for life to be fully and truly human it had to be lived in freedom and that involved the meeting of varied and different viewpoints and interests. He saw there was need to allow great freedom of manoeuvre and conflict within the human and political sphere. Within the Church it was important to distinguish between the confession of faith in which Christians must be at one, and the debates and discussions of the theologians in which there must necessarily be differences of view. Only through the free interplay of varying positions is progress made. But these vital distinctions do not imply the complete separation of the one sphere from the other. Indeed it is on account of the prior, given unity of faith that the discussions and conflicts can in the end be fruitful and creative, can lead towards life and wholeness, not towards disintegration and death. Within the life of the Church as a community of faith, that priority of the oneness of faith is pre-supposed and itself makes possible the fruitful interaction of very varying views. Vital interconnections remain, but Grundtvig came to understand that these matters needed to be seen in a more open-ended, diversified way than he had realised before.

The reason for this underlying unity is to be found in the second basic element in Grundtvig's thought, and, we might add, in his life as a whole. 'God is the focal point in all Grundtvig's thinking. If one takes the divine Trinity out of this thought, the whole falls apart'.[15] As Prenter remarks, once one has done that, one has a mass of fragments out of which a great variety of different systems and 'isms' could be constructed. Grundtvig's mind and imagination were so unquenchably productive that the raw material is there for a great variety of Grundtvigs, a secular Grundtvig, a green Grundtvig, a feminist Grundtvig, a romantic Grundtvig, a conservative Grundtvig, certainly a Marxist Grundtvig, an exclusively Nordic and ultra-nationalist Grundtvig and even, on an extremely reductive view, a Nazi Grundtvig (certain of the 'German Christians' made that move in the early 1930s).

Doubtless there is something to be learned from all these different interpretations, but none of them can be more than partial at best and some of
them may be misleading to the point of perversity.

For the God-centredness of Grundtvig's thought is anchored in the revelation of God in Christ through the life of the Holy Spirit in the Church. This
is the third fundamental point which Prenter discerns.

The acknowledgement and understanding of the triune God — and thus strictly
speaking *all* understanding — is anchored in the Christian Church's means of grace,
baptism, the preaching of the Gospel and the eucharist. In Grundtvig's lifetime there
were many, especially among … Hegel's disciples, who speculated about the
Trinity. Grundtvig's trinitarian teaching is not speculative in that way, not
something that rests on human reason itself. It is a light which falls over everything,
over human life and over God, its Lord, from the specific place where God has
drawn near to humankind and has made his covenant with humanity in definite
words, i.e. the covenant of baptism, the Our Father, the eucharist's declaration of
love. Beginning at that point and remaining at that point, Grundtvig, by the tireless
use of Holy Scripture, the Church's unique book of instruction, and by constant reference to the experience of life of the people of God, saw a steadily clearer light fall
on the divine Trinity and over everything else as seen in that light.[16]

It may be useful to underline that this centredness, this anchoredness of
Grundtvig's thought in the given reality of the Church's life of sacramental
worship does not mean that his thought is something static and fixed in the
sense of complete and fully defined. The sacraments themselves are not static
but dynamic, not exclusive but inclusive, and are always pointing beyond
themselves. Both baptism and eucharist though celebrated within the communion of the Church have their meaning and finality in relation to human
life as a whole, as becomes very clear both in Grundtvig's sermons and in his
hymns. The Lord gives himself for the life of the world.

Both baptism and eucharist are, at their core, a movement, a passover from
death to life, from time to eternity. As Luther says, the eucharist is a ship, a
door, a way which leads us into the world to come. The Lord's prayer as the
core of Christian prayer is full of an eschatological longing and an
eschatological hope. The prayer is that God's will may be done and his
kingdom come throughout the whole creation, now and in the end of all
things. It expresses the tension between that which is already given and that
which is still to come. But it looks through the tests and trials of the last
things, to the final hallowing of God's name. It is a prayer which can only be
prayed truly in the power of the Holy Spirit, that Spirit who speaks the
unspeakable longings not of humanity alone but of all creation. These are
longings for rebirth in a new creation, for the revelation of the great deed of
love which the Trinity will do on that day.

The truly ec-static nature of the Church's shout of praise and thanksgiving
is wonderfully expressed in the great body of Grundtvig's hymns, which

carry us out beyond ourselves into the anticipation of this feast which is to come.

> Yes, let your font and your table so work
> With the consecrated tongues,
> So we may hear that your Spirit and Word
> Are those who are speaking and singing.
> Yes, let us feel it and taste it
> The Spirit is better than flesh and blood,
> The Lord is delightful and in every way good,
> He crowns all our days with his gladness.

It is the Word and the Spirit who speak in the sacraments of the Church. In their praise and prayer Christians are brought into the circulation of the divine life, which underlies and sustains all human life. In finding God and being found by him we also find and are found by his whole creation.

Prenter concludes his article with the words, 'Is there not something for contemporary theologians and others to learn here?'

IV

There are two sides to this vision, both of which are important for our understanding of Grundtvig. One is found in the way in which his whole life and thought is anchored in the revelation of God made known focally in the gathering of God's people for worship. The other is seen in the fact that this centring of all in the Church's worship has a totally inclusive and not exclusive purpose and intention. The God who is revealed is the God in whom, for whom and towards whom all things exist. For Grundtvig both affirmations are vital and both reveal that special characteristic of his thought which identifies him with the life and tradition of the first Christian centuries. We have heard Martensen saying that he thought that Grundtvig owed more to the ancient Catholic Church than he did to the Church of the Reformation. Insofar as Martensen was making a polemical point here, and trying to suggest that Grundtvig was not a true Lutheran (whereas he, Martensen, was), I am suspicious of his judgement. Whether Grundtvig or Martensen was truer to the best and deepest insights and intentions of Luther is for Lutherans to judge. But, insofar as Martensen is recording his own genuine and surprised impression of the importance of the early centuries for Grundtvig, I am inclined to take him very seriously. Irenaeus, and not only Irenaeus, was of decisive significance in Grundtvig's spiritual development, and in Irenaeus, no less than in Paul, we see the fully cosmic scope of the Father's revelation of himself in Christ and in the Spirit.

The first point then underlines the centrality of worship in the life and faith of the Church from the beginning until today. It is a point which is made with admirable clarity and precision by a contemporary Danish Church historian, Jakob L. Balling, in relation to the early Church and its *lex orandi lex credendi*.

The law of prayer is the law of faith, is the saying of the early Church. By that is meant that every thought about God and humanity springs out of what is experienced as reality in worship, and that only what means something there can have relevance in this way of thinking.

But, as Balling goes on at once to point out, this affirmation is not to be taken too absolutely and without any qualification. The Church's life and thought is not only determined from within. There are also pressures from without, which effect its development.

Christians of the early centuries had more ideas about history, Christ and the Church than those to which worship directly gave rise; impulses and challenges coming from outside not seldom made these subjects into urgent theological problems. But the starting point for the reflection with which those challenges were met was more than anything else to be found precisely in this history of salvation, this Lord made present and this praising, praying and learning people who express themselves specifically in worship.[17]

What is more, it is not only the perspective and the conviction of the early Christian centuries which we find here. We find here something which, to a great extent, was the common conviction of all the major Christian traditions down to the eighteenth century, and as Balling points out, it is something which, in a very particular way, remains characteristic of Eastern Christianity.

Here we have touched that which characterises Orthodoxy more than anything else, the primacy of worship and its significance for all other expressions of Christian life. In worship it is the common Orthodox conviction that the heavenly world becomes visible on earth; here past and future are gathered together in the present; here the meaning of theoretical affirmations is made manifest in the practice of proclamation and adoration.[18]

Grundtvig's understanding of this mystery of the triune God, revealed and communicated to us in the life of Christian worship, and in particular in the celebration of the sacraments, (the *mysteries* as they would be in Greek) is central to his understanding of the world and humankind, it is the one thing above all else which gives coherence and unity to his thought and writing in all its many strands. It is also the one thing above all else which gives him a place at the centre of the one Christian tradition, linking him with Ethiopia and Armenia, with Romania and Russia, no less than with Rome and with Canterbury, with Wittenberg and Geneva and the more familiar traditions of the West. Indeed by a blessed paradox at the level of faith and prayer it may perhaps link him more closely with those who are geographically and historically further off than with those who are humanly speaking nearer to hand.

But here again is the second point which is vital for any at all adequate understanding of Grundtvig's life and work; this apparently narrow centering of the whole of the Church's life in the act of worship in which the living God is present and makes himself known — 'Only at the font and the altar / Do we hear God's word to us' — opens out to include the whole of creation. For the God who saves and the God who creates are one and the same. The Word who takes flesh in Jesus is the light who lightens everyone who comes into the world. The Spirit who descends at Pentecost is the Spirit who, now as at the beginning, broods over the elements of creation and makes them fruitful of life.

Grundtvig's constant concern for the whole common life of his people, for the position of the marginalised and powerless, of the young and the old, his passionate conviction that God's Spirit and God's Word are at work in all times and in all places shows that his thought is in no way confined to the history of God's people recorded in the Scriptures and continued in the Church. The power of God at work in history is seen not only in the specific acts of redemption, but in the whole underlying structure and nature of things and events. There is a trinitarian pattern of 'being-withness', a movement towards communion built into the structures of the world and human history. The whole fabric of human life and development, indeed the whole fabric of the created order is to be gathered together into the kingdom of the Father. Here again, in this desire to respond to all that is good throughout creation we find that quality which links Grundtvig so closely with much that is most characteristic of the earliest Christian tradition, and gives practical expression to his trinitarian faith.

CHAPTER 9

The Earth made in God's Image

Even a first acquaintance with Grundtvig's theology reveals that the doctrine of creation, of the world in general and of humankind in particular, has a peculiar importance for him. Only in the light of our understanding of God's work in creation can the divine work of redemption be properly understood. No less important than the doctrine of creation, in his vision of Christian faith, is the doctrine of the person and work of the Holy Spirit, in the life of each believer, but still more in the life of the whole Christian fellowship, the Church through the ages. Just as the work of redemption is for him a matter of universal import which has its effects backwards in time as well as forwards, so the work of the Spirit is not confined to the specific history which begins at Pentecost. In the beginning, the Spirit presided over creation, throughout history the Spirit is seen as the giver of life and growth to all things, moving towards the day of fulfilment in God's kingdom. The work of the Spirit is all-encompassing; it touches the realms both of history and nature.

As we have seen in many places, as a theologian, Grundtvig was constantly fighting a double battle. On the one side he was combatting a new German theology being developed in his own day. This was a theology which he regarded as speculative and insubstantial, for which the doctrines both of the Trinity and of creation in God's image and likeness were of little or no significance, often considered, then and indeed throughout the history of liberal Protestantism, as unhelpful and mistaken lines of thought taken up by the early Church. On the other side he was distancing himself from major aspects of the older Lutheran orthodoxy, in particular the radical pessimism of its view of the fall and its understanding of the death of Christ in strictly forensic and sacrificial terms. But while there were elements in the classical Lutheran position of which he was highly critical, there were large parts of it which he took for granted, notably its powerful reaffirmation of the classical doctrine of the Trinity and of the Chalcedonian teaching about the union of human and divine natures in the person of Christ.

In his preaching and in his hymns Grundtvig was seeking to build up a middle way in which he would be able to affirm afresh the meaning both of creation and redemption by the Word and the Spirit, 'the two hands of God' to use Irenaeus' phrase. This way centres on the understanding that men and women are made in God's image and likeness with a calling to share in the divine nature and life, but it extends to the work of the Word and the Spirit, throughout the natural order, in bringing the divine plan to fulfilment, in the ultimate *forklarelse* of all things. This *forklarelse* involves both their clarification and their transformation into the glory of the kingdom. This is a theology at once trinitarian and incarnational; affirmative of creation and humanity; seeing the goal of all things in the marriage of heaven and earth; the real participation of the divine in what is human and of the human in what is divine.

For Grundtvig, humanity is, from the beginning, a great and unparalleled wonder, riddle, mystery, experiment. All the words are necessary to express his attitude towards our common humanity. There is wonder and amazement at the mixture of littleness and immensity in the human calling. We are earth clods, we are fashioned out of dust, yet we aspire to the divine. Humanity's life is a riddle, never fully explained, never immune from conflict and tension. The intermingling of wisdom and foolishness, of self-sacrifice and destructive self-seeking, of ardour and coldness in human history, personal and universal, these are not things which human beings can in themselves explain, clarify, let alone transfigure. For this we must wait upon God.

Yet humanity is not only a riddle but also a mystery, because at the heart of the conflict and confusion there is also a deep and often deeply buried longing for the divine, an intuition about the universal power of love, a re-flection in the created order of the love which is at the heart of the godhead. Women, and men too, have a heart which can respond to the heart of God and in this response things can come together into unity.

I

Perhaps it is in his view of human life as an experiment that Grundtvig reveals himself as most original. This term is used in his famous description of humankind, in the introduction to the *Norse Mythology* of 1832,

For humankind is no ape ... but is a unique, wonderful creation in whom divine powers shall make themselves known, shall develop and clarify themselves through a thousand generations, as a divine experiment, which reveals how spirit and dust can interpenetrate and be clarified in a common divine consciousness.[1]

In these words we see something of Grundtvig's constantly repeated con-viction about the interpenetration and interaction of flesh and spirit in human history. This is something working itself out in ways both personal and universal, something in which we are taking part. There is nothing static in this view of human nature. He sees humanity developing through the vicissitudes of history, he is aware that he himself is living through a time when not only external factors but also deep internal elements of the human situation, are altering radically.

But the development and flux of human affairs are not only the result of the inherent movements of human history. They are that, and as time went on Grundtvig was more willing to allow these movements their own autonomous existence. Still more, however, they are the result of the fact that God has breathed his own life into humanity from the beginning, has made for himself an image and likeness in the dust of the earth. If humanity cannot understand itself, finds itself unable to achieve its own ends, is constantly baffled in its attempts to reach completion and fulfilment, that is because the purpose for which human persons were made is in the end beyond our ends, nothing less than the union of heaven and earth, the gathering together of all things into a new and hitherto unexpected harmony and life. This is an end which only God can reveal and accomplish.

For this end to be fulfilled humankind has again to wait upon God, to wait upon the divine action, already revealed and made present in the world of space and time, in the presence of the Word made flesh and in the work of the life-giving Spirit. The events of the Gospel mark a turning point in the human story and these events point us to the end of all things. In the worship of the Church we celebrate in joyful anticipation that end, in riddles and symbols. But the end is not yet; already towards that end we, and all things, find our way through struggle and disaster, through achievement and gift.

This view of humanity carries closely with it a view of the whole material creation as itself being apt for God, in its own way capable of God. One can see this in Grundtvig's use of natural imagery in the hymns, which is far more than a simple matter of literary convention. It is a way of asserting the essential God-relatedness of the whole living world. Such a view of things has its roots in the Old Testament, not only in the psalms, but in many places where God's covenant with all creation is celebrated (e.g. Jeremiah 31:35-36, 35:25-26, Hosea 2:18). It finds expression in the liturgical texts of East and West, many of which Grundtvig himself translated. We might think, for instance, of the Easter hymns of John of Damascus, in the eighth century in the East, or in the Alleluia sequence of Notker Balbulus, in the tenth century, in the West. The whole creation praises God, for the whole creation is full of God. In the great dictum of Maximus the Confessor, 'The Word of God who is God wills in all things to work the mystery of his embodiment.'[2]

This sense of the participation of the whole creation in the praise of God and the activity of God, is expressed by Grundtvig in a number of sermons preached on the fourth Sunday after Trinity, an occasion when he takes the opportunity, not only to expound the gospel for the day but also to preach on the epistle which comes from Romans 8. It is interesting that no less than three of these occasions occur during the eighteen sixties. This is a theme which Grundtvig developed more and more strongly in his last decades. His basic convictions about it come out clearly in the sermon for 1866 when he insists that the whole scheme of the divine action, from the beginning to the end, needs to be seen in the light of the original creative will and purpose of God, which provides the essential line of coherence and continuity in the whole. Having spoken of the reality of the resurrection of the body and of the incorporation of our bodies into the body of Christ, he goes on,

So, Christian friends, although this is certainly enough, as the apostle writes, a great and for us here below an incomprehensible mystery, yet it is also evident that it is only a part of that great mystery which is God's whole marvellous creation both of heaven and earth, a creation which will grow old and be worn out as a garment, but will yet be renewed to last forever, because the all-good, the all-powerful, the all-knowing God, who will rejoice over all his works, neither could nor would create the visible from the invisible, the temporal from the eternal, for its sorrowful destruction and ruin, but only for its transfiguration and the full revelation of his glory and his salvation in the perfect love, which would rather give than take; it follows of itself, of the depth of the riches in the wisdom and knowledge of the living God that his unfathomable counsel for the world and for humankind could not be frustrated by sin and death, but that they must also serve to glorify him and to set his wisdom as well as his love in the clearest light.[3]

All, from the beginning to the end, is held in the purposes of a God who sees all that he has made and sees that it is very good. He will not let his creation come to nothing. Life, not death and destruction, is his ultimate goal. He will draw all things to their conclusion in the fulfilment of wisdom and love.

This theme had been expounded at greater length in a sermon preached almost thirty years earlier in 1838 on the same Sunday. Here he begins by saying that the text from Romans 8, 'The whole creation groaneth and travaileth ...' is often regarded as very obscure and difficult. In part he says this comes from the obscurity of the old Danish translation, but when we understand that the translation should read

'Nature waits with longing for the revelation of God's children', then we find that there is nothing obscure in it, apart from what is inherent in the nature of things, in our body's obscure but certain connectedness with the whole of nature; for so long as this connectedness or solidarity has not become clear to us we can have no clear idea of what it is to say that the whole of nature shares our distress and sighs with us over the law of death and decay, to which all bodily things are subject, from the flower which is born today and dies tomorrow, to the shining heavenly bodies which seem incorruptible and were therefore worshipped as gods by the heathen in their blindness, but which according to our prophets and apostles are to grow old as a garment and fall to pieces, just as our bodies decay and just as metal is dissolved and smelted in the fire.[4]

This paragraph is at once very remarkable and very characteristic of Grundtvig. It is characteristic in that the language used is full of reminiscences of Scripture; it is very biblical both in its content and in its manner of presentation. Yet at the same time it speaks from an experience of bodiliness and of the coherence and connectedness of our bodiliness with that of nature as a whole, which seems of a somewhat exceptional kind. Grundtvig feels in his flesh and his bones that he belongs together in this universe with the most ephemeral forms of life on the one side and with the shining heavenly bodies on the other, which though they seem permanent are also changing and in the end moving towards decay. He has, as it were, a bodily awareness of his relationship with all creation. Perhaps this is a particualarly poetic gift. We may think, for instance, of some of the expressions of John Keats or in a traditional Christian context, of the awareness which is expressed in St. Francis' Canticle of the Creatures, implying a particular gift of solidarity and fellow feeling for the creatures.

This being so it is not strange that for Grundtvig it is simply self-evident that our bodily resurrection which follows on from our solidarity in Christ's resurrection, implies the resurrection of the whole creation.

When we see that the law of nature, under which we sigh, is not, as the wise of this world think, eternal and unchangeable, but only a temporary slavery which will be taken away, and which will set the whole of nature free together with ourselves, when we see that, then in a wonderful way light comes over the grave and over all death and decay; although a complete clarity about these things is impossible in our dust.[5]

Often we are troubled and frightened by the world's proclamation of the unchangeable laws of nature. But this will frighten us no more

when we become confident in the apostle's way of thought, in which there is certainly a law of nature, which stands in the way of the redemption, liberation and immortality of our body, but that law of nature, to the eternal joy of the whole of nature, will certainly be taken away by his power, who proved both that he could and that he would, when he raised up our Lord Jesus Christ from the dead, and gave us his Spirit, as witness with our spirit, that we are his children and heirs, fellow heirs with Jesus Christ to the divine fullness, which according to the Father's good will dwells bodily in him.[6]

All this is part of Grundtvig's fully developed understanding, both of our faith and of the creation. It means

that we should not, like our fathers, consider nature in us and around us, as the property of the Enemy, but as the work of God, which never fell from his hand or slipped from his care ... [at this point a phrase in the original manuscript is unclear] however much it was spoilt by sin and put to shame by death as the wages of sin. Yes, we shall consider nature as God's work, in us and around us, which shall in no way be hated, mistreated and destroyed, but loved, cleansed, healed and sanctified, yes, which should share in that same glory, which in the Spirit we already rejoice in, in that liberty and blessed incorruptibility, for which, as the apostle says, the whole of nature, as well as our hearts, sigh, for which the whole of nature longs with a wonderful hope. In no way then should we set *nature and revelation* [italics original] in opposition to one another, as things incompatible with each other; rather, we should call revelation nature's light and salvation, as our Lord Jesus Christ calls himself the light and saviour of the world, without troubling ourselves that unbelievers misuse our expressions just as they misuse our Lord's and twist them according to their own false conceptions, as if we either said or meant that nature could enlighten, heal and save itself ...[7]

So Grundtvig maintains clearly that while revelation and salvation are always God's free gift, they are in no way opposed to God's work in sustaining and giving life to creation. Revelation and nature go together. We must respect and love the nature which is God's gift, both within us and around us. Here is a basis, alike for a Christian understanding of the inner life of the spirit and of the outer life of the world around us with which we are called to live in solidarity. Psychological and ecological consequences very evidently flow from these insights.

We have here a very interesting point about Grundtvig which needs to be explored further, i.e. the similarity which is evident between major aspects of his vision of Christianity and some of the characteristic features shared by many of the primal religions, which we find in different cultural and ethnic contexts across the globe. Grundtvig is so assured of the specificity and uniqueness of the Christian faith that he has no anxiety in recognising the features which it has in common with other and earlier religious traditions. Amongst others, for instance, we observe the feelings of respect and wonder before the creation, a sense of oneness with all living things, a sharp awareness of our human interrelatedness and an awareness that our life now is supported and sustained by the presence of former generations; above all he sees the need to take what has been called 'the sacred journey from the head to the heart'. Since in Grundtvig's theology there is no pressure to set God and humankind, revelation and nature, in opposition to one another, it becomes possible not only to see but to welcome correspondences and complementary qualities in a great variety of places.[8]

II

What is here stated in general about the relationship of grace to nature can be seen in one particular instance in a sermon preached at Septuagesima in 1834. Again here we have a beautiful example of the consistency and coherence of Grundtvig's vision. His theology is not, in a formal sense, systematic. It is too free and too living to be fitted into a total system. But when we examine it in detail in any particular place we are often astonished at the way in which what he says in one context confirms or illustrates what he says in another. What he says in general about the relationship of flesh and spirit, of nature and revelation, in his preaching whether in the 1830s or the 1860s, is here worked out in detail in one particular aspect of the eucharist.

The text for the sermon is taken from Psalm 104, the Old Testament psalm of creation which Grundtvig particularly loved; 'Wine which maketh glad the heart of man so that his countenance becomes joyful.' The prayer before the text is announced, already plunges us into the midst of our subject,

We thank you, great master of the vineyard, who existed before the mountains were and before you *created the earth in your image after your likeness* [my italics], we thank you in Jesus' name for the wonderful vineyard which you created and hedged in, cultivated and guarded in the midst of the desert, and for your call in grace to us, who for long stood by idle, but who then had a share in your holy day's work ...[8]

The earth itself is created in God's image; God himself has planted his vineyard in its midst. He summons his human creatures to share in the work of his vineyard. In order to exemplify this faith the preacher turns at once to the subject of the eucharist and in particular to the place of wine, the fruit of the vine, in the eucharist.

In Western Christendom theology has not reflected much on the particular significance of the use of wine in the sacrament. Because in the middle ages, in the West, the laity ceased to receive communion from the chalice, traditional theologians as a consequence found it necessary to work out a doctrine of concomitance; to urge that because Christ was fully present in either kind, therefore there was no pressing need for the wine to be used in the communion of the people. This development which was used in the sixteenth century to defend the Roman side of the argument discouraged positive reflection on the matter, and while the controversies over the question in the fifteenth, sixteenth and seventeenth centuries, gave a great deal of attention to the question of the authority by which the Church either used or did not use both bread and wine in the communion of the people, little time was spent on the particular sacramental significance of the wine as an inherent part of the whole action.

The situation had of course been different in the East. Here the laity continued to receive communion in both kinds and the fact that in the Eastern middle ages the practice grew up of giving communion to the laity from the chalice (the fragments of consecrated bread being put into the wine and the people receiving both from a spoon) has made the thought of the chalice and its contents the source of more devotional and theological reflection than in the West.

Moreover in the theology and practice of the Christian East the role of the Holy Spirit in the celebration of the eucharist and in particular in the consecration of the holy gifts, was also affirmed more strongly than in the West. The eucharist has been thought of, not only as the presence of the Christ's death and resurrection, but also as the constant renewal of Pentecost. Naturally enough this has led to reflection on the image of fire as present in the eucharist, descending on the altar, filling the chalice. The fire of Pentecost crowns the Church's prayer and offering. The words which are said in the Eastern liturgy at the moment, just before communion, when hot water is poured into the chalice, whatever the origin of the practice may be, are also highly significant, 'the fervour of faith, full of the Holy Spirit'. If the broken bread of the sacrament naturally suggests the broken body and our solidarity in that body, so the wine in the chalice naturally suggests the joy and ecstasy which the Spirit brings to the Church and to each of its members. We need not suppose that Grundtvig was much aware of these developments in the East. As in so many places his mind seems to have developed on its own in surprisingly similar directions.

'Wine makes glad the heart of man, so that his countenance becomes joyful.' So says the psalmist, and although drinking songs say the same thing that does not mean that psalms become drinking songs nor that drinking songs become psalms. It only shows that the Spirit, who inspired the psalmist and all the prophets and apostles of the Lord, understands how to speak gracefully and how to choose images for himself and his divine activity where they are rightly to be found and where they are fore-ordained for this purpose from the beginning of the world. Yes, my friends, we do well to give heed to this as to the lamp of God shining in the darkness of night, that it is not just the psalmist who praises him who created wine which gladdens man's heart, and not just the prophets, who liken God's planting in Israel to a vineyard, no, nor is it only that the Lord himself in today's gospel continues the prophetic comparison so that it lasts until the end of time, nor that on another occasion he compares himself with the vine, and his father with the vine-dresser, no, just as he really changed the water into wine at the marriage at Cana in Galilee, so he has really consecrated and blessed wine together with bread on his table, so that the cup of blessing which we bless is the communion of the blood of Christ.

Although therefore we ought, as Christians, always to remember the apostle's warning not to be drunk with wine wherein is excess, but to be full of the Spirit, so it is also true that at the Lord's table both bodily and spiritual realities are at work. It is true both in a bodily and a spiritual way — as the psalmist sings — that wine rejoices man's heart and bread strengthens it, because there the bread and wine are not just images of the Lord's body and blood, in which we share spiritually; rather they are incorporated and taken up into them by his word which says 'take this and eat it, drink ye all of this'. Therefore, one of the early fathers rightly said, that the Lord in the eucharist took to himself the first creation and put the seal to his word, that he had come, not to destroy, but to fulfil, just as he sent out his servants not to break down but to build up.[10]

Thus from the beginning the sermon contains a remarkable statement about the interaction and reciprocity of sacred and secular, human and divine. Drinking songs are not hymns; nor are hymns drinking songs. They must not be confused, but the two worlds are often surprisingly interrelated. In actual fact secular songs have often been adapted (words as well as music) to sacred use and the reverse also has happened and happens.

The Spirit uses imagery from nature to speak of the things of God, because nature itself comes from the hand of God. In this case the imagery used is not only a matter of natural metaphor. It corresponds to a more than natural

Gospel pattern. Just as at Cana the water really became wine, so here the bread and wine are really blessed and consecrated so as to be the communion of Christ's body and blood. This happens, not because Christ's body and blood as it were come down to the earthly elements and are embodied in them, but because the earthly gifts are taken up and incorporated into the heavenly reality of Christ's body and blood.

Grundtvig, in his earlier writings, reacts strongly against the classical Lutheran teaching about the real presence of Christ in, with and under the consecrated bread and wine. To him it seemed to imply some kind of restriction and limitation of God's action. For him the mystery involves the elements being taken up and incorporated into the heavenly reality which they have always themselves foreshadowed. For him it is clear that the Christian doctrine of the sacraments and the practice of using material elements to represent divine realities presupposes in those material elements a sacramental and divine potential which is there from the beginning. 'God puts his seal to his word', the word of creation, in which the final goal of the whole creation is already foreshadowed. In the moment of worship, which is the moment of the real presence, that which was at the beginning and that which shall be at the end come together and are fused into one.

Writing at the end of the nineteenth century in the famous collection of essays, *Lux Mundi*, Francis Paget too quotes Irenaeus,

As bread from the earth receiving the invocation of God is no longer common bread, but the Eucharist consisting of two things, an earthly and a heavenly; so our bodies also receiving the Eucharist are no longer corruptible, having the hope of the resurrection.

Paget goes on,

Alike in us and in the Sacrament the powers of the world to come invade the present and already move towards the victory which shall be hereafter.[11]

Such teaching was not easily received in a century like the nineteenth, when a gulf was set between spirit and matter, and the word spirit was commonly taken to mean what is abstract or immaterial. Here, as in other places, Grundtvig finds himself impelled to protest against what he regards as the wholly inadequate and misleading character of these contemporary ideas of the spiritual.

The world, I suppose, can certainly not bear to hear this, for its conceptions of spirit are so fine and empty that for even the least evident reality to be linked with the spirit seems to the wise of the world something coarse or crass, as they say, something which not only weighs down and dishonours the spirit but scares it off and drives it away. This, however, only follows from the fact that the world, as the Lord says, in no way knows the Spirit of truth and cannot receive him, but is deceived and blinded by its own spirit, which is the spirit of the air, i.e. the spirit of delusion and deep emptiness. We Christians however, who are baptised in the name of the Holy Spirit, that is to say plunged into and rooted in his divine personhood, as well as in that of the Father and the Son, should naturally only smile at the world's superstitious faith in a ghost under the name of Spirit.[12]

Thus in the course of this sermon we can see Grundtvig's conviction that the purpose and the economy of God is basically one and the same through all the vicissitudes of his relationship with the world which he has made. From the moment of creation and through all that follows from it, the final consummation of all things in God's kingdom is never lost to view. And this is the work of God the Holy Trinity, and in its fulfilment the activity of the Holy Spirit is particularly evident.

On the other hand we also see something of the consequences of this for human life here and now. The resurrection of the body and the trans-figuration of the world are not only mysteries to be revealed at the end of all things. They are at least in part already at work and making themselves known. Just as the meals which Jesus, during his ministry in Galilee and Judea, shared with unlikely and disreputable people, were themselves anticipations of the feast in the kingdom of God, so our meals now, not only our sacramental celebrations, but our ordinary sharing with each other round the table, can afford glimpses of a future glory. Even here and now we find that wine rejoices the human heart and mind.

This present, this-worldly significance of the eucharist, as an anticipation of a feast which will be known in its fullness only beyond this world of space and time, is beautifully set forth in a hymn from the first volume of the *Sang-Værk*. In it Grundtvig brings together sacramental themes with thoughts about the work of agriculture and the distribution of human resources, in ways which seem strangely relevant to the world we are living in, with its anxieties about the environment and its sense of baffled impotence before the problems involved in a just sharing of the material resources of our planet.

As in other places, so here, Grundtvig's vocabulary covers a very wide range of registers. The word translated 'bread for life' is in Danish *levebrød*, a common expression which refers to the bread and butter of our existence, our job, our livelihood. The first three lines of the hymn could therefore be taken perfectly literally as a statement about people's working life. Work in the fields, in the factory, in the office, gives us the things we live on. It is this which is then brought into the tents of the Word, placed on an eternal and heavenly table. Even in his choice of words Grundtvig underlines the paradoxical mixture of strangeness and earthiness which the poem conveys.

Yet this same hymn with its evocation of the work of ploughing and the cultivation of vines, also looks to the fulfilment of all things in the end. It is at once ecological and eschatological. Twice Grundtvig uses the word *sammensmelte*, (fuse together) a term which, for him, nearly always brings with it the thought of the final coming together into one of flesh and spirit, earth and heaven, the gift of the human heart and hand and tongue, and the gift of the life-giving Spirit of God.

> The care of vineyards and the tilling of fields
> Makes for men upon earth
> Bread for life and the strength of the heart,
> Above all on the Lord's Table;
> For there, in the tents of the Word
> Earth and heaven are fused together.
> He who takes the Lord
> At his word, as it sounds out here,
> Rejoices in nectar and ambrosia.
>
> 'Wheat corn' and 'vine-stock'
> My Lord calls himself,
> So deliberately leading our minds
> To the bread and wine of the Table,
> Where the heavenly in the Spirit
> And the earthly in the hand
> Fuse together, basically one
> As in the word, so in the mouth,
> To the benefit of soul and body.
>
> Wheat cake and the juice of the grape
> Are found on every king's table,
> But only on the Lord's do they have the strength
> Which is in God's Spirit and God's Word.
> Only there, in the Church's gathering
> Does daily bread become eternal.
> Only there does the wine's fruit
> Have the taste of heaven and the power of God,
> And create with blessing the joy of the heart.[13]

III

In his later preaching Grundtvig comes more and more to dwell on the thought of the final marriage of heaven and earth, the union and communion of divine and human as the end for which in the beginning all things were made. These were not new themes in his preaching. Already, in 1832, in his sermon for the feast of the annunciation, he had said that the fathers made the mistake of thinking more about

how the divine and human natures were united in Christ than about what for us as Christians follows on from this just as joyful as wonderful union — something which we can and shall realise;[14]

how also in us and for us God and humankind should be joined together, in just as joyful and as wonderful a union, should fuse together and be united by the Spirit of Christ, who gives us new birth and new life as branches of the true vine and limbs in the body of the only-begotten.

But as the decades pass these themes receive new emphasis. In a very characteristic way Grundtvig sees that the union of human and divine in Christ which takes place in the life of Jesus in Galilee and Judea is only the beginning of a history which will go from now into the end times, a history in which again and again human and divine are brought together by the power and presence of the Holy and life-giving Spirit. To describe the final consummation of history, Grundtvig as an old man does not hesitate to draw on pre-Christian mythology in order to find the images for what he wants to say. Here too what is to come takes up and clarifies what was there from the beginning.

So, preaching on the nineteenth Sunday after Trinity in 1862, he declares,

So, when the Greeks would tell us of their poets' most splendid visions, in which the first divine wedding was the wedding of heaven and earth, then we would answer; that indeed is so, for this divine marriage is both the first and the last; but what you do not know is something which we, the children of Sion, can teach you; that is how this divine marriage bond was first joined, then broken and in the end restored again for time and for eternity.

For this divine marriage between heaven and earth was established when God, by his Word, created humankind out of the dust of the earth in his image, and breathed his heavenly Spirit into dust; and it necessarily followed on the fall that there was a divorce between heaven and earth as between Spirit and flesh, as it is written, 'You take away your Spirit and they die and turn again to dust.' But when God took mercy on sinful man, then the divine marriage was renewed, as it is written, 'You send out your Spirit and they are made, and you renew the face of the earth'. Thus God the Father has now sent out his Spirit in the name of his only begotten Son our Lord Jesus Christ to his believing people, who are therefore with right spiritually called his bride and his body.[15]

It is very striking that Grundtvig again uses here, to enforce his message about the fall and restoration of humankind, two verses from Psalm 104. It is a psalm which is above all devoted to God's care for the whole of creation, and in which the calling of humanity is seen in the context of the whole living world. In such a vision the restoration of humanity by the coming of the Spirit is understood as the central element in the radical renewal of the creation as a whole, a renewal which in fact carries the first creation to a fulfilment beyond that which it had already attained.

Again Grundtvig sees, in this consummation of all things, two aspects, one which is eschatological, deep and unfathomable to us while we live within the world of time, but another which he says is already clear and evident to us now. This second aspect concerns the interaction of divine and human, of eternity and time, which we see portrayed in the gospels and which we know as a reality of our own life and experience. Already now, amidst all the imperfection and fragmentariness of our life in time, through the work of the Holy Spirit the life of God is present among us.

Yes, Christian friends, this divine marriage between heaven and earth, between the Lord and his people, as between the Word and faith, that is the deep mystery of eternal life and love and blessedness which we should not demand to be clear and evident to us here below. However, in faith in Jesus Christ, the only-begotten Son of God the Father, our Lord, conceived by the Holy Spirit and born of the Virgin Mary, the mystery has a clear aspect from which to be considered. For the Holy Spirit has proved that he who came forth from the Father and came into the world, as one of us in all things, save without sin, and who left the world and returned to heaven with a body of flesh and bone — in him has the Holy Spirit proved that he, in man, both can and will make all that is heavenly earthly and all that is earthly heavenly; not so that in a popish way the one is changed into the other, but so that they are fused together with one another in the heart, in love, as soul and body in our Lord Jesus Christ, Son of God and Son of Man. In him the heavenly indeed became earthly and the earthly heavenly, the eternal temporal and the temporal eternal, as it has happened and shall happen in the whole of the community of faith, which on earth in time carries eternal life within itself and in heaven shall eternally carry its temporal life within it.[16]

Grundtvig does not hesitate to spell out more clearly the meaning of these affirmations in speaking of the ministry of Jesus in Galilee and Judea. In a sermon from the eighteen forties he had declared,

and when we now believe that this Jesus of Nazareth was the only begotten Son of God the Father, to whom all power was given in heaven and on earth, then we cannot possibly consider this his wonderful humility and friendliness, his way of being with the simplest of people, his concern for their physical nourishment and his share in their poor cares, without seeing a glimpse of paradise, where God speaks with man face to face, and treats him as his neighbour.[17]

In this human simplicity and accessibility of Jesus, God himself draws near. In it we see an image of the divine-human community which was in the beginning, which shall be in the end. The gospel narratives, when read with the eye of faith, tell us more of this nearness of God to his creation, which is for Grundtvig the heart of the gospel, than many volumes of theology.

Yes my friends, one can read many learned works and ponder for many years over the union of the divine and human natures in Jesus Christ, without getting so clear and living an impression of it, as comes from considering him in today's gospel by the sea of Galilee, where he speaks God's word, which is life and breath for heart and soul and speaks a word of almighty power when he says to the fishermen 'let out your nets', but for the rest is not just as human as any one of us, but simpler, more natural, more plain than any of us.

In such moments we truly feel that it is not the distance between earth and heaven, nor the great difference between flesh and Spirit, creature and creator, but, as it is written, only our sins, which make a division between God and us and prevent him from doing what otherwise he could and gladly would do, setting up his tabernacle among the children of men, and when they truly desired it, taking them up with him into the everlasting habitations.[18]

This sense of the intimacy and simplicity of the relationship between divine and human, heaven and earth, was not only something which Grundtvig conveyed by his preaching. His whole way of being spoke of it. It was something which touched the whole Grundtvigian movement and made very simple practical projects, the reclaiming of heathland, the planting of fruit trees, the improvement of methods of farming, the development of education for those who had not formerly had it, in particular for women and for peasants, the celebration of anniversaries with singing and dancing — all these things seemed full of an eternal presence. Heaven and earth were not far apart.

Here too in the later sermons the figure of Mary is never altogether forgotten. She again is present in an eschatological perspective but also as a constant reminder both of the facts of the Gospel and of the fact that woman, no less than man, has a vitally active part in the whole divine-human process. In a sermon from the eighteen sixties Grundtvig says,

Adam called his wife's name Eve, i.e. life, since she became the bodily mother of all living and our forefather evidently called his wife by her right name, for despite all the disturbance which sin has placed in the original order of human nature, it was in a daughter of Eve, the Virgin Mary, that God's only begotten Son sought and found the earthly human life when he humbled himself to bear the image of the earthly so that we could be raised to bear the image of the heavenly.[19]

So, in another, even later sermon, Grundtvig expresses, in striking images, his faith that something of paradise has remained at the very heart of human life throughout human history.

Although fallen humankind was chased out of paradise so that they should not eat from the tree of life and live forever, yet there was a way of escape, so that the tree of life could spiritually blossom and bear fruit on earth for the benefit of humankind, because a handful of paradise-earth was preserved in the heart of humanity wherein the tree of life could put down its roots.

Even at the darkest times

when the tree of life was, as it seemed, hopelessly lost, the garden of God was not altogether forgotten, but here and there the rose of paradise grew up wild, betraying through its sweet scent the motherly soil from which it grew.[20]

Even at the darkest times of the history of our race, some inexplicable potential for goodness, some totally unlooked for manifestation of beauty reveals itself and proclaims that there is still hidden in the human heart a
handful of the earth of paradise, the earth which carries in itself God's image
and likeness. This is, Grundtvig says, a motherly soil, our mother earth, a
phrase which reminds us that it was in the heart of the woman of faith and
love, the mother of all living, above all others, that the tree of life put down
its roots.

The Christian tradition, in the course of its history, has not always been
notably generous in recognising the gifts of goodness and beauty which have
been manifest in the world beyond its own borders. Too often the virtues of
the heathen have been seen as 'splendid sins'. Here, in the image language
of the Old Testament and the earliest Christian centuries, Grundtvig seeks to
redress this niggardliness. Even when the situation seems most helpless,
when God has seemed most definitively estranged, the deeply planted
yearning to turn towards goodness reasserts itself. We may think in our own
century of the accounts of many writers, perhaps above all in Alexander
Solzhenitsyn, of the way in which in the desert of the concentration camp
suddenly, growing wild, acts of kindness, moments of relief, can be
discovered. We may think of a poem like Edwin Muir's vision of 'The Good
Man in Hell', the good man who has been doomed to damnation by reason
of a bureaucratic error in the heavenly places, yet who, by his patience
kindles a spark of hope even in the pit of hell and begins to undermine the
frozen immobility of evil.

> One doubt of evil would bring down such a grace,
> Open such a gate, all Eden would enter in,
> Hell be a place like any other place
> And love and hate and life and death begin.[21]

It is above all, as Grundtvig has said, in the heart that the handful of
paradise-earth is found. We have seen enough of Grundtvig's use of language
to know that for him to speak of the good earth of the heart is more than a
matter of rhetoric. His view of humanity centred in the heart is also rooted
in the earth. The interrelatedness of the whole of creation is affirmed yet
again.

But there is more that needs to be said about this image of the handful of
paradise-earth preserved in the human heart. In it Grundtvig shows at the
end of his life the extraordinary esemplastic capacity of his mind and
imagination, its capacity to bring together into one and restore life and
meaning in places where there had been forgetfulness and death. In this passage Grundtvig recapitulates and makes new a theme which had its place in
the thought and prayer of the early Christian centuries, particularly in the
Syriac East.

In these centuries, in the Syriac tradition, the story of the fall, as recounted in the first chapters of Genesis was understood and expounded, not so much as a single catastrophic event, but as a gradual process in which the alienation of humankind from God and from paradise took place bit by bit. One aspect of this gradual fall from grace and glory is the gradual distancing from the earthly paradise itself. Certainly after the fall in Eden the gates of the garden are shut and the angel stands at the entrance with the flaming sword. But all contact is not lost. Adam and Eve continue to live on the lower slopes of the mountain of paradise.

Living close to paradise and still being steeped in memories of that place Adam and Eve were still able to continue some sort of paradisiac life. Despite their sin, the transmission of the generation of the righteous was preserved in them and the divine blessing was passed to Seth.

Particularly striking is the expression of Aphrahat,

although he [Adam] had sinned, the seed of the righteous had been preserved through him and the blessing had been preserved in Seth and in all his generations.[22]

These stories of the nearness of the human race to paradise in the ages before the flood, move, in the writing of the greatest Syriac theologians, Aphrahat and Ephraim in particular, into a more general reflection on their meaning, as showing the links between God and his creation which continue even after the fall.

As a close neighbour of paradise, man still is, despite pain and suffering, God's intimate ... The closeness of paradise, occasioning memories, repentance, longing and comfort may therefore become an important theme in the characterisation of early human history.[23]

And this applies not only to the very first generations of humanity but more generally. It involves more than a simple nostalgic memory of what is past. Even if it is clear that paradise is not to be regained on earth, yet the neighbourhood of paradise awakes in humankind some desire for movement towards a future paradise.

This view, that paradise is still in some ways very close to us, is in full accord with the view of God in the writers of this period. For them his justice is always counterbalanced by his grace and there is in the human race not only evidence of fallenness but also some promise of future blessing.

It is striking how these passages, from a scientific article written by the Leiden scholar, Lucas Van Rompay, to elucidate the nature of the early Syriac tradition, evoke memories of passages in Grundtvig's writing. For him also paradise is very near, always about to appear in this world yet never fully

realised, always giving birth to an unfulfilled longing. For him some
memories of the earthly paradise remain at the heart of human life and
experience. In the light of such a theology, expressions about Denmark itself
as a little paradise, which can easily seem sentimental, and which frequently
embarrass contemporary Danish readers, can be given a new and more
serious interpretation.

To understand such expressions in Grundtvig we need to think again of
the context in which they occur. We need to think, for instance, of the summer landscapes of the painters of the Golden Age, a Peter Christian Skovgaard, or a Johan Thomas Lundbye for instance, with their own particular
form of the contemplation of nature. We see in them how the beauty of the
world reveals itself to us in many unexpected ways. Still more we think of all
those small acts of human generosity of which Grundtvig's contemporary,
William Wordsworth, speaks,

> That best portion of a good man's life,
> His little, nameless, unremembered acts
> Of kindness and of love ...[24]

In such things something of paradise is glimpsed as close at hand. Already
here and now a joy is sometimes given which this world cannot contain and
which therefore points us to a world beyond this one. Grundtvig speaks of
an interchange of human and divine in the life of the Church 'which on earth
in time carries eternal life within itself and in heaven shall eternally carry its
temporal life within it'. In such ways as these the image of God, in which the
world is made, is at times transmuted into a shining likeness.

CHAPTER 10

A simple, cheerful, active Life on Earth

We have seen in the former chapter how Grundtvig envisages the history of humanity in an eschatological perspective, as beginning in God and ending in him, and we have also seen how for him, when seen in this way, the history of humanity cannot be separated from the history of creation as a whole, of which humanity is an essential and constitutive part.

But what will he say when we come to look more closely at the nature of human society and the relationship of human beings with one another? Here again we shall find that the concepts of active interrelationship and living interaction are of vital importance. Not only in the relationship of humanity with the whole created order, but in relationships within human society, where human beings are necessarily in living interaction with one another, his view of human nature is, as we have already seen, ineradicably personalist and not individualist; persons cannot be understood except in relationship. As an outstanding authority on Grundtvig's ideas about education and society, a former principal of Askov Folk High School, Hans Henningsen, has written,

Grundtvig himself was incapable of thinking individualistically. Reality everywhere consists of relations. Freedom must therefore always rest on reciprocity, he believed. Whoever would be free must also grant his neighbour freedom. Neither individuals nor social classes can liberate themselves at the expense of others without freedom being lost in the end.[1]

It is difficult to stress too much the importance of these affirmations for understanding Grundtvig's attitude toward social, political and educational problems. First we notice that this relational view of human society and personality is set within the context of a relational view of reality as a whole. Indeed for Grundtvig it is rooted in the very nature of a God who is at once three and one. Then we may observe that such a view implies a radical critique both of the Marxist theory of the necessity of the class struggle, and of the capitalist ideology of the primacy of individual rights and the value of unregulated competition.

Another leading exponent of Grundtvig's educational ideas, K.E. Bugge, insists,

It is, however, characteristic of Grundtvig's independent way of thinking that he did not accept the tenets of liberalism uncritically ... As a positive alternative to the revolutionary French conception of freedom, and as an alternative to the British economic theory of liberalism, Grundtvig advocated what he called 'a Nordic concept of freedom'. Concerning this concept he writes: 'I know from my own personal experience that it can be very difficult indeed ... to be satisfied with the amount of freedom that leaves some freedom also to my neighbour.' The liberty that Grundtvig advocated is therefore a liberty which is actively constrained by responsibility towards one's fellowman. Liberty is closely knit together with a commitment to care for the well-being of other people.[2]

This constraint upon the immediate freedom of the individual, political and economic, which Grundtvig himself recognises has its difficulties, is not in the end hostile to true human freedom and development. On the contrary it promotes it, for it is based on a true perception of the nature of society and indeed of reality itself. 'Reality everywhere consists of relations. Freedom must therefore always rest on reciprocity'. Such a view thinks not of quick, short term, immediate results, it looks to the longer perspectives of social and national life and history. It is such basic premises as these which underlie the development in Scandinavia and specifically in Denmark, of a particular kind of democratic socialism which has in the end as little in common with the ideology of the free market economy as it has with Marxist Leninism.

These social and political developments have often had no explicit or direct reference back to the underlying principles of Christian faith. More often, particularly in this century, the theological basis of such a view of human society in the doctrine of God as Trinity, God already carrying sociality within himself, has been unexpressed or indeed denied. But for Grundtvig the two things, the divine and the human, cannot be kept apart. For him the work of God the Word throughout creation, bringing into being a world and a humanity which are made in God's image, gives the underlying pattern to all human history. As a contemporary theologian puts it,

this divine ordering is what ultimately implants in the human condition, the 'being-with' which is natural to it ... Hence it is to this dynamic that we trace the capacity of human beings to generate richer more open-structured forms of order in a social universe of consistently expanding complexity.[3]

For Grundtvig of course the possibility of realising such a society of open-structured order, in which different groups and interests respect one another's viewpoints and recognise one another's rights, and so work together in harmonious disagreement is bound up with the existence of an historically rooted national community. For him a nation is a community of people who, across all their differences, are joined together by common memories, a common language and a shared and inherited territory.

Grundtvig's view both of society and education, is as he constantly says, both historic and poetic. It allows for the importance of objective factors, geographical, historical and economic, but it also allows for the importance of subjective factors, knowing that the understanding and appreciation of what history and geography mean cannot be achieved without awakening the imagination. We need to *feel* our relationships with our fellow human beings as well as to acknowledge them with our minds, if we ourselves are to become active and responsible members of the people to which we belong.

This vision of personal and national rebirth and renewal which Grundtvig formulated in the circumstances of nineteenth century Denmark is the one aspect of his thought which has, up till now, received a certain international recognition and response. In a great variety of places, in Bangladesh, in the Philippines, in Nigeria and Japan, for instance, people have been captured by a Grundtvigian ideal of education for life, or in twentieth century terms 'consciousness raising', encouraging people to become aware of their own latent, often unrealised, resources for thought and action. Amongst the different initiatives which have been taken in this field, two deserve particular mention, the Education for Life Foundation, in the Philippines, directed by Edicio de la Torre, and the Grundtvig Institute in Oba, in Nigeria and its founder, Dr. Kachi E. Ozumba.[4]

It is not within the scope of this book to begin to assess these developments, but one cannot help but be impressed by the way in which something of Grundtvig's vision and personality has evoked a response in such widely separated places. How far Grundtvig's ideas have been understood, in at least some of the cross-cultural encounters which have taken place, is not always easy to see. In two closely argued articles, Holger Bernt Hansen has looked at the variety of ways in which these ideas have been received, and has shown something of the complexity of the process of cultural, intellectual and human exchange which takes place across the continents.[5] What seems clear is that Grundtvig's combination of the traditional with the radical, of the popular and practical with the visionary and spiritual, can speak powerfully to people outside Western Europe and North America. These are people who have often been dismayed by many of the dominant western ways of doing things, and by western ways of education in particular. Grundtvig provides a kind of alternative or third way.

Already in the 1930s a prominent Chinese thinker and social reformer, Liang Shuming, thought he had found, in a somewhat idealised view of Denmark, something refreshingly different to what he had discovered more generally in the western, and mostly English-speaking world. As he bluntly remarked to some Danish visitors, 'We often feel that there is too much competition between Westerners and too little friendship'. The Grundtvigian ideal of holding together thinking and feeling, heart and head, of seeking for a collaborative, rather than a competitive model for society, particularly attracted him.[6]

At the present time it is striking to see how the emphasis on practical and living experience has been vital for Edicio de la Torre in his work in the Philippines. At the end of a lecture given in Copenhagen in the summer of 1996 he asked,

Shall Grundtvig be for the scholars alone, and shall they tell us what he is or is not? I believe that experience has taught me, that Grundtvig is understood more deeply and in a more living way, in our time, when learning and experience of life work together. Light and life — and yes — hope.[7]

The note of hope is particularly significant. There is something in what Grundtvig was as well as in what he said, which engenders new hope in those who come into contact with him. He encourages people to feel that new life is possible for them, through a new understanding and a new realisation of the importance of interdependence and interaction.

Thus, if Grundtvig holds together freedom and mutual responsibility in a way which is very much his own, so also does he hold together feeling and thinking. Here again there needs to be interaction and reciprocity. This is true not only in general but specifically in regard to education. The emotional and intuitive aspects of knowing are needed to complement the rational and objective ones.

Normally reason and feeling are regarded as phenomena that must be kept apart from one another in regard to education.

This is not at all Grundtvig's view; we learn to know because we first love.

All living knowledge or knowledge about life is nothing other than a feeling within us that comes to light and thus itself becomes clear ...[8]

Often Grundtvig's approach to this question of the unity of human knowing and loving is expressed in biblical and poetic images rather than in abstract concepts. So for him the triad of heart, mouth and hand, which we have seen in his theological thinking, provides a vital tool for speaking about the unity and wholeness of human knowing and perception. The inner work of the heart must be expressed outwardly in words and thus become articulate and clear. What is dark and unclear though deeply felt, comes to light and is clarified in thought and in speech. Then what is spoken and expressed in words must become embodied, made practically real in the work of the hands, in skilful deeds.

We see in this way something of the primacy of love in Grundtvig's thought. To say that we know what we love is to say something directly about the process of education. We learn what we are attracted to, what fires our imagination. Hans Henningsen sums it up by saying, 'all true enlightenment is gentle and soft so that it pleases our heart'[9], an affirmation which, if we take it at all seriously, overturns many of the presuppositions of our society. It gives us not only a holistic but a strangely optimistic view of human nature, very much at odds with the hardness and pessimism which has come to characterise much of late twentieth century life.

Writing some twenty years ago, the Anglo-American theologian Daniel Hardy, whose words we have already cited in this chapter, noted the tendency to lose hope in relation to basic elements in the current social and political situation. The questions he asked in 1975 are no less pertinent today.

Are there any symbols of hope, symbols of community, symbols of individuality-in-community, which transcend both the system of a warring conflict of interests and the system of central planning of society by the state? Are there here any resources for hope? Since sooner or later we shall run short of that fundamental human emotion and outlook, are there any resources in the Christian tradition which, recognising man's creativity as ambivalent, nevertheless help us to promote not only individual salvation but also the future well-being of mankind?[10]

These are questions to which Grundtvig's view of human nature and society is strangely relevant.

Such a vision of human nature is personalist and holistic. It sees a unity in the human person and in human society which holds together all the different faculties which go to make up our human nature. The process of education involves them all and not only the mind. So the Folk High Schools have always aimed to be primarily communities in which a living interaction can take place between teacher and taught and in which both learn from one another. This educational process takes place in the context of a common life involving living and eating, singing, playing and working together as well as studying and learning, in which hard realities and difficult topics can be understood in a way which is not altogether out of harmony with the deepest longings of the heart. It is a process which is apt to give birth to unexpected hope.

I

This vision is expressed by Grundtvig in a poem written in 1839 for his two elder sons at the time of their confirmation, a poem which contains some of his best known and best loved lines,

> A simple, cheerful, active life on earth
> Which I would not exchange for that of kings,
> A way made clear in the path our noble fathers trod
> With equal worth ascribed to cottage and to castle,
> With the eye, as it is created, turned towards heaven,

> Wide awake to all that is beautiful and great here below
> But well acquainted with the depth of longing
> Only satisfied with the radiance of eternity.
> Such a life I desired for all my descendants
> And pondered diligently how to prepare it,
> And when my soul was tired of its effort
> It found rest in praying the Our Father.
> Then I felt confidence from the Spirit of truth,
> That blessings hover over our life's garden,
> When our dust is placed in its creator's hand
> And all things are awaited in nature's order.[11]

This is a passage that seems at first sight simple but proves to be more complex than we might have expected. The unity which it describes is manifold; it has many facets or dimensions. It speaks of a balanced, active, cheerful life on earth, and it speaks of equality of worth given to all in society, but yet in a society which is conscious of standing in an ancient and noble tradition. It goes on at once to speak of the human eye as created with a view towards heaven. We are standing on earth looking to heaven. In doing this we do not for a moment cease to see and rejoice in all that is good and great here below. Indeed perhaps it is implied that it is out of the deep longing for eternity, a longing which will only finally be satisfied with a glory which comes from eternity, that we are be able to see and rejoice in the many gifts of this world of time and change. There is in these lines no sharp opposition between time and eternity but rather a mysterious interaction.

Grundtvig goes on to speak further of the quality of life which he desires for his descendants. It is a life in which effort and achievement are complemented by prayer and contemplation. Here again there is a striking interaction of the active and passive elements of human experience. It is indeed a thoroughly human and humanist vision which he sets before us, but it is also a deeply religious one. We might perhaps say a theocentric humanism is at work here, for it is noteworthy that even here where Grundtvig seems to want to speak primarily in natural terms, the trinitarian nature of the prayer he makes comes very close to the surface. The prayer which he prays is the prayer of sonship addressed to God as Father and over it the Spirit of truth presides.

Yet again we are reminded that to be truly lived our human life needs to be lived in harmony with things as they really are. We may work hard and strive diligently, but we also need to cultivate a spirit of expectancy which finds that all things will in the end be given us 'in nature's order.' Two lines before, it is said in the original that *lykken* hovers over the garden of life; that word could be translated as good luck or good success, or, as Charles Williams would have put it, 'holy luck'. All in the end is gift and grace. In the lines which follow the poem goes on to speak of the growing maturity of human life in images taken from the growth of the natural world through the seasons of the year. Such a vision of human development seeks to do justice to the many dimensions of human existence and yet to reveal its underlying unity.

It is not surprising that among Grundtvig's contemporaries, and particularly among his younger contemporaries, those who in some sense became his disciples, we should find that some were more attracted to one side of the picture and some to another. Grundtvig himself was so complex and manifold that it was almost inevitable that after his death there should be different interpretations of his teaching which gave rise to different and sometimes conflicting groups among his followers. There were those who moved to the left and became political activists; there were those who became theologians with a deep fascination for liturgy and sometimes found themselves on the right politically. Above all there were those who took the lead in the growth of the Folk High School movement, and who tried to work out the meaning of his ideas in terms of human development and the growth of a just and participatory society.

II

It is one of the many paradoxes of Grundtvig's life and work that this one aspect of it which is known internationally, the foundation of the Folk High Schools, was not really his own at all. Certainly the ideas and inspiration of the movement came from him but their realisation was the work of a group of younger men who, in various ways, initiated a new kind of educational establishment; small, residential schools or colleges which worked, for the most part, with young adults who would have had no prospect of entering university. All the leaders of the first High Schools were disciples of Grundtvig, though none of them were uncritical or unreflective disciples. Among them one stands out as a personality in his own right. Certainly not a man as complex or many-sided as Grundtvig, but yet a man with a highly memorable genius as a teacher.

Christen M. Kold (1816-70) was the son of a shoemaker in northern Jutland. As a young man he was converted to a living Christian faith under the influence of a popular lay preacher of Grundtvigian convictions. He discovered that Christianity was a religion of life and joy, not of fear and death. 'I thought earlier that God was policeman, a strict schoolmaster, who watched over us and gave us a good box on the ear when we were bad.' The discovery that God loved him came as an altogether astonishing surprise.

I have never experienced anything like the life, the joy, the strength and power that suddenly arose in me. I was so happy over that discovery, that I didn't know which leg I should stand on.[12]

There was of course no possibility for a peasant like Kold of getting to the University. He became active in the revival movement. He worked as a teacher, spending five years in Smyrna (Izmir), in Turkey, as assistant to a Danish Lutheran missionary there. In 1851, when he was thirty-five, he came back to Denmark and managed to see Grundtvig. He impressed Grundtvig so much that he gave him financial and moral support. With this and with his own savings Kold managed to open his first school in November of that year. He had fourteen students in the first year and sixteen in the second.

Kold's schools were famous for many things, not least for their spartan regime. Most of the early High Schools took in the sons of the somewhat more prosperous farmers. Kold would take the poorest. All lived together, teachers and students alike. They shared the same dormitory, ate porridge out of the same bowl, couldn't afford the luxury of tea or coffee, wore wooden clogs and homespun clothes. In this society Kold began to work out his educational methods. The boys came for the winter months, when there was less work to do on the farm; in the summer, from the beginning, there were courses for young women as well. Mostly the students were around the age of eighteen to twenty. Reading, writing and arithmetic were taught, as useful tools, but in a quite secondary way and often by Kold's assistant. Kold's own work was to encourage his students and to bring them to life. In a letter to his brother, Ludvig P. Schrøder, himself the head of the school at Askov, speaks of Kold like this,

It is a sort of Socrates who sits in his chair surrounded by a large number of farmers and farmgirls who come from far and wide to visit the school. And all the day long — apart from when he is lecturing in the school — he talks to all these people in such a way as always to stir something in them. He has a wealth of experience and of stories, and with these treasures he enriches his audience, with the clear purpose of encouraging their active efforts. They are establishing free schools for children round about in the parishes. He lets them have his former pupils as teachers, but the peasants take care of the teachers' board and lodging and consider it a privilege to be able to sacrifice something in a good cause. He lectures for an hour or an hour and a half every morning, at which time the schoolroom is full of pupils and visitors. He prefers to take a chapter out of world history, but the main point is its practical application, which he has a particularly good grip on. He aims to stir us ... to open our hearts to the spiritual world so that it can come to use us as willing instruments to proceed with the task of our people and the whole of humanity.[13]

The world of the spirit is to come to us, to use us in the service of the common good, at home and abroad. Although it was not always explicitly said, the thought of the Holy Spirit, the encourager and strengthener, is not far away from this message.

Encouraging and bringing to life was indeed Kold's great gift. Grundtvig had spoken of the schools as a source of enlightenment, *oplysning*, the old eighteenth century term for education. For Kold another word seems to have been particularly vital, *oplive*, a word which can simply mean encourage but which has as its root meaning 'to bring to life'. It is in this deeper sense that Kold constantly uses it. Some of the schools, he once said, sought to fight against privilege, others against the pressure of Germany felt in southern Jutland.

The enemy I have set my sights on is Death, and that enemy is closer to us than either the Germans or the Estate owners, because it lives in our hearts, side by side with Life. All other battles are lost in the ripple of time's waves, but this battle lasts for all time, and to prepare oneself for it, this is the one that really counts.[14]

One sees at this point how deep is Kold's affinity with Grundtvig. For Grundtvig also the struggle of life with death was the guiding thread which led him through all the complexities of his long career. In Grundtvig's metrical paraphrase of the Agnus Dei, still commonly sung at the time of communion in Denmark, the third verse reads, 'In spite of our death, give us your life.' This for him is the heart of the matter. We may see here, in the actual educational practice of Kold, a practical outworking of Grundtvig's stress on the doctrine of Christ's descent into hell which we shall find so fully developed in Grundtvig's Easter sermons.

We can also see his deep affinity with Grundtvig in the way Kold formulated his basic ideas about teaching and learning. For him it was clear that all instruction should take account of the real needs and capacities of the students whatever their age.

The children's school has been guilty of the mistake, that it almost exclusively has tried to talk to *understanding* and only partly to *feeling*, while *fantasy*, the power of the imagination, has been as good as forgotten.[15]

He held that both children and adolescents were given too much of the wrong sort of written instruction which deadened and de-sensitized their minds and hearts, turning them into enemies of both the school and its learning. What they needed instead, he held, is the right kind of oral instruction, one which will bring them to life and widen their feeling for the world in which they live. Grundtvig's own basic preference for the living word and for an educational process which involves reciprocal interaction between pupil and teacher, clearly came to life in practice, in Kold's schools. It is a remarkable fact that in all the variety of Folk High Schools to be found in Denmark today, and they are many and various, this basic option for the living word, this belief in the personal interaction and exchange of the teacher and taught remains constant and unquestionable.

III

We have looked at one of the most remarkable figures of the first generation of the Folk High School movement. We come now to a figure of a later time, but one who, in her own way, was no less central to the movement and representative of it. Ingeborg Appel (1868-1948) was the daughter of the first Principal of Askov High School, the Ludvig Schrøder, whose description of Kold's socratic method we have just seen. Since she was to marry her father's successor, Jacob Chr. L. Appel, Ingeborg's long life was identified with the school to an exceptional degree. Speaking shortly after her death in November 1948, Holger Kjær, one of the senior lecturers at the school comments specifically on this aspect of her life. She had taught there, he tells us, for fifty years. From 1906–18 she had been Women's Principal. At times during that period, when her husband was away serving as a minister in the government at Copenhagen, she had been in sole charge. She had brought up her own family in the middle of the school community. She was clearly a woman deeply devoted to family and home, but not in an unreflective way, for since her own family was placed at the centre of the life of a large residential school community, she had needed wisdom to see how to hold the two things together without confusing them. With her death, Kjær tells us, a whole epoch had passed, for her memories went back to the great figures of the first generation, to Trier, Nørregaard, la Cour, and Christian Flor, and via her parents further back still to Grundtvig himself, to the pioneering days at Rødding before the war of 1864.[16]

In his memorial address Kjær asks himself how he is to describe her? In her maturity she had become a person of great authority, a formidable person, not to be trifled with, 'manly in her deep womanliness', *'mandig i sin dybe kvindelighed'*. It is a phrase which speaks of a remarkable degree of human maturity, an interaction of complementary powers, a reconciliation of opposites. Since he is speaking in a Grundtvigian milieu, an historic-poetic milieu, it is natural that Kjær looks to the past for parallels to her life and for possible comparisons. Not surprisingly he looks to the history of the North. Yes, she is a *sagakvinde*, a woman of the sagas, Bergthora, Njal's wife in the greatest of the Icelandic stories; true and steadfast, loyal to the end.

But he admits that this comparison is not, in the end, enough. It does not bring out the deeply Christian character of her life, nor its complexity. There was in her a reconciliation of light with darkness, of strength with human frailty, of faith with fear and trembling. For, he insists, she had known much of fear and trembling; it was that, in part, which had given her such a remarkable combination of strength and sensitivity.

It is this fear and trembling which is the explanation of her authority. She had authority, it is true, by nature, but ultimately her authority was rooted in something else. Those who do not know fear and trembling in relation to their call are afraid of every possible human threat; but those who know true fear find in it the courage to overcome the fear of men which we all must struggle with; find courage to take responsibility and, if need be, to take the knocks.

The true fear of God can cast out all other fear. So rather than the past of the sagas, he looks to the high Middle Ages to find a figure to compare her with. No, he says, she is a Brigitta of Sweden. Though she is no nun, and though she would have repudiated utterly the idea of being a saint, yet, in the end, Kjær finds he must compare her with the foundress of the community of Vadstena, the critic and counsellor of popes.

   In a way which may surprise us he finds in the rule of St. Benedict, the rule which provided the underlying framework for the development of monastic life in the medieval West, the terms he needs in order to capture the essential quality of her life. In her, we see an outstanding example of *stabilitas loci*, a steadfast stability and loyalty to one place which can result in a deep unity and fruitfulness of life.

Our life is so short, and there is a great danger that it may fall apart in different episodes and so come to nothing.

The monk is committed to remain true to one place, and to persevere in the task which he has begun. Appel knew the *samlethed*, the gatheredness or integration, that that can give. *Conversio morum*, that second principle of Benedictine life, that daily conversion, she had indeed pursued day by day, a daily turning to God with a sometimes almost frightening intensity, through all the details of the common life, of school and family alike. There was little that the monks could have taught her about self-discipline and regularity. *Obedientia*, the attentive listening and the active response to the call once heard, that she had never neglected. She had not been disobedient to the heavenly vision. She had sought to respond to the will of God as it had made itself known to her in a life singularly dedicated to God's service.

   So, he tells us, she was a mother in Israel to young and to old, to her own children and grandchildren, to generation after generation of students, to the teachers and their spouses and their families, and indeed, far beyond Askov, to the whole world of the Folk High Schools in Denmark and beyond. And Kjær, in his address, suddenly gives us a glimpse of the details of her life, how she would get to know the children, come to see them when they were ill, tell them fairy stories, 'bring a picture book for a birthday with pictures which she herself had cut out and stuck in.' He tells us too how she also took care to visit those who were old and failing. 'She came and she came regularly. She listened to them, let them unload the things which worried them, and sang for them when the end drew near.' At the last, it was the hymns, not only those of Grundtvig but also those of Jakob Knudsen which expressed the deepest and most lasting things by which she lived.

   It is in many ways an extraordinarily pre-modern picture with its perceptive evocation of the rule of St. Benedict, and yet it also seems to point us towards the future. It raises many interesting questions about the nature of the Grundtvigian movement in which the Folk High Schools played such a central role. For if the figure of Ingeborg Appel in some ways speaks to us of a remote past, it also shows us an authority which can enable and set free, an integration which can hold together the clashing archetypes of male and female, married and celibate in a tense but fruitful harmony, a way of being mother which is really that of a mother of life. It leads us to ask where we are to place the Grundtvigian movement in the whole spectrum of Christian movements of revival which are characteristic of Protestantism both in northern Europe and the English speaking world in the eighteenth and nineteenth centuries.

Grundtvigianism evidently has many things in common with those varied movements of pietist and evangelical revival. There is its intense seriousness, its dislike of any kind of pomp, its love of a certain frugality and simplicity of life, its overwhelming sense of personal responsibility. But whereas in many, if not most, strands of evangelical pietism, there is a deep suspicion of the world of the intellect and the imagination, here both intellect and imagination are welcomed and acknowledged as gifts of God. New lines of thought, new areas of study, new methods of education, all have their place. Music and poetry, yes, acting and dancing, are all to be cultivated. At Askov itself, Ingeborg Appel played a pioneering role in developing physical education for women. The young men were not to have a monopoly on the gymnasium, though naturally in the nineteenth century the two sexes exercised in strict segregation. There is something here of the largeness of spirit which has characterised the Society of Friends over the last three centuries and made their own educational establishments so innovative and encouraging.

The spirit of innovation and willingness to take up new ideas manifested itself in the life of the farming communities of nineteenth century Denmark. The Folk High Schools gave the farmers new confidence in their own capacities to promote new methods and to work out new structures of co-operative action. Within the farmhouse there would be a surprising array of books, not only on religious topics. Whereas the pietist family would have its harmonium to lead the singing of hymns, in the Grundtvigian home there would be a piano. Hymns would certainly not be lacking in a Grundtvigian milieu, but was not the music of Schumann and Brahms also worth cultivating?

Grundtvig had sought to promote a way of life which would value and appreciate the things of this world because it was always half aware of the things of heaven shining through them. For more than a generation after his death this way of life became a reality for many people in Denmark. It coloured, and to some degree still colours, large areas of Danish life. It is, as we have suggested earlier, a deeply human vision of life, but also a God-centred vision. It is striking that within this movement, which has grown at the heart of Lutheran Denmark, the rule of St. Benedict should provide a privileged way of approach to the understanding of its character and particularly to the interpretation of a person such as Ingeborg Appel. For the Benedictine rule provides the classical Western form for that monastic tradition which is itself rooted in the baptismal covenant on which Grundtvig meditated so deeply. It is one particular way of knitting together the clashing archetypes of male and female, human and divine, in a renunciation of evil and an embracing of all which is good and on the side of life, a way of making real in the frailties and imperfections of flesh and blood a deeply theocentric humanism.

Part III

The Celebration of Faith

Introduction

In the two previous sections of this book we have necessarily been extremely selective. The quantity of material which Grundtvig has left behind him is of daunting proportions. In this third section we can be a little more representative in our treatment of the subjects as we come to them, the different articles of Christian faith, as they succeed one another in the course of the Church's year. If this book has any originality it lies in part in the fact that, so far as I know, it is the first time that the recently published volumes of sermons have been used to fill out the picture of Grundtvig's understanding of Christian faith as a whole.

After a preliminary consideration of the interaction of eternity and time, we begin with Advent, with three sermons from 1836 which show us not only the deeply trinitarian quality of Grundtvig's preaching, but also its insistence that Christian faith and prayer not only ends in God, but begins in God. It is God who comes to us before we can come to him. We learn in these pages two things which are fundamental to Grundtvig's exposition of Christian faith and worship; first that *God is mighty, he is near, he is good and his mercy endures forever*; secondly that *the past is only important to us for the sake of the present and the future*.

At Christmas we see in a special way something of the vital significance of childhood in Grundtvig's view of human life, and something too of the way in which popular piety and solemn doctrinal affirmation are constantly linked in his presentation of Christian faith. We see too how the particular moment of the birth at Bethlehem has for him a universal significance, how it reveals something of the way in which, in God's hands, all time tends to pass from darkness into light.

It may surprise some readers that the following chapter, headed 'Annunciation', is longer than the chapter on Christmas. Surprise, however, is not appropriate here, for one of the places where Grundtvig is most original and has most to offer readers today is in his vision of the place of women in the scheme of human redemption. In this section, we look not only at the sermons which speak directly of Mary, but at others in which the role of women in the Bible story, and especially in the Gospels, is given consideration. But at the end it is the calling of the whole Church 'to be a Virgin Mary', which is central to these pages.

The two following chapters, which speak of Christ's triumph over death by death, and the coming of the Spirit at Pentecost, are necessarily the longest and fullest in this section. Both themes are developed by Grundtvig with a wonderful inventiveness which can only be suggested here. In the Easter section we look in detail at two contrasting sermons for the crucial year 1837, both in their different ways influenced by the work of translation which Grundtvig was then doing with the Greek hymns. One of the most striking things about both the hymns and the sermons of this period is that the Eastern influences are felt not as bringing in something new or intrusive, but as strengthening and deepening lines of thought and intuition which are already there.

The sermons on Pentecost again reveal to us something of the many-sidedness of Grundtvig's vision. The joy of Pentecost is for him something rooted in the life and history of his people. It is the fulfilment of the hidden, deepest longings of the heart. It is also a liberating energy which loosens tongues which have been dumb and sets up communication between the many different languages with which God has endowed humankind. But then, in another mood, it is presented as the moment in which we are to stand still and look deep into the unfathomable abyss of the divine love, 'both the source of our salvation and our salvation itself, both the source of life and the river of life.' Finally, it is at Pentecost that we remember the gift of the Spirit given through the course of the centuries in the history of the Church, and rejoice to commemorate our own particular apostles, as well as the apostles of the universal family of God.

I have taken a certain liberty in the two shorter chapters which follow and which are linked to two of the feasts of September, the fourteenth and the twenty-ninth of that month, the Feast of the Holy Cross and the Feast of St. Michael and All Angels, since neither of these festivals occur at the present time in the calendar of the Danish Church. But in the course of the Christian year Grundtvig frequently finds himself drawn to preach on the Cross, and particularly on the second Christmas Day, the Feast of St. Stephen, the first martyr. In these sermons we find more of the wealth of his meditation on the central mystery of our salvation, and we also see his insistence on the value of outward signs and gestures in Christian worship when they express the inner life of faith.

As to the ministry of angels, it is a theme to which Grundtvig returns in a variety of contexts. Their feast day was observed in the Danish Church until 1770; it must still have been remembered in his boyhood. He thinks in the first place of the angels as God's messengers to this world of space and time; messengers of hope and redemption. But he thinks too of the angels as those who accompany the Lord of all, not only in heaven but also in the days of his flesh, and therefore as those who accompany us on our earthly journeys, sometimes revealing themselves to us outwardly, sometimes inwardly. Here, as in many places, Grundtvig shows himself to be at once 'an old fashioned believer' and an original thinker, who speaks out of his own experience both as a poet and a man of prayer. The conjunction of faith and imagination with which these sermons present us is strangely compelling.

CHAPTER 11

Eternity in Time

I

In the final section of the book we shall seek to expound something of Grundtvig's understanding of the Christian faith by way of his hymns and sermons. In doing this it will be natural to arrange the material according to the pattern of the Christian year. The sermons were preached Sunday by Sunday in the gathering of the Christian people to celebrate the Lord's death and resurrection, by singing his praises, hearing his word and acting out the mystery of his sacrificial love, in the sacraments which he himself had given. The hymns were written in order to articulate the celebration of that mystery and to enable the congregation to take its full part in the liturgy. Liturgy is a word which itself indicates that the act of worship is intended to be the work of the whole people. In the Lutheran tradition as a whole this popular aspect of worship has, since the time of Martin Luther, been sustained above all by the singing of congregational hymns.

But, for Grundtvig, this weekly celebration of the mystery of the faith was deepened and strengthened by the annual celebration of particular moments in the whole history of God's dealings with his people, the birth, the death and rising again of Jesus Christ and the coming of the Spirit at Pentecost. So Christmas, Easter and Whitsun have a special place in establishing the pattern of faith and teaching, and around them gather other commemorations, among them, for instance, the Annunciation or Maundy Thursday, which have a special importance in Grundtvig's life. What we have here in the calendar of the Danish Church is a great simplification of the old pre-Reformation order of the Church's year. By the removal of a multitude of secondary commemorations, the christological and trinitarian character of the scheme shines out clearly. That christological and trinitarian character of Christian worship is something that Grundtvig always wishes to make clear.[1]

This cycle of feasts is part of what, for Grundtvig, is simply given, the framework in which Christian prayer and faith grows, something as unquestionable and as taken for granted as the medieval church buildings where in so many places in Denmark the congregation still meets. In Grundtvig's days the overwhelming majority of church buildings in use dated from before the Reformation. The Lutheran Reformation, particularly in Scandinavia, had been much less iconoclastic than the Reformation of Geneva. In many places pre-Reformation statues and paintings remained in the church;

there was no hesitation about introducing new statues and paintings in the style of the times. The old eucharistic vestments continued in use, and although in most places side altars were removed, the main altar of the church remained and remains the focal point of the church's worship. This given framework included, as well as the church building, the traditional elements of worship which made and still make up the content of the Danish Liturgy, the structure of the Sunday Mass, a service which today is liable to include the celebration of both the gospel sacraments, baptism and holy communion. But this framework of weekly and annual celebration is itself in constant interaction with the changing times and moods of the seasons of the natural year. For Grundtvig grace and nature, redemption and creation are never separated or opposed to one another. There is a constant exchange between them, an interpenetration of time and eternity, which is sometimes harmonious and joyful, sometimes difficult and full of pain, but never a total estrangement. Thus it is, that in his great festival hymns, natural imagery and seasonal themes are juxtaposed with biblical and liturgical elements in ways which at first may startle us. They certainly have no parallels in Watts or Wesley, or in the classical hymnody of the eighteenth century in England or America. On the other hand, from a literary point of view, they have much in common with the hymnody of the first Christian centuries, both in East and West, where natural and biblical images are constantly intertwined.

For Grundtvig, God's eternity carries time within itself, and human time is seen as full of potential for eternity. Eternity redeems and transfigures time, clarifies it in innumerable ways, while the realities of time give their colour and feeling to the mysteries of eternity. There are great transcendent and eternal events which stand at the heart of Christianity, events of universal significance which take place in time, yet are full of the presence of eternity, from the annunciation of the Word at Nazareth to the coming of the Spirit at Pentecost. These realities which proceed from heaven and return to heaven touch our world of space and time at particular moments, creating those intersection points of the timeless with time, moments within our world of time which cast their light backwards as well as forwards, gathering up past and future into an eternal present, a fullness of time. They are once for all moments by which the world of time is decisively changed. As Christian Thodberg puts it, 'God's great deeds bind all times together. Past, present and future times fuse together in God's time.'[2]

These moments by which the world of human history is transformed are also moments at which the world of nature is established and made firm and its true structure revealed and made known to us. Grundtvig is not simply a romantic poet promoting a sentimental religion of nature and then colouring it with biblical and Lutheran images, as some non-Danish commentators have thought.[3] On the contrary, he is a theologian and prophet who is making much stranger and more challenging affirmations than that. For him it is the incarnation of the Word and above all the resurrection of

Christ from the dead which provide the true foundation and direction for the
world both of human history and of universal nature.

> Like the dawn of the sun in spring
> Jesus rose up from the earth's lap
> With life and light together;
> *Therefore* so long as the world stands
> Now after winter comes the spring
> Blessed in God's kingdom.[4] (my italics)

In some mysterious way the events of redemption precede those of creation,
or at the very least decisively clarify and transfigure them. On Christmas
night we see why it is that every day, light follows on after darkness,
darkness tends towards light. It is Christmas, Easter and Pentecost, the birth
of Christ, his resurrection from the dead, the coming of the Spirit, which
provide the foundation and the framework for our human experience of time.
These great focal points of the intersection of the timeless with time do not
destroy or supersede the temporal realities which they redeem and fulfil.
They reveal the meaning and purpose of the ages which went before them;
they show their finality, their ultimate outcome. Our human experience of
time remains frail and fragmentary, full of frustrations and times of longing
for an eternity which seems unattainable. So it is that the mysteries of eternity
need slowly to be worked out, little by little in the course of human history
and in the course of the history of each member of the human family; and
already those eternal realities are at work within us and around us.

So, in the round of the church's year, the annual celebration of the mysteries of the faith, the constantly turning circle of the seasons is, as it were,
open to receive the riches of eternity, and the fragile fleeting moments of
human life in time are taken up into the splendour of the eternal realm. The
seasons themselves are God's gift in creation, as in the biblical story of the
covenant made with all humanity after the flood; 'While earth lasts, seed-time
and harvest, cold and heat, summer and winter, day and night, shall never
cease.'[5] The freshly confident colours of spring, the wounded burnished tones
of autumn, the darkness and cold of winter, the long warmth and light of
summer, these things are part of God's promise to all things living. All
human societies have celebrated their passing with stories, songs and poetry,
with drama, dancing and celebration. The work of grace does not destroy the
natural order of things. It completes and perfects it.

In nineteenth century Denmark the careful loving attention given to the
moods of the changing year by the landscape painters of the golden age of
Danish painting reveals something of this vision in the field of the visual arts.
The work of the painters shows a particular form of natural contemplation,
physike theoria as the Greek fathers would have called it, a contemplation of
God's gifts in creation.[6] It involved a very particular, detailed study of the
smallest things, of commonplace scenes and objects which the classical art of

the eighteenth century had thought unworthy of notice. It saw God in what is small and apparently impoverished.

This painting was part of the fabric of culture and of the perception of things which marked the society in which Grundtvig lived and moved. It demanded a constant attention to change and difference as well as an ultimate awareness of the one light shining out in the variety of all things. The world is infinitely varied. As the greatest English landscape painter of that time put it,

The world is wide; no two days are alike, not even two hours, neither were there ever two leaves of a tree alike since the creation of the world; and the genuine products of art, like those of nature are all distinct from one another.

And Constable was prepared to go further than that. The world is also full of the promise of new life. In the spring of 1819 he wrote to his wife,

Everything seems full of blossom of some kind and at every step I take, and on whatever object I turn my eyes, that sublime expression of the Scriptures, 'I am the resurrection and the life', seems as if uttered near me.[7]

For Grundtvig every season speaks of some aspect of eternity. Sometimes for him, it is autumn with the harvest which speaks most clearly of the final gathering in of all things into the gladness of heaven. At other times it is the clarity of spring which suggests to him most forcibly the eternal newness of God's kingdom, the lasting spring of that eighth day onto which the seven days of our world of time and change will finally open. At times it is the height of summer with its moment, in the North, when the night is almost wholly swallowed up as dusk and dawn come very close to one another, which speaks most clearly of these realities to him. And then, paradoxically, the depth of winter has its own irreplaceable gift.

For Grundtvig, the joy of winter has a very special place within the picture as a whole. It is a joy which can coexist with cold and darkness. It is the joy of littleness and beginnings, the joy of Christmas and of childhood. It speaks of an intimate interaction of joy and sorrow, two things closely associated in the experience of childhood, two realities which remain with us, inextricably intertwined throughout our life, so long as we continue to live with the openness and the vulnerability of childhood, discovering day by day how

> Joy and woe are woven fine
> A clothing for the soul divine; ...
> And when this we rightly know
> Through the world we safely go.[8]

The reality of eternity is so much richer than that of time that we need to gather together all the gifts of the seasons if we are even to begin to approach the joy which is present at the heart of heaven itself. This is a theme which Grundtvig develops in a remarkable sermon preached on the third Sunday after Easter in 1838, on the text from John 16:22, 'Your heart shall rejoice and your joy no-one shall take from you'. In it we shall find that though he is preaching in the season of Easter, the thought of Christmas is never far from his mind. The eternal realities overturn the measures of time.

This is a blessed prophecy to which all the Lord's disciples who heard him must necessarily have said Amen in their hearts. Indeed that is what we all do, we who believe in the Lord, as soon as it strikes us that his word is not law but gospel, not a command that despite all the sorrowful things which meet and surround us, we should be happy, but the good news, the divine assurance, that our sorrow will be turned into joy by him who made the water into wine, and that that joy which he gives and grants to his own is so deep and constant that no-one can take if from them.[9]

This joy is pure gift, just as the gospel is pure gift; it has all the un-expectedness of Jesus' rising from the dead. It is a meeting of human and divine in the power of the Holy Spirit. It can coexist with times of deepest grief and sadness; in the end it overcomes them.

Yes, also for this reason the saviour in the city of David was born at night time and in the dead of winter, so that even in dark times and under the shivering cold, we should not be without confidence, but should always at least have a good hope in a clear thought which as an angel from heaven announces a great joy which we await, like the hope of morning, which naturally visits us whenever we hear:

> Now dark night goes away
> The dawn is rising up ...

Yes my friends, just as in natural life the joy of winter is one thing, the joy of spring another, the joy of summer a third, and again the joy of harvest a fourth, so also it is in Christian life; joy upon joy, and joy beneath sorrow, and each has its own colour. These are different, and the perfection is not the first but precisely the last, and harvest joy is not here but there where the wheat is gathered into the barn and where the seed which was sown in tears becomes a harvest with songs of gladness. But what our annual festivals point to, that is what we truly find in the Lord's house. We find there winter, spring and summer joys, and these are not as with the world, only for a moment, not just on Christmas, Easter and Whitsun days, but lasting joys which do not change with night and day, with the time of the year or our age in life, but which only rise and fall according to the will of him who knows our making, who remembers that we are but dust. He always gives us what serves us best, perhaps summer today, winter tomorrow, or perhaps the reverse, but by preference and most often spring, for that suits us best and is in Christianity as in nature here below commonly the time of the highest and most lasting joys, the joys which encourage us for powerful endeavours.[10]

There is a contrast here between life in the world and life in the Lord's house, between the joy of earthly seasons and the joy of seasons which are wholly in God's hand. Is Grundtvig here contrasting earth with heaven, does the 'Lord's house' refer to the kingdom of eternity, or is he comparing life in this world without any conscious awareness of God's presence, with life in company with God here and now, that is in the anticipation of eternity which is given already in the Church's life and worship? As we read on it seems increasingly to be the second alternative which is meant, for already here and now the Lord is with us, bringing his joy with him. This is a joy which goes beyond all our expectations, something which the world can neither give nor take away, which is immeasurable and sure. The most daring human hopes cannot come to its measure. But what is given from the outset in a potential fullness, is something which yet we need to appropriate gradually; through the changes of the seasons God enables us to grow. Above all through the experience of winter he helps us to regain the openness, the vulnerability, the trust of childhood without which development is impossible.

When the Lord gives us winter, when he makes it cold and dark about us so that sorrow naturally seeks us out, that he does, only because in no other way can he bring us back to that childhood time in which sorrow and joy quite evidently go together. This we learn as soon as we humble ourselves and become like children again, then we find at once the Christian childhood-joy, the joy of night and winter, the joy of Christmas with the child born in Bethlehem.[11]

This is a joy which is not only born in the cold and darkness of winter but which is born out of the cold and darkness. Grundtvig never forgets the words of the beatitude, Blessed are those who mourn, for they shall be comforted. The joy of which he speaks is never something superficial or rootless. It puts down its roots deep into the darkness of sorrow and anxiety. As he says in a sermon preached fifteen years earlier, in 1823,

The sorrow, the anguish, the fear which presses out of us a great cry and a heartfelt sigh, that is something born only at night, when darkness appals us, in winter when the cold oppresses and shakes us, and when precisely with these sighs of the earth of longing for heaven, the hard crust of the soil is broken up and crumbles and is prepared to receive the dew and the rain, the light and warmth from above, then we can easily understand why the seed grows most at night and in winter, though it is only in the light of day and in high summer, only towards harvest, that we see it.[12]

Underlying the experience of darkness and loss which prepares us to receive anew the descent of God's grace, the hidden joy remains, waiting to be revealed as times and seasons turn.

So, in the sermon on the many colours of joy Grundtvig can go on

Thus we confidently await the well known and dearest joy of springtime, when the birds sing and everything reveals a power of life for which only death is unreasonable and for which eternity is the true element. It is only in these ways that joy changes its colours and its times of year for Christians, it never leaves them and cannot abandon them when they remain with the Lord. For he himself, the Lord, is our joy, who takes away all our sorrows when we cast them on him, lamenting our need and praying to him with confidence in his promise that he will change our sorrow into joy, which nothing, neither grief nor the world, neither death nor the devil, can take from us.[13]

This assurance of joy we have from the word which the Lord speaks directly to us in the sacraments which we celebrate, in which he comes and is present with us. It is the assurance rooted in the birth at Bethlehem and before that in the annunciation at Nazareth, in the littleness of that moment of conception when the unbelievable, wholly new, God-given life is first conceived, as the little word, the human *fiat* responds to the great word, the divine *fiat*. Here is all the mystery of the necessity of our free human response. God who can create the worlds by the word of his mouth, cannot and will not recreate them without the free responsive word of his creature. The life and joy which the Gospel brings is a life and joy which comes into being in the free and wholly personal response of faith and obedience, comes into being in the exchange between Mary and the angel, in which the promise of God is met with that wholly personal free response. It comes into being again in the exchange which takes place in the sacrament of baptism, in which again the promise of God is met with freely given faith and obedience so that baptism may be above all the sacrament of new birth.

Through a word from the Lord's own mouth in baptism, Grundtvig says,

he has accepted us as his disciples, incorporated us into his people and given us the right to rejoice with the gladness of his people ... in baptism we have made a covenant with him that we should be his people and he should be our God, to dwell in us and live in us, to be our joy, our gladness, our power of life, our light and our salvation. This therefore is the childlike faith which begets winter joy, Christmas joy which is dark but deep, out of which all joy of the Lord proceeds. This is the childlike faith to which we must daily turn back as to a source, so that the streams of the river which make glad the city of God shall not dry up in us; this is the mother of joy, to which we shall never turn in vain, in dark hours and days of sorrow, for with faith in the little word from the Lord's mouth, faith in his welcome brought by the angel who says 'Hail thou who art highly favoured, thou hast found favour with God' — in this faith confidence is reborn. This is the childlike boldness with which the heart makes its own all the good words of the Lord and in them the joy which no-one can take from us.[14]

In a poem written in 1851 about God's initiative and our response, Grundtvig concludes with the lines,

> The great word reveals to us
> That heaven is near to earth
> The little word in the soil replies,
> God's paradise right now is here.

Poul Borum comments on this last line *'Guds paradis jo nu er her'*,

four of the very smallest words in the Danish language are brought up close together, *Jo* and *nu* and *er* and *her.'*

'Jo' which could be translated 'yes' is taken by Borum to mean 'affirmation and fellowship in what is taken for granted.[15]

It is joined with *nu*, a word which speaks of the temporal dimension of existence, the present moment, the given time; it is also joined with *her*, which speaks as directly of the spatial dimension of things, this very place, Denmark, this world in which we live. All this is where paradise is found, is truly given. This is a vision, both of fulfilment and of truth; it speaks of a quality of joy which is not to be taken away.

II

The interaction, the interpenetration of grace and nature, of creation and redemption, is to be seen, not only in the content of Grundtvig's sermons and hymns but also in their form. This is particularly clear in case of the hymns. It is much more difficult in Denmark than in England to know where hymns begin and poems end. The dividing line is not clear. At least at times the case is the same in the sermons, which can suddenly modulate into extended prose poems. Because hymns are more firmly established as part of the literary tradition as a whole in Danish, it is common for a major hymn to have more poetic density and to be more assured technically, more complex in its imagery, than a comparable hymn in English would be. Of course this does not apply to all hymns. There are hymns which in their simplicity and directness rival the classical restraint of Isaac Watts; there are in Danish, as in English, hymns of great simplicity and sometimes of a certain banality. But if we think of some of the greatest of Grundtvig's hymns there is a luxuriance of metaphor which is disconcerting to the translator; and behind these hymns of Grundtvig there lie the major triumphs of his seventeenth and eighteenth century predecessors, Thomas Kingo (1634-1703) and Hans Adolph Brorson (1694-1764).

On the other hand there is also in Grundtvig's production a whole world of songs; songs which tell Bible stories, songs which tell national stories, songs which celebrate the seasons of human life. These may sometimes function as hymns in church but more often they are used in more informal situations; at home, at school and particularly in Folk High Schools. The occasions on which people sing together are many and more varied in Denmark than with us; at the end of a lecture, at the beginning of an annual general meeting, at a twenty-first birthday party, at a reunion of old friends. Social verse making still exists today, as it did in the nineteenth century, in a way which is now rare in the English-speaking world. Grundtvig was skilful at this kind of verse making too. One of the characteristics of such popular pieces is that they often reflect, frequently in fairly obvious and sentimental ways, on the passing of time and the keeping of anniversaries. There is a kind of continuum here from the lowest to the highest, from the most ephemeral to the most lasting. In Danish social life what is serious, indeed solemn, and what is comic and altogether grotesque can come together in ways which a foreigner finds surprising, sometimes disconcerting and sometimes deeply moving.[16]

To give an example of a work which is at first sight a poem but in the end turns into a kind of hymn, we shall look at a set of verses called 'Autumn'. We ask of such a work, is it to be read or sung? Is it private or public? The last three verses could perhaps count as a hymn in English, but hardly the first six. Yet it is in the last three verses that the point, the conclusion of the whole, is contained. What is clear is that for the greater part of its text the poem is about our human experience of time in its frailty and its constant sense of loss. Only in the end are the affirmations of faith in the presence of eternity made explicit. Yet throughout, in defiance of the inevitability of death, we are celebrating at least the possibility that life and meaning can continue, to be carried across the gulfs between the generations and the centuries.

> 1. The clouds become grey, the leaves fall,
>   The birds sing no longer.
>   Winter threatens and night calls,
>   The flowers sigh, 'it is snowing'.
>   And yet we carry the flame with joy.
>
> 2. Winter comes, the snow falls,
>   The flowers wither in the earth.
>   The ice is not thawed by weeping for Balder
>   The tears freeze in the cold.
>   And yet we carry the flame with joy.[17]

The first two verses tell us in the simplest terms that all things die in autumn. The tears of sorrow which the season brings themselves stiffen and become dead. Even the heart's compassion is frozen. The flame which is carried through the winter night has many meanings. Perhaps its most literal reference is to the torches and candles which people carried through the early dark to the service held on Christmas Eve, and which then served to light up the church and make it festive. This practice of carrying light through the winter darkness was of great significance for Grundtvig. It seems to have been common in pre-industrial Europe. The Danish practice is exactly paralleled in the lights which were taken through the dark very early on Christmas morning to the plygain services in eighteenth century Wales.[18]

> 3. The solstice comes, the leaf is turned,
>   The days grow longer again.
>   The sunshine grows and winter ends,
>   The larks sing in the sky;
>   Therefore we carry the flame with joy.

> 4. The years change for fear of old age.
>   The poets are in accord with them,
>   All the birds moult every year
>   Or else they cannot fly freely,
>   Therefore we carry the flame with joy.

The return of spring brings with it the promise of new life; but the carefree happiness soon passes. This life in time is caught up in a constant returning circle of birth and death. We hurry on under the pressure of impending old age. The poets are bitterly conscious of the transitory nature of things. Always we must be moving on; like the birds abandoning the comforts of our former habits if we are to fly at all.

There follows the central verse of the poem. In the original surely the finest and most striking stanza, in which the poet's role is first fully acknowledged and celebrated:

> 5. The birds fly like wind on the wings
>   Freely over the wild sea,
>   Poets fly as the rhymes ring
>   Smoothly over the graves of generations.
>   Therefore we carry the flame with joy.

The poet carries the flame across the ages, linking century to century, generation to generation with living bonds of understanding and love. Commenting on this verse, Andreas Haarder says 'The key note is *coherence*'. The difficult word *sammenhæng* (which I have here translated in this way), can also mean consistency, context, connectedness, it is a very rich word in the Danish language. 'Whatever does not rhyme cannot be carried further.'[19] Only what makes sense, what resonates, what awakens an echo in the other can be carried across the gulf of the years. Here Grundtvig the translator speaks from his own deep experience. He speaks out of the labour of his work with the old Norse texts and the medieval Latin chronicles, bringing them alive for his frequently heedless contemporaries. He speaks out of the labour of his work with the ancient hymns, Greek, Latin and Anglo-Saxon, bringing them to life again against all expectations, in the worship of ordinary Danish congregations. But all this is precarious. Affirmations may be made, light does conquer darkness, but never without anxiety, uncertainty.

> 6. Hearts stagger, when they beat high,
>   Are drawn to the track of the birds.
>   Yet light conquers; the dark thought
>   Fleeing sinks in the earth.
>   Therefore we carry the flame with joy.

But now suddenly the mood changes, we are no longer alone or even in company with a few friends on the shore of the northern sea in winter, with the snow falling and night coming on. Certainly it is still winter and night-time but now at the heart of the darkness there is the bright light of the church shining out. We hear the clear sound of the bells ringing and we hear voices singing.

> 7. The hymns resound, the bells ring out
>   Mock the Christmas snow.
>   Winter must rhyme itself with spring
>   Melt before the sun which is hiding;
>   Therefore we carry the flame with joy.

The church is not only before us, warm, light and full of song, we are drawn into it. Now we are entering another world. The sun which is there, hidden behind the clouds, the divinity of the Son hidden in the flesh, melts the ice of winter, makes winter rhyme with spring; the passing of time is redeemed. 'Mid-winter spring is its own season' (T.S. Eliot). The two following verses speak repeatedly of hearts that believe, who have entered into the mystery of faith.

> 8. Hearts that believe, in the course of winter
>   Give birth to the delight of spring,
>   Clasp it to themselves in swaddling clothes
>   With a happy new year.
>   Therefore we carry the flame with joy.

> 9. The child of Bethlehem in the crib,
>   He is the eternal spring.
>   Believing hearts have gathered that
>   Christmas makes a happy new year.
>   Therefore we carry the flame with joy.

Christmas makes a happy new year. One could not have a better example of Grundtvig's amazing capacity, to take the simplest most ordinary, everyday, used up words and fill them with incalculable meaning. This is indeed transubstantiation. The daily bread of language becomes the vehicle of divine truth and life. It is the birth of the Christ-child in the darkness of winter, which makes our new year a source of gladness. The birth of the eternal Word at the lowest point of time, alone in the end conquers the iron law of time and death, creating in the midst of our world, a lasting spring. Or rather it is he who is that lasting spring. As Grundtvig says in another place, each one of us has his own birthday for sorrow, trouble, defeat and ultimately death. It is the birth which takes place on Christmas night which is for each one of us the moment of our own birth into eternal life. It is the moment of the Word's rising from the grave which is for each one of us the moment of our entry into that life.

We see in this poem not only the way in which in Grundtvig natural and liturgical imagery are combined and interchange, but also the way in which a very personal expression of the mingled joy and sorrow involved in the passing of time and the round of the seasons, comes to fuse with a very direct expression of the corporate experience of the whole Christian people. The solitary poet wrestling with the enigmas of human experience discovers that, despite the barriers of time, words and meanings can be carried across the generations and can rhyme across the centuries. In making this discovery he finds his own story to be part of a longer ongoing story; the story of the faith and hope which moves towards Bethlehem and then opens out into God's future. The joy which is rooted there redeems the ravages of time and thus creates not once but constantly 'a happy new year'.

CHAPTER 12

Advent

We have been looking at the way in which, for Grundtvig, time and eternity constantly interact, in which the mysteries of Christ are made present and active in the lives of his people. We come now to three sermons preached in Advent 1836 at the very start of the Church's year. They underline for us in a striking way, the absolute priority of the divine action as Grundtvig understands it. They show us the imperative need to see the Church's year, not primarily in natural or purely human categories, but in strictly theological ones, for in the things of God we find it is necessary to start at the end, to see everything in the light of the ultimate point to which it tends.[1]

This insistence on the priority of God's action is particularly striking, because as we have seen, Grundtvig allows very readily for the many dimensions of the Church's life of worship; the world of nature comes in, no less than the world of human history. The order of creation and the order of redemption are both involved, and the word liturgy, as we have already noticed, itself speaks of the work of the people. All this is true, but only on condition that before and beyond it all, there is the unfathomable initiative of the divine love, the active presence of God three-in-one.

The first two sermons follow a rather similar pattern. Both begin with a discussion of the gospel passages set for the Sunday in question. In both cases the choice is not obvious. What, Grundtvig asks, was in the mind of 'the Fathers', when they established this order? On the first Sunday we have Christ's entry into Jerusalem, the passage which is also read on Palm Sunday. It might well have seemed more fitting to begin the Church's year at the beginning of the story of Jesus, with the birth at Bethlehem or the annunciation to Mary. He recognises that the major part of the Church's year does in fact follow this narrative pattern, following the story of the Lord chronologically from Christmas to Easter and then on to Whitsun.

This chronological way of doing things is, as he sees it, particularly valuable 'for the childlike and simple'. It is basically a catechetical method, but it does not take us to the heart of the matter. More important is the point which the first Sunday makes; it is the present action of God now in the midst of his people which is the one vital thing. Certainly the Christian year contains an element of historical commemoration within itself, but that is not the whole of the matter, nor even is it primary. Grundtvig sums up his vision in the words, 'The past is only important for us for the sake of the present and the future.' Thus the first sermon becomes a powerful expression of faith in the present action of the Holy Spirit as the foundation stone of Christian worship.

The gospel for the second Sunday in Advent is no less surprising from the point of view of historical commemoration. It is the passage in the twenty first chapter of St. Luke which speaks of the Son of Man as 'Coming in the clouds with power and great glory.' Here we are seeing everything from the end. As in the previous sermon Grundtvig takes familiar biblical material and gives it a startling new interpretation. The coming of Christ at the end of all things is only incidentally a coming in judgement. It is before all else the coming of Christ in triumph into the presence of the Father, the entry into the kingdom of heaven. It is a moment of ultimate fulfilment. Here is the inner and eternal significance of the story of the entry into Jerusalem which was read the week before.

If the first sermon had concentrated on the person and work of the Holy Spirit, the second concentrates on the person and work of the Son, he who dwells within us, the hope of a glory to come. Here again the sermon is turned towards the future. It is not difficult to see where the third sermon will take us as we follow this trinitarian pattern, in the Spirit, through the Son to the Father. This sermon is full of the thought of eternity; it is an extended meditation on the primordial mystery of the divine love, the love of the Father. For Grundtvig, it is always the Father who is understood as love, and of that love we are here and now made participants. The sermon concludes with the words, 'Here at the Lord's table, we receive from the Father the love of Christ which ever unites us with him.' These three sermons taken together give us a remarkable statement of the meaning of faith in the tri-une God, and in the divine action as a reality of here and now.

I

So it is with these words that the first sermon begins, 'Hosanna to the son of David, blessed is he who comes in the name of the Lord, Hosanna in the highest.'

This popular acclamation of Jesus of Nazareth was, as we know, heard between the Mount of Olives and Jerusalem, through the streets of the capital right up to the temple and in the temple itself, from the voices of children, at the time when Jesus went up to Jerusalem for the last time, to the feast of the Passover. He went up, as Luke writes, in order to be taken up, indeed to be raised up as a prince and saviour at God's right hand, but first of all, as he himself said to his apostles, to fall into the hands of sinners, yes of devils, to be betrayed to the high priests and to the scribes, condemned to death and handed over to the gentiles, to be mocked, beaten and crucified. Therefore this gospel is read on the Lord's day which is still called Palm Sunday in memory of the palms which the people scattered in that thorny and royal path.[2]

At first sight, therefore, it seems unreasonable that the fathers also began the Church's year with this reading, but just because this strange arrangement is so striking it cannot possibly have escaped their attention. For that reason we can be certain that they had good reasons for what they did, even though we cannot understand them, yes even though they themselves could not have given us any other reason, except that it seemed that it must be like that! Among us Christians the question is not how much or how little any one of us knows or understands or can clearly express himself on any particular thing; rather the question is if the hidden man of the heart is precious and worthy in the sight of God, as the apostle writes, and the Holy Spirit bears witness. Now, that hidden man of the heart, who shed tears every time he vividly considered what the Lord had to suffer for our sakes, and who on Palm Sunday looked not at the palms scattered at the Lord's feet, but at the cross hanging over his head, that hidden man of the heart has, under all skies, and not least in our sea-girt fields and meadows, rejoiced numberless times at the great Hosanna with which the Church's year began and announced the coming of Christmas with all its heavenly joys for the believing and childlike heart. So I can dimly remember how wonderful it still sounded in my childhood, when they sang on the first Sunday in Advent 'Rejoice now bride of Christ' with the blessed refrain 'Hosanna, glory and honour shall be to this King.[3]

It certainly does not follow from this that Christians to the end of the world will necessarily begin their church year with this same reading, for Christ makes no-one a slave but loosens all the bonds of the soul ... and with us far too little of the Holy Scriptures is read in the public service of the Holy Church. So it must be arranged otherwise in the future; but I suspect that even then the Church will want to begin its year with this old reading on account of the sacred memories it evokes ...[4]

Grundtvig thinks that at all events Christians will want to use this gospel reading before they come to the chronological account of Jesus' life, because it contains such a powerful reminder that all that Jesus did for us in the past must become living for us in the present through the action and gift of the Holy Spirit.

This is the Christian foundation truth, the ultimate force from which come all the living springs of water, which on the first Lord's day in the Church's year we will unforgettably impress on believers who have not yet understood it, and which we will renew and strengthen in the minds of those who already possess it, for we could not possibly find a word in the whole of Holy Scripture which we would rather pray to the Holy Spirit to enliven and inscribe, as the finger of God, on the tables of the heart, than this great Hosanna to the son of David, blessed is he who comes in the name of the Lord, Hosanna in the highest.[5]

Why, for Grundtvig, are these words so vital and why have they come to take such a central place in the worship of the Church? Hosanna, in Hebrew, means 'save now' and Christian worship, this word tells us, is about salvation and about salvation now, it is about the presence and activity of God himself, in the midst of his people, for it is he alone who can bring salvation, and it is about that presence as a contemporary reality. The Church's worship is rooted in the past but it lives now towards the future. As Grundtvig will say in a subsequent sermon *'The past is only important for us for the sake of the present and the future'*. It is in the Church's worship that the risen Christ comes to meet his people and that his people become contemporary with the events of the gospel. It is here that the gulf between past and present which was felt so acutely by the theologians of the nineteenth century and has not ceased to be felt ever since, is constantly overcome through the power of the Spirit. It is here that we become contemporary with the events of the gospels, both as gathered congregation and as individuals within the congregation.

Here, as in many places, he speaks not only out of the experience of his childhood, but out of the experience of the Church through the ages. For in all the varieties of eucharistic worship in a divided Christendom some things remain remarkably constant, in particular the central place given to the thrice-holy hymn of the angels, 'Holy, Holy, Holy' and the following acclamation 'Hosanna in the highest, blessed is he who comes in the name of the Lord'. Why should these elements remain firm when so much changes? They speak to us of foundation truths which are so basic as to be often overlooked. The cry Hosanna speaks of the nowness of God's action and its speaks of it in a cry from the heart, a cry to God to act now, and more precisely a cry to God the Holy Spirit to make his presence known in the midst of the congregation.

In this passage therefore, Grundtvig stresses that the note of invocation or epiklesis is central not only to the Church's worship but to the whole of the Church's life, the epiklesis of the Holy Spirit to come and make his dwelling with us. Here again Grundtvig shows himself unexpectedly close to the tradition of the Eastern Christian world. As the Anglican-Orthodox International Commission pointed out

Although the epiklesis has a special meaning in the eucharist, we must not restrict the concept to the eucharist alone. In every sacrament, prayer and blessing the Church invokes the Holy Spirit, and in all these various ways calls upon him to sanctify the whole creation. The Church is that community which lives by continually invoking the Holy Spirit.[6]

How far Grundtvig can have been aware of the specifically Eastern Orthodox theology of the action of the Spirit in Christian worship, is difficult to say, but its basic principle is clearly central for him. The importance of this invocation lies in the fact that it signifies the nearness of God's action to his people. It gave him a way of speaking of that overwhelming sense of the intimacy of the divine presence in the life of the Church and in the life of humanity as a whole, which is one of the most striking characteristics of the whole of his theology.

So he continues,

What is it other than the cry for salvation to the Son of God and of Mary, our King at God's right hand, the cry which every Lord's day will fill his house and which will at every moment echo in the secret chamber of the heart? This is a cry not of despair but of childlike faith and trust, daily filled with joy, peaceful even in the midst of anguish, because the heart feels *he is mighty, he is near, he is good and his mercy endures forever* (my italics). What is it that makes our heart able to believe this Hosanna to the son of David, what is it that makes us able to put our firm un-shakeable childlike confidence in his salvation, now and in eternity, what or rather *who* (original) is it who does this? Is it not he the blessed one who comes in the name of the Lord with the kingdom of our father David, the kingdom of God's be-loved son. And Christian friends, who is this blessed one who comes in the name of the Lord?[7]

He is the Holy Spirit.

So, for Grundtvig, it is the Holy Spirit in person who works all these things in the midst of the Christian people. Words which are usually taken to apply to Christ are applied to the third person of the Trinity who comes in the name of the Lord.

Who is this blessed one who comes in the name of the Lord? Is it one of us, even if we come to you as the obedient servants of the Word, with the word of faith and the gospel of peace, and will know nothing among you but Jesus Christ, born under the law and laid in a crib, the crucified one? …

No, it is no human agent who can bring this fullness of blessing, it must be the Holy Spirit himself

who comes in the name of the Lord, bringing the fullness of the blessing of his gospel, yes, who comes with the kingdom of God, which is righteousness, peace and joy in *the Holy Spirit* [Romans 14:17] (italics original). Yes, here we have named him with his own words, with the humble description he gives of himself, not with the world's false humility as if he should deny his own power and behave as if he effected nothing, but with the true divine humility he has learnt from the Son who sought not his own glory but the Father's who sent him. For thus the Spirit seeks not his own glory but the Lord's and Saviour's who sent him and so it is with the Father, in the eternal days of his kingdom, he does not seek his own glory but bids all the angels and nations and languages eternally praise his beloved Son in whom he finds his good pleasure and praise his Holy Spirit, through whom he has worked all things in all. So the Holy Spirit comes to us divinely humble, not in his own name, but in the Lord's name, just as the Lord comes in the Father's name, and when he is about to describe God's kingdom the Spirit begins not with himself, although it is he who creates it in us, but with the kingdom as the home of righteousness, peace and joy and he names himself at the end so that we can know with whom we shall seek and find it.[8]

At the beginning of the Church's year we have then this remarkable piece of trinitarian theology. It is a living trinitarianism in which the interchange of the divine persons is described in terms of the humility with which they give way to one another, and in which this movement of giving way to one another is seen as the basis of their dwelling in us and ours in them. The ancient doctrine of the mutual indwelling of the persons of the Trinity in one another, known by the Greek term *perichoresis*, comes to life in this presentation of it. The humility which we see in the person of the Son of man, the humility of the one who empties himself in order that he may take the form of a servant, reveals to us in a unique and particular way something that is eternally true of the relations of the persons of the Godhead with one another.

In words of the greatest simplicity Grundtvig shows us something which is true of the nature of personal being as opposed to individual being, at every level, divine as well as human, something of the way in which persons dwell in one another and make place for one another. He shows us that this is as true on the level of divinity as it is on the level of humanity. Just as the divine persons live in a mutuality of exchange and love, so it is that we are called to live together in Christ and in the Spirit in the mutuality of the Church, making way for one another in love. This indeed is how all Christians should be towards one another. It is in a very particular way how the ministers of the Church should act and be in face of the divine action, ever more transparent and humble. That it is not always so now and has not always been so in the past is palpably evident to him, but no less he declares that this is how it should be.

It is therefore in no way sufficient that we in our way of speaking give the Holy Spirit the glory for all that we achieve, for he will in no way take the shame which is the greater part of things and which alone belongs to us, no, we will give him his glory again and take the shame and blame on ourselves, by teaching the congregation to recognise the blessing which he brings every day, so that they can distinguish it from all that we do on our own behalf. It is therefore not sufficient that we insist that it is only the Holy Spirit as the great messenger who comes in the Lord's name who is able to bring you the kingdom of God, which is righteousness, peace and joy. No, we must tell you where and how he brings the Kingdom — the Lord's life in holy baptism, the Lord's light in ordination, the Lord himself in the holy Supper in Jesus' name Amen.[9]

Grundtvig here declares that the preacher must explain to the congregation where and how it is that the Holy Spirit himself comes as Christ's messenger. He does this very briefly but quite decisively by pointing us to the sacraments of the Church. It is there in baptism and the eucharist, in the actions given us by Jesus Christ, that the Holy Spirit is present and made known. This is a point which he will take up again in the third sermon. It is not at all by chance that to the two great sacraments of the gospel he here adds a third rite, giving us an interesting and for him most unusual juxtaposition of baptism, ordination and holy eucharist. It is unusual for him in that in his writing the middle term of the triad is much more often filled by prayer, the Lord's prayer in particular, than it is by ordination. Here he seems to be thinking of ordination as itself a gift of the Spirit, indeed we may dare to say as a gift of a sacramental kind, a gift which in a very decisive way demands to be received in terms of this humility of mutual giving.

II

The opening of the second Sunday's sermon makes these points yet more clearly. It is as if in the intervening days Grundtvig's thoughts on the way in which the Church's year should open had developed very rapidly. Now he has no hesitation in commending the traditional order of readings. The end must come first. He does not of course deny an element of historical reference in the liturgy, its reference back to the things which happened in Judea and Galilee. The early centuries of the Church were right to make the main course of the Church's year, from Christmas through Easter to Whitsun, follow the historic course of the life and ministry of Jesus,

the old, long past, yet eternally note-worthy and unforgettable days, so fruitful for salvation, when the Word became flesh and revealed his glory, a glory as of the only begotten of the Father

As he said before, there is an educational purpose in this arrangement. The Church does this principally for the sake of children and for the sake of child-like faith, following

the Lord's course through life from the stable and the crib to the cross and the grave, through hell to heaven, so as in due order to await with the apostles the Father's promise, the Spirit who proceeds from the Father, and whom the Word promised to send to those who believe in him, as their advocate and comforter forever.

Nevertheless the early centuries were even more right not to begin simply historically, not to begin the year 'with Zachariah in the temple or with the annunciation to Mary' but with the Lord's entry into Jerusalem.[10] We have already recognised, he says, that they were justified in doing this and so we were led to see Jesus' entry into the holy city itself from two different sides, the one temporal, the other eternal, the one sorrowful, recognising that he is going to his passion, the other joyful seeing him as entering into the eternal kingdom which the Father prepares for him. Grundtvig insists that it is this second meaning which is the vital one.

This is the eternal joyful side in which this entry represents the great festival in the city of Sion, with the establishment of David's kingdom, and the Holy Spirit's coming in the name of the Lord for endless comfort and redemption.

The choice of the entry into Jerusalem as the gospel for the first Sunday in Advent came not from the inspiration of an angel but from the inspiration of the Holy Spirit.

Yes, we will today add that this feeling was not only right, but so deep that it could scarcely have been caused by an angel troubling the waters, but only when the Spirit himself who searches the deep things of God, moved the depths of the human heart, so this is for me one of the great proofs that while our Sunday gospels, as we now have them were not the Church's readings from the beginning, yet they are a precious survival from the public worship of the apostles' days ...[11]

That Grundtvig may be historically inaccurate in this particular point is surely less interesting than his conviction that the traditional patterns of Christian worship contain insights and understandings which go back to the very origins of Christian history.

So the gospel for this second Sunday in Advent is again a passage which speaks of Christ coming into his kingdom, this time in terms of the Lord's coming on the clouds in power and great glory in the end of all things (Luke 21:25-36). It is, he maintains, no less appropriate than the former Sunday's gospel. Here still more it is made clear that we are seeing everything from the end and not from the beginning.

Just as it is natural, yes spiritually necessary that the Christian people should begin their year with praise to Christ's divine viceroy on earth, who not only comforts us during the king's absence but makes us happy to feel that this absence is in the end only apparent, all the time we have his Spirit with the divine authority, the Spirit who can and will unite us with the Father and the Son, with whom he himself is and makes us divinely one, so it is just as natural and spiritually necessary that each year we should begin with a living hope of the king's public and solemn home-coming, with great power and glory, his home-coming on the clouds which form his triumphant chariot, with all angels as his servants and all saints as his followers.

For it is not in Christ's kingdom, as it is in the kingdoms of this world, that on account of the present viceroy one forgets the absent king, as has happened in Christendom only when men tried to create for the Lord a kingdom of this world and gave it a viceroy. No, the viceroy whom God himself has established as the Spirit of truth can neither lie nor boast and as the Spirit of love who proceeds from the Father, he cannot abide those who forget the Son, even though they should overwhelm him, that is to say the Spirit, with the most flattering praises![12]

For this reason, after the first Sunday, when we have celebrated the coming of the Spirit himself and his work of uniting us with the Father and the Son, it is only right that now on this second Sunday we should hold a feast of expectation, looking toward the coming of Christ as king who we know is to come though we do not know when.

We saw in the first sermon how Grundtvig took the familiar words 'Blessed is he who comes in the name of the Lord', and gave them a totally

new meaning by applying them to the Holy Spirit rather than to Christ. Here
he acts in a very similar way. He takes the gospel passage which speaks of
the coming of the Son of Man in judgement and makes it speak rather of the
coming of the Son of Man into his kingdom in triumph. He is showing us
that we should not think of the last day principally in terms of judgement,
still less of condemnation, even though of necessity he says it must be that for
the unbelieving world for whom it will seem to be judgement and
condemnation. For the Church, for the people of Christ, the last day must be
seen as a time of fulfilment, the triumphal entry of the king into his kingdom.
This is the eternal and joyful side of the event which in time we celebrate on
this Sunday. So if the first Sunday had been the Sunday of faith and had
centred on the work and presence of the Holy Spirit, this Sunday is the
Sunday of hope which centres on the person and action of Christ in us who
is himself our hope, the hope of a glory to come (Colossians 1:27). It is only
in the strength of the first Sunday, that is to say in the power of the Spirit,
that we can proceed to the second.

Grundtvig goes on to say that in the order of Christian faith and life, faith
always comes first and is followed by hope. So again he insists that to make
of the last day simply a day of judgement is to mistake its nature altogether.
It is so necessarily, 'for the unbelieving world, but in no way for Christians,
whose great, whose eternal victory is precisely this, that the Lord comes again
to judge the living and the dead, wherefore the Lord also says 'When these
things begin to come to pass then look up and raise up your heads for your
salvation draws near.'

Yes, when our life which is hidden with Christ in God, shall be revealed with him,
then shall there be gladness, both as there is in summer and as there is in harvest.
As the corn and the flowers teem up from the earth and cover it, so shall the dead
rise up like waving corn fields, after the seed has rotted in the graves, the seed
which was sowed in dishonour and now rises up in glory. The harvesters are ready
and the angels will harvest and gather the wheat into the houses in the Lord's
chariots of cloud, gather them into the starry barn, and then we shall harvest the
fruits of the tree of life in the paradise of God.[13]

The fear of judgement has been transformed into a joyful expectation of the
coming of an eternal spring and an eternal harvest. One is reminded inescapably of the figures of the angels of the last day to be found in one of Rub-
lev's frescos, serenely joyful figures who look almost like a personification of
the spring.

Grundtvig allows that the Lord's coming in judgement cannot be altogether without fear. For only love in its perfection casts out fear entirely.

And our fear of doomsday is much greater than it ought to be because love is much
less than it ought to be, but we shall thank God, and with him, our fathers and
mothers in their graves and in their unseen lodging places with the Lord, because

the hope of God's glory has not been altogether lost in the fear and terror of judgement day, while the world both laughed and mocked at both. Yes my friends, the Scripture teaches us that the hope of God's glory in the time of the new covenant is Christ himself, as he is spiritually born within us in baptism and daily grows in his faithful people ...[14]

From a Sunday which celebrates the gift of faith and centres on the work of the Holy Spirit, we have come to a Sunday which anticipates Christ's entry into his kingdom in glory and therefore centres on the gift of hope. We thank God and we thank our fathers and mothers in their graves, who have lived in God and who still live in God, and in whom God lives, that this gift of hope has never altogether been drowned by fear of the day of judgement.

III

If the opening of the first sermon has been hesitant, and the opening of the second full of conviction, the opening of the third is a curious mixture of the two. The gospel for this Sunday should give us a sermon about John the Baptist, for it contains the passage in the gospels in which John bears witness to Jesus. But it is clear that the internal development of Grundtvig's thought is leading him elsewhere, to the final statement of his view of the trinitarian basis of Christian worship, the Church's worship as based in the action of God the Trinity now. So John the Baptist provides Grundtvig with a starting point, but no more than a starting point. For he at once goes from the witness which man bears, to the witness which God bears, and he looks again at the way in which the persons of the Trinity bear witness to one another within the coinherence of the divine life. Here, as in other places, he confirms the words of Scripture with the words of a popular proverb. It is a very characteristic strategy for him.

If it has become a proverb even in the world that 'all good things are three', then how much more should it be used and followed in the Lord's house and in the Church of Christ. Not only because the so-called great festivals are three, but insofar as there are three that bear witness in heaven, the Father, the Word and the Holy Spirit, though these three are one, and there are three that bear witness with us on earth, the Spirit, the water and the blood. Although they all work together for one end, yet their effects on earth are also three, i.e. faith, hope and love, which only when that which is perfect is revealed fuse together into one, that is to say in love which is the only one which never ceases. Yes, with us certainly, all good things are three, and therefore there should be at the beginning of the Church's year, not two but three Lord's days, as festal exceptions to the historical order, which our thoughts otherwise rightly follow through the seasons.

For these three, faith, hope and love, which still are and constitute till the end of time all our Christian strength and good fortune, which prepare us for a blessed eternity, not only merit each on its day to be constantly impressed on the congregation and brought to their mind as the only true and living Christianity, but their joyful remembrance must, at the beginning of each new year of the Church, become vivid and living and strengthening among us in the same degree as light and life grows within us. For thus the deeper we may feel and the clearer we may see that although the ground of all our Christian good fortune in time and eternity was laid in the ancient days when the Word was made flesh and dwelt among us and the wellspring of our eternal life was made open when the Lord rose up from the dead, ascended to heaven and sent his Father's life-giving Spirit, these things can neither profit nor rejoice us if faith, hope and love do not make us vitally participant in good fortune and life; yes all that is past is dead and powerless for us, with the fathers who have fallen asleep, unless we have the life-giving Spirit and the Lord with him who awakens from the dead everything which he will.

But when we now speak of faith, hope and love we are not like those who beat the air, for we neither imagine that we can catch them out of the air nor that they are airy shadows drifting in what is undefined, which we commemorate, praise and commend under these great names. No, it is the definite Christian faith which we all confess; it is the hope of eternal life and the hope of the glory of God that springs out of it; it is love to him who loved us first and to all that is born of him, love for the heavenly Father who so loved the world that he gave his only begotten Son that whoever believes in him shall not perish but have everlasting life. For this faith, hope and love, which are the living expression of our Christian childhood, youth and manhood, we naturally give thanks first of all to the three witnesses on earth, the Spirit, the water and the blood, but not as if they were things which we could expound on our own account and according to our own ideas, but things which refer back to the living remembrance of his wonderful deeds in former times and the unchangeable means of grace given by him for the completion of the good work, the means of grace which the Lord instituted in his Church on earth. So these three witnesses, the Spirit, the water and the blood are for us the living pro-clamation of the gospel of our Lord Jesus Christ, our baptism with water and the Spirit and our participation in the one bread and in the cup of blessing at the Lord's table as the communion of the true body and the true blood of Jesus.[15]

Thus in this sermon Grundtvig insists again that the trinities of which he is speaking, the trinity of faith, hope and love, the trinity of the Spirit, the water and the blood, the trinity of the three persons of the divinity; Father, Son and Holy Spirit, are in no sense abstract or indefinite. He is talking not in terms of speculative philosophy but in terms of historic Christian witness and experience. There is almost certainly an element of polemic here against any form of speculative, philosophical theology, a thing not uncommon in nineteenth century Germany, a theology involving a kind of intellectual dialectic which would make the doctrine of the Trinity the final term of a fully developed human speculation 'worked out on our own account and according to our own ideas.' For Grundtvig the doctrine of the Trinity is anchored in the historic Christian Church, in faith in Jesus Christ come in the flesh, in the sacraments which are a constitutive part of the Church's life and structure. Thus this is a faith which is rooted in baptism and fulfilled in the supper of the Lord.

So it therefore follows that if we are to begin both our Christian life and our Christian enlightenment from the right end, then we must begin with him who came in the Lord's name, with the Holy Spirit who preaches the gospel and speaks not of himself but calls to mind all the words of the Lord and seeks not his own glory but that of the Lord who sent him, and when we have received from this Spirit the faith which resounds in our confession, then he brings us to the Lord in baptism where we receive the hope of God's glory and fly with it to the ends of the world, when he shall come again to judge the living and the dead. Then we are brought by him to the Father in whose name he came, in whose place he judges, in whose house he has prepared a place for us, making us to sit down at table with Abraham, Isaac and Jacob. And here, at the table of the Lord, we receive from the Father the love of Christ which forever unites us with him. Amen, in Jesus' name.[16]

In the first of these advent sermons Grundtvig had spoken of the coming of the Holy Spirit as the key to Christian worship. All the commemorations of the Church's year, all the things concerning Jesus from the Annunciation to the coming of the Spirit at Pentecost, are not to be understood only, or primarily, as historical events in the past. They are historical events in the past, that is true. But they are also present and eternal realities at work in the life of the Church and of each of its members, and this is the thing which matters most to those who live now. In the second sermon we saw how the reference of Christian worship is not only to the present and to the past. It is no less vitally to the future. What we do in the Church's worship helps us to grow in the knowledge and understanding that Christ himself is born in us and that Christ in us is the hope of a glory to come. Therefore our Christian worship is also forward looking. It is an anticipation of the home coming of Christ and the end of all things. It looks towards his entry into the kingdom of heaven, a kingdom from which neither his earthly people nor his earthly creation are excluded.

These two Sundays, which dwell first on the present action of the Holy Spirit awakening in us the hope of a glory to come and then revealing to us the presence of Christ within us and amongst us, lead us on to a third Sunday in which much of what has been said earlier is recapitulated and confirmed. But here the main aim is the movement towards the Father. The Spirit leads us in the Son, to the Father. It is the love which the Father has which draws all things to himself. It is in love that faith and hope find their fulfilment. The clear trinitarian structure outlined in the first sermon, in which we hear of the humility of the persons of the Godhead making way for one another, and of the humility of God himself in making possible the redemption of his creation, all this is here worked out more fully and is directly rooted in the Church's sacramental life and practice. Time and again in this sermon Grundtvig emphasises in opposition to any kind of speculative doctrine of the trinity that it is not any Spirit that he speaks of, nor any Christ. It is the Christ who was incarnate of Mary at Bethlehem, it is the Spirit who was given to the apostles in Jerusalem at Pentecost, to whom the whole

Christian tradition bears witness. It is this Christ who is speaking and working through his Spirit, leading us to the Father.

In the eucharist the life given in baptism, the life which grows through the expectant prayer of the Church and is guided by the inspired ministry of those who have received the Spirit's light in ordination, is nourished and finds its fulfilment. In a most remarkable way Grundtvig ends his third sermon by showing us the Holy Spirit leading us to Christ in baptism and Christ leading us through our Christian life into the Father's house where he has prepared our place and sits us down at table with Abraham, Isaac and Jacob. Then he concludes with the simple but all inclusive affirmation, 'And here, at the table of the Lord, we receive from the Father the love of Christ which forever unites us with him. Amen, in Jesus' name.'

The table of the Lord is here and now. Already here and now we are brought by anticipation into the banquet prepared for all when all things are brought to completion, when heaven and earth, things human and things divine are brought together and fused together in love. *Guds paradis jo nu er her.*

IV

The overwhelming message of these three Advent sermons is to do with God's presence with us now. He is mighty, he is near, he is good and his mercy endures forever. In answer to the cry of the heart, to the cry of the whole creation, Hosanna, Save now, there is the Advent of our God. In recalling the deeds of the past we discover that the acts of God are eternal and present. The past is only important for us for the sake of the present and the future. Rejoicing in this presence and activity of God now we look towards a future when our life which is hidden with Christ shall be revealed with him. Then shall there be gladness, both as there is in summer and as there is in harvest.

Even more powerfully, and certainly more succinctly than in his sermons, Grundtvig expresses these convictions in his hymns. Amongst them there are hymns like the first to be given here which adapt material from the period from before the Reformation. Here we have echoes of a carol welcoming the New Year which speaks of the people's hope for the time which is coming. There are also hymns, which like the second and longer piece we shall quote, are more immediately and deeply rooted in the Bible. This, one of the greatest of the Sunday hymns, gathers up the exaltation of the Old Testament psalmist in one of Grundtvig's most ecstatic utterances.

These hymns were not written by a man living in retirement, seeing visions and dreaming dreams, a man unrelated to the burdens of the common life of his time. They were written in the thirties by a man who in these very years was fully immersed in a national struggle to find new ways of education to fit people for the task of responsible democracy, a national struggle to maintain the identity of a small nation in the face of an expansive and uncomfortably large neighbour. It is in these circumstances that Grundtvig is able to look to the present and future with hope, and to express that hope in a form which speaks not for himself alone but for a multitude of others. He can look out in this way because he finds in the year, feast by feast, Sunday by Sunday, day by day, hour by hour the coming of God.

> 1. Welcome to you, year of the Lord
>   Welcome here with us,
>   Christmas night when our Lord was born
>   Then light was kindled in the heart of darkness
>   Welcome New Year, you are welcome here.
>
> 2. Welcome to you, year of the Lord
>   Welcome here with us,
>   Easter morning when the Lord arose
>   Then the tree of life put down roots in the grave
>   Welcome New Year, you are welcome here.
>
> 3. Welcome to you, year of the Lord
>   Welcome here with us,
>   Whitsun day when God's Spirit came down
>   Then God's power descended to our frailty.
>   Welcome New Year, you are welcome here.
>
> 4. Welcome to you, year of the Lord
>   Welcome here with us,
>   The year of the Lord with our God's good pleasure
>   Now brings us joy every day of the Lord.
>   Welcome New Year, you are welcome here.[17]

In this hymn we see very simply how the entry of eternity into time enables us to live the passing of time with confidence and joy. Every year the Church celebrates the three great feasts, Christmas which brings light into darkness, Easter which brings life out of death, Whitsun which brings strength to our weakness. But this threefold cycle of celebrations is repeated week by week in the keeping of Sunday, the first day of the new week. And the joy of that new day is not confined to one day in seven, it overflows into the whole passage of time.

The second hymn makes the same affirmation in greater detail and with more subtlety. It is, as we have said, among the greatest of Grundtvig's Sunday hymns. While in no sense simply a paraphrase of the last eleven verses of Psalm 118, it nevertheless follows the psalm closely, especially in its affirmation that this is the day which the Lord has made, and in its cry of exultation, Hosanna, Save now.

19. Open for me the gates of righteousness,
    I will enter into them;
    I will offer thanks to the Lord.
20. This is the gate of the Lord
    He who is righteous may enter.
21. I will give thanks to you, for you answered me
    And have become my salvation.
22. The same stone which the builders rejected
    Has become the chief cornerstone.
23. This is the Lord's doing
    And it is marvellous in our eyes.
24. On this day the Lord has acted;
    We will rejoice and be glad in it.
25. Hosanna, Lord, Hosanna!
    Lord send us now success.
26. Blessed is he who comes in the name of the Lord;
    We bless you from the house of the Lord.
27. God is the Lord; he has shined upon us;
    Form a procession with branches up to the horns of the altar.
28. You are my God, and I will thank you;
    You are my God, and I will exalt you.
29. Give thanks to the Lord for he is good;
    His mercy endures forever.[18]

There are a number of vital points here which turn on the translation of the Hebrew. The older translations in Greek and Latin, and they are followed in this by the older translations in our vernacular languages, read at verse 24 'This is the day which the Lord has made'. A more recent study of the original has led translators to prefer 'This is the day in which the Lord has acted'. Both renderings are possible and both can support and complement each other. As we have seen, Grundtvig's sermons are full of the thought of the present action of God, and in this sense, although the version which he knew is the older one, the newer one supports his interpretation strongly. Verse 23 perfectly represents his fundamental attitude; again, at verse 25 the older translations have tended to render the Hebrew directly, 'Save us now Lord, Lord grant us salvation', and in at least some of the modern versions, as here, the original Hosanna is kept. Just as verses 24 to 25 are centrally placed in this section of the psalm, so their content is central both to the psalm and to Grundtvig's reading of it.

Of course Grundtvig's hymn is through and through christological and trinitarian. To him, as for the whole Christian tradition down to his time, the latent meaning of the old covenant is only revealed and made plain in the new. The opening of the temple gates of Jerusalem, allowing the worshippers to go into the holy place, the place of God's presence, is here understood in terms of God's own action in Christ, opening to all who believe in him the gate into heaven, the eternal place of the fullness of God's presence. The reversal of human decisions, and of human perspectives, by which the stone which the builders rejected becomes the chief cornerstone in the temple, whatever exactly we understand the original reference to have been, for him refers at once to the exaltation of the Word of God on Good Friday and Easter. The thought that verse 24 speaks of the day in which God has acted rather than the day which the Lord has made, in fact fills the whole of the second stanza of Grundtvig's hymn and is worked out in some detail. God is at work on Sunday, his people in their millions — there is a nineteenth century touch in this reference to millions, as in Schiller's 'Ode to Joy'; the human family was becoming more aware of how rapidly it was growing — people in their millions are rested and refreshed, precisely because their part in the day is only responsive. The initiative is God's, and the work is his. In the Church's worship, in the preaching of the word, in the singing of God's praises, it is the Spirit who speaks and strengthens God's people, giving them the blessing of peace.

The point is made again more insistently in the last verse of the hymn. The sacraments themselves, in the original *dit bad og dit bord*[19] are active in such a way that God's people are able to understand and experience that it is the Word and the Spirit, God himself who is speaking and singing. The substance of Christian prayer and liturgy is God's work and not our human activity or speech. We have a part in it, a necessary and a vital part, but again our part is that of response, a response called out by and sustained by God's prior activity in Christ and in the Spirit. These are affirmations central to the whole Christian tradition of prayer, corporate and personal. They are rooted in the New Testament itself, for example in the eighth chapter of the epistle to the Romans, and have been remade in many ways through the course of Christian history. Here they are affirmed anew with inimitable force and emphasis.

But there is one phrase on which we have not yet commented, the words which I have translated as 'With the consecrated tongues'. The translation I have given is purposely somewhat bland, and is intended to suggest that the tongues referred to are those of the whole Christian people, consecrated to God by their baptism. That interpretation is, I am confident, perfectly possible but perhaps it is not altogether adequate. It is possible to give another translation, which would be more controversial but which I am now inclined to think might be more correct, that is 'With the ordained tongues' or 'With the tongues of the ordained'.

For a variety of reasons, not least because he felt that the Oxford Movement was making a fatal error in making the Church depend on the ordained ministry, rather than the ministry dependent on the Church, as time went on, in the thirties and forties, Grundtvig was inclined to say less and less, theologically, about the role of the ministry in the Church. As a result one has a curious ecclesiology in which the celebration of the sacraments is absolutely vital to the being of the Christian community, but nothing is said about the ministry which presides at those sacraments, which pours the water on the child's head at the font, which picks up the chalice and patten on the holy table. It looks as though, at this particular moment, Grundtvig's mind was working rather differently. At least for a moment he looks at the place of the ordained ministry within the worshipping life of the Church, the place of those who have to proclaim the word of God and actually perform the acts which are central to the celebration of the sacraments. The Holy Spirit, as he says in the first of the Advent sermons, brings us the kingdom in three ways, granting us 'The Lord's life in holy baptism, the Lord's light in ordination, the Lord himself in the holy Supper in Jesus' name.'

As we have already noted, such a reference to ordination, immediately between the two gospel sacraments is, in Grundtvig, very unusual. It should perhaps be seen in connection with the phrase about the tongues of the ordained in this hymn, written in the same period as the sermon. It is precisely through the gift of the ordained ministry, when it is properly lived and understood as a ministry of service and not domination, that we discover in the Church's life and worship that it is not we ourselves but the Spirit and the Word who are speaking and acting. The ordained have their necessary part to play in enabling the whole of God's people to discern between what is human and what is divine.

This is in one sense a detail, though not an insignificant detail. The main substance of what Grundtvig is saying is, however, clear and incontrovertible. It may of course be nonsense. The public voice of our largely secular society would be obliged to say that it is nonsense, nonsense and potentially dangerous nonsense, because in these last two stanzas Grundtvig is employing all his not inconsiderable skills as a poet to say that human life finds its fulfilment in a literally ec-static movement of praise. Ec-static that is in its original meaning, taking us out beyond ourselves, into a life which is eternal and divine. Only in that ec-static movement does human life discover its true purpose and potential.

> 1. This is the day that the Lord has made,
>   This gladdens the hearts of his servants;
>   Today he opened the gate of heaven,
>   This every Sunday resounds;
>   For in these thrice sacred hours
>   Triumphant from the grave, God's Word arose
>   Gracious from heaven his Spirit came down.
>   Now do you see why the bells ring?

> 2. Save us now Lord give good fortune and luck,
>   The work today is your own;
>   Let millions thank you at evening
>   For granting them rest and refreshment.

Yes, let them praise with rejoicing
The Spirit who freely speaks and comforts,
Blessing the people in your name
Showing your peace to be present.

3. Lord our God, visit us in your glory
Wherever in your Church we meet.
May our tongues weave you crown upon crown
Just as our hearts are on fire.
May the festival grow with the day,
Easter and Whitsun grew out of Christmas,
So let the joy which was hidden in faith,
Ask in vain for its equal.

4. Yes, let your font and your table so work
With the consecrated tongues
So we may hear that your Spirit and Word
Are those who are speaking and singing.
Yes, let us feel it and taste it
The Spirit is better than flesh and blood,
The Lord is delightful and in every way good,
He crowns all our days with his gladness.[20]

CHAPTER 13

Christmas

Christmas was, and still is in Denmark, as in other Northern European coun-tries, the most popular of the Christian festivals. Indeed it is the only one which in our late twentieth century, despite all its secularisation and com-mercialisation, remains in some ways a major public event. It is a festival which mingles sacred and secular in a great variety of ways. Centering on the birth of a child, it is of course, in a particular sense, a festival for children. It is a moment when parents try to provide some special delight for their children, especially for young children. It is again a time of singing, when popular hymns, carols and Christmas songs still convey something of a sense of tradition when the past comes alive.

Clearly, in Grundtvig's Denmark, both in the village of his childhood and in the city of his adult years, Christmas remained a festival of great sig-nificance. For Grundtvig himself it awoke vivid memories of his childhood at Udby. As we know, for him childhood was a very special and a very important time in human life. It is not surprising that some of his most popular hymns are Christmas hymns, and particularly his Christmas hymns for children and about children. One of the best known of these was written as early as 1810, before the moment of his return to Udby and his experience of an evangelical conversion. Throughout his life from the beginning to the end, Christmas was important for Grundtvig. But here at the outset we meet a difficulty, for there are elements in these hymns which in translation can scarcely fail to sound sentimental, images which remind us too readily of the prettiness of conventional Christmas cards. These are problems which we shall come to in due time.

Grundtvig himself was not unaware of a tendency, even in his own time, to trivialise Christmas. It is perhaps not a mistake to see the opening of his first Christmas sermon at Præstø in 1821, his first sermon as an incumbent of his own parish, as a reaction against any such tendency. What is evident is that it is a highly solemn as well as a strongly theological statement of the meaning of the feast. When one remembers that it was preached in a pro-vincial market town on the coast of Zealand, south of Copenhagen, its highly structured quality is even more striking. Grundtvig is not going to speak down to his congregation; he wants to give them the full weight and glory of the occasion. We begin with the prayer before the sermon and note its carefully worked out trinitarian structure,

Hallelujah. Heavenly Father, you from whom all fatherhood takes its name, in heaven and on earth, and who loved us so beyond all measure that you gave your only begotten Son, so that whoever believes in him should not perish but have eternal life; pour out now in Jesus' name, your Holy Spirit into our hearts, so that we can learn truly to value your unspeakable grace, and honour, thank and praise you for it in time and in eternity. Yes, grant him to us, your Spirit of truth, that he may enlighten us to know your living word and your eternal truth in the child in the crib, to see the light of the godhead in the face of our Lord Jesus Christ your image. Grant us to have him in our hearts, the Spirit of grace and comfort, of peace and joy, so that we, reborn as your dear children in Christ Jesus, with childlike faith and hope and Christmas joy, may follow the song of the angelic host, 'Glory to God in the highest', and go singing along the way of life, which your Son has opened up for us into the sanctuary, to the paradise which he has opened anew for us, until there with angel tongues we shall sing before your throne the new song which you yourself will place in our mouths, to the praise of your love, to the expression of our blessedness in your fellowship, O our God, you who are Father, Son and Holy Spirit, praised to all eternity. Hallelujah, hallelujah.[1]

This prayer already tells us much. At Christmas we celebrate the mystery of the incarnation. God the Word takes flesh of the blessed Virgin Mary. A new covenant, a new relationship, is inaugurated between God and humankind, indeed between God and all creation. This event, or rather this series of events, is not an isolated incident in the past. It is the beginning of something radically new which goes on now, our adoption as God's children, our new birth in Christ through the work of the Holy Spirit. This adoption allows us to live as God's children now. We can live our life in childlike confidence in the Father, and this implies living our life in time already in communion with the life of heaven and eternity. In our life on earth paradise is already being opened to us. This, as we shall see, is one of the most persistent themes in Grundtvig's preaching. Here and now we can begin to share in the joy which shall be ours in its fullness only beyond this world of space and time. We have here a realised, or perhaps better, an anticipated eschatology.

I

The sermon itself opens in an unusual way. The preacher reads to his congregation the whole of the last three of the Old Testament psalms (148, 149 and 150). We need to remember that, because the daily Offices fell out of use in the Lutheran world, much sooner than in the Church of England and its sister churches, the Old Testament psalms are not nearly so well known among Lutherans, even among regular church goers, as among Anglicans. There is moreover a point of terminology which is of interest here. The Danish word *salme* means hymn. To speak of the Old Testament psalms one has to use a phrase such as 'David's psalms'. As we might have guessed these psalms were of the greatest significance to Grundtvig. As he himself grew as a hymn writer and as a translator, he seems more and more to have found himself identifying with the Old Testament psalmist and taking up his characteristic themes. Here he quotes verses which stress the cosmic significance of the event which is being celebrated. All the heavens, all the earth, join in this one act of praise. So after the reading of the psalms the sermon begins,

Oh friends, to this the angels answered in today's gospel, 'Glory to God in the highest'. But we too are encouraged by the heavenly notes of David's harp, to praise the Lord, in communion with the whole creation, in chorus with everything that has breath. We are encouraged to praise the Lord for his marvellous acts and for his salvation upon earth, and when, my friends, should we feel ourselves more awake, more in tune to praise the God of our salvation in holy songs of praise, than today on Christmas Day? Christmas Day, which from generation to generation, is hallowed as a solemn memorial of the favourable time, the day of salvation, the great and blessed hour when the heavens literally proclaimed God's glory on earth and when the night became as day, darkness as light, when celestial spirits in their garments of light came down to proclaim with joyful voices, the great saving message which day shall proclaim unto day unto the ends of the world, yes which eternity itself should gladly re-echo, the wonderful gospel that the virgin has born a Son whose name is Emmanuel, that is God is with us.[2]

The preacher could hardly underline more strongly the universal nature of the feast. All creation is involved in this birth, heaven and earth together. He dwells with evident delight on the participation of the angels in the Christmas story. For him the angelic hosts are a vital part of the whole Christian scheme of things, our association with them is a sign of the opening of the way into paradise here and now, for as he says in another place 'A paradise without angels is like a wood without birds, or a beautiful hymn which no-one sings or hears'. To him too it is significant that Christmas occurs at night time and in the dark. This is the moment when night turns to day, when darkness turns towards the light. It is indeed the moment of a new creation, when again God says, let there be light. Finally he underlines the fact that this is an event whose meaning grows, a feast which re-echoes down the ages, which is passed on from generation to generation, above all in the repeated songs of praise.

But if the opening of Grundtvig's Christmas sermon at Præstø in 1821 has a solemn and weighty feel to it, we find a somewhat surprising change of tone in the sermon for the following year, this time preached to the congregation of his church in Copenhagen. Here, in an urban milieu which we might imagine would be more sophisticated, Grundtvig seems to wish to invoke the popular, informal quality of the feast, its character of unrestrained and spontaneous excitement and joy. Here he starts, not with the last three psalms of the Old Testament, but with the traditional words of popular Christmas greeting.

'Happy feast, happy feast; happy Christmas and a blessed New Year.' These are words which we have all said and heard very often, but it is with these words, as with all words; they are known as they resound. So Ethan also sings 'Blessed are the people who understand the joyful sound, Lord, they shall walk in the light of your countenance, they shall rejoice in your name all day long' (Psalm 89). The deepest and finest words which are perfectly formed to express spiritual things and to enliven their hearers' thoughts about them, lose their life and power when they lack their right resonance and tone; for the tone is the life of the word, and the resonance is the power of the tone which reveals the Spirit.

Perhaps that sounds strange to many people, though it is something we all know, a quite well known thing, which only sounds strange because, alas, we realise so little of what we have learned, consider so little of what we say. Who does not know that when we talk together the tone is the most important thing in our conversation, and that it can give words a meaning they otherwise would never have, that it can turn the most outspoken words of praise into scorn and mockery? Thus tone is the life and soul of speech, and if this is the case in small things, in talk of earthly and visible things, how much more is it the case in the great, in talk of spiritual and invisible things, which words can only describe in a shadowy way and which must necessarily fall to the ground when there is neither resonance nor tone to carry them to heaven as on the wings of the Spirit.[3]

It is very striking that this reflection of Grundtvig on the fragility of words, on the way in which they may mean different things, according to the context in which they are spoken and the tone with which they were spoken, should also have a major place in the thought of Keble and Pusey. Here is one of those places where Grundtvig and Keble in particular seem to share a common, poetic sensitivity to the aura which words can carry with them. If both men seem, from a late twentieth century point of view, still extraordinarily and almost naively confident in the power of words to convey meanings and establish conclusions, in divine matters no less than in human affairs, nonetheless at times they come much nearer to our own time in their readiness to recognise how varied and sometimes contradictory the meaning of words can be, and also how much their comprehension depends on the context in which they are used and the tone in which they are spoken or sung; in the end how much they depend on the person who speaks or sings them.

So Keble writes

Consider how very differently the same words sound in our ears, according to our different moods of mind; how much more meaning we find, not only in a text of Scripture, but in a chance passage of a book or a stray remark of a friend, when we recall it by and by, more seriously than when at first we listened to it; nay, and how much beyond what we suspected we discover occasionally in our own words, uttered perhaps at first by instinct, we hardly know how; so that not only are we always uncertain whether any two persons receive exactly the same impression — the same moral impression that is — from any given words, but even whether to the same person the same ideas are conveyed to them twice. And yet there is truth and definite meaning in the words so spoken, although they go much deeper with one man than they do with another.[4]

Grundtvig goes on to reflect on how, in their original usage, the conventional words of the Christmas greeting must have had all the freshness of a new creation. Indeed, he maintains, it was the very strength of their original use which has since turned them into conventional phrases which are handed on from generation to generation. And then there comes one of those amazing moments of personal recall, where we suddenly find ourselves back in a Zealand village of the 1780s. Here we have a picture of very unsophisticated people who express all their pleasure at meeting one another as they come out of church at Christmas time, as they turn towards home, and the thought of Christmas dinner, shouting their greetings, embracing one another. Surely here too we see the astonished observation of the small boy, overwhelmed by the size and the sound of so many grown-ups, deafened by the volume of their mutual greetings.

From this note of village rejoicing, Grundtvig passes at once to the thought of how the generations gone by still greet us through the centuries in their Christmas hymns and carols, songs which resound through the years. It is a reflection which may easily come to us also perhaps at the end of the twentieth century as on occasion we are almost choked by the transparency and spontaneity of the joy which is conveyed from the past into the darkness of our cynical and sometimes despairing spirits by popular and traditional Christmas carols,

> On Christmas night all Christians sing
> To hear the news the angels bring
> News of great joy, news of great mirth
> News of our merciful king's birth.[5]

Happy feast, happy Christmas and a blessed New year. These deep beautiful words are therefore now nearly always mere formulas ... but it was not always so; for at least we know that the one who first used these words as a solemn greeting, was not following a form of words, but spoke from the Spirit's urge and the overflowing of the heart. Only afterwards it became a custom of words, handed on from generation to generation among millions of people to greet one another with the same words. This fact witnesses with what tone, with what a beautiful resonance these words were once spoken first of all; so spoken that they should find so sweet an echo in their hearers' hearts and on their tongues.

So it is, my friends, that there certainly was a time when crowds of people met on Christmas morning and competed with each other in wishing each other a joyful feast, and all their faces lit up as the words were repeated and the sound got louder and louder and moved all hearts to join in a joyful hallelujah. This is so much the more certain, since the bygone generations in spirit and in truth wish us such a joyful feast with the delightful sound of their Christmas songs and hymns about the child born in Bethlehem and the joy of all Jerusalem. But to hear this greeting from the past, to feel how sweetly its echoes move the heart is something we learn late, if it has never sounded through us in those childhood days, when the heart is tuned with it. But if it has been so, then we are lucky; for as we feel the lack of what we have lost, so the slumbering notes will awake again on our lips and break out with a joyful resonance, so that it shall be heard from our greeting that the heart takes a living part in this joyful feast which we proclaim.[6]

At this point Grundtvig shows us something of his understanding of the popular nature of Christian tradition. The continuity of the Church's life and worship is not only, or perhaps even primarily, to be found in its regular, ordered ministry or in its systematic teaching of the gospel. It is also to be found more democratically expressed in the songs of praise which belong to the whole Christian people and which echo back and forth across the centuries and across the generations. Here again we find new insight into the importance of hymn-writing in his vision of things. It is clearly important for him that this popular song of praise is something which undergirds the divisions of Church history and can be heard across the chasm made by the Reformation, and across all the differences of theological understanding which have followed in the centuries after it.

It is for this reason that Grundtvig's adaptation of popular pre-Reformation hymns and carols is particularly significant at Christmas. Here is one such carol which he had first prepared for use in 1820. It was twenty-five years before it truly came to life in the worship of his congregation at Vartov in 1845, causing something of a commotion to the staid Danish gathering that year, as more and more members of the congregation got caught into the tune and began to sound out the hallelujahs at the end of each verse,

> A child is born in Bethlehem,
> Jerusalem rejoice at it.
> Hallelujah, hallelujah
>
> A poor virgin hidden
> Gave birth to the king of heaven's son.
> Hallelujah, hallelujah
>
> He was laid in a crib,
> God's angels sang with joy
> Hallelujah, hallelujah
>
> Wise men from the East
> Offered their gold, incense and pure myrrh.
> Hallelujah, hallelujah

All our afflictions are now overcome
Today for us a saviour is born
Hallelujah, hallelujah

We are again God's dear children,
We shall keep Christmas in heaven.
Hallelujah, hallelujah

On light blue carpets of stars
We there gladly go to church
Hallelujah, hallelujah.

God's angels there at once teach us to sing
As they sang that night.
Hallelujah, hallelujah

Then we shall become angels like them.
God's kindly face we shall see.
Hallelujah, Hallelujah

Him be praised eternally
For our strong saviour, our kind brother.
Hallelujah, hallelujah.[7]

This hymn and these sermons were written early in the eighteen twenties. It was, as we have seen, a decade which ushered in rapid changes in Grundtvig's life and thought, seeing the publication of one of the greatest and most original of his poems, and certainly one of the most controversial and powerful of all his occasional writings. It was at this time that he wrote a Christmas hymn which has been, ever since, one of the most popular of all his compositions. It is a hymn which seems at first full of a childlike joy. It is only at the end that we gather something of its depth and darkness. If the writer of the hymn has recaptured something of the joy of the child's Christmas, he has not lost the grief and longing of the adult whom he has become. The two things are reconciled within him.

With this hymn there are more than usual difficulties of translation and interpretation. There are lines which it is hard to prevent sounding sentimental in English. There is the whole question as to who the small angels are who take such a central part in the poem. In so far as angels have any place at all in a Christian imagination today — and they certainly do not have a large place there — they tend to be thought of as large and impressive beings. The baroque *putti* of counter-Reformation art are almost our only models of small angels. But they hardly fit into our picture of the Danish countryside in mid winter! Edvard Lehmann saw in the angels, in these verses, a christianised version of the spirits of the departed, who were sometimes supposed to visit the house at Christmas time in medieval Scandinavia. Others have suggested that the background to these little angels is to be found in the popular belief that the *nisser* 'the little people', the 'leprechauns', come to visit us at Christmas time, and that as long as they are well received, with bowls of porridge and cream and butter, prove generally benevolent.

The role given to the angels in Grundtvig's hymn, singing to the children, playing with them, promising a good year for birds and seeds, certainly seems more consistent with this second interpretation; they are friendly spirits whether of earth or of heaven. Above all it is the children who are more likely to see and understand the *nisser* than the grown-ups are. It is not of course suggested that Grundtvig's angels are nothing more than *nisser* slightly Christianised. As in other places the presence of angels on earth tells us that paradise is already made known. But it may be that the thought of friendly earth spirits provides a background to these verses, a natural preparation for the arrival of friendly spirits from heaven.

Either way this is a poem which celebrates the recovery of a childlike faith in the union of heaven and earth, of God and humanity, in the birth of the child at Bethlehem. It celebrates this recovery of childlike faith but without in the end sacrificing the complexity of adult experience,

> Welcome again God's little angels
> From the high hall of heaven,
> Wearing your sun-bright robes of light
> In the dark valleys of earth.
> Despite the hard frost you promise a good year
> For birds and seeds lying dormant.
>
> Well met on the road to church
> Across the snow at midnight,
> Do not have the heart to refuse our welcome.
> We dare trust you not to do that;
> Do not pass by our door,
> Do not cause us that distress.
>
> Our cottage is low and so is our door,
> Only poverty is within,
> But you have visited such places before,
> That is something we remember.
> If the cruse is earthenware, the bread is dry,
> Yet angels are to be found there.
>
> With friendly blue eyes
> In their cradles and their beds
> We have children in every corner,
> Like flowers which grow in the meadow.
> Oh sing to them as the larks sing
> A song they have not heard for a long time.

So they dream sweetly of Bethlehem
And even if it is still dark,
Yet they dream truly of the home of that child
Who lay in the crib.
They dream that they are playing at Christmas with those
Whose song they have heard.

Then they will wake gently with the dawn
And no longer count the hours,
Then we shall hear the Christmas song anew
Which rhymes with the rhythms of the heart,
Then it will resound sweetly through high heaven
When the Christmas bells ring out.

And then suddenly Grundtvig takes off. The harmony of heaven and earth in the celebration of Christmas leads to the thought of Jacob's ladder where the angels ascend and descend, as a type of the incarnation, of the coming in flesh of the Son of God. As a mystery which the angels accompany and welcome, this understanding of the incarnation is found in many places in Grundtvig's sermons. Here the ladder of Jacob becomes a ladder of sound, the scale of notes in the hymn. The angels go up and down this ladder of the Church's worship, carrying our praise on high, bringing God's message to earth. At the top of the ladder heaven's gate stands open, the Lord himself awaits us, gives us the greeting of peace. The kingdom of God comes on earth as in heaven, and heaven and earth are at one. And then comes the final verse with its infinitely more direct petition that we might truly taste that joy in this life, so that our grief, like that of a woman in childbirth, should be turned forever into rejoicing.

Then God's angels go up and down
On the ladder of the hymn tones,
Then our Lord himself bids God's peace
To those who long for it,
Then the gate of heaven is opened
Then God's kingdom truly comes.

Oh if only we could see that joy
Before our eyes are closed.
Then, like the labour of the mother in childbirth
Our pain would be gently cradled away.
Our Father in heaven, may it come about,
May Christmas sorrow be quenched.[8]

III

Grundtvig's famous Christmas hymn of 1824 ends with the thought of the sorrow of Christmas being quenched, the pain of childbirth turning into the joy of the birth itself. This pattern of moving from darkness into light, of sorrow making way for joy, is one which Grundtvig sees throughout the work of creation and he takes up this theme in a remarkable sermon for Christmas Day which dates from 1832, preached on the text from the first chapter of the book of Genesis, 'There was evening and there was morning, the first day'. Grundtvig begins:

So it stands written in the book of creation and we can read it there a thousand times without thinking anything about it apart from the fact that it was strange that it was not first morning and then evening. But if, like the Lord's mother, we keep the word in our heart, and if it then rises up alive from the heart into our mouth, then it will become clear to us that we have never heard a word so unusual and yet so true, so simple and so deep, so short and pithy, in order to express the whole economy of God's grace and his loving deeds on earth, as this little word 'There was evening and there was morning.' Above all it strikes us that we can never express more vividly than in these words what happened in the great Christmas night when our Saviour was born, the marvellous night which the angel of the Lord called day, when he said to the shepherds 'See, I bring you a great joy, for to you this day a saviour is born in the city of David, the Lord Christ.' Yes, here we are reconciled with night and with all darkness in which a star shines, with all except the utter darkness, there where there is weeping and gnashing of teeth; for here it was in every way evening and it became night, the blackest night that ever brooded over the earth but in the middle of that night it became morning when the Saviour was born and his angel stood before the shepherds and his glory shone round about them [9]

Here we see one of Grundtvig's deepest convictions about Christmas, that is to say, about the mystery of the incarnation. God comes to be born in the heart of our world of space and time, at the centre of our human life, in the darkness of night, in the dead of winter. This fact is for him of universal import and in itself it reconciles us to night, to darkness, to cold, to littleness, to death itself, so long as in these things at least a star shines, at least a messenger is found of the greater light which shines in the darkness and is never overcome by the darkness. Only the ultimate darkness of the abyss is excluded from this great affirmation. Here, as always, Grundtvig acknowledges the possibility of hell, and indeed he affirms its reality. There may be, indeed for him there is, a situation which is beyond this law of alternating light and darkness, but it is an ultimate boundary situation. Within the world of human choice and human possibility, not only is the dark not to be shunned, it is to be embraced for there in the darkness we find the hidden promise of light.

This experience of winter cold may be deep and dark indeed. Perhaps our twentieth century has known it even more intensely than the century in which Grundtvig lived. So a poet of our own time can underline the darkness and deadness in which the new and eternal light of heaven is born.

> In the starless night, no moonlight,
> The pit of winter, in the year's
> Senility — behold a baby,
> The Son of Mary. Oh Sibyl,
> The king of heaven was born.

It is striking that for Saunders Lewis, as for Grundtvig, this birth while firmly situated in a particular time and place, in the history of Israel, in the House of David, is yet explicitly of universal import and gives rise to universal acts of praise.

> Let a robin sing in the snow,
> Let Melchior sing to his camels,
> Let Virgil sing with the Buddha,
> Son of Mary, Alleluia
> Eia Jesu, Alleluia
> Praise to his name, all praise.[10]

The three wise men from the East, Virgil with his prophetic eclogue, the Buddha with his God-given wisdom, join with the robin and all the natural world in acknowledging this birth.

All following times have shown that it must be thus here below, especially since the fall of man. First comes evening with a living afterglow of a wonderfully beautiful, paradise day, and then comes morning for those who wait on the Lord. So it went at the beginning of our life on earth, and so it will go at the end when things go best.

And Grundtvig again looks back to his childhood experiences and recalls a saying 'A child is happiest at twilight', a happiness which in those childhood days included both the evening of Christmas Eve and the morning of Christmas Day itself.

Just as we may say of our life until now that there was evening and there was morning, so it is also all that we can wish to be said over us with truth when we have departed out of this life, for when our life on earth is most filled with light and gladness then it is, spiritually speaking, only as it were a Holy Eve, a vigil in which we rejoice in an expectation of what shall come, rejoicing in the hope to see God's glory in which we have believed. So it is our triumph when once it shall be said over us from the Lord's mouth 'it was evening and it was morning for these;

they rejoiced in that prophetic word about my day, as in the light from a lantern, until the day broke and the dawn arose in their hearts'[2 Peter 1:19].[11]

In speaking of the light here, Grundtvig adapts words from 2 Peter, words which follow on directly from the passage in which the writer speaks of the transfiguration, of the divine glory which shines out from the person of Christ. Grundtvig wants to underline that it is an eternal and eschatological glory which is in question here. The whole course of our life on earth, however long it may be, is necessarily brief and fragile, but since Christmas, it has this quality to it that it is always looking forwards, tending towards an eternal day, moving towards an ultimate promise which is not yet fully known. The world's time runs down into darkness and death, the Christian's time turns always towards the future, to the promise of new life. Christmas looks towards Easter, already speaks of death and resurrection.

So as Grundtvig goes on in his sermon, he comes inescapably to the thought of the resurrection and Sunday, the first day of a new week,

So the word 'there was evening and there was morning', hovers not just over Christmas night but over all our days, as many as the Lord has called out of darkness into his marvellous light, so it is no wonder that these words sound out over the whole Church and people of the Lord, throughout the course of time, or to sum up all together into one, that they apply most appropriately to the Lord's day, to Sunday which is the first day of the new week, 'There was evening and there was morning the first day'.[12]

IV

We have seen in these pages something of the variety of Grundtvig's preaching on Christmas Day. There are the solemn doctrinal declarations; there are the rejoicing, the popular singing and the unaffected joy of village people; there are the reflections on the universal law that in God's dealings with his creation light follows on darkness, joy follows on sorrow. But in his preaching at this feast Grundtvig can also concentrate quite simply on the story itself and on the people involved in it. As we shall see in greater detail when we come to look at his sermons for the Annunciation, he is fascinated by the person of the Lord's mother and her part in the whole mystery. And this fascination can come to the fore at times, in his sermons on Christmas Day. This is the case, not least, in 1845, a year when, as we recall, for the first time Grundtvig's Christmas hymn 'A Child is Born in Bethlehem' was sung in the worship at Vartov and caused a great sensation.

'All generations shall call me blessed', said the Virgin Mary in her song of praise, before ever she saw the fulfilment of God's promise. Necessarily the Lord's mother must be as blessed as it is possible for a weak mortal human being on earth to be, with the day spring from on high resting in her lap, he who should be the glory of Israel and the light of the gentiles, he who should as Lord of Lords and King of Kings possess his father's throne to all eternity. It would be impossible to think of a greater joy on earth, and since it rests on eternal truth, how could it ever be taken away? When therefore, we read about all, that, as it explicitly says, gave the Lord's mother sorrow and distress, from the night when Joseph got up quickly and fled with her and the child from the angel of death, until the night which took place at midday, when she stood beneath the cross, the wound in her heart, which bled not less because it was hidden from the world's eyes, when we read of all that, how can we doubt for a moment that the joy which Mary felt, either when God by his angel called back his exiled son from Egypt, or when Jesus, at the marriage at Cana revealed his glory so that his disciples believed in him, or finally her triumphant joy when she saw him who had been crucified, risen, when she saw him whom she had swaddled and laid in the crib ascend beyond all the heavens to his father's house to prepare in those lovely places a place for her and for all who believe in him — yes, who can doubt that the perfect joy with which in God's time she entered into the joy of her Son and her Lord, was in the end the same joy with which she had received the angel's message and with which she had embraced the newly born infant, swaddled him and laid him in the crib, the same joy only tried and tested in many ways, often darkened but through each trial purified and transfigured, once indeed dead and gone but only for a little while, in order to rise up incorruptibly into eternal life, that is to say simply subject to the same conditions as is everything that is clothed in dust, as was he himself, who had the glory with the Father before the foundation of the world, when he humbled himself and became as we are in all things, save without sin.

And as it was now with Mary's joy as a mother, so it is now and always with our joy over the Lord's birth, both with the little and the great, if only they keep the faith, and do not fall in time of temptation, that is as the Lord explains, when the soil in the heart is deep enough for the joyful message, like a heavenly seed, to put down its roots there. Yes, all the sorrow and anxiety which seems to take away the joy of Christmas will only be like clouds before the sun, and when they gather most thickly, as when the sun was darkened over the Cross, yet they soon give way to the perfect joy, the joy of Easter which rises up from the grave:

> As the golden sun breaks out
> Through the dark black cloud
> Shooting out its rays of light
> While gloom and darkness fly.

See Christian friends, we have an image of that and a new security of it in the old Christmas hymns whose joyful sound often sank down in the course of time but always came back again, like angels who descend and rise up again. In the recent times they were dead and gone from us, but now they rise from the dead so that we, like the disciples of old, scarcely dare to believe our own eyes and our ears for joy and wonder.[13]

As in the very first Christmas sermons which we looked at, so here again, in 1845, Grundtvig is full of the thought of the way in which the hymns preserve the living tradition of the Church and echo the joy and thanksgiving of the Christian people across the centuries, linking our congregation now with the shepherds in the fields at Bethlehem. And here as in many other places he seeks to show how the initial joy which is known when God's presence and will are revealed, is not destroyed by the sorrows which follow after in the course of human life, but in the end only deepened, clarified and strengthened through experiences of darkness and loss.

There is, he insists, an underlying unity in the growth of each human life, just as there is in the history of humanity and in the life of the Church. The joy which Mary knows in the resurrection of her Son is the same joy which she had known at the beginning at his conception. The long and in some ways clumsy sentence with which, in this sermon, he expresses this thought, may itself be seen as a way of making the point about the underlying unity which holds together a great variety of circumstances. Form and content here go together, at least in intention. For this joy is itself an eternal thing, a gift from heaven, which yet needs to be tested and filled out through the passage of time and the encounter with sorrow and loss. Only in the perfect union of what is divine with what is human, present and at work in Jesus Christ, can our human life come to its fulfilment. This for Grundtvig was not an intellectual speculation, but a living conviction based on his own difficult and at times stressful experience of light and darkness, joy and sorrow.

It is often remarked that, psychologically speaking, Grundtvig himself was of a manic-depressive tendency. What we see in his preaching, as indeed in his life, is that he succeeded in a remarkable way in holding together the conflicting forces which made up his complex and many-sided nature. So when, towards the end of his life in 1867, the equilibrium which he had established seemed finally to have broken down and even his friends feared that he could never recover his balance, the episode of Palm Sunday proved only to be an episode. As we have seen, after that strange and uncontrolled outburst of rejoicing which was followed by a period of deep weakness and humiliation, within a few months the two forces were brought together again in him, reconciled through some strange inner power of healing.

CHAPTER 14

Annunciation

We have seen that the rejection of any purely abstract view of humanity forms a constant theme in Grundtvig's preaching. It is one of the places where he is most at odds with the spirit of the Enlightenment. He of course recognizes that the human race is one. But he always wants to consider human beings in the particularity of flesh and blood, as this man or this woman located in these circumstances, in this time. Hence comes his sometimes disconcerting insistence on the importance of national identity. Human beings live and develop in particular historically shaped communities which are characterized by their own unique language, the vehicle which conveys their sense of identity and their memory of the past. For him language is a vital and constitutive part of our humanness, for we cannot exist as human beings except as part of a community, a people, except in relation to one another. Thus differences between languages, which do so much to form the character of particular nations, point to permanent differences between peoples and cultures.

But what is true as regards national difference is still more profoundly true of the difference between men and women. To a degree uncommon in traditional theology, Grundtvig sees humanity as embodied either in man or in woman, not in a way that takes little account of sexual differentiation. For him it is clear not only that women and men have different callings but also that they have different ways of relating to God. As we shall see he is often inclined to think that women have a more direct relationship to God than men have. Of course Grundtvig's position on this matter is of his own time and place. If there are some aspects of it that may appeal to contemporary feminism, there are other aspects which are likely to be less acceptable. What is undeniable is that for him the whole question of women and men and their relationship to one another assumed an importance unusual in nineteenth century theology. It led him into areas not much explored by Protestant theologians, and it may still have things to say to us today despite our necessarily different perspectives.

Grundtvig himself was deeply influenced both by the society in which he lived and by his own personal temperament. If he finds it natural to associate women with the human heart rather than with the human head, we have to remember that he lived in a world in which it was virtually impossible for a woman to be a professional scholar or writer. The universities of western Europe had never been open to women and the small openings towards a life of learning which the monastic and religious orders made possible in the middle ages were firmly closed off in the world of the Reformation. It was not by chance that in his later life, Grundtvig became a strong advocate of the education of women. Almost from the first the Folk High Schools admitted young women as well as men.

In terms of Grundtvig's personal character it is clear that all his life he was a man easily moved to the love of women. He had a powerfully emotional nature and he found in feminine beauty a constant source of inspiration. But there is more; he seems to have been a man in touch with the feminine side of his own nature in a way that is not very common. It was perhaps this combination of masculine and feminine elements within himself which was one of the facts that gave rise to his own astonishing productivity. The fusion of male and female within him was extremely fruitful.

In looking at this topic in his sermons and his hymns I shall proceed from the general to the particular. I shall look first at his discussion of the relationship between male and female in humankind and in all creation, then at his view of the place of women in the Gospels, and finally at his attitude to the woman who stood closest to Jesus at his death as well as at his birth.

I

The fact that in the Danish Church the feast of the Annunciation is always celebrated on the Sunday nearest March 25th gave Grundtvig an annual occasion on which these themes would come before him. In his Annunciation sermon for 1836, he begins with a summary of the apostles' creed and then continues,

That, my friends, is in brief all that we believe to salvation, to true blessedness both here and hereafter. This is the faith in which we are all baptized so as to live by the Son as he lives by the Father. Yes, as the Apostle says, not as man's wisdom but as the Holy Spirit taught him, to live no more our own life but his who died and rose again not for himself but for us. This is the depth of the riches of the wisdom of the knowledge of God, which no one can fathom except the Spirit who fathoms all things even the deep things of God, that is the depth of the Godhead, the eternal, incomparable fatherhood, which on earth has its living image only in the motherhood, which is the depth of our human riches, which also needs the heavenly wisdom and knowledge to fathom.[1]

Here at the outset Grundtvig declares that over against God the Creator, revealed as father, humankind discovers itself as woman, as mother, and that just as the divine nature is in itself unfathomable and infinite so too within our humanity created in the image of God there is also an unfathomable depth. For Grundtvig it is love which unites the two:

This is because the heavenly fatherhood and the earthly motherhood have a name in common in which they are livingly fused together, and that name is *love*, the depth of the heart which is obviously unfathomable for human understanding, which in us is a mystery to itself, which can explain everything to us but is itself inexplicable. Therefore the Lord praised the simple and unlearned as blessed, those to whom the Father revealed what had been hidden from the wise and prudent, that is the depth of those riches which one profits from the more, the more unfathomable one finds them to be, when one only believes in them and remains near to them in the way the Lord ordained. For it is the same with the depth of God's riches as with those of humanity; yes, as with all riches, that it is just their virtue that in the passage of time one never comes to the end of them, never empties their treasure chambers.[2]

We have here a typical Grundtvig affirmation of the depth and mysteriousness of our human nature, mirroring the infinity of the divine nature. It is not at first easy to see what are the other human riches to which Grundtvig refers in the last sentence. They are certainly not the riches of this world in the sense of our financial or economic resources. These are not at all endless as the Danish people had felt very keenly at the time of the state bankruptcy of 1814. The clue lies perhaps in Grundtvig's suggestion that we are to remain near to the mystery of God's disclosure of himself to the simple and unlearned and not to the wise and prudent. Human self-sufficiency is always in the end poor. Those who know themselves to be poor and vulnerable find themselves to be rich on account of their openness to the divine initiative. Certainly, as we shall see, it is in this context that he understands the call of Mary, stressing her littleness and her humility and yet seeing in her 'the amazing depth of the human heart, as heavenly as it can be found on this fallen earth.'

   This stress on the littleness of the creation before the Creator can take us further. There are unmeasurable and unsuspected riches latent in the apparent poverty of the handicapped, the marginalised, the unregarded. In the depths of compassion latent in the human heart there are also unforeseen possibilities of growth in understanding and clarity of perception and wisdom, human and divine. In our own time the intuitions and experience of the communities of L'Arche, founded by Jean Vanier, with their varied experience of the gifts of the handicapped, are relevant here.[3] Perhaps in the end we are to understand that in all that God has made, not only in humanity but in all creation, there is an indefinite wealth of possibility and life, and that it is of the nature of the physical universe as well as of the human creation to be an open flexible system, not a rigid and finally fixed one. And so Grundtvig continues:

But, dear Christian friends, there lies in this and there flows from it — from this both heavenly and earthly depth of riches — much, much more than one usually recognises, so that I most strongly wish that I could lay that fact unforgettably in the heart of all my hearers.

There follows from this sense of the mystery of things a reflection on the futility of controversial theology, which is not altogether typical of Grundtvig. As we have seen he was only too likely to become involved in disputes. The combative quality of his nature, his at times naive reliance on the logic of his arguments could easily betray him into controversies which one would have thought he had better avoided. In this sermon he reflects on the quality of mystery as leading us to choose to affirm rather than to deny,

For what evidently follows is that when one has Christian faith and right reason, then one never takes it into one's own hands to fathom the depths of God, and this is so straightforward and clear that both I and the older ministers of the word have repeated it much too often and insisted on it much too strongly, partly because it is unnecessary to say it and even more because it feeds the unhappy pleasure that one takes by nature in pulling down others rather than in building up others as well as oneself. This is a hateful practice which reaches its climax when we seek to build up ourselves by pulling down others, as if we could win a house on the rock for ourselves by scorning and criticizing those who build on the sand, or as if we could become rich simply by scolding thieves.[4]

How deeply ingrained this habit has become in the Christian world in the centuries following the Reformation can be clearly seen in the places where the old adversarial arguments are still commonly used between Catholic and Protestant, as in Northern Ireland. Such arguments are also still in use in the older and no less hardened schism between Christian East and West. They recur in surprising places wherever we are too lazy to discard old and un-profitable habits of mind, at times when we affirm our own position primarily by denying that of others, so that long after we have ceased to be-lieve positively in what is either Catholic or Protestant or Orthodox we know in our hearts that at least we reject the other.

In this sermon Grundtvig speaks of God as Father and of the earth with humanity at its centre as mother; but it is evident that he would not want us to press these terms too hard. In his insistence on the unfathomable character both of God and humanity we have a warning against any too speculative development of this theme, any taking of it upon ourselves to fathom these depths through our over-confident theology. There may be an echo here of older Lutheran reticence about the development of doctrines of divine predestination in Calvinism and a more recent reluctance to become involved in further flights of Hegelian dialectic. What does seem to be present is a desire to underline his belief that the role of humanity and of all creation is to respond to the initiative of God. The heart of God calls out to the heart of the world, calling for a response of love.

II

This theme is powerfully expressed in a long hymn from volume five of the *Sang-Værk*.[5] Here the masculine-feminine contrast is secondary, since the primary image used is that of the word and its echo. But as we shall see it is not altogether absent. The birth of the Word in flesh, demands a mother as well as a father, and the response of humankind is therefore necessarily maternal:

> 1. In the beginning was the Word,
>   Was divinely with God,
>   Went out from the heart, in God's voice
>   Enveloped with the Spirit's power,
>   Created all with divine capacity
>   In the heights, in the depths,
>   Created life and light
>   And in the end created the echoing-word
>   In its own image.
>
> 2. In the beginning was the word,
>   The echoing-word in our breast,
>   Not buried but earthed there,
>   Heaven-born with an earthly voice,
>   Empowered to name all things
>   But not having creative capacity.
>   Yet with humble prayer
>   Able to borrow light and life
>   From God's Word and God's Son.

In creation the Word proceeds from the heart of God. As always for Grundtvig it is the Father who is thought of first of all as love. From the heart of God, the Word goes out enveloped with the Spirit's power. All things are made by the Word through the Spirit, including in the end the echoing or responsive-word in the heart of humanity, 'heaven-born with an earthly voice'. The creative power of this word is not unlimited. It can name things but cannot create them out of nothing. Its own life depends on its relationship with God, on its dependence in prayer on the Son. In the third verse we see that when that relationship is broken, the responsive-word becomes cut off from its origins and loses its creative capacity. It is reduced to a sigh and a womanly sigh at that. The tears of Eve are hinted at here, tears which were wiped away only at the resurrection. However, where even a weak memory of God's voice in paradise is retained, all sense of direction is not lost. And, as we see in verse four, in the coming of the Word incarnate new creative powers are laid on the tongue of dust. At the annunciation Mary responds with her free and obedient *fiat* to the word which God speaks to her. In the life and teaching of Jesus and in his death and resurrection, light and life are brought back into the world of death and darkness,

> 3. In delusion, the echoing-word
>   Was cut off from its root,
>   Uttered only what can be revealed
>   Through flesh and blood,
>   Became a plaything for every wind,
>   Except where in poverty,
>   With a woman's sigh,
>   It fastened itself
>   On a vague memory
>   Of God's voice in paradise.

> 4. But God's Word in the fullness of time
>   Itself became flesh and blood on earth,
>   Let itself be hailed by God's angels,
>   Wrapped in the echoing-word of dust,
>   Laid new creative powers
>   Marvellously on the tongue of dust
>   So that with them the ancient *fiat*
>   Kindled light and breathed life
>   In the midst of death and darkness.

> 5. Then there sprang up for the Word's mystery,
>   Which only God's Spirit can resolve,
>   A new year's time of God's grace
>   When, in the bond of love,
>   The Word of God from on high
>   Humbly united itself
>   In a heaven upon earth
>   With the weak echoing-word
>   On the earth-clod's tongue.

In the concluding verses, Grundtvig declares how at Pentecost the Word of God goes forth again, now in the fullness of the Spirit's power. In the Church and in the Church's sacraments the Spirit and the Word always work together. The Son and the Spirit come and make their dwelling at the heart of the redeemed community. But the history of the Church is not simple. Darkness follows light, the word is imprisoned, almost choked in earth, but by God's gift is finally made free. In the final verses Grundtvig looks to the renewal of the Church's life which he believed was beginning in his own ministry, and was moving towards its fulfilment in God's kingdom, but he warns that only when the word is received and heard at the font and at the altar and only when it is treasured in the heart then will it be clear that God has made his dwelling on earth.

In this hymn we have a whole theology of the call of humankind to become co-creator with God, not on an equality with God but always in dependence upon God. The responsive power given to men and women in the beginning is restored and enhanced in the incarnation. There are new creative powers laid on the tongue of dust. This includes the powers of the imagination, which for Grundtvig no less than for Coleridge are seen as in part divine powers, mirroring the word of the Creator. Here they are given new capacities so that humanity can sing a new song to the Lord.

<h1 style="text-align:center">III</h1>

It is not only on the Sunday of the Annunciation that Grundtvig develops his teaching on the special role of women in the scheme of salvation. He seizes upon the occasions when the Gospel for the Sunday brings a woman to the fore, to take up this theme again. Some of his most powerful sermons were preached year by year on the sixteenth Sunday after Trinity when the reading recounts the raising of the widow's son at Nain. He loves to dwell on the words which Jesus speaks on this occasion, 'Weep not'. They are words of power which are addressed to us now. Another occasion which comes each year is the Second Sunday in Lent, when the Gospel is the story of the Canaanite woman who comes to ask for healing for her daughter, and Jesus responds, 'O woman, great is thy faith.' It is again a word which he loves to expound. For him, faith is above all God's gift to women. And if faith and love are both the properties of the heart, and if the heart is woman's special possession, what is there left for men? So, on this Sunday in 1837 he says,

If we consider therefore what the Spirit witnesses, that faith, hope and love are the three things which include all that is truly Christian within themselves, then it will soon strike us that two-thirds of Christianity are womanly, i.e. faith and love, and that while faith is the first and love is the greatest, hope — which is the manly quality between them — remains necessarily an empty, spiritually dead and powerless fantasy when what is womanly is missing, while the womanly, that is to say faith and love, without help from any man will conceive and give birth to a living hope, just as the Virgin Mary conceived and bore him who will be the hope of glory in us all. This, Christian friends, is the deep reason why the people of Christ on earth are called the bride, and why the Church is called our mother, for womanliness, as faith, stands in a motherly relation to us and, as love, it stands in a bridal relationship to the Lord and this, as the Apostle Paul reminds us, is a great mystery; and while experience teaches us that this truth has been distorted and misused very shamefully, yet nonetheless it remains a divine truth, out of which our Christian life grows, and by which it is fed and develops.[6]

The truth, as Grundtvig declares it here, is that all Christians, men no less than women, need to grow in faith, hope and love, to find ways in which their inner capacity of being born again and of giving birth may be renewed. All have to discover what it means to give birth, and since all are members of the Church which is Christ's bride, all have to share in those virtues and attitudes which are particularly characteristic of women. If for much of Christian history women have been silently incorporated into a religion which has been thought and spoken of almost exclusively in masculine terms, here we see an affirmation of a very different kind, which is also part of the tradition, though an element which is often almost totally forgotten. Here men are to acquire the character of women, and for Grundtvig, as we have seen, woman stands for the heart, for faith and for love and humility. These are qualities which are needed by men as well as by women for any human and Christian growth. But they are qualities which are likely to be despised in a civilization, like that of the nineteenth century, which prides itself on qualities which it thinks are primarily masculine, the use of reason and the cultivation of confident self-assertion; as Grundtvig had already said earlier in his sermon,

We all need greatly to remember this, because according to the natural man we live in a time of reason, when people are constantly tempted to despise the deepest and best feelings of the heart, partly because they are dark, but still more because they are humbling, like those of the woman in the Gospel when she said, 'the little dogs eat the crumbs which fall from their master's table'. Yes, self-opinionatedness and arrogance are nowadays the ruling vices of our world so that everything which is naturally attractive to us has to appear to be crystal clear and to put our own precious personages in a favourable light ...[7]

The feminine perceptions are *dark* and *humbling*. They speak to the hidden, unconscious side of human nature. They relate to the earth, the body, the things that are thought to be low and of little importance, and to that dark but lifegiving aspect of things which Grundtvig spoke about at Christmas. Out of the humble, hidden things a truer perception of light and life can come, for God delights to reveal himself to the simple and unlearned.

More central to Grundtvig's preaching than these general considerations about the relations between women and men, and perhaps of more immediate importance in his work as a theologian, are topics which rise directly from the text of the New Testament itself. Grundtvig is fascinated by the role of the women in the Gospel narratives. So he says in the remarkable paragraph which concludes this Lenten sermon of 1837,

When we now again follow with our Lord on his incomparable priestly way, then we not only find women constantly in his company but we find it explicitly noticed that women from Galilee served him with their belongings and took care of his needs. These are things which most of the men even among his best listeners seldom, if ever, thought about because they lacked the women's love. Again if we ask who was his best listener, we may perhaps think it was the disciple whom the Lord loved, but yet it is only said of a woman, Mary, the sister of Martha and Lazarus, that she sat at his feet and followed his words and according to his own testimony chose the better part which she would never lose.

If we go a step further, to the cross and grave, there we find at the foot of the cross not only the Lord's mother by the side of the disciple whom he loved, but along with that one man a whole company of Galilean women, who were not only with him until they saw him give up his spirit, until his body was laid in the grave, but continued to think only of him. Although they knew that he had been anointed by Joseph and Nicodemus, only the Sabbath hindered them from going at once to offer their own anointing too. Sunday morning while it was still dark they hurried to the tomb to offer him their last respects. Yes, one of them, Mary Magdalene, could not even satisfy herself with the angel's song, 'He is risen', but anointed the empty grave with her tears when she did not find his body. Thus it was the women who saw angels at the tomb, when Peter and John saw only the grave clothes, and Mary Magdalene was the first who saw the risen Lord, so that just as the Lord was born of a woman so the great Gospel about the crucified and risen Lord was born of a woman's lips, while the apostles still doubted. Long live the believing women! Amen, in Jesus' name, amen.[8]

IV

Clearly the Lent of 1837 when this sermon was preached, was a time when Grundtvig's thoughts turned often to this question of the place of women in the Gospel narratives and in particular in the stories of the resurrection, since this was the time when he was translating hymns from the Byzantine office-books. Among them he found a number of pieces which sang the praises of the women who came to the sepulchre bearing spices on the first Easter morning. But his mind also turned at this time to the place of Mary in the Christian scheme of things as a whole, and the Annunciation sermon for this year is amongst his finest statements on this subject.

Grundtvig, so far as I know, writes more about Mary and her place in Christian faith and life than any other nineteenth century Protestant. Certainly among the theologians of the Genevan Reformation I do not think we could parallel his development of this theme.[9] Grundtvig finds it necessary, needless to say, to differentiate his position very sharply from that of Rome. He lived at a time when Christians still felt obliged to distinguish their understanding of the faith from that of their opponents by strong denunciations of the errors of the other tradition. It was a point of honour among Protestants that Rome was in grievous error on the question of Mary. Had not Rome made her into a goddess? Did not the Roman Church indulge in idolatry giving her the worship which was due to God alone? That there was at least some truth in these accusations seems on the face of it probable. That something had got out of proportion in devotion to Mary is recognised implicitly in the documents of Vatican II. But this is not to say that such exaggerations had ever wholly obscured the true proportion of things.

Although this is an area in which Christians of different traditions still disagree with one another, such extreme accusations are hardly likely to be made today, particularly by those who have taken the trouble to examine the matter carefully. But then our situation today is altogether different from theirs a hundred and fifty years ago. It is important to remember that until the earlier part of the twentieth century it was rare for Catholic and Protestant theologians in Europe even to meet one another, let alone to sit down together to discuss calmly the things on which they differ. When at Malines, in Belgium, in the 1920s a small group of Anglican and Roman Catholic churchmen did this they suddenly realized that it was the first time for almost four centuries that such conversations were taking place. They found, as has been regularly the case in the last fifty years when such meetings are held, that though differences do not disappear at once, they are usually discovered to be less absolute and final than had formerly been thought.

I make these points because I do not want to linger over the way in which in this sermon Grundtvig finds it necessary here and in other places to denounce Rome. His protestations are doubtless wholly sincere though they sometimes seem rather routine. He himself had probably never met a Roman Catholic theologian and certainly had never had the chance of an extended conversation with a Roman Catholic scholar of anything like his own ability and range. How far his position on the role of Mary is at variance with that of the Roman Catholic Church, or for that matter of the Orthodox Church, it will be for representatives of those traditions to discern. That there are real differences of theological emphasis and interpretation is evident enough. Whether they are differences of faith which touch the heart of that apostolic faith about which Grundtvig cared so passionately is a different question.

Grundtvig takes as his text the words of the angelic salutation, 'Hail thou that art highly favoured, the Lord is with thee', and his sermon begins,

Christian friends, when we believe that an angel of God, Gabriel, who stands eternally before the face of God, really brought this greeting from the throne of heaven to a Virgin on earth, then we must indeed praise her as blessed, even if we did not know what the result of this signal favour of the highest would be; for life, eternal life is in his good pleasure and there is great joy before his face. Therefore there can be no human being on earth whose eternal happiness and salvation should be surer to us than the Virgin's, whom he who will never flatter and can never lie calls the blessed one.[10]

As we have seen Grundtvig's whole life and teaching stresses the reality, the nearness of God's presence with us. But he is far too good a theologian to emphasise the accessibility of God without at least at times also insisting on his transcendence. So here at the moment when he is about to celebrate the coming together of heaven and earth he discreetly underlines the distance between the two realms by insisting on the intervention of the angel, and stressing the element of transcendence by speaking both of heaven's throne and the face of God in whose presence there is fullness of joy, before whom Gabriel stands.

But of course the angel's salutation is only the introduction. It is what follows which is the real heart of the matter,

> But when furthermore we believe that the Holy Spirit came upon her and that the power of the most high overshadowed her so that this Virgin of the house of David should really become the mother of the saviour of the world, God's only begotten Son, king of the house of David forever, then it is clear as the sun that all Christian generations must, as it says in her own song of praise, call her blessed, since it is not to be thought that anyone who believes and is grateful can dwell on the memory of God's Son, born of a woman, without praising with great wonder the womb that bore him and the breasts which were blessed to nurture him. And that is so much more certainly the case because none of us can remember our baptismal covenant and our common Christian faith without the Virgin Mary at once standing before us, as the one who gave birth to God's only begotten Son on earth, for we all confess our faith in Jesus Christ, the only begotten Son of God the Father born of the Virgin Mary.[11]

In these opening paragraphs, as often happens in Grundtvig's sermons, the preacher evidently chooses his words with special care and precision. It would be difficult to make a more balanced statement of the theological basis on which devotion to Mary both in East and West alike is based. It is impossible, he says, to ponder on the mystery of the incarnation with faith and gratitude without praising the faith and courage of the young woman who gave birth to the Son of man who is Son of God. Indeed, when in the first paragraph Grundtvig said, 'there is no human being born on earth whose eternal happiness and salvation should be surer to us', one cannot but wonder whether he has not hit upon the root out of which, after a very long and complex process of development, the two most disputed Marian doctrines have grown; the immaculate conception and the assumption. The first is an attempt whether wholly successful or not, to articulate the traditional assurance of Mary's salvation. The second is an attempt to express the meaning and the consequences of that assurance for her eternal happiness. I do not for a moment suggest that these implications were consciously in Grundtvig's mind, as he preached this sermon, but it seems at least possible to recognise their presence here.

If the position of Mary is central in this way, then, Grundtvig goes on, you might have thought that the exaggerations of the pre-Reformation past were preferable to the silence of the Protestant present. But Grundtvig will not admit this for, he maintains,

Experience has taught that in the last centuries there has been without comparison much more true and living Christianity where people have almost forgotten the Lord's mother than where people have made a goddess of her.

And it is this, he maintains, that Rome has done, and nothing could have horrified the Virgin more than this,

for what made her pleasing to God was just her faith and hope in him alone, and her humility, seeing God as everything and herself as nothing.[12]

The essence of the Roman error, as he sees it, lies in isolating Mary from her fellow human beings, and elevating her alone to a quasi-divine status, making of her a kind of goddess. For Grundtvig, on the other hand, to understand the mystery of Mary aright, we have to consider not only what makes her different from all other human beings but also what unites her with all her fellow men and women, and that is 'the amazing depth of the human heart, as heavenly as it can be found on this fallen earth.' In her capacity to love Mary stands in solidarity with all creation and reveals its true potential. In another place Grundtvig speaks of Mary as the queen of the heart, comparing her with Abraham the father of faith and John the Baptist the hero of hope. In this context we can see that this title has nothing sentimental in it. It needs to be understood theologically. It is the heart which focuses the response of humanity to the initiative of the heart of God, a response of love to an initiative of love.

So that what made the Virgin Mary acceptable to God and made it possible that she should be the mother of the Son of the highest, was only this hidden person of the heart, which, as the Holy Spirit witnesses, is to be found in all devout believing women and is very precious to God. Certainly this does not make the great mystery of godliness, that God was revealed in the flesh and that God's only begotten Son was born of a woman, comprehensible to us. But it does teach us that there is no unnatural mystery in it, that it has its roots in the whole deep secret relationship which there must necessarily be between the Creator and the creation, made in his image and likeness, a relationship which it is evident we have to be God fully to understand.

To understand what Mary shares with all the other members of the human family, to see her not in isolation, placed on a pedestal, but identified with the hope and longing of humanity, and especially with the faith and ex-pectation of her own people, enables us to see her place in the life and prayer of Christian people today. And to recognize all that unites Mary with us does not mean that we shall fail to see what is specific, unique to her. What it does is enable us to understand that she pleased God 'because she had the most humble, godly, devout and loving woman's heart that ever beat on earth.' It shows us, Grundtvig says, how to value all that is heavenly in Mary without falling into idolatry. Above all, it means that we can,

learn much better to know and follow God's way on earth and his order of salvation amongst all peoples, learn again to value the heart, and especially the devout
woman's heart, at its true worth. Thereby alone it becomes possible that Christ can
rightly be formed within us; for although he will be with us always and will be
reborn in all who believe and are baptized, yet it will always be only to that degree
in which our mothers and the whole people of God have a heart in common with
the Virgin Mary. That is the same as to say in drier words, that Christian hope, the
hope of God's glory which is Christ in us, will always be found to be either dead
or living, weaker or stronger, to the degree in which our faith is more or less a
matter of the heart, childlike, humble and loving.[13]

It would be difficult to express more clearly the reason why in Churches where Mary is explicitly loved and honoured Christian people do not feel that that practice is a kind of optional extra to their religion, but rather is something which in a mysterious way touches its innermost meaning. If Christ is to be born within us, if he is to live in us, then we have in some way to become like Mary. Men and women alike, we have to celebrate the qualities which we see in her, and discover within ourselves possibilities of giving birth which we had never suspected.

To say such things certainly has a traditional, indeed a Catholic, sound to it. Grundtvig himself is aware of this. He admits that to say as he does,

that we can never in a living way express the heart which must reign in Christ's
Church, if he is to be spiritually born and to grow there, without saying that the
Church must be a Virgin Mary,

may easily seem to justify the Roman Catholic view of the whole matter. But, he asserts, this is not so, and he claims that attempts to use the writings of Irenaeus and the apostolic fathers in defence of the Roman position are of no avail.[14]

He insists further on, that the situation was not always so negative among Protestants as it had become by the early nineteenth century. Within the post-Reformation centuries he feels called to distinguish between an early and a later period, and clearly he gives the preference to the earlier time.

But if it is really so that the Virgin Mary as the Lord's mother must be constantly
praised and called blessed in the Church of the Lord, that the Lord's people must
see in her the model they must resemble in order to imitate God and her Son, we
may well ask with full justification how it could be that our Lutheran fathers who
lacked neither humility, faith, nor love, should have been blind to this. The answer
is simple; they were in no way blind and still less unfeeling about this as we see in
the Lutheran hymn 'Mary is a pure Virgin' and in the many hymns among us even

as late as Thomas Kingo, whose hymn for the Annunciation, 'Now came the message from the angel choir', would alone be enough to show how confident our Lutheran fathers were in feeling that the Virgin Mary became the mother of the Lord through that same disposition of heart which must also be found in us if the Lord is spiritually to be born and grow among us.[15]

The last two verses of the hymn of Kingo, which are referred to and which are to be found in the current Danish hymnbook, read,

> O Lord Jesus, may your Spirit
> Powerfully overshadow me;
> Prepare my heart with your hand,
> That you therein may build,
> So that I also may spiritually
> Conceive you
> And never turn from you.
>
> So shall your heaven in me here
> Begin with the Spirit's power,
> My heart and soul and all my desire
> Shall hasten up to God
> Until I become like the angels
> In heaven
> And never sin any more.[16]

Grundtvig goes on to attribute the eclipse of this understanding of the place of Mary to the rationalism of the eighteenth century. In the paragraph which follows we see a typical statement of the things which he constantly reacts against in the religion of the Enlightenment,

The Virgin Mary only disappeared from the preaching and the hymns among us at the same time and for the same reason that all mention of the Church as a living communion, of the congregation as the daughter of Sion and the bride of Christ, and of the Lord as our brother and of us as members of his body, also disappeared; in other words, only in the same degree and for the same reason as living speech about Christ in us and the Holy Spirit with us was silenced and died out, that is to say, in the same degree as childlike and heartfelt faith in God's word perished. So it necessarily follows that to the same degree as this faith again comes to life and grows in us, to the same degree our speech and song must also express the early Christian way of thought and feeling, and we cannot then possibly remain standing at the Reformation which is in no sense the birth of faith or the creation of the Church, but only the first step on the way home to the apostolic Church after centuries of deviation, the apostolic Church where the Holy Spirit is in truth the priest and Jesus Christ the shepherd and bishop, not far from but near to all who call on him, the Lord in whom as Christians we live and move and have our being.[17]

In this sermon Grundtvig has expounded forcibly his faith that if Christ is to live in us, then he must be born and grow in us, and that if this is to happen then the heart of each one of us must become a truly loving and believing heart. That is to say that our innermost being, that which is most characteristic of us as humans and as persons, has to be open for the coming of the divine, and for transformation by the divine. This is a transformation to which we can put no limit. But this, at the same time, involves us in recognizing our littleness, recognizing in particular how little even the cleverest of us know of the mysteries of the world around us and in us, let alone of the mysteries of the world beyond this one. It will involve a willingness to be open and surprised, to acknowledge our need to grow and to learn, and that not only in our earliest years but throughout our life. Implicit here is a view which sees the capacity to grow, to change, constantly to be going further, as constitutive of personal life. There is within the human person a capacity for self-transcendence which gives us a clue to the nature of humanity.

Certainly this faith in the birth of Christ in the human heart or soul, which is implicit in the letters of St. Paul and explicit in the writings of Origen, has a long history in the development of Christian spirituality. Grundtvig longed to renew and reawaken this faith in the interpenetration and interaction of human and divine, this faith in the unsuspected capacities of human life on earth. He longed for these things to become real for the ordinary members of his Copenhagen congregation. Like Eckhart in the fourteenth century Rhineland he was not afraid of confronting his congregation with the innermost secrets of Christian doctrine. We may perhaps conclude that this teaching was not merely abstract for Grundtvig. He himself seems to have had to the end of his long life a remarkable capacity to continue to grow.

V

But if Christ lives and is born in us, we also live and are born in him. Both movements, he in us, and we in him, have their roots in the witness of the New Testament, both in the Pauline and Johannine writings, and the second movement is no less important to Grundtvig than the first. Whereas in the first we are called to realize our likeness to Mary by ourselves giving birth to Christ within us, in the second we find our likeness to Christ by being born with him and finding that with him we have Mary as our mother. Here we remember that it is the Church as mother which gives birth in the waters of baptism. The font becomes the womb in which new life is conceived, as Lancelot Andrewes puts it, commenting on the name Emmanuel,

And this indeed was the chief end of his being 'with us'; to give us a *posse fieri*, a capacity, 'a power to be made the sons of God', by being born again of water and the Spirit; for, *originem quam sumpsit ex utero virginis posuit in fonte baptismatis*, 'the same original that himself took in the womb of the virgin to usward, the same hath he placed for us in the fountain of baptism to Godward'. Well therefore called the womb of the church, *sustoichon*, to the virgin's womb, with a power given it of *concipiet et pariet filios* to God. So his being conceived and born the Son of Man doth conceive and bring forth our being born, our being the sons of God; his participation of our human, our participation of his divine nature.[18]

This side of the mystery is expounded by Grundtvig in an exceptionally fine hymn which dates from this same period of the 1830s. It begins with a reference to the sixty-sixth chapter of Isaiah, in which it is said that Sion gives birth in a single instant to a whole people,

> Shall a woman bear a child without pains?
> Give birth to a son before the onset of labour?
> Who has seen any such thing?
> Shall a country be born after one day's labour?
> Shall a nation be brought to birth all in a moment?
> But Sion, at the onset of her pangs, bore her sons.
> Shall I bring to the point of birth and not deliver?
> The Lord says; shall I who deliver close the womb?
> Your God has spoken.

There follows in the prophet a passage of prophetic exultation in which the abundant maternal imagery reminds us that Grundtvig is not unbiblical in making use of such language to describe the mystery of God's activity. Particularly striking is the use of the image of the child dandled on the knee. In Grundtvig the image of the mother's lap is to be found in many places. If it has no precise biblical equivalent it certainly has some likeness to what is said here,

> Rejoice with Jerusalem and exult in her,
> All you who love her;
> Share her joy with all your heart,
> All you who mourn over her.
> Then you may suck and be fed from the breasts which give comfort
> Delighting in her plentiful milk.
> For thus says the Lord,
> I will send peace flowing over her like a river,
> And the wealth of nations like a stream in flood;
> It shall suckle you,
> And you shall be carried in their arms and dandled on their knees.
> As a mother comforts her son,
> So will I myself comfort you,
> And you shall find comfort in Jerusalem.[19]

1. All Christians have their birthday
   In common with Christ,
   Therefore in the company of his friends
   Great is the joy of Christmas.
   Yes, the whole people,
   Young and old, far and near,
   Are born with their king.

2. Isaiah, now has come to pass,
   What in old time
   Only the prophets saw,
   A wonder without equal.
   Sion, now as all can see,
   Has given birth without birth-pangs
   To children numberless as the stars.[20]

The hymn is a hymn for Christmas. It celebrates the birth of Christ, and in it we see the further development of themes which we have already considered in the previous chapter. Christmas is a moment of great joy. Now at last the common destiny of humanity is fulfilled and human solidarity is restored. This destiny had been frustrated by the fall, with all its consequences, which held the generations of the human race in fear and peril, at war with one another, no longer mindful of their common lineage. Mary's calling and her response is seen in the context of this whole long history of human servitude and destruction,

3. Before with Noah there was born
   A very great multitude
   Whom sin and death
   Always held in fear and peril;
   And from Babel's day till now
   The people of Noah no longer
   Remember their common lineage.

4. But when with his angelic message,
   The Father in the highest
   Found himself a bride on earth,
   Beautiful in his eyes,
   Then, secretly with the Spirit's power,
   The maiden conceived with God's Son
   The whole Christian people.

There follows one of those verses in which with extreme simplicity Grundtvig succeeds in saying a very great deal, a verse which is all the more moving in that it speaks out of a lifetime's experience of pain as well as joy. Each one of us has his or her own birthday, a day which leads to disappointment, defeat, pain, and ultimately death alone. But at Christmas we share in another birth, a birth which brings us out of death into life, out of isolation into communion, restoring our awareness of our common heritage which brings us through hope and love into eternal life together,

> 5. Each of us has his own birthday
>   For this world's troubles,
>   That is for struggle and defeat
>   And in the end for death;
>   But for life and peace and joy
>   Christmas night with the angels' songs
>   Is the hour of our birth.

There follow three verses celebrating the beauty of Mary, who in Christ is the mother of us all. The use of the three Old Testament images in verse seven has behind it a long history through the centuries of Christian praise and celebration. Grundtvig takes them and makes them new.[21] In verse eight we begin to see the same point which was made in the sermon of 1837. Mary is blessed above all, as St. Luke makes clear, in that she is the one who believed, the one who heard the word of God and kept it. It is in her faith that she gives birth. In this sense we may say that faith itself is the great mother.

> 6. Therefore, following the Lord's word
>   As our twin brother,
>   We have no father upon earth
>   But like him only a mother,
>   Only his mother, the pure Virgin,
>   Wonderfully dear to God the Father,
>   Fruitful by his grace.

> 7. She is like the gentle cloud
>   Though melted into dew,
>   She anew in the desert
>   Is the ark with heaven's tent.
>   She is the beautiful gate of the temple
>   Which opens only for David's Son,
>   Who is also God's Son.

> 8. Scornful are the words of unbelief
>   About the beautiful woman.
>   Superstition makes of her
>   A goddess upon earth
>   Faith takes the scorn patiently
>   Is comforted by the king of grace,
>   Is itself the great mother.

Being born of woman, as is each one of us, Christ shares fully in our humanity, our creatureliness, our temporality. He becomes sharer in the love of that tender believing heart, which from the days of creation, in and through the darkness brought about by the fall has never ceased to beat. At the moment of the incarnation all the maternal expectations of the people of Israel are fulfilled. Those expectations themselves are only the focus of the baffled longing which is characteristic of humanity through all ages and all races. Without that remaining trace of divine longing, he implies, the human race could hardly have continued. We should have died of despair.

> 9. Straightway now the thing is clear
>   Which for long was dark,
>   That our Lord has his birthday
>   In common with the flowers of the field,
>   Shares with us as a kind saviour,
>   His mother in dust and earth,
>   Eve's woman heart.

> 10. A tender heart which believes in God
>   Is from the days of creation
>   Mother of kings, an emperor's bride,
>   A queen beyond compare,
>   The pure Virgin of Bethlehem,
>   Sion and Jerusalem,
>   The mother of us all.

It is very clear that Grundtvig will not allow us to see Mary in isolation from all who have been mother, and that he will remind us forcibly that it is by faith alone that she enters into her maternal calling. But at the same time he does not lose sight of her in her particularity, her uniqueness. He is not celebrating abstract principles, but a living person of flesh and blood, who made a unique personal response to the initiative of God,

> 11. The heart beat highest on earth,
>   Turned to God, and bled
>   When from heaven with God's word
>   Gabriel came to meet it
>   Then in secret it conceived
>   God's Son and David's Son
>   Spiritually betrothed.

In the last three verses of the hymn, which we do not reproduce here, it is the Church which is seen as the mother of us all. Grundtvig sees each believing mother within the Church as a representative person by whom the Christ-child is born again in each child who is brought to baptism and thus mysteriously incorporated into Christ. But, in the last verse, we are again reminded of the uniqueness as well as the representative nature of Mary's motherhood. The tender woman's heart, he says, present to a greater or lesser degree in each one who brings her child to birth and baptism, is renowned on earth *almost* like Mary. Mary's role may be inclusive and self-effacing; it is still unique.

Taken together with the sermon of 1837 we have here a very full and balanced statement about the place of Mary in the economy of redemption, and of the way in which we are to relate to her as a model insofar as we are to let the Christ-child be born within us, and as a mother insofar as we are to let our whole life, our birth and our dying, be taken into his. Throughout, Grundtvig has avoided any tendency to isolate Mary from her son or from the people of Israel or indeed from the whole human family. Her part is seen as being that of response; the response of faithful and loving obedience to the prior initiatives of God's will. This means that she is always seen in relation to other greater mysteries than her own, and often she seems almost to disappear. But nonetheless her presence and her figure are still to be discerned; she is present in her silence, her faithfulness and her love. It is difficult not to think that there is theological material here which will be useful in the future, in the dialogue between Rome and Orthodoxy and the Churches of the Reformation.[22]

In the opening years of the second Vatican Council, a Roman Catholic theologian who was to have considerable influence in the council's deliberations, Charles Moeller, published a book suggesting the ways in which the faith should be presented in the twentieth century. Charles Moeller was not at all unaware of the tendencies to exaggeration and disproportion which had marked a good deal of pre-Vatican II Mariology. It was in that context that he wrote,

It would seem that the mariological mysteries tend, just as Mary did in her earthly life, to efface themselves in the light which comes to them from beyond, and with which they shine. They seem to efface themselves for they show us how to go beyond them, not doubtless in order to forget them, but so that thanks to the divine light with which they are filled, we may enter more intimately into the mysteries of Christ, of the Spirit, of the Church, and of the end of the ages and yet, we know that these Marian mysteries, which seem content to gravitate around the greater mysteries are mysteriously the source of these mysteries themselves. If everything comes from the initiative of God in Jesus Christ nonetheless it remains true that without Mary the Word could not become incarnate; there is the unfathomable mystery of the love of God which respects and re-creates his creation to such a point that he has, as it were, need of the *fiat* of Mary in order that the incarnation may take place.[23]

I do not think that Grundtvig would have found it necessary to disagree with that.

CHAPTER 15

Easter

I

Faith in the resurrection of Jesus Christ from the dead, in his destruction of death through dying, is so central to Grundtvig's life and teaching that it is difficult to know how to approach it as a separate topic. Traces of it are to be found everywhere in his writing. I have chosen to examine the theme in the light of three sermons dating from the 1820s and 1830s, Easter sermons which throw a special light on Grundtvig's understanding of the death and resurrection of Christ, and on his vision of the risen Christ as the centre and dynamic power of the Church's ongoing life in time.

The first sermon, which is taken from a volume published by Grundtvig in 1830, is based on the sermon preached on Easter Sunday in 1825. It reveals the new insights on this central point of Christian faith which were to come to Grundtvig in the unparalleled discovery of that year and which were examined in the first chapter of Part II of this book. There is a certain po-lemical element in it in the insistence that the Church is founded, not on the Bible, but on the presence of the living Christ made known in the power of the Spirit in the Church's sacramental worship. There is also a sharp criticism of the flatness of a rationalist understanding of Christianity, symbolised for him by the 1798 Hymn Book, and a less sharp but no less clear differentiation of his own way of preaching the Gospel from that which had been dominant both in the time of Lutheran orthodoxy and in the century of pietism. The second two sermons date from Easter 1837, from the time at which we have already looked, when Grundtvig was working on translations from the Byzantine office books and was increasingly aware of the affinity between his own thought and that of Eastern Orthodoxy.

All three sermons show the way in which hymns form a vital background to his preaching and all three give evidence of the poetic nature of that preaching. This is particularly clear in the first of the sermons at which we shall look, the one published in 1830.[1] In this case, as in that of some of the other sermons which Grundtvig wrote up for publication, we find a style which is more highly wrought and more literary than those of the sermons actually preached. In this case it is also much longer and more fully deve-loped than the original sermon was. I have from time to time set out passages in this text in the form of a prose poem, in this following the example of

Professor Christian Thodberg in his current edition of the sermons. For the sermons as preached, though less elaborate stylistically, are hardly less poetic in form. It is interesting and perhaps not altogether surprising that in this sermon Grundtvig himself finds it necessary to defend himself from accusations of an excessively poetic style of preaching.

In all three sermons we find the idea, which we have already met at Christmas, that it is through the worshipping life of the Church that the living tradition of the faith is carried on. The hymns echo back and forth across the generations and across the centuries; they are the work of the one Spirit making present the triumph of the one Lord. Together with this we find again the conviction that the Church's worship is not a mere recollection of a past event, it is the presence of that event with us now. Most interesting of all perhaps is the absolute refusal to separate cross from resurrection. The resurrection is a triumph over death which is inaugurated in the death on the cross. The element of conflict with death and triumph over death, powerfully present in the old Lutheran hymns to which Grundtvig appeals in the sermon of 1825, is no less present in the hymns of the Greek tradition to which he appeals in the sermons of 1837. This victorious conflict is seen not only as something of one particular moment, but as something which is for all places and for all times; its power and its meaning stretch back into the past and extend into the future.

Grundtvig of course had never been present at the Eastern Orthodox paschal vigil service, that most amazing of all affirmations of the triumph of life over death. In that service a verse from St. John of Damascus is repeated over and over again. It is a verse which makes three simple and clear affirmations, each one of which is vital to Grundtvig's preaching at this feast,

> Christ is risen from the dead
> By death he has trampled down death
> To those in the tombs he gives life.

II

It is not only that Grundtvig had never taken part in the worship of the Orthodox Church, his whole experience of worship, apart from a number of sometimes not very happy occasions in England, was in the context of the Church of Denmark. It was in the parish churches of his native land that Grundtvig had come to know the mystery of Christ, and above all in the villages of Udby and Thyregod where he had lived as a child and as an adolescent. So in this sermon there is much reference to the hymns which were sung at Easter, hymns taken from the old Kingo hymn book, before the introduction of the moralising verses of the new book of 1798, which Grundtvig so greatly resented. Grundtvig had known the old book 'by green beech woods' i.e. at Udby in Zealand, and 'on the barren heath' at Thyregod in

Jutland. Now, however, its contents were to be heard only in Jutland where certain small dissenting congregations called the 'Strong Jutes' refused to use any other hymn book than that of 1699. It is from one of these hymns, a late seventeenth century Danish translation of an earlier German original, that Grundtvig quotes to begin his sermon,

> In death Jesus slept
> In the grave he was laid down,
> But now he has conquered
> All the bitterness of death;
> Now rises up so clearly
> The sun with light and gladness,
> Which in its earthen clothes
> Was altogether darkened.

It is indeed only on Jutland's heath, the Christians amongst us may say with truth, that the fathers' beautiful Easter morning hymn sounds out like this. For only there is it still heard in church after it has been banished with all its family, through almost a whole generation's silence with us, who yet dwell by the lovely woods where the nightingale joins in chorus with the lark, and where one would have thought that such sweet and animating sounds in the dawn of Easter, once heard, could never have been forgotten. Such sounds, one would have thought, must of necessity have transplanted themselves from mouth to mouth and from generation to generation as long as there was in all the wood an eye for May, an ear for song and a heart for longing for eternal life in God's garden.

Yes Christian friends, he who in his childhood days has drunk in, as with his mother's milk, the sweetness of this cup of gladness as I have done, both by green beech woods and on the barren heath, such a one cannot possibly, without a sigh and without pain mingled with anger, think of the Easter hymns we inherited from our fathers and then exchanged, as Israel exchanged its glory, for what, to put it at its kindest, can never profit us, never encourage any Christian soul, never gladden any believing heart. If the action which then was taken could not be revoked, if we and our children were doomed to do without what in madness we have rejected and to be satisfied with what we chose when fast asleep, I for my part would say farewell to the woods and build my nest between myrtle and heather or amongst Norway's rocks where on Easter morning it still resounds,

> Away you sealed stone,
> Which hid Jesus' bones,
> You cannot lock him in,
> God's Son will not so bend,
> You too must learn his strength
> Whose name is ever blessed.[2]

This second verse comes from a long hymn of Kingo's and although this particular verse is not contained in the present hymn book, the hymn from which it comes, or at least six verses of it, is. And then, having quoted Kingo,

Grundtvig bursts out into an exclamation of joy in which the series of scriptural quotations and allusions lead on to an evocation of midsummer in the North, midsummer in which darkness is almost wholly swallowed up in light,

But we are blessed in that we have a God of mercy, yea indeed of great mercy,
Who does not torment and grieve the children of men from his heart (Lam. 3:33),
But whose pleasure it is to overlook transgressions.
Righteousness and judgement are the foundation of his throne,
But grace and truth go before his face,
And so blessed are the people with an ear for the triumph song
And for the hymn of exultation,
They shall walk in the light of his countenance.
Yes, for our God is a God of great salvation,
And with the Lord are the issues of death,
His wrath endures only for a moment,
But with his favour there comes eternal life;
Weeping may last through the night
But joy cometh in the morning.
We are children of his beloved, of the King of kings,
In whose kingdom the sun never sets,
The night is there as with us in midsummer
When evening and morning kiss one another,
And the dawn springs out of the twilight,
Like a rosy cheeked son from the lap of a pale elderly mother,
Yes as Sarah bore Isaac in her old age.
And as the sun arises so do the birds
However short their sleep has been,
And so the morning hymn rises directly out of the echo of evensong.
The evening lark goes sweetly to sleep,
Like a child in its mother's arms,
At the first sound of the summer night's birdsong,
And the morning lark awakens with the last.
Such is the state of Christ's kingdom,
Which not only has a star of blessing,
But a king who commands the sun, the moon and all the stars,
For there grace always goes before justice,
There grow healing herbs for mortal sickness,
There a transfigured life springs out of corruption,
And the people who had grown old becomes young like an eagle.

I know well, dear friends, that such language sounds fanciful and is not unlike that with which both before and now heathen poets have adorned their grey haired idols and tickled the ears of their effeminate kinsfolk in lazy degenerate times. But I have not at all forgotten what befits my grey hairs and how far such empty clangour with its vain hope should be from the Lord's house, from the temple of truth and from the high station of deep seriousness. No, what I have said here is a truth to

which the past bears witness so strongly that it is impossible for the future to deny
it, that is the psalmist's ancient prophecy (Psalm 89) about God's gracious dealings
with his people and the revelation of his fatherly tenderness, a prophecy on which
three thousand years have cast so joyful a light that its entire manifestation in
complete fulfilment is as sure as if we already saw it. The whole of this economy
of God's grace in a sinful world must naturally be still more wonderful than the
Spirit's certainly wonderful course in dust would have been in an unfallen race.

Even the least glimmer of the sun of love in the land of the sinful is something
    strange,
Where after the law of nature only the lightning of wrath should have pierced
    the darkness,
And where not only the voice of the lark or the nightingale,
But even the sparrow's twitter is a miracle,
There where only the eternal thunder of the law
Should have drowned the weeping and wailing and gnashing of teeth.
Therefore friends we can easily see,
That to be a Christian without belief in the Lord's resurrection from the dead,
Is not more impossible than it is
To speak in a living way of the hymns of Easter,
Of the joyous songs of praise of the heart-bird in the sun's uprising,
When it rises up from the gloomy deep of night,
Without one's words sounding still more fanciful
Than the wildest flights of fancy to which man's imagination ever gave birth.
For what the Spirit says to the Church about the great resurrection,
Which holds true for all God's people
Dispersed across the earth and under the earth,
And in the kingdom of possibilities
Which will first become real with generations yet unborn,
What the Spirit says about the Lord's resurrection
Which is for them all, for the whole fallen race of man,
Sent down in death's boundless abyss,
A restoration into the likeness of the creator, to an ascension upon dove's wings
To a royal state in the land of the living,
What the Spirit revealed to the Lord's apostles about this,
And to us with them,
What the Father has granted us in his only begotten,
And what he has prepared for us as his beloved children in him,
That surely is what stands written (1. Cor. 2:9)
'Eye has not seen, nor has ear heard
Nor has it entered into the heart of man on earth'.
In comparison with this
The most daring flights of the human mind
Become like the fluttering of a bat;
The most wonderful poems become small and trivial
In comparison with the simple tidings of what really happened on earth,
When the Lord's angel came down from heaven
And unlocked with the royal key

The sealed door between the kingdom of the dead and the land of the living,
Because the prince of life had come as if by error,
To lie in the chains of death,
Which must necessarily then be broken.[3]

This is indeed to try to overcome poetry with poetry! Just as God's revelation of himself goes beyond human reason, without rejecting that reason, so too it goes beyond human imagination however creative that imagination may be. The sermon is certainly dazzling but it is difficult to know how successful it is and difficult to know how we should react if we heard it. But Grundtvig continues,

Yes, my friends, you hear for yourselves
And all the world has heard it,
That the plain faithful narration of this,
Which the tax gatherer of Galilee has written in today's Gospel
Sounds more fanciful than any of the world's heroic epics
And when you add to this,
What has happened since on earth
That more stones than any but God can number
Have been rolled away from the doors of men's hearts
Through faith in the wonderful opening of Joseph's rock hewn tomb,
And that a stronger and more loving human life,
A clearer, broader and more comprehensive view of things, both earthly and
    heavenly,
Than there was before on earth,
Has come to birth from faith
In the one who was crucified and is risen again,
Then it can clearly be seen that nothing can be said too marvellous
About the Church of the risen Lord,
That it should seem incredible on account of its wondrousness.[4]

Having stressed this quality of amazement, which should characterise our response to the resurrection, and the way in which the resurrection has made possible a quite new awareness of the depth and quality of human life, Grundtvig comes to speak in more detail of the way in which the previous centuries had failed fully to grasp this. Here he criticises the centuries immediately preceding his own, the time of what in Lutheranism are called 'orthodoxy' and 'pietism'. His criticism is not and cannot be total. The hymns which he is quoting themselves come from the earlier part of this period. Yet he cannot help seeing in the past centuries a stress on the death and passion of Christ, at the expense of the resurrection and the ascension. There was moreover a stress on the Bible and the reading of the Bible, which was maybe not a bad thing for the learned, but which was very hard on women, the young and children, that is to say on the great majority of the Church's members, many of whom would in fact have been illiterate. And then he tells us how in 1825 he had come to see new light on the whole matter, 'new light from the old sun', and thus he expounds his understanding of the Church as dependent directly upon the living Christ made present in the faith and celebration of his people now. He had come to see the resurrection not only as something of the past but as something which is happening among us, something which is full of God's promises for the future.

Yes indeed it is a word of deep truth and seriousness, however it may sound, that this has been a time which was certainly rich and joyful, in comparison with what the world can give. But in comparison with what God can give and has given in Christ Jesus, it was a poor and sorrowful time for Christian women and children and in fact, on the whole, for the heart of humankind, this last time, when the Lord's sufferings and death were, so to speak, the whole portion of the heart while the resurrection, the manifestation and the ascension, and the whole life of the Lord, only unfolded its strength through the thoughts of old, tried, learned disciples and individual crucified, contrite thieves whom the Lord himself took by the hand to bring into paradise. In the days of our Lutheran fathers the whole of Christianity was derived from Bible learning and it was connected with the terror of a fearful soul at Sinai and its comfort under the cross, so that only those who were dead to the world and those who were lying on their death beds felt themselves at one with the message, while it fell heavy and dead, like great tombstones on the hearts of children, women, inexperienced youth and therefore the great majority. I do not know whether my fellow Christians understand me yet, but I know that they will come to understand that the Church's situation in those days was just as little natural in the Christian as in the human sense, except insofar as death is the natural consequence of sin and life in death a natural consequence of faith in him who while dead in the body was alive in the Spirit.

After all we know that what attracted us, as many of us as have been Christian children, was not the explanations or the teaching of books but the Bible story itself and the festival hymns, and above all our three articles of faith, with Martin Luther's childlike comments on them; therefore all glimmer of a living Church communion among us must necessarily disappear when the Bible story was distorted, Luther's catechism set aside and the festival hymns done away with.[5]

Grundtvig goes on to personal memories of his own sermons at Udby in the two years he spent there, from 1811 to 1813, as his father's curate, and at Præstø in his brief incumbency there in 1821 and 1822. That his preaching in those places had a powerful effect on his congregation is something for which we have a good deal of evidence.

Yes my friends, whoever heard my preaching ten or twenty years ago will remember how especially the old festival hymns were constantly in my mouth and in my heart. The highest expression of a living communion in the Church, which I have witnessed as a priest, was there in my youth, when the hymns and the catechism became glowing on my lips and resounded so strongly and re-echoed so livingly in the hearts of grey haired men and women that their eyes sparkled, and their words broke forth audibly or they sobbed like children while the heart melted in my breast and the Lord as it were rose before my eyes.

It is therefore not merely today or yesterday that I have begun to consider our fathers' Easter hymns to be much more prophetic songs about the resurrection we await than historical songs about our fathers' feelings of life in Christ. But it was not until this later time, during my difficult ministry in a strange circle, and with the passing of the last of the old Christian people, that there dawned a light for me, on the ground of all this, yes it was a new light from the old sun, which rose before my eyes over the living Word of which all Scripture, even the holiest, is only a shadow, and above all over the Word in baptism which creates our communion, creates the Church's body, to which the Spirit gives soul and life, but which brings death for us when we will not have that communion created by the living, sure, vocal, audible word, which the Spirit speaks to the Church, but instead will have it created by the dead, uncertain, written, silent signs in the book.

This light alone was new to me and with greatest amazement I now saw the resurrection of the Church body in which I had always believed but which I had never been able to picture to myself, save in the most fantastic forms. I saw it happen in a way which in the kingdom of Christ is so natural and simple that it was no longer this but its death which amazed me. That is to say, how Christians could ever have forgotten that it was not the Scripture but baptism that made them Christians, and that the living solemn witness of the whole Church at baptism, to that faith which we all are to have and confirm, is much surer than anything one can find in all the books in the world ...[6]

This assurance about the living word spoken in the proclamation of the Gospel, spoken again in the sacraments of baptism and eucharist is, of course, at the heart of Grundtvig's new discovery about the nature of the Church; it is very striking to see how he roots it in convictions which he had already held, ten or even twenty years before. The origins of the new discovery were there already, given in his exposition of the old festival hymns, and in his living experience of a way of preaching which was a true proclamation of the risen Christ, an integral part of the Church's worship, rooted in the sacrament of baptism. He goes on to expound it further.

Thus we must needs hold unshakeably our baptismal covenant if we wish to remain Christians, and we must base our whole Christian life, both here and beyond, on our regeneration in baptism, by the living word of God which lasts eternally and does not wear out as all books do and which does not even shrink away when the heavens are rolled up as a scroll. How Christians could ever forget this basic apostolic teaching, which is clearly enough taught in all the apostolic letters, was a great puzzle to me and indeed still is. What in the meantime I still find much more unreasonable is that most of my fellow Christians, far from rejoicing in this light, shut their eyes to it and determine to have the Church body lying in the Scripture grave.

I must speak freely, this comes from the fact that they have not believed the prophets, nor have they even had an eye for the child angel, who both Martin Luther

and all childlike believers have always seen at the entrance to the grave and thus
let themselves be guided and shown where the Lord lay. For it was this angel who
before my eyes rolled away the stone from the grave of the Church, sat down on
it, yes it was he who blew away the smoke from my eyes, so that I discovered as
a great mystery, what a child can see and understand. That is, I discovered that if
the Church is to stand recognisable and rock sure for us, we must allow it to remain
standing on the foundation which the Lord and the apostles have really laid when
they founded it. This was not with pen and ink but with their word of mouth, their
word which was life and spirit. They built it as little of paper as of stone and brick,
but they built with living men who believed what was the Lord's will and
thereupon were baptised in the name of the Father and the Son and the Holy Spirit,
before any apostle had set pen to paper. They saw the Son of Man standing at the
right hand of God while he whose letters men wish to build the Church on, the
apostle Paul, was still Saul breathing out fire and slaughter against the Lord's
disciples, the one who wanted to force them to break their baptismal covenant and
to deny the Lord.

Yes my friends, I know that the angel of childlike faith will work this miracle for
all those who love him, so that they will see that it is the Word in baptism which
has sustained the Church and created the community from generation to generation
and that thus it is foolish to give the glory for this to something else. Thus it was
no wonder that the congregation became dead when men wished to have it created
by a pen, it was no wonder that the Church seemed ready to collapse when men
wanted to have it founded on a book, no wonder that the fellowship amongst us is
almost dissolved, when not only do men despise and fail to appreciate baptism and
the baptismal covenant but change the word, on which everything depends, to their
own measure.[7]

After the passage of confrontation with those who would not receive his message, Grundtvig concludes, as he had begun, with a passage of almost ecstatic
celebration of the mystery of the resurrection, a mystery which looks back
from Easter day to the mountain of transfiguration, and forward from it to
the mountain of the ascension,

> Must not the Easter hymns of our fathers
> Indeed become sweet in our mouth,
> When we feel that what was uncertain for them,
> Is fulfilled in ourselves,
> When we taste the sweetness of the Lord's cup,
> Of which for the most part they tasted only bitterness,
> Yes when we are ourselves the living proof
> Of how he who is grace and truth,
> Gives always grace upon grace?
> Oh how shall we thank him worthily,
> How shall we find words for a hymn,
> Yes for a thousand psalms and hymns and spiritual songs,
> Which will answer to that Easter morning,
> When Mary Magdalene stood at the holy grave,

And sowed tears but reaped songs of joy,
When the tears in her eyes were turned into smiling angels,
And became in the grave a mirror-like sea,
From which the dayspring from on high broke forth,
With the word Mary, from the Saviour's lips.
Yes as the visions overwhelm me in this holy morning hour,
So shall the dear feelings of amazement, joy and gratitude
Overwhelm the people who now are created to praise the Lord,
To see light in all graves,
To see smiling angels at the head and the feet
In the holy grave of the Word
Which our Holy Scripture is in truth,
And not only to see them but to hear them sing,
He is not here he is risen,
But come and see the place where he lay,
And then to hear the Spirit proclaim to the Church,
That self same Word only now living and revealed
Which they had seen crucified and dead,
Shrouded in death's gloom and laid in the grave.
Oh what days of the Lord,
When the word of faith which we preach,
Shall thus spread abroad vital and vivid
On the wings of the Spirit, as on the wings of the wind,
And make his presence known among us,
He who is himself God's Word from all eternity,
The living Word whose life is the light of men.
Then shall it be known that what we have preached
Is no brainchild of ours,
But comes from the Holy Spirit,
No flower of speech, but his whose words are all life and spirit,
That the Lord repeats the course of his life
With all his wondrous deeds, before our eyes.
For the living word of God sets it forth for us,
And either we remember that which spiritually corresponds within us
As something we have experienced,
Or we experience it in the hearing of the word,
Or we see it coming in the light of the Spirit,
With the divine certainty which he imparts,
Who calls the yet unborn by name,
And speaks of that which is not as if it were.

I will not speak here of visions of every day
When all the graves of speech are opened at once,
And the nations of the world repeat their lives,
Before our eyes, in the living word —
But all Christians shall see, even in this morning hour,
That already it is good to be here,
As with the Lord and Moses and Elijah in the Holy Mount,

Yes as in paradise,
When only we make our own the apostle's word,
God who is rich in mercy,
In his great love with which he loved us,
Has also made us who were dead in sins,
Living in Christ, has also raised us up
In union with Christ Jesus,
And has appointed us to sit down in the heavens,
So that in his goodness towards us he might show the ages to come
The exceeding riches of his grace;
For salvation is of grace through faith,
A gift of God undeserved so that no-one should boast of it,
For we are his work created in Christ Jesus,
To good works which God has before ordained
That we should walk in them (Eph.2:4-10).
Therefore let us keep the feast,
Not with the old leaven,
Nor with the leaven of malice and wickedness,
But with the unleavened bread of sincerity and truth,
Singing the fathers' beautiful hymn,

> Come dearest soul up and wake
> For the gloom of death and hell
> By Jesus' death is already dispersed,
> And victory for ever is won.
> Amen, yes Amen, in the name of Jesus Amen.[8]

III

We have seen how Grundtvig's deepest convictions about the nature of the Church as the Church of the living God were shaped by his experience of the worship of that Church as he had known it as a child at Udby and Thyregod and as he knew it again as a young man in the first years of his pastoral ministry. It was out of that experience that all the subsequent growth of his faith and insight came. It was from there that the deep wellspring of joy had its origins.

But now we are to look at a moment when he made direct contact with another older and more widely spread liturgical tradition than that of Denmark, that of the Orthodox East. Admittedly he only knew that tradition through books, but there is no doubt that he resonated to it. The early months of 1837 mark a high point in his assimilation of specifically Greek patristic ideas and images. In January of that year, in the course of his work on the *Sang-Værk*, he borrowed from the royal library in Copenhagen an eighteenth century Venetian edition of some of the basic liturgical texts of the Byzantine Church. The results of his work on that book are to be seen in the hymns which he translated or adapted from the Greek. There are thirty-eight of them in the *Sang-Værk*. They can also be seen in original hymns of his own written at this time, which show clear marks of Greek influence and also, as we shall see, in his sermons preached during this year. As often happened, the work on the hymns stimulated his preaching and the preaching can sometimes be seen preparing the way for new hymns.

If Grundtvig was deeply impressed by the faith of the Greek fathers, his attitude towards the Greek Orthodoxy of his own time was distinctly ambivalent. His admiration for the hymns did not extend to the contemporary Church of Greece. He had the distinct impression, as he says in this sermon, that 'nowhere is Christianity more dead than among the Greeks'.

Grundtvig's combative nature, with its love for argument and controversy, could easily lead him into sweeping judgments on people and things, judgments which were sometimes ill founded. Such is the case here.[9] It is true that in the 1830s, after four centuries of Turkish oppression, the state of the Greek Church was not outwardly flourishing. During the period of the Ottoman domination, the Christian populations of the empire had lived a ghetto-like existence as second class citizens. The Turkish authorities adopted a policy of indirect rule, using the clergy and especially the bishops as the representatives of the various Christian communities and making them responsible for their good conduct. This led to innumerable problems in the Church. In Istanbul itself, for instance, the government constantly interfered in the election of the Patriarch, demanding the payment of large bribes whenever a new Patriarch was installed.

A long period of pressure amounting at times to overt persecution has the effect of disfiguring and maiming important aspects of the Church's life and work. Outwardly, at least, the Church has to compromise in many ways with the ruling power. Inwardly also, many elements of its life may be paralysed or cramped. There was, for instance, in these centuries, no possibility of developing centres of learning or making use of the arts of printing in Greece itself. Books had to be published outside the Turkish empire, often in Venice. The experience of the Orthodox Churches under communist rule in our own century has had much in common with the experience of many of these Churches under Ottoman rule in the five preceding centuries. Such times can leave Churches gravely wounded.

But, as we know from contemporary experience, such a time of suffering can also bring out wonderful qualities of faithfulness and devotion within the persecuted Church. So it was in Greece and the other Balkan countries during the Turkish domination. There were those who gave their lives for their faith, the new martyrs. The monasteries both of men and of women were centres of spiritual life and of charitable activity. Clandestine schools were carried on in many places. Only a generation before 1837, a monastic scholar on Mt. Athos, St. Nikodemos of the Holy Mountain, had gathered together a great anthology of Orthodox spiritual writings known as the Philokalia, a work which is now being eagerly translated into the languages of Western Europe.

Certainly the Church did more than any other institution to maintain the
Greek sense of national identity and human values during the period of
oppression.

All this history was almost wholly unknown in the contemporary West.
We should not be too hard on Grundtvig for his ignorance of it. It was easy
for a cultivated western European not to see beyond the unfamiliar exterior
of Orthodox Church life, the beards, the icons and the candles. John Henry
Newman, like Grundtvig, a theologian and a scholar with a passionate love
for all things Greek, seems, in his travels in the Mediterranean in the winter
of 1832-33, to have seen very little beneath the surface of the life of the
Church in those parts of Greece which he visited. Grundtvig himself had probably never actually met a member of the Orthodox Church and certainly had
never had the opportunity for a quiet conversation with an Orthodox scholar
or theologian of his own calibre.

In fact, Grundtvig's almost total ignorance of contemporary Orthodoxy in
many ways makes his enthusiastic response to the liturgical texts of that
Church even more remarkable. Across the centuries he felt an identity of faith
and experience. So his sermon begins with a verse from a hymn, but this time
it is not a hymn by Kingo,

> Today Hell sighs and mourns,
> 'Alas, Adam and the whole of his race
> Now defiantly march out in troops,
> Redeemed by the hidden Son of God.
> I gleaned them carefully with joy
> Now he has snatched them away altogether
> Now at the word of the crucified
> They journey from hell up to heaven.'
> Glory to the God-man
> Who was crucified and is arisen.[10]

Grundtvig continues in triumphant tones, 'So, Christian friends, sounds out
for us the joyful morning song of God's people from most distant times ...'
Here was confirmation of his own innermost convictions about the over-
coming of death, from a remote part of the Church's history. Across the centuries he felt an identity of faith and experience. He was not, of course,
devoid of a strong sense of historical change and development. Later in this
sermon he speaks of the way in which many of the peoples and languages of
the old Christian world were now dead. We may think for instance of the
Churches of Asia Minor or North Africa which had simply disappeared.
Grundtvig saw the centre of the Church's life moving West and North, 'so
that a new Christendom has arisen in the desert amongst Scythians and
barbarians.' But in all this history he sees the power of the crucified and risen
Christ at work, through the gift of the one life-giving Spirit;

not just the generations of past, but also peoples, tribes and languages have changed, and although the gifts were different, yet the Spirit as well as the faith and hope have remained the same.

It is this gift of the Holy Spirit which creates the unity of the Church through space and time in despite of the divisions made by human blindness and sin. So it is that he can so warmly commend to his Copenhagen congregation, this ancient Greek vision of the resurrection. So it is that he can expound it so powerfully, since he is sure that the Spirit that inspires him, and who lives in the Church and people which he serves, is one and the same Spirit who spoke through the apostles and the fathers of the Church.

'So', he declares,

it is joyful beyond measure that the Church's ancient psalms and hymns and spiritual songs can find a living resonance in our hearts and on our lips. So that we can feel and prove that the gates of hell have not had power over the house set on the rock, and that time, which devours everything, has not been able to damage the living memorials which our Lord Jesus Christ left here below, consecrated by his blessing and animated by the life-giving Spirit of the Father. Yes, Christian friends, on this glorious feast of the resurrection may we, who feel the Lord's presence, diligently and joyfully recall to his glory that the life of his Church and people upon earth, the perpetuity of the people who worship the crucified Jesus Christ, is not just what is called a witness to his resurrection and ascension, but a constant reiteration of his victorious struggle with death and a crystal clear proof that Jesus Christ has power to lay down his life and take it up again ...[11]

Here we have again one of Grundtvig's deepest convictions, at least since the great discovery of 1825, which we have seen in the previous section. The life and worship of the Church is not only a witness or sign which points us towards the reality of Christ's death and resurrection as past events. It is a constant reiteration, the original word could also be translated as repetition, of that death and resurrection. The memorials which Christ has left behind him are brought to life as present realities by the action of the Holy Spirit. So, through the power of the Spirit, Christ repeats throughout the ages, the mystery of his love in the lives of his people. He lives in them and they live in him. His people participate in that same mystery of sacrificial love which they celebrate in the sacraments of the new covenant, both in baptism and in the Lord's Supper, and in which they enter, by faith, into the life conveyed by his word. The new life which is theirs, in baptism and eucharist, is to be lived out in all the circumstances of every day. The worship of the Church on Sundays is an inclusive and not an exclusive focus of it.

In our own century there has been a long standing discussion as to whether the Church's life and worship should be thought of primarily as a sign pointing towards the mystery of Christ or as its actual embodiment on earth here and now. It has often been thought that the first position, which sees the Church as a John the Baptist, pointing toward the Christ who is still to come, is the typically Protestant one. The second position has been maintained with insistence by Catholics and above all by Orthodox. There is no question where Grundtvig stands on this issue. At least in its life of worship the Church embodies the presence of the risen Lord.

This sense of the resurrection, as a present reality, can be illustrated by some of the verses which Grundtvig translated from the texts of Easter. It is interesting to notice that whereas in many places Grundtvig makes a free translation of the Greek original and in some places simply paraphrases it, in this particular instance in the three first verses from the canon of St. John of Damascus he sticks quite closely to the original,

> Come let us empty the cup anew,
> Not from the water which sprang from the rock,
> But from the living spring which comes from the grave,
> The spring of blessedness which wells up into heaven,
> Jesus the strength of our life who stablishes our hearts.
>
> Light now arises in its fullness over all things,
> Heaven and earth and hell are made bright,
> The foundation of all things is suddenly revealed,
> The whole creation now accepts the paschal feast,
> Feels itself stablished in the uprising of the Word.
>
> Christ our Saviour as God and as man,
> Crucified with you and buried yesterday,
> We shall arise and as light already here below
> Shine with you in the land of the living,
> You who for our heart are both rock and strength.
>
> Suddenly, Lord, you stood among your own,
> Bade them God's peace, and gave comfort in sorrow,
> Created anew in them a temple for the Spirit,
> Gave them the life with which you arose;
> Great is your grace, our light and our strength.
>
> As you began so continue now
> Come also to us through the locked doors,
> Now act in the way that you did at first,
> Promise us your gladness, give us your peace
> Graciously breathe into us your life and your strength.
>
> The old shall now give place to the new,
> Which you won for us on the cross and gave us
> So that we are renewed to eternal life
> And may journey towards it and meet in the sky
> You who for eternity are our life and our strength.[12]

In these verses we see the writer's insistence that the work initiated on the first Easter morning is continuing now in the life of the Church. The mystery of Easter is constantly renewed and links the believers across the centuries, bridging the gulf of death. But this is a reality which exists not only on the plane of history. It has cosmic dimensions. We see also the way in which what is personal is united with what is universal. Both elements are essential, Easter is celebrated as a festival of all creation and a festival of the whole of humanity; but it is also celebrated as the festival of each person who partakes in the feast. All things are established and made firm in Christ's triumph over death, for the creation is made subject to death only for a time. Its true destiny is life and eternity in God. The resurrection of Christ reveals the true nature of all creation, the true nature of all human life.

This cosmic victory is also intimately personal, the risen Christ shares his life with his disciples, breathes his Spirit into each one. Each one becomes a temple of the Spirit and at the same time the whole community of faith is built together and raised up as such a temple. All the baffled longings of the human race are finally fulfilled in this moment of new life. What is personal and what is universal do not merely coexist. The whole divine economy is summed up in the life of each one; in a mysterious way each one is called to embody the whole work of salvation.

We could not have a more powerful expression of the faith that what is central to Christianity, what is the heart of the life of the Christian community, is of universal power and significance. It is in no sense confined to the explicitly Christian world because God's act in Christ is always overflowing into the whole creation. The resurrection awakens echoes in the whole fabric of the world which itself comes from God's hands. What is specifically Christian and what is universally human is always and necessarily in a state of interaction and interchange. In these very years, when Grundtvig is writing these hymns, he is also becoming more and more involved in the problems of the social, economic and cultural life of his nation. This most practical involvement in the issues of his time is not something which happens in despite of his celebration of the victory of Easter; it is something which happens on account of it. For him there is no opposition between the life of prayer and worship on the one side and the life of active social concern on the other. His commitment to the struggle for the life and freedom of his people, for the growth of their sense of responsibility for the life of society, springs out of his faith and experience of the resurrection.

We see here how the combination of what is personal and human with what is universal and cosmic is characteristic alike of the eighth century Greek and of the nineteenth century Danish writer. For both, in their very different intellectual situations, find here, a way of speaking about the fullness of God's work in Christ. The first three verses which we have quoted above are not part of the current Danish Hymn Book, the book which is used in all the parishes of the Church of Denmark, but the second three verses, from

'Suddenly Lord you stood among your own', are frequently used to a magnificent tune by the early twentieth century composer Thomas Laub, a man who devoted himself to the music of the Church and who produced a large number of fine congregational hymn tunes.[14] It is a moving and powerful experience to share in the singing of such a hymn, a manifestation of the unexpected presence of Orthodoxy in the West.

For Grundtvig, this fullness of the risen life in which we share, is imparted through the sacraments of baptism and holy communion, each of which is a sacrament of life through death in Christ. This, which is part of Grundtvig's basic conviction about the faith, finds particular expression in these hymns translated from the Greek. So, in two verses, one from Palm Sunday and the other from the Monday in Holy Week, which Grundtvig has taken and combined into one long irregular verse, we read,

> Faithful souls
> Come let us dwell
> With reverence on the memory of our Saviour's passion,
> In order to find comfort.
> We will not weep for the pain and the death
> Which has granted us the blessed hope,
> But we will worship our Saviour and sing,
> Thanks for the deep, the holy baptism,
> Where we are crucified, dead and buried
> With you, so that from you we may receive life,
> You who arose from the dead again
> Friend of humankind.
> As our God and our Lord we glorify you,
> Blessed forever and highly praised,
> For that of your compassion
> You suffered death,
> And will give us life from the death of sin,
> And grant us heaven,
> You who died for us, that we might live with you.[14]

Through dying and rising with Christ in baptism we are brought into the fellowship of the meal of the new covenant, the feast of the Kingdom, in which the risen Christ makes us sharers in the powers of the age to come.

Edvard Lehmann, commenting on this verse, regards it as a typical example of Grundtvig's preference for seeing the mystery of salvation in terms of life and death, rather than in terms of sin and forgiveness. He stresses how congenial this view is to the Greek way of looking at things, which tends to understand salvation primarily in terms of our renewal through our participation in the life and immortality of Christ.[15] All this seems to me true enough, but it does not follow from it that either the Greek fathers, or Grundtvig, ignore or underestimate the reality of sin and forgiveness. Both in their different ways stress humanity's need for the freedom which forgiveness brings. They see the conflict of sin and forgiveness as included within the larger categories of life and death and in no way excluded by them.

What they seek to avoid is a primarily external reflection on the passion of Christ, weeping for his passion and death, something which in Western Christianity, both Catholic and Protestant, had become very common; an emotional and moralistic consideration of its lessons for us. Rather, they stress our incorporation into Christ, our dying with him and our letting his death work itself out in us. That is something which implies a radical repentance, allowing the old man to die so that the new may come to life, a change deeper than any purely moral approach would be able to bring about, a change where we are crucified, dead and buried with Christ so that from him we may be able to receive the new life which he gives. This is part of what is involved in Grundtvig's insistence on baptism as the sacrament of new birth.

The eucharist itself comes into the picture in a three verse hymn which Grundtvig has gathered together from scattered texts used in the liturgy of the pre-sanctified in the first days of Holy Week. It is very striking here that the presence of Christ's sacrifice in the eucharist is underlined, since this is an aspect of the sacrament about which the Lutheran tradition has been on the whole very reticent. Here, it is Grundtvig who introduces it into the first verse of the hymn. Every time the eucharist is celebrated, he says, the high priest enters the holy place, the good shepherd gives his life anew for the sheep:

> Angels in hosts
> Gladly descend
> Kneel around God's table with us,
> Every time in the Word
> The high priest enters the sanctuary,
> The shepherd offers himself for his sheep;
> With us they joyfully cry,
> Praise be to God Hallelujah.

> Faithful souls
> So let us kneel
> Hungry for the feast on the table,
> The Lord in his Word.
> Eat and drink his flesh and his blood,
> So we can taste that the Lord is good.
> Thus we all sing with the angels,
> Praise be to God Hallelujah.

> We praise him now,
> To be blessed in his likeness,
> Always on our tongues will be
> What we now sing,
> We have all tasted that the Lord is good
> We have drunk of the stream of God's blessedness
> With the angels we all journey henceforth
> Praise be to God Hallelujah.[16]

Always when he speaks of the eucharist in his hymns and in his prose writings, even when most influenced from beyond his own milieu, Grundtvig has in mind the rite which he actually knew with the communicants kneeling at the altar rails, the priest standing in their midst at the altar, the intending communicants standing a little further back in the chancel. It is part of his totally unselfconscious acceptance of the liturgy as he had experienced it, that he sees no difficulty here or in other places in seeing the angelic hosts kneeling with the communicants at God's table where the Lord in his Word offers himself to his own.

IV

The Easter sermon for 1837, which we have just examined, is followed on Easter Monday by another, no less remarkable but carefully contrasting utterance.[17] Here again Grundtvig begins with a verse from the Greek, and again, one which unites cosmic and personal themes. It is a verse which affirms that the earth was shaken when the Saviour died, and so was the human heart. Now both are made quiet and strengthened in the resurrection of Christ. Then the preacher begins,

This expression of the gentle joy of Easter also comes to us from ancient Greece, where in the days of heathendom the feeling heart had been shaken more than in any other place, at the sight of the dark, silent, joyless kingdom of the shades. It was there, therefore, that the prospect of heavenly immortality, the joyful hope of everlasting life which sprang from Jesus' resurrection, must necessarily have made the deepest impression and given rise to the most joyful song of praise.

Yesterday we praised God because we could share the manly gladness of the early Christians over the defeat of death and the overthrow of hell by the God-man, who the heavenly Father gave to us as our champion and our Saviour. Today we shall praise him because we can share, not less but even more, their womanly gladness over the comfort and peace which the first Son of Man, who triumphantly rose from the dead, brought to the women who wept at the tomb. And through the women he has brought comfort and peace to all mortals, to all who from the ground of the heart have a desire to live and see good days, have a longing too deep to feel satisfied with the span of days and the passing pleasures which are the natural lot of fallen humanity here on earth. Theirs is a longing too deep and a seriousness and love of truth too great to be quietened by fairy tales and fantasies about the isles of the blessed on the far side of the world's sea.[18]

Grundtvig goes on to expound his dearly held conviction that 'There has scarcely ever been a people so like the Greeks in this respect as the little nation to which we belong.' For him Greek mythology and Nordic mythology have it in common that they express an intense longing for eternal life and a common revolt against the mortality of our human condition here below, a longing and a revolt which express themselves in myths and legends, stories and images which, while they testify to the heart's desire for immortality, in the end fail to satisfy it. Here again, as in other places, he witnesses to his sense of a special affinity between Greece and Denmark.

In the Byzantine Easter hymn just quoted, Grundtvig goes on, 'We hear an echo of the Hallelujah of the heart.' The angel has not only rolled the stone away from the grave, he has taken away the great stone which lay on the human heart and

another Greek Easter verse expresses it thus, that when the risen seed of woman met the women who came to the grave and said to them 'All Hail' which words mean rejoice, then and only then did Eve, the mother of all living, cease to weep. There can be for us no more delightful image of the blessed effect of Christ's resurrection than this. For we too, by nature, have the feeling that the heart is at all times what Eve was at the beginning, that is to say the mother of all living, for as Solomon says 'Life issues from the heart'. So it is a deep and moving truth for us, that Eve wept in the language of the Spirit and of the heart, from the fall in Eden to the resurrection in the garden of the dead, till the seed of woman came back victorious from the kingdom of the dead and met his mother and said,

> Rejoice, I have broken the serpent's head,
> I have taken away the sting of death
> And the triumph of hell,
> You shall not die but shall live
> And proclaim the works of the Lord;
> For I remembered you in the grave
> And they gave thanks to me in hell,
> Yes I worked wonders for the dead
> And saw the dead rise up and thank me.
> My mercy was made known in the grave,
> My truth in the land of corruption
> My secret was made known in the darkness
> And my righteousness in the land where all is forgotten.[19]

In this magnificent passage there are many things which demand our attention. There is first, in the very opening of the sermon and its contrast with that of the previous day, an expression of Grundtvig's conviction about the complementarity of men and women. The two halves of the human race both need to have their full share in the life of humanity; both are to make their own specific response to the revealed mystery of God's love. Then there is his long held view of the special affinity between Greece and Denmark and between Norse mythology and the mythology of ancient Greece. Those who feel the bitterness of death most sharply will be most deeply filled with the longing for immortality. Thirdly there is his equally long considered opinion that there is something specifically feminine in both the Greek and the Northern spirit. In both there is a particular depth and strength in the life of the heart. This is a quality which makes these peoples particularly sensitive to the horror of death and therefore particularly eager to find signs of hope for an eternal life beyond the barrier of death.

We may be inclined to find some of these views artificial or extreme. Surely, we may question whether these qualities are to be found only in a few peoples and not throughout the human race. That is perhaps something which Grundtvig would have been willing to recognise. As we shall see in his treatment of Pentecost, at times he sees the action of the Spirit everywhere in human history. Meanwhile we should at least recognise the importance of these particular views about Greece and Denmark for Grundtvig, and acknowledge that they are based on an extensive first hand knowledge of the literature of ancient Greece and the world of Norse mythology such as few contemporary scholars could claim.

Beyond these points lies the connection made between the grief of the women who came to the sepulchre and the grief of Eve, the mother of all living. Here it seems that Grundtvig's eye had been caught by the Kontakion for the second Sunday after Easter, the Sunday of the Myrrh-bearing women,

With your greeting, Rejoice, to the myrrh-bearing women, O Christ our God, you put an end to the mourning of our first mother Eve, through your resurrection.

Here the grief of Eve is seen as the grief of all humanity, the grief of mothers weeping for their children through all the ages. Here a motif out of the mythology of ancient Greece, the mourning of Demeter for Persephone for instance, is taken and transformed, fulfilled and made universal in the women's response to the death and resurrection of Christ. The age-old sorrow of the human heart is transformed by the mystery of Christ's dying and rising in which, as the hymns for Holy Saturday declare, 'All things are changed'. All humanity grieved over its fallen condition, its alienation from God, its subjection to sin and death. All humanity's grief is assuaged in the light of Christ's resurrection victory, a resurrection which is for all.

There is a rather remarkable parallel to Grundtvig's vision of the lasting grief of Eve in the well known passage of a great spiritual writer of our own century, St. Silouan of Athos, in his meditation entitled 'Adam's Lament'.

Here it is Adam who weeps over his lost communion with God and the whole of creation weeps with him. In his prayers the saint associates himself with Adam and feels himself incorporated in Adam, the father of all. On this view of things we are all of us included in Adam and Eve, representative figures of our common humanity. It is they who are shown being drawn up out of the place of death in the Orthodox icon of the resurrection. It is they who come to share in Christ's rising, as in Grundtvig's rendering of the old Anglo-Saxon poem on the harrowing of hell.[20]

We have here an example of the unselfconscious way in which Grundtvig uses the image language of the Bible and Christian tradition to articulate his vision of the Christian faith. In the last passage of the sermon which I have quoted, and which I have set out as poetry, it is interesting to note that almost every line contains either a quotation from or an allusion to a passage of the Old Testament. This intensely biblical and traditional expression of the faith is set within the wider context of the expectation of the whole of humanity, an expectation which for Grundtvig is most eloquently expressed in the pre-Christian mythology of ancient Greece and the stories of his own pre-Christian ancestors. One could hardly have a more striking illustration of the comprehensive and all-inclusive nature of Grundtvig's understanding of the work of God and of the response which it calls out in the hearts and minds of men and women of all nations and all ages.

The question of the relationship between the Christian faith and the other religions of humankind had not, in the nineteenth century, acquired the pressing urgency it has now at the end of the twentieth century. But it is not difficult to see the way in which Grundtvig could have responded to it. For him it is clear that God has been at work throughout the whole history of humanity, despite the reality of the fall. This divine activity can be seen focally, centrally in the history of Israel, which leads directly into the coming of the Messiah. But it is by no means confined to that particular historic process. It is also to be seen, less clearly perhaps but sometimes no less powerfully, in the history of other peoples, and especially in the history of those who have received a particular calling within the whole drama of God's dealings with humanity. Once again the mystery of the resurrection is seen inclusively and not exclusively.

This theme of the Easter greeting brought first by the angel, then by Christ himself, to the women who had come bearing spices to the tomb, is one that figures prominently all through the Orthodox liturgical texts for the season of Easter. As we have seen, one Sunday is devoted particularly to the commemoration of the Myrrh-bearing women. This was clearly an idea which attracted, yes indeed, fascinated Grundtvig. We can illustrate this by two more of his translations from the Greek. The first a single verse hymn with very short lines, particularly effective in Danish,

The angel like lightning
Fearful to the eye
Had a word to speak,
Gentle as falling dew.
He said, Devoted women
You come with ointments
Seeking among the dead
The dawning light of life.
He has departed from the cave,
He has risen in glory.
Death fled before him,
The graves were emptied,
He, the undying one,
In the kingdom of the dead.
Declare, this is great
This thing God has done
Adam's fallen race
Has been raised up by God's Son.[21]

The five verse hymn which follows soon after this in the *Sang-Værk* is more conventional in form, but its content is equally clear and outspoken. It is a hymn in praise of the women who were the first to greet the risen Christ and who went to tell the apostles, thus becoming apostles to the apostles. In Danish it is possible to make a feminine form both of the word friend and of the word apostle. It is this form which is used in the opening lines of the hymn,

Friends of the Lord,
Women apostles,
We praise you as blessed today;
Light from the grave
The rose from the garden of the dead
You have brought first into the house of sorrow.

The most golden of words
Resounded among you
The living voice of the Resurrection,
'The Saviour man
Jesus our friend is risen',
You broke out in joy to the comfort of all the earth.

Angels revealed to you
The joy that was swaddled,
The Lord himself placed this joy in your breast,
Then with wings
At once to the apostles you went to proclaim
Joy from the grave in the name of the living.

Never do we forget
That the women's voices
Gave a foundation for the apostles' message,
Theirs the first fruits
Of the life which had come from the dead;
The word of the resurrection is born of a woman.

Friends of the Lord
Women who are blessed
You bade the apostles at once proclaim
Easter Day,
Smile against sorrow and grieving
Powerful witness from the land of forgetting.[22]

V

We said at the beginning of this section that the theme of Christ's death and resurrection is so omnipresent in Grundtvig's hymns and sermons that it is difficult to know where to begin. A sign of that omnipresence of the resurrection is to be seen in Grundtvig's Sunday hymns, hymns which are in constant use in the Danish Church and which forcefully express the idea that every Sunday is an Easter Day. Some of the finest of these hymns date from this same amazing year 1837, and in them we see how Grundtvig has made his own emphases drawn from the Lutheran tradition, from the medieval Latin West and from the worship of the Byzantine East. We see something of the ecumenical quality of these liturgical proclamations,

Sunday morning from the dead
Jesus rose triumphant.
Every Sunday's dawn
Now brings healing in place of death
And wonderfully recalls
All the days of the Lord's life.

Thousand tongued the Lord's words
Are now reborn throughout the land,
Wake now from sleep and sloth
Every ear that can hear,
Arise soul from the dead
And greet the dawn of Easter.

Every Sunday death shudders
Darkness trembles beneath the earth
For with glory then Christ gives light,
The Word of life has giant tones
And victoriously does battle with
The prince of death and the kingdom of darkness.[23]

CHAPTER 16

Whitsun

I

We have already seen that the combination of natural and scriptural imagery is a constant feature in Grundtvig's hymns. This is particularly the case in the hymns for Whitsun. Here we see most clearly the Spirit's role as giver of life in bringing together both inner and outer, flesh and spirit, grace and nature in a new and creative fusion. Here again we find that the imagery of the changing seasons is used to illustrate the growth of the life of grace.

It was characteristic of the popular religious revivals which touched northern and western Europe in the eighteenth and nineteenth centuries that, though their appeal was primarily to the individual conscience, they affected not only individuals but the life of whole societies, sometimes of whole nations. In eighteenth century Wales, for instance, the Welsh-speaking part of the population, at that time the great majority, was powerfully affected by the Methodist revival which in the course of sixty or seventy years radically changed the nature of Welsh society, creating a way of life and social and cultural attitudes which survived well into the twentieth century. For a time, in such a movement, heaven and earth, time and eternity seem to come dangerously close together, not just for individuals but for a whole people. The dangers of pure fantasy and of unbalanced fanaticism can become real. Yet, at the same time, remarkable forces of individual and social transformation are let loose. Movements which in their original form and motivation are primarily other-worldly can have strong this-worldly affects. Movements which, at least at the outset, make a strong appeal to the emotions, can give rise to all kinds of new intellectual initiatives.[1]

If this was the case in eighteenth century Wales, where the Methodist preaching had a strong element of doctrinal and other-worldly Calvinism in it, still more was it the case in nineteenth century Denmark where the message which Grundtvig proclaimed was professedly for this world as well as for the next, where there was a new idea of school and all that that stood for in terms of human development, as well as a new idea of Church and congregation. Of course the Grundtvigian gatherings which multiplied from the middle of the century onwards, were not the only, or indeed the earliest, indications of popular religious revival in nineteenth century Denmark. There had been older movements of revival amongst the farmers and peasants, some of which had their origins in the pietism of the eighteenth century and which had a strong puritan streak in them, not unlike what we find in the

English-speaking world at the time, but the movement which had Grundtvig as its inspiration, while it had a number of features in common with these earlier tendencies, had also its own particular quality, a quality which gave value to the things of earth as well as to the things of heaven.

And if it was the case that, in the preaching of the Methodists, heaven and earth seemed at times to become unbearably near to one another, what would be the case with the followers of Grundtvig, where the old man insisted so much on the real presence of God with us here and now, in the midst of our daily life, in the midst of our ordinary occupations? Jakob Knudsen, whose description of the impression which a Grundtvigian hymn could make on children when sung in the intimacy of the home we have already seen, has an equally vivid description of the impression such a hymn could make on a child when heard out of doors in a country gathering for preaching and exhortation. He is speaking from the experience of a rural society in which people still lived very close to the natural world, in which lives were inevitably shaped by the changes of the seasons, and he is describing the impact of a well-known Whitsun hymn which itself is full of a characteristic Grundtvigian blending of natural and scriptural themes and images. He tells us of a time when as a nine year old boy he had accompanied his father to a gathering in a nearby village to hear two noted local preachers.

I heard this hymn for the first time — so far as I can remember — in Salling. I am fairly sure it was in 1867. Old Sveistrup and Peder Larsen Dons were there. I had been allowed to go with father; we stayed with Pastor Konradsen in Nautrup. The two travelling speakers arrived there too; I have the impression that Sveistrup spoke in the churchyard; perhaps there were too many people for them to get into the church. Afterwards a lot of people gathered downstairs in the vicarage along with the speakers. I went out into the courtyard and suddenly they began to sing 'You who proceed from the living God, Spirit of spirits in the highest …'. How varied and rich was the feeling that seized me. Varied; there was something of a beehive that came to my mind — partly because there were so many people in the little low rooms of the vicarage — partly because of the spring breeze, which easily leads one to think of bees. Yes, but it was also the memory of the hill which lifts itself on glowing pillars — perhaps it was the powerful song which burst out and seemed about to lift the roof — and then the memory of the fire of Pentecost and the glowing tongues which the hymn itself mentions — but above all it was the thought of that strong rushing wind from heaven which filled the whole house where they were sitting. And then once again the spring breeze which soon, yes very shortly, would become warm and bring summer to Denmark.[2]

We are not to imagine that the nine year old boy had all these impressions so articulately in his mind as the adult who writes up the incident some forty years later. Yet somehow they must all have been there, and together they go to make up a remarkable picture. The description begins and ends with what is purely natural, the warm spring breeze that brings with it the promise of summer. By the time the reference to spring and summer comes again, the words have been filled with such a multitude of associations that the summer which is to come to Denmark is not just a season which returns each year, it is some universal time of fulfilment which seems to be promised.

In between, Knudsen has filled out his description, first with the thought of the beehive and its swarm of bees. This image, in part at least, must have been suggested by the eager buzz of conversation that preceded the singing of the hymn. Something was actively at work here in the long low rooms of the country vicarage. Then there is the piece of popular Danish lore which will easily escape the foreigner, 'the hill that lifts itself on glowing pillars'. When the little people, the spirits of the earth, the fairies, really start celebrating in the barrows where they live, when the singing and dancing really get going, then the top of the hill lifts off and the merry-making becomes visible and mortals must be careful not to let themselves be drawn in. At such moments a hidden world, which lies just below the surface of our everyday experience, is suddenly opened to us. Its attractive power is very great.

From this palpably pre-Christian image, we pass at once to the upper room in Jerusalem and to the mighty rushing wind which came upon the apostles on the first Whitsun Day. Knudsen is indeed a disciple of Grundtvig. Grace, nature, popular mythology, scriptural teaching are all blended together, all reinforce the feeling that summer has almost come. Yes, the mild, friendly Danish summer. But also the suggestion of an eternal summer, a heavenly season which will know no end. Knudsen goes on,

Yes, that summertime of the Spirit in Denmark which at that time so many were waiting for — none of them seemed to think that they really came to experience it. There was something in that expectation which after all suited the eternal kingdom of heaven more than life on earth. But they had difficulty in giving up that hope, in realising that it was not going to happen already here in this world. I remember, early one morning, I was lying in a room beside my father's study, and he came into his room, the door being shut, and he sang but wept at the same time, wept and sang, 'The barren fields will blossom like a rose-garden.' I think that it was from sorrow that he would have to leave to the eternal kingdom so much of what he had hoped for and which Grundtvig also apparently had thought would happen already here on earth, yes, here in Denmark.

The words which he was singing come from one of Grundtvig's most evocative hymns,

> The golden year announces aloud
> the joyful new year's singing,
> The barren fields will blossom
> Like a rose-garden.
> The glory of Lebanon and Carmel
> The delights of Sharon
> Will gather in a dance of light.

Yes indeed, but not in this world, and this is why he wept, although both the words and the melody were so full of joy.[3]

Who is to say whether the tears were not tears of joy as well as of sorrow? *Paradis jo nu er her*, paradise is here right now, and it is precisely because it both is and is not that we can only weep for sorrow and for joy. If paradise were altogether here, sorrow would be totally overthrown. If paradise were altogether absent, we should have no experience of it and so no reason to sorrow at its absence. The tears are ones of sorrow and of joy. 'Joy and woe are woven fine, a clothing for the soul divine' (William Blake).

As Knudsen remarks most perceptively elsewhere, it was Grundtvig's immense love for his people and his profound knowledge of them that made this possible,

Through that love Grundtvig became the instrument through whom years ago a joy was brought to birth in the people of the Danish Church, greater than was known anywhere else at the time. This was so truly a thing of the people, that it was felt most strongly by children ...[4]

The echoes of that joy, when the full power of its original manifestation had faded, continued to resound through the years. It gave a particular quality to the Danish love of celebration and festival. Indeed it still touches those things even today.

II

Something of the warmth and something of the universality of the description of Jakob Knudsen is, as we might expect, to be found in Grundtvig's preaching at Whitsuntide. On Whitsun Day in the crucial year of 1837 Grundtvig preaches on the text, 'We hear them speak in our own tongues, the wonderful works of God', and he begins directly,

Such an exclamation was not unusual in ancient times, when the poets of every people, inflamed with invisible fire, spoke to them with winged words, in parables and image language about the ones who dwell in the heavens, yet who come down to consider the earth, sometimes in a wonderful way to visit the children of men, regarding them as their distant relatives, all of them impoverished and yet not all wholly degenerate. It was not unusual, I say, for this happened not only in Israel, when the prophets spoke, but also amongst all the heathen who had not altogether forgotten that humankind is originally one family with its Creator. It is the Creator who breathed the breath of life into man's nostrils and with it placed the word in man's mouth, the word about the unseen world, the wonderful expression of thought and feeling with the stamp of deity, by which we can be distinguished from all creatures who do not speak ...

So, my friends, what happened on the great feast of Pentecost, when the apostles spoke with fiery tongues about the Saviour crucified and risen again and ascended, and what constantly shall happen in the Church which the fiery tongues created, this is certainly enough unparalleled; but yet it is not altogether or essentially different from what has happened numberless times, when the Spirit came on the gifted, so that they took up their speech, their image speech, and spoke in it in such a living and fascinating way about the secret relationship between heaven and earth, between God and humanity, that their hearers felt that they were visited by the divine, and were powerfully reminded that humanity is made in God's image and after his likeness, in order to reveal his glory and rejoice in his fellowship, who alone has immortality but who wills to share it with us who are the work of his hands and the dwelling place of his Spirit. No, what the Spirit of Christ did on the great Whitsun Day and continues to do until the Lord comes again visibly, as he ascended, is only in degree unparalleled, for the Spirit of Christ worked and works, not only in one single people, but in all the nations under heaven, and he enlivened and enlivens those who receive him, not just for a moment but for eternity, yes enlightens them not just to see a glimpse of salvation, but actually to gain it.[5]

The theme of the sermon is, as we see, a double one. It treats both of the particularity and of the universality of the coming of the Spirit at Pentecost. Indeed the preacher seems to experience a certain tension between the two affirmations, at times stressing what is unique and unparalleled in the event in Jerusalem, at times insisting that it is only an example, even if the supreme example, of something which has been liable to happen at all times and places throughout the course of human history.

When Grundtvig here says that all the nations under heaven have had their poetic and visionary voices, we recognise at once the inclusiveness of his vision. At all times and in all places the creator Spirit has been at work; he has spoken by the prophets not of one but of many peoples. He is, as the Orthodox liturgy maintains, 'everywhere present and filling all things'. But we should not on this account think that Grundtvig had a totally egalitarian view of human history, which ignores the vital distinctions of time and place. Just as there was something unique in the experience of the Jewish people, which gave them a central role in the whole human story, so too, he would argue, there were particular peoples who at particular times had received special poetic gifts and for that reason had become bearers of major historic movements in the story of mankind. Clearly the Greeks were one such people. The people of the North were another. And indeed Grundtvig will argue about the primacy of the Jewish people in precisely this way. In the first version of the World Chronicle of 1814 he says,

The importance of a people depends on the influence it has had in the world, and its good reputation on the character of that influence; now it cannot be denied that through their holy books, and through Christianity which arose amongst them, the Jews had an influence greater and more lasting than any other people can boast of, and moreover the life not only of Christian but also of Mohammedan peoples cannot be understood without some knowledge of the history of the Jews.[6]

Though Grundtvig would not deny to any people a share in the vision and burden of history, there were also peoples, he believed, the nations of Africa for instance, who in his time had not yet fully emerged into the stream of human history. Their time maybe was yet to come.

Grundtvig goes on to stress the inwardness of the relationship between the human and the divine, created by the coming of the Spirit. The feeling of kinship between earth and heaven was, he says,

not wholly foreign to any people who had a word in their mother tongue which expressed what we call Spirit. In all languages this word is derived from the feeling that there is a strange unseen power which even less than our bodily breath can be investigated or described, but which when it is active puts us in a wonderful relationship with another and higher world. Yes, it opens up such a world in our own inmost being, in our mind and in our heart, so that we discover a whole world of new thoughts and feelings, not as something foreign to us but as something which was fast asleep and almost dead, but which now awakens in us and begins, as it were, to draw breath. This is how it was when the apostles' hearers, on that great feast of Pentecost, exclaimed in amazement, 'We hear them speak in our own tongues the great and wonderful works of God.' In this respect what happened to them is not something alien, but something altogether human, something which makes it clear that what is above nature in the Church of Christ is in no way against nature, but rather a divine blessing and transfiguration of the glorious and deep, but deeply fallen and corrupted nature of man, which it pleased our heavenly Father to raise up, to regenerate, to renew, bless and transfigure in his only begotten Son, the seed of woman, our Lord Jesus Christ.[7]

In this view of the latent inner capacities of all human beings we see the origins of Grundtvig's poetic-historic views about education. There is a hidden, unrealised capacity within men and women which the Spirit can release and cause to grow. It is the work of the teacher to assist that liberation. We see also the importance of his own historical songs, both biblical and national, within that educational process. By singing these songs the young will have become participant both in the vision which formed the universal people of God, the Church, and also in the particular calling of their own nation. Sharing in the vision they also became sharers in the responsibilities for action which the vision brings with it. This vision and these responsibilities are not things imposed on them from without. Rather they are the unfolding and articulation of potentials for life and understanding which are already there within them.[8] The whole Grundtvigian method of education was intended to enable people to discover their own hitherto unrealised capacities for action and endurance, for growth and development. This is one reason why it appeals so strongly to people working in the third world today. This method was itself based on a coherent view of human nature and of the action of God within human nature. This is a divine action which raises up and gives new birth, which renews, blesses and transfigures the fallen nature of humanity. We may note here again the happy ambiguity of the Danish word *forklare* which I have translated as transfigure; it could also be translated explain and clarify, but it seems that here the third and fullest meaning is most appropriate.

We see here also, something of the root of Grundtvig's views about national language and national identity. Each nation has its own language. That language is not a private possession. Languages exist within communities, indeed in many ways they shape and even create those communities. The gift of the Spirit at Pentecost draws out and confirms the God-given nature of human diversity and differentiation. Each people has the right to hear the Gospel in their own language, indeed each person has that right. Here there is an interesting counterbalance in Grundtvig's thought to the apparently elitist nature of his views about leading peoples with historical destinies. In his sermons, from time to time, he stresses the rights of the poor and the uneducated; it is time, he repeats, for women and children to hear the Gospel in their own terms. From one point of view, this insistence is part of his constant and relentless criticism of the learned preaching of academically trained pastors, whether they are adopting an old and dogmatic mode, as that of Lutheran orthodoxy, or a modern and speculative one as that of contemporary idealist theology. In either case their words are addressed to the brain alone and not to the whole person; but the words which are empowered by the Spirit must come from the heart and go to the heart. They are to be accessible to all, and they are to affirm the value and capacity of all.

It is interesting to see how a contemporary theologian writing about the missionary activity of the Church and the relationship of faith to culture can make a very similar point in commenting on this passage of Scripture. John D. Davies speaking out of his own long experience of the meeting of major and minor languages in Southern Africa, and of the clash between dominant international cultures on the one side and threatened local cultures on the other, can say, in words which shed light on the reason why Grundtvig's ideas can speak in third world countries today,

The miracle of Pentecost is not just that people are enabled to understand each other... the point is made with considerable emphasis that communication comes to them, not in the international language of the powerful, but in the local languages of family, region and nation ... the most native and deeply running symbol-system inherited from parents in children's earliest years of formation. This is the heart of the miracle. Our own language however insignificant in the eyes of the empire builders and the powerful advertisers, is claimed as a suitable vehicle for the good news ... if your learning is limited to what you can learn through someone else's language where the someone else dictates not only the answers but the questions, you will be losing your human dignity and value. Your faith will not be yours; it will be the faith of the authority which draws up the catechism ... those who heard the apostles' words did not only get information about events external to themselves; they also got an assurance of their own value through the affirming of the language which shaped their basic perceptions.[9]

This point is reiterated in a striking way by Edicio de la Torre, in relation to the struggle for independence and social justice carried on in the Philippines during the last hundred years. Words which have one meaning and resonance in Spanish or in English have a different set of meanings and echoes when translated into the vernacular, e.g. Tagalog. The familiar tongue, the mother tongue, with its imaginative warmth and strength, empowers people to think and act for themselves. The foreign tongue, the technical vocabulary, serves as the instrument of control and, ultimately, of oppression.[10]

III

If the sermon which we have been looking at gives us a strong sense of the coherence of Grundtvig's thought, of the way in which his views on education or on national language are related to his central theological affirmations, the sermon to which we now turn, preached on the second day of Whitsun in the subsequent year, reveals something of the inner coherence of his theology, of the way in which the different elements of Christian belief hold together in his vision of the faith.

The text of the sermon comes from the Gospel of John 3:16, 'For God so loved the world that he gave his only begotten Son to the end that all that believe in him should not perish but have everlasting life.' This is one of the best known and best loved verses in the Bible, especially for evangelical preachers of every persuasion. It is also, as we shall see, a verse of supreme importance in Grundtvig's own understanding of the faith.

Grundtvig begins with a particularly impressive and solemn opening,

This divine summary of revelation, made by the Lord himself, by the only begotten Son, who was given and given up to death, and after the resurrection was given away and left to us, so that we being planted in him might become branches of the tree of life in God's paradise, and through eating his flesh and drinking his blood should have life in ourselves, so that we might live by him as he lives by the Father, this little masterpiece of the Word, the Divine Word who became flesh and dwelt among us, is something we can never sufficiently admire and love and raise up, for there is clearly no equal in the world to this sentence, so short and clear, so simple and distinct and yet so high and deep, so rich and pithy. No other Bible word has so clear and blissful a history as this.[11]

It is fascinating that Grundtvig speaks of this word's history. For him words are living things which come to life and fulfil their true function when they are spoken or sung, when they are at work in human lives and actions, not when they are simply resting on the page. Grundtvig at once goes on to speak of the way in which through all the varied circumstances of the Church's history, in all the places where the Gospel has come, this word has brought the promise of new life in Jesus Christ, and has played a central part in building up the life of the Christian community. But interestingly, and perhaps strangely, his own sermon comes fully to life only when he brings this supreme word of the Lord into contact with another word which he calls 'a beautiful proverb among us' and this is the phrase 'Love is stronger than death'. Grundtvig can hardly have forgotten that this saying too has a Biblical origin, for in the 'Song of Songs', Chapter 8, we read 'Love is strong as death'. But it is from the interaction of the Johannine word with the popular Danish proverb, the word from the Scripture and the word from the people, that the rest of this sermon develops.

Yes, my friends, we have a fine proverb 'Love is stronger than death', and it is the deepest natural sorrow and lament of the human heart that experience only half confirms this, only confirms that love can be strong enough to defy death, and despite of death to continue to love those who in their life time we found attractive and loveable, and even to hazard our life for the one who is deeply loved. It is, I repeat, the deepest natural lament of the human heart that love, although it is evidently in some ways stronger than death can never really overcome or conquer it, can never finally disempower or destroy it. This is the heart's sorrow and lament at the grave of those who are dear to us, and again it is its sorrow and lament in the death throes among its bereaved loved ones from whom it cannot tear itself away.

This sorrow is ended, this lament silenced, only when the heart hears and believes the great Gospel message, that God so loved the world that he gave his only begotten Son to the end that all who believe in him should not perish but have everlasting life. This divine word proclaims from first to last that love is in every possible way and meaning stronger than death, but that this almighty, victorious and ever triumphant love is not that with which we naturally love God or our fellow human beings but that with which God has loved us and sent his Son as the redeemer of our sins. Yes, Christian friends, God our Father did this not because he loved or could love us poor sinners more than his only begotten Son. He did it and could do it only because his love even towards us fallen, defiled, perverse creatures really was stronger than death, stronger in his and in his Son's heart, so that death itself, with all its horror and agony, was less to them than our disaster and loss. Furthermore, this love is stronger than death when in conflict with it.

So not only could the Father's love break the bonds of death for his only begotten Son, but the Son's love, which brought him to die for us, could also free us from the tyranny of death, so that all who believe in him crucified and risen should not perish but have eternal life.[12]

In his desire to stress that there is nothing unnatural in God's work in the world, Grundtvig sometimes seems in danger of wiping out the crucial distinction, crucial that is, in the whole history of Christian theology, between created and un-created, between human and divine. Here we see very clearly that he never really makes that mistake. Here, at the deepest point of human existence, where our human life comes up against its final enemy, death, it is clear that our human love is insufficient. Only the divine love will be adequate. The fact is that as women and men we feel that love could be stronger than death; we long that it should be so and struggle to make it so, but in the end we find that it is not so. This, in Grundtvig's terms, is a sure sign that we are made in the image and likeness of God and that our love itself is in the image of the divine love. It has an infinite longing and desire, but not an infinite capacity and power; that belongs to God alone.

For our love, being created, is always limited, and being fallen it has been fatally flawed and weakened. Only God's love can suffice, which is that love, the love in the Father's heart which is also in the Son's heart, which is both the motivating force and the effective power which enters into combat with death and overcomes it, thereby bringing about atonement between God and his creation. We see in this passage that Grundtvig's view of the death and resurrection of Christ as a triumphant conflict between God and the forces of death and evil implies a view of the atonement which is wholly motivated and effected by love.

Since at least the time of Augustine, when particular attributes of the Godhead have been linked to particular persons of the Trinity, it has been common in the West to associate love especially with the third person. If the Father is power, and the Son wisdom, then the Spirit is love, the bond of love who unites the Father and the Son with one another and with us. Grundtvig always avoids such language. For him it is the Father who is particularly associated with love, and the Spirit with life. Of course, within the Trinity these attributions or associations can never be final or absolute, for what belongs to each belongs to all and what belongs to all belongs to each.

But as, for Grundtvig the Father is always the ultimate source of love, so perhaps we might suggest that the love in the Father's heart, which is also in the heart of the Son, and which brings the Son, in union with the Father's will, to give himself to death for the life of the world, this love is indeed the Spirit who proceeds from the Father and is sent by the Son. Grundtvig does not say this explicitly, though perhaps we may see it underlying his words. What is clear is that we have here an understanding of Christ's atoning death expressed entirely in terms of a triune God whose love for his whole creation makes him give himself entirely to his creation. As a Russian theologian of our own time, Vladimir Lossky, writes,

It is in this context of the divine economy — the love of the Holy Trinity made manifest in the mystery of the Cross — that Philaret of Moscow speaks of, 'the love of the Father crucifying, the love of the Son crucified, and the love of the Holy Spirit, triumphant in the invincible power of the Cross'.[13]

What Grundtvig says directly about the Holy Spirit — and remember this is a sermon at Pentecost — comes in the following paragraph.

This is the first part in the great Gospel, the Christian revelation that God's love, with which he loved us, is stronger than death, and can and will through the faith of our Lord Jesus Christ, in defiance of death grant us eternal life. So for the believing heart the great sorrow is ended, and an imperishable hope is born into this world, which gives us heavenly comfort at the graves of our fellow Christians and at our own. But this faith in the power and greatness of God's love over death would always be hesitant and our hope for life weak if already here we were not at all able to learn from experience to know this love which is truly stronger than death.

So the second part of the Gospel, the revelation that God's love is poured into our hearts by the Holy Spirit who is given to us, assuredly belongs to it, as the apostle says, 'That our hope shall not be ashamed'; but it also lies in the fact that whoever believes shall have eternal life, shall not only hope for it but shall have it. For we cannot possibly have that eternal life except in a love which is stronger than death, and since faith is the only requirement for it then it must be, if God's word is not to be made void, that his love should be born in every believing heart, not just as the natural love to our divine Father, Saviour and benefactor, but as the divine love wherewith he loves us, a love which in us as in him is stronger than death.[14]

So it is that through the action of the Holy Spirit we now become participant in this divine love and can say with St. John,' we know that we have passed from death to life because we love the brethren.

There follows a passage in which we see again that Grundtvig is no less a poet in prose than in poetry, and where what is said reminds us forcibly that however much Grundtvig by his life and being emphasised the social, communal and this-worldly aspects of Christianity, what is often called its horizontal dimension, he never lost sight of its vertical dimension. The heights and depths of the human experience of God are there in his vision as well as the length and the breadth.

And now, Christian friends, let us remain still in the Spirit and gaze into the depths of love both above and below. Of that love we have only a weak but nonetheless a beautiful image in the visible world, when the sky is arched above our head, deep and blue without a cloud or any mist and when it is mirrored in the motionless, clear, sky-blue sea. Let us gaze into that blessed deep, which is both the source of our salvation and our salvation itself, both the source of life and the river of life. Let us see so as never to forget that just as we with our sins deserved not a grain of the amazing love with which the Father loved us and gave his only begotten Son, the love with which the Son so loved us that he gave himself as an offering and sacrifice for us, so there can be not the least merit in our loving in return him who first loved us, loved us with that great and indescribable love, stronger than death. As the Lord says, 'if you love those who love you, what reward will you have for that, do not the tax gatherers do the same?'

There is then not the least merit in this but only incalculable gain because this natural responsive love of ours, this childlike thankfulness, which can in no way fill or satisfy the depths of the heart, does open and expand it, showing our heavenly Father an emptiness which he will gladly fill, a poverty which he will gladly supply. It makes it possible for God to pour out his love into our hearts in the Holy Spirit, who is granted to us in Jesus' name. This divine love with which the Father loves his only begotten Son and us, is the love which as a source of everlasting life becomes stronger than death even in us, and teaches us gladly to know that love with which God loved the world when he gave his only begotten Son, the love which grants eternal life to all who believe in the Son. This is the love with which the Saviour loved his disciples and loves them to the end and with which he will be loved in return by his own, so that they will lay down their life for him and for the brethren just as he laid down his life for us.[15]

If we have been tempted to think that Grundtvig is so taken up in the length and breadth of the divine love as to neglect its height and depth, a passage such as this makes us think again. It reveals a contemplative delight in simply gazing into the depths of the divine love above us and below, the all embracing mystery of the Father's heart. The human mind and heart is invited to be still and to enter into the stillness of the sky and the stillness of the sea on a day of perfect summer calm. Here again there is no denying the reality nor the place of the natural human response of love and gratitude before the immensity of the divine love. But again it is seen that that love in itself is totally unable to make an adequate response to the divine initiative. What it can do is to open and expand the human heart to receive what God has to give, so that God perceiving the heart's poverty and emptiness can overwhelm it with the riches of his bounty. And this God will do, gladly and willingly.

Here Grundtvig goes beyond the language of the fear of death, which he has used in the first part of the sermon, and speaks instead of a sense of radical disproportion between God and humankind. Before God humankind is always poor and empty, aware of its nothingness. Certainly this is language which has been loved by the Christian mystics throughout the centuries, and which commentators have sometimes wished to contrast with the different register which speaks of the conflict between life and death and of our human anguish before death. But the language of poverty and emptiness is there in the gospels no less than the language of the conflict of life and death. We remember the words of the Beatitudes, 'Blessed are the poor in spirit, blessed are those who mourn, blessed are those who hunger and thirst after righteousness.' Perhaps it was the very greatness and multiplicity of his natural gifts — who was richer and fuller in them than he? — which made Grundtvig at times aware of an inner emptiness and poverty which only God's love could fill. He was, as has often been remarked, at all times aware of the reality and anguish of death which puts its question mark against the affirmations of human life, but it is clear that he also had a sense of the absolute littleness and nothingness of humanity and creation before the transcendence of the divine.

IV

We turn now to a third sermon, one which reveals yet another dimension of the Spirit's work in Grundtvig's understanding of it. If the work of the Spirit is to be seen both in the horizontal and in the vertical dimensions of human life, so too it is to be seen in the development of human society in time and in particular in the history of the Church. At Pentecost in 1832 Grundtvig took the opportunity of preaching, on the second day of the feast, on the commemoration of the thousand years of the Danish Church's life, a celebration which had first been held in 1826. It was in that year that he had resigned his ministry and he had therefore been unable to preach on that occasion. Now, at the first opportunity offered him, he takes the subject up and makes good the omission.

Grundtvig begins by saying that there seems to be a great and glaring difference between the universal feast, which we celebrate on Whitsun Day, and the particular commemoration of a thousand years in the life of a single Church which follows it. In the first place we think of the Spirit coming upon all human languages, in the second of the Spirit's work 'confined to a mother tongue which in the world is disregarded and almost unknown'. If this difference between the first and second day really became a kind of rivalry of one with another, 'if what we call our Church wants to be a building alongside the Holy Universal Church which the Lord founded on the rock', then indeed this difference would become a total separation. But thanks be to God this has not happened.[16] Instead Grundtvig turns to the first foundation of the Church in Denmark and to the man particularly responsible for it, Anskar.

In truth, this is not what we learned from our fathers and not what that resident alien taught them, he who laid the foundation stone of the Danish Church and first planted the Whitsun lily on our lips, Ansgarius the man of God; may his memory be blessed. Yes, his memory hereafter shall be solemnly renewed every second Whitsun Day in these lands, so long as the second day humbly bows before the first, so long as the Danish Church sets all its glory in the fact of being an extension of the Holy Universal Church, that longs fervently to lose its own name there in its universal name, and thereby to win the fullness of the blessing of Christ's Gospel which only flows out from the fiery tongues in the midst of Jerusalem, and which only flows into the communion of saints, who call nothing their own, but are of one heart and one soul in Jesus Christ our Lord.

Yes, my friends, when I say that this is how the one, who alone therefore is rightly called the apostle of the North, our evangelist Anskar, considered his work and the Church of Christ, it is no empty flattery or vague rumour which I promote, but the trustworthy witness of his dearest disciple Rimbert. He describes his spiritual life in such a true and blessed fashion, that in so far as what is small and imperfect may be compared with what is greatest and incomparable, so we may compare Rimbert's description of the life of his beloved father in Christ with John's description of the Lord himself. Yes, we can still read among so many other testimonies, what a childlike believing soul, what a tested Christian, what a humble worker in the vineyard and yet an ardent claimer of a martyr's crown, God created for us, and among many such things we may read how that dedicated man dreamed himself in paradise, where all was gathered together in the rays of glory which shone forth from Jesus Christ as the eternal light of the Godhead, the dawn from on high.

So was it with him, our first father in Christ, and so was it also with the second, Martin Luther, the man of God whose blessed memory we will always henceforth join together with Anskar's. Neither the one nor the other of them was or would be anything other than a servant for the spread and strengthening of the faith, preaching not themselves but Jesus Christ their Lord and the Lord of all, to the glory of God the Father. For both would wish that what Paul said of himself and of Apollos should be true of them, 'neither of us was crucified for you nor were you baptised in our name; I planted, Apollos watered, but God gave the increase, and he that plants and he that waters are nothing, but he that gives the increase is all'. Yes, in speaking hereafter of God's planting among us we will say, 'Anskar planted, Luther watered, but the Lord gave the increase', praise be to him in the heights. For it is true that at one time people invoked Anskar as a mediator between the Lord and themselves, and so also at one time people were not free of thinking of Luther as a middle man between themselves and Christ, who should not be invoked but who yet should be believed on his word and followed blindly.[17]

But this is not an error we need fall into if we recognise the work of the one Spirit, active in them both.

These paragraphs are interesting for very many reasons. In the first place they show us how Grundtvig sees the continuity of the Church's history through the ages. He does not hesitate to make a parallel between the work of Anskar and the work of Luther in the growth of the Church of Denmark. Even the greatest moments, for instance the sixteenth century Reformation, are to be seen as events within this continuity. Indeed he positively underlines this parallel by pointing to the danger that there is in trusting to the work of particular apostles or reformers rather than to the Lord himself and to the Spirit who comes from him. Grundtvig is, as we might expect, critical of the medieval cult of the saints, but he is also critical of a certain glorification of Luther which in his view has no less obscured the real meaning of the Gospel. It is very striking at such a point, that he does not criticise the medieval Catholic world without also criticising the world of the Reformation which was so much closer to him.

Still more striking is his evaluation of Rimbert's life of Anskar. On the one hand he makes a very Lutheran distinction between the life and witness of the man of God, small and incomplete, and the Gospel itself, great and incomparable. Then, having made that distinction, he goes on to recognise in the medieval text a genuine intention to show the life of Christ shining out in the life of Christ's servant. He treats the work of Rimbert with the greatest respect. As we have seen in his use of the poetry of Anglo-Saxon England, Grundtvig has a strongly developed and sympathetic respect for the thought of the early Middle Ages as well as a remarkable understanding of it. In a way which is rare in the nineteenth century, he seems able to take these writers of the first millennium with unconditional seriousness.

This high evaluation of the medieval source material is characteristic not only of Grundtvig, but also of the work of some of the nineteenth century historians who were inspired by his ideas. It is interesting to see how differently these particular texts are handled in the contemporary standard history of the Danish Church, where Rimbert's life is treated with far less sympathy and also with less understanding.[18] Grundtvig's approach is startlingly different. Both as a theologian and as a historian he is working with different presuppositions.

This stress on the person and work of Anskar in the history of the Danish Church, and in the history of the action of the Holy Spirit in the Danish Church, was very powerful in Grundtvigian circles, as can be seen in the example of an altarpiece painted in 1872 for a newly founded Grundtvigian congregation on the island of Mors. The painting, which is the work of Christian Dalsgaard, dominates the sanctuary of the church. In a woodland setting we see a young woman holding her baby over a stream so that the child may be baptised by the Benedictine monk, Anskar, who forms the central figure in the picture. Just behind Anskar another Benedictine is to be seen, holding a processional cross over the event.[19]

The choice of the subject, and the prominence it is given as the centre of attention in the church's room, would be surprising in most Protestant Churches and indeed, one might suggest, in much of the Catholic world as well. Certainly in Eastern Orthodoxy it would be unthinkable to place a non-Biblical event in such a crucial position in the church building, however acceptable it would be in a different setting. Here, in the context of a parish community built up around Grundtvig's teaching, it seemed not inappropriate, as an expression of the faith in the continuing life of the Church through space and time, a life which has always been lived in the power of the Spirit and which has been active above all in the sacraments of baptism and eucharist. Certainly, the picture expresses in a very striking way the sense that God himself is at work in the history of a particular Church and people, and the sense within that history of the closeness of the interaction between eternity and time.

We must remember, that at the time when this sermon was preached, Grundtvig was particularly sensitive to charges that he himself was acting in a sectarian way. Many of his admirers had hoped that he would set up a congregation of his own in defiance of the state church. This he would not do, instead accepting the compromise put forward by the church authorities in Copenhagen that he should hold services in the evening in Frederikskirken. These were 'prayer services' which lacked something of the Church's full authority; indeed it was not until 1839 that Grundtvig was again allowed either to baptise or to celebrate the Holy Communion, but these services were not set up in opposition to the Church or in protest against it.

In these three sermons we have seen something of the richness of Grundtvig's teaching about the work of the Holy Spirit, but it is here especially that he excels as a hymn writer and so we must turn from his Whitsun sermons to consider two of his Whitsun hymns.

V

Of Grundtvig's many hymns for the Holy Spirit, here are two. One is brief, simple and yet very typical; the other considerably longer and certainly among the finest of all Grundtvig's Pentecost hymns,

1. The power from on high,
   In the likeness of fire,
   With the delight of all tongues
   Came down on God's people.
   Let us all thank God for his gifts.

2. May the power from on high,
   God's Spirit, join us together,
   From east and west, from south and north,
   As guests at the table of our Lord.
   Let us all thank God for his gifts.

3. May the power from on high
   Rejoice us in our mind,
   As the Lord's people with heaven's peace
   Chosen for God's blessedness.
   Let us all thank God for his gifts.[20]

The hymn is in the same metre as a medieval Easter carol, 'Christ Rose up From the Dead'. That is a hymn originally written in Latin, but translated into Danish before the Reformation, and then re-translated more than once, eventually by Grundtvig himself. Grundtvig's version of this Easter hymn was highly successful and its tune became very popular. Grundtvig therefore wrote hymns for Christmas and Whitsun which would follow the same pattern and use the same tune. The hymn is therefore a mid-nineteenth century composition, but in its form it has its roots many centuries earlier.

The content of the hymn, for all its simplicity and directness, is considerable. The first verse states the mystery of the feast. The Spirit descends in tongues of fire on the people of God; the Spirit descends with the delight and the joy of all tongues. There is multiplicity as well as unity granted by his coming. It is not only the apostles who receive the gifts of the Spirit. Those who are with them share in the same experience. All are gathered together as God's people, God's Church.

The second verse makes this gathering together of the Church more explicit. God's people are to be gathered from the four ends of the world. The prophecies of the Old Testament are to find fulfilment. They are to be gathered together not in one place, but in the sacrament of the eucharist. In sharing together in the feast of the Kingdom, the many members of the body, in all their diversity of origin, are brought together into one.

The third verse opens us towards the world to come, the kingdom of eternity. Our minds are to be renewed by the joy of the Spirit, which brings to us the peace of God which goes beyond all human calculation, and opens up our minds and our eyes to the eternity and infinity of God, an eternity and infinity which are made known in part in this world but are only to be known fully in the world beyond this one. We are chosen out for that blessedness, that ultimate blessedness of life in God himself.

This brief hymn is at once an act of proclamation, of praise and thanksgiving and also of invocation. It echoes, in its own time and place, the sounds of the Easter hymn which preceded it by seven or eight centuries. At the same time it renews, in the West, the Eastern tradition of epiclesis or invocation of the Spirit. It hands on a tradition of Christian celebration which is both universal and particular, rooted in one place but constantly reaching beyond it.

The second hymn is altogether longer and more complex,

1. In all its strength now shines the sun
    The light of life over the throne of grace,
    Now comes our Whitsun lily time,
    Now we have summer sheer and mild,
    Now more than angel voices foretell
    A golden harvest in Jesus' name.

2. In the short coolness of the summer night
    The woodland nightingales sing loud,
    So that everything which the Lord calls his own
    May sleep sweetly and awake gently,
    May dream sweetly of paradise,
    And wake up to the Lord's praise.

3. It breathes in a heavenly way over the dust,
    It flutters gently through the leaves,
    It blows deliciously beneath the sky,
    From paradise opened anew,
    And at our foot there wells up with delight,
    In the meadow, a brook of the river of life.

4. All this is caused by the Spirit who comes down
   All this is worked by the Spirit who speaks
   Not of himself, but to our encouragement
   Out of love, with the voice of truth,
   In the name of the Word, who here became flesh
   And ascended into heaven in flesh and blood.

5. Awake all deep sounds
   To praise the Saviour of mankind,
   Gather together all languages
   In the sacrificial cup of thanksgiving,
   Sound out now over the Lord's table,
   The full choir of God's Church.

6. In Jesus' name then tongues catch fire
   Amongst heathens as well as Jews;
   In the sacrificial cup of Jesus' name
   All mother tongues are fused into one;
   In Jesus' name there then bursts forth
   The eternal hallelujah.

7. Our God and Father without equal,
   Then the rose blossoms in your kingdom,
   As suns we rise and set
   In the glory of your only begotten;
   For you for the heart which we gave you
   Gave us with him your heaven.[21]

The hymn falls into two parts, the first dominated by natural imagery, the second by imagery drawn from Scripture and from the Christian tradition of worship. The fourth verse, the central verse of the poem, is relatively simple in terms of imagery, it is a kind of open declaration of what the first three verses have been constantly pointing towards. For the first time the Spirit is mentioned by name, despite the fact that all the earlier verses have been full of his activities.

These first three verses give us a vivid picture of early summer in the Danish countryside. Because in the north spring comes late, many of the associations which in England gather around May Day are in Scandinavia associated with Whitsun. Leaves are cut down from the newly green trees and brought in to decorate the church. After the long and hard winter, the summer, when it comes, is all the more gratefully embraced. As we have seen in some of Grundtvig's Easter sermons, the short twilight of the northern summer is for him full of significance. Just as at the moment of the crucifixion there was darkness, night, in the middle of the day, so here in the middle of the darkness of night, there is already the first promise of dawn. In the poetry of the seventeenth and eighteenth century, summer was often taken as a symbol of paradise. This is particularly the case with the hymns of H.A. Brorson.[22] Grundtvig here seems to be drawing upon these associations. It is of paradise that we dream in the summer night, the paradise within us, the buried memories of childhood, which Grundtvig believed are in all of us, but also the paradise beyond this world which we long for so blindly. Here too there is a hint of the verse from 'The Song of Solomon' which meant so much to the spiritual writers of the middle ages, 'I sleep, but my heart wakes.' When the senses and the discursive intellect are laid to rest, the deeper places of the heart may come to life and speak.

We have seen in Jakob Knudsen's memories of his first hearing of a Grundtvig hymn, the feeling that the mild warm breeze of the Danish summer was about to usher in some time of cosmic fulfilment. This is what the third verse suggests here. Again, and certainly on purpose, the Spirit's name is not mentioned. The third person of the Trinity is so close to us, so much the heart of our heart, the breath of our breath, that often we do not observe him, often he does not disclose himself openly. Each of the first three lines of this verse speaks of this warm refreshing breeze; only in the fourth line is a more theological affirmation ventured. The breeze comes to us from paradise. No longer locked against us, but opened anew, so that there is no longer a barrier between God's garden, Eden, and the rest of God's world. Paradise is regained. There is a transfiguration, a clarification of nature, as the light of God's creative love shines through. So we see that even the brook, which ripples at our feet, is full of water from the river of life which flows out from the garden of Eden.

There follows the fourth verse, which after all the hints that have gone before, makes a plain bold statement and is comparatively prosaic in contrast to the verses which go before and follow after it. All this, it declares, is the work of the Spirit, who speaks not of himself but in the name of the Word who became flesh, the Word who is now ascended in that flesh into the glory of heaven. This verse leads us on and launches us into the second half of the poem which is as full of the language of the liturgy as the first half was full of the language of the countryside.

In the fifth verse all deeply sounding voices, all the peoples and languages of the world, the full choir of God's gathered people, are summoned to praise the redeemer of humankind. The specific images of the Book of Revelation are not used here, but the atmosphere conveyed has in it something of the rejoicing of the heavenly chorus as it is depicted in that last book of the Bible. But the centre of the verse, the centre of this praise is explicitly eucharistic. It is *i takkesangens offerskål*, in the sacrificial cup, or the offering cup of thanksgiving, that all languages are gathered together. The full choir of the Church of heaven and earth is to sound out over the table of the Lord.

These same motifs are repeated in verse six, but here in an even more insistent tone. Three times it is said that all this is done in Jesus' name. It is as if the anonymity of the earlier verses is now suddenly and finally removed.

Hitherto the Saviour's name has been mentioned only once, and that in a rather conventional way in the first verse of the hymn. In verse four there is a reference to the Word made flesh, in verse five to the Saviour of human-kind. But now all barriers are broken, three times the name of Jesus is repeated, the name which in itself unites the two natures, human and divine, into the one person of the divine redeemer. Here, in this more ecstatic and eschatological context, the languages are no longer said to be gathered together into one but fused together into one, the term which Grundtvig delights to use when speaking of the ultimate coming together of human and divine. This ultimate coming together, this fusion of human and divine, oc-curs in a love which is in itself God's love made perfect in us and our love made perfect in God, that is to say, in the Holy Spirit himself.

The hymn as a whole is of course a hymn of the Holy Spirit, but the penul-timate verse is dedicated particularly to Jesus the Son. As we might expect the final verse therefore arrives at the person of the Father. From a literary point of view this verse is a tour de force. It combines in one the natural imagery of the first section of the poem with the biblical and liturgical image-ry of the second. Whether consciously or not it leads us to think of the end of Dante's great work where the poet sees heaven as an open rose. It takes up the imagery of summer and of the sun which shines in summer, which had dominated the first verse, and uses it to bring the hymn to a close. But here we have entered fully into the world of eternity, and that world is not empty of time. Time is taken into it and so it is said that as suns we rise and set within that Kingdom, clearly suggesting the passage of time and the cycles of the seasons. All the changes and the gifts of time are taken up into that heavenly rejoicing, and so are the changes and gifts of human life and histo-ry. All that is gathered in, into the glory of the only begotten Son, because in return for the heart which we gave to the Lord, God the Father gives to us his Son and with him he gives us all things.

What is implied for Grundtvig in this offering of the heart? It is something which he writes about in many places, and with a particular eloquence in a sermon for 1822 from his years at Præstø. Preaching on the text, 'What shall we render to the Lord for all the benefits he has done for us', he says,

See, this is what we shall render to the Lord, we shall give him our heart, so that it may be his dwelling place, a holy workshop of his Spirit for good works to the praise of the Father. Yes, we must belong to him our Saviour, a people for his own possession, active in good works, if he is to belong to us, as the one who reconciles us to God, as the only begotten Son who will share his inheritance and his glory with those who belong to him, but only with his true and obedient servants. Each soul which will have part in him, and live blessedly with him in his kingdom, must also be his own, as a particular possession; this is what St. Paul expressly witnesses when he says, 'You are bought with a price, you are not your own', and in our text 'He died for all, so that they who live should live no longer for themselves, but for him who died and rose again for them'; yes, and what the Lord himself says, 'Dwell in me and I in you, as the branch cannot bear fruit unless it abide in the vine, no more can you unless you abide in me; I am the vine, you are the branches, whoever abides in me and I in him, he bears much fruit, for without me you can do nothing ...[23]

That Christ is ours and we are his, that he who knew no sin became sin for us, so that we should become the righteousness of God in him, that is the wonderful word, which did not occur to any human heart, but which God reveals to those who love him, through his Spirit, who searches all things, even the deep things of God. This is the word of the Cross, which is scandal and foolishness to the world, but to us who believe, is the power of God to salvation. This is the word of life which the Lord in his Church and people seals with the most holy sacrament of the altar, the wonderful communion in his body and his blood, by which his faithful people become one with each other in him, the members of whose spiritual body we have been made in baptism.[24]

All this is the work of the Spirit in whose love this wonderful exchange of human and divine takes place, in whose love the Father and the Son come and make their dwelling place at the heart of human life. It is very typical of Grundtvig that to express this central mystery of the faith he uses the language both of the Johannine and the Pauline writings in the New Testament. This dwelling of God in the heart of human life is nothing esoteric or strange to the message of the Gospel. It is its core.

CHAPTER 17

The sign of the Cross

I

It may have seemed strange that in following the way of the Church's festivals, we came to Easter without stopping at Good Friday. That was done principally because, for Grundtvig, Good Friday and Easter can never be separated. The cross and the empty tomb, the death and the resurrection, are seen by him not as two things but as one. The thought of the descent into hell is so central for him that it could not be otherwise. The element of conflict, of the struggle with death, is strongly present in the celebration of Easter itself. It is by his death that Christ has overcome death. But it would be false to suggest that for Grundtvig, as for the whole Christian tradition, the cross is anything other than absolutely central to Christian faith and life. Although the Danish Church has not, since the Reformation, celebrated the feast of the holy cross on the fourteenth of September, it seems perhaps appropriate to make use of that traditional commemoration to consider Grundtvig's devotion to the cross, as we can see it not only in his Good Friday sermons but also in his sermons for the second Christmas day i.e. the feast of St. Stephen, the first martyr. It is there that he develops one of his favourite themes, 'the Son of God in the crib, and the Son of Man at God's right hand'. It is by the cross that the crib and the heavenly throne are united.

One of the many surprising facts about Grundtvig's life is, as we have seen, that he had a strong devotion to making the sign of the cross. The formula which was quoted in the last chapter of Part I and which was used in the daily prayers of his household during his latter years, has something of the character of a *lorica* or breastplate, the kind of prayer for protection from evil through the power of the holy cross, which we find in early Celtic Christianity. With its emphasis on our separation from all hostile powers, it carries within itself something of the old formulas of exorcism. It certainly implies the power of the sign when it is made with faith and understanding.

We arrive at another of those areas where Grundtvig was faced with the need to do battle on two fronts. On the one hand there was his determination to maintain, against all tendencies toward a rational explanation of the death on the cross, the full weight of the mystery as it is rooted in the New Testament and deployed throughout the Christian centuries in various forms. On the other hand there was his determination to avoid features in the preaching and exposition of the cross, as he found it both in Lutheran orthodoxy and pietism, which to him seemed profoundly disproportionate; on the one side, the primarily forensic theories of the atonement, on the other, the long detailed meditations on the incidents of the Passion, almost forgetting the glory of Easter. These were things with which he felt great unease. Something of this unease reveals itself in his Good Friday sermon for 1846,

Yes, my friends, ... when we look back over the years we ourselves have left behind in the Lord's house, or when we look to the many centuries which the Church of Christ in its old age has left behind it, then we find much bombastic and much unreal wisdom coming out in the preaching of God's counsel for the salvation of sinners. We find many unsuccessful attempts to explain the great mystery of godliness, in the incarnation of the Word, in our justification by faith in the only begotten, in the life of the Son of God in us and our gathering to him. Yet we always find beside this, first and last, the constant confession and the heartfelt witness, that salvation comes in no way from our explanations or from our wise or foolish thoughts and conclusions, but only from faith in Jesus Christ crucified, the heart's faith in him active in love. However much misuse there has been, both of the sign of the cross and of the word of the cross, yet the whole people feel and the Spirit impresses on all true preachers of the Gospel, that whoever in time and in eternity will have gain and gladness from Jesus Christ, must above all believe in him, confess and proclaim him as the crucified one, as the apostles have shown him to us. He was counted amongst evil doers, nailed to the cross between two thieves, wounded and done to death, mocked and rejected ... We all feel that it must be so, both because the word of the cross is at all times, as in the days of Paul, a foolishness and scandal to the world ... and also because we never come to feel the true Gospel power of God to salvation, before with a whole and heartfelt faith we make our own the word of the cross about the Righteous One who died for the unrighteous, by whose punishment we can have peace as by his wounds we have found healing.[1]

Before and behind all theories and explanations of the meaning of the cross, wise or foolish thoughts and conclusions, there is the plain fact of the death of Christ in all its paradoxical starkness, a mystery whose contours we seek to discern with the aid of the basic affirmations of the New Testament. It is a mystery, whose depth we are not to explain away but to which we commit ourselves in faith, not paying too much heed to the theories which the preachers or the scholars have produced, which only too often have obscured and darkened its true meaning.

In Grundtvig's preaching of the cross we at times feel the presence of the historian, a man who was aware of both the continuities and discontinuities in the Church's movement through the centuries and of the many and various ways in which the cross had been celebrated and proclaimed through the course of Christian history. Particularly interesting in this regard is a Good Friday sermon for 1855. Here Grundtvig begins with the question about the possible existence of the wood of the cross itself. We do not expect Grundtvig to want to encourage a cult of relics, nor do we find him doing so. But we do find him unexpectedly sensitive to the devotion of previous ages, and as always critical of the shallow scorn with which the eighteenth century looked at the earlier stages of church history. Grundtvig affirms that though the cross, like all the other trees on the Mount of Olives and in the Garden of Gethsemane, has by now perished,

we can in no way take part in the mockery of those who long ago, with loving thoughts, dug deep into Golgotha in order to find, if it were possible, a splinter of the cross on which the saviour of the world suffered and died.[2]

Why, he asks, should not the worshippers of the cross look for its remains, when the worshippers of the Roman Empire are always excavating in search of the chains with which Rome bound the world to itself? But this search can have little or no significance for us, for, he maintains, even if we found the tree of the cross or indeed the seamless garment for which the soldiers diced, this would itself be of no importance for those who worship in Spirit and in truth, and who now no longer know Christ after the flesh, even if once they did so know him.

If we now come from the tree of the cross to the sign of the cross, that is already something different, for the sign of the cross is the same for all times and hovers on the boundary of the visible and the invisible, of the bodily and the spiritual, and we are all marked with that sign on our forehead and on our breast in holy baptism, so that among Christians there cannot possibly be thought or talk about mocking the sign of the cross, however much fleshly misuse of it there may have been or still may be today ...

It is moving to know, Grundtvig says, that in the crusaders' time soldiers from the north coming to the Mediterranean could establish themselves as Christians with the use of this sign, even when they had no common language with the people amongst whom they were travelling. He says too that the only way a deaf and dumb person could profess their faith would be with the sign of the cross, and this too underlines its importance. 'The sign is necessarily dear to us all for the sake of him whom it signifies'. Thus again, though in itself it has no worth, any more than the water, the bread or the wine have worth apart from the name of Christ which is joined with them, in its proper use it is to be respected and used.

When the name of Christ is added to it, only then does it become the sign of Christ's cross, when it is explicitly said as at baptism that we acknowledge with this sign that we belong to the crucified Lord, Jesus Christ.[3]

We note that in this paragraph Grundtvig says that the sign of the cross 'hovers on the boundary between the visible and the invisible'; it is a phrase we shall examine again. As we shall see in a hymn written in the following decade, Grundtvig underlines the power of the visible sign to defend us from invisible foes. This visible sign made with the hand, yet has an invisible power when it is linked with the word of faith which proceeds from the heart. Hand and mouth together express the innermost thoughts and movements of the heart; the inner and the outer, the visible and the invisible are linked together into one.

II

If the choice of the Gospel reading for the first day in Advent seemed at first sight difficult to explain, no less problematic to common sense is the placing of the feast of St. Stephen, the first martyr, directly after Christmas Day. Grundtvig is not the first, or indeed the only person, to be struck by the paradox of this arrangement. In the centre of 'Murder in the Cathedral', between the two acts of the drama, T.S. Eliot places a sermon, preached by Archbishop Thomas Becket in Canterbury, on St. Stephen's Day 1170. At the end of his homily the archbishop points the audience towards his own coming martyrdom, and refers to that of his predecessor St. Alphege. But the primary theme of his sermon is the appropriateness of the feast of the first martyr, following immediately on the feast of Christ's nativity. It is only, he declares, in the Church that we are able to grieve and rejoice at once and for the same reason: to grieve over the sins of men which kill God's servants and crucify the Son of Man and at the same time to rejoice and give thanks for the love of God which makes out of their suffering the means of our redemption.[4]

In his 1830 collection of sermons Grundtvig has a sermon for the second day of Christmas which takes up a very similar theme, 'The Cross Over the Crib and The Crown Over the Cross'.[5] It opens up the way which takes us from the feast of Christmas through Good Friday to the crown of life which we celebrate at Easter. In Grundtvig's view these three moments are inseparable from one another in the scheme of our redemption. Throughout the gospel narratives the shadow of the cross is constantly present. Indeed Grundtvig suggests the shadow of the cross is to be seen even in the natural order of things, where we need constantly to moderate our first sense of joy and confidence in life in case it ensnares us into acts of blind foolishness.

However, to speak of the cross over the crib, inevitably, with Grundtvig, leads to the thought of the baptism of children, and to the prominent place which the sign of the cross has in that sacrament in the Danish rite. Before the baptism itself the priest makes the sign of the cross first over the child's face, then over its breast. And it is not only at baptism that in the Danish Church the sign of the cross has a prominent place, it is also evident in the sacrament of communion. Here it is the custom that each railful of communicants waits until all have been communicated before anyone leaves the altar. Before they depart, the priest who is distributing the sacrament, stands at the altar with the chalice in his hand and solemnly makes the sign of the cross over those who have just received the sacrament, saying, as he or she does so,

The crucified and risen saviour, our Lord Jesus Christ, who has now given you his holy body and blood, with which he has made atonement for all your sins, himself strengthen and uphold you therewith, in true faith to eternal life.

This sacramental blessing with the chalice can hardly fail to impress those who from other traditions attend the Danish eucharist.

It is striking, therefore, that in both the gospel sacraments the sign of the cross has a central place. So it is not perhaps surprising that Grundtvig goes further, to discuss the value of acted signs in general and of the sign of the cross in particular. He maintains strongly that the sign is of itself of no value without the word which goes with it. That is not in itself surprising. More unexpected is the parallel he makes between the use of the sign of the cross and the use of the letters of Scripture. Neither, he says, is of any value without that which they signify, both have their value only when united with it. As always with Grundtvig hand and mouth are to go together to express the thoughts of the heart, and so the sign and the word are to be united. The word declares the inner reality in one way, the gesture in the other, the two together confirm and strengthen one another. He maintains, moreover, that the Holy Spirit will create in us, if we let him, 'a deep reverence for the living signs ... and a living use of them ...'. This certainly is a more positive evaluation of the traditional gestures associated with the Church's worship, than is commonly found in Protestantism. They are not, he says, only to be maintained by reason of their historical character. Their use and their meaning is to be renewed through the gift of the Holy Spirit. As Professor Christian Thodberg has pointed out, every element in the Church's ritual, and particularly in the Church's rite of baptism, had its significance for Grundtvig and finds its way into his hymns and his preaching. We have here a striking proof of the way in which, for him, the rite is a whole in which inward and outward both play a vital part.[6]

In the light of these considerations we can turn to Grundtvig's sermon for St. Stephen's day, 'The Cross over the Crib and the Crown over the Cross', and see how he will expound this theme;

At first sight it may seem strange why our fathers in the Church, precisely during the joyful feast of Christmas, should make a solemn commemoration of the first of the suffering witnesses of the Lord, Stephen, who signed his faith with his blood, according to the Lord's prophecy about the sorrowful fate of his servants amongst his raging enemies. And so our Asaph [i.e. Thomas Kingo] begins his lament at Stephen's grave in such a sorrowful way,

Sweet Jesus, Lord of the Feast,
Shoot of the stem of Jesse,
Will men thirst so hastily
After your blood and that of your friends,
Yesterday with angel songs
We welcomed your birth with joy,
Shall we now sigh and weep and today sing a lament?

But we will let the same singer answer us with his lovely lines,

Sorrow and gladness come together,
Fortune and misfortune walk side by side,
Success and failure face one another,
Sunshine and shadow follow each other.

By this we are reminded of the old truth of experience which makes it foolishness to be intoxicated by the joy of the moment, however innocent, however heavenly it may be, for sorrow always stands at the door so long as we have not passed through the valley of the shadow of death and entered into that house from which sorrow and sighing must forever flee away. Nor are we ever weaker to bear sorrow than when it surprises us in the midst of the intoxication of happiness. The fathers, therefore, were right in planting the cross over the crib, for children who are as deeply confident in joy as in life, so that they have no thought at all of sorrow and death except in the moment when they weep them away — children are not frightened at the sign of the cross. And in our growth we must become accustomed to all that will afterwards befall us easily and naturally, and still more to the thing which is for nature most difficult of all for us, the one thing necessary in the discipleship of Jesus, to deny ourselves and take up the cross.[7]

This being so, it ought never to surprise us that the fathers at Christmas have added the words of the cross to the tidings of joy. To do that was in every way Christian, for how often did not the Lord himself grieve his apostles by foretelling what would happen to the Son of Man and to all his true servants? It was not only in the night in which he was betrayed, or on the day when he wept over Jerusalem, because its children would not understand the things which belonged to their peace and would not seek shelter with him, who so lovingly called for all troubled souls as the hen calls to her little ones to gather them to her breast and be guarded under her wing. No, not only then did the Lord take pains to prepare his disciples for the grief and tears they were approaching; he did the same at the first joyful outburst of their faith in him as the Son of the living God, who had the word of eternal life, he moderated their excess of joy with the word of the cross when they saw him transfigured on the mount and already in their thoughts built a paradise hut of branches on earth before his dazzling countenance. And when he stood on the plain, as a God, before all men's eyes, surrounded by his glory and looked upon with wonder, then he said to his disciples, 'Take note of this, the Son of Man shall fall into the hands of men'.[8]

But, Christian friends, this is eternal life
That we know God and him whom he has sent, Jesus Christ.
This cross of Christ which we shall take up in order to follow him,
Is our ladder to heaven, which we raise up in order to come to him
Where he is, the Lord crucified but risen again, ascended into heaven,
And when we are in this way lifted up from the earth,
Then heaven opens to us, as to St. Stephen,
And we see the Son of Man, standing at God's right hand,
Where he lovingly beckons us with his glorious hand to come up,
And put our finger into the print of the nails,
And feel eternally that the sufferings of this time
Were not worthy to be compared with the glory which was to be revealed in
    us.
If it is so with the cross over the crib,
That the crown does not only hover over it,
But grows out of it, like the May-green crown of beech leaves,
Whose precious stones are singing birds,
If this is the connection between the cross of Christ and the Crown of life,
Then it is no wonder that Paul would know nothing
In the Church save Christ crucified,
And no wonder that the fathers let the lament for Stephen
Merge with the hymns of Christmas,
So that the Spirit could make from them both the new song
For the redeemed of the earth,
The song answering to the sound of David's golden harps, the stringed
instruments,
The song worked out with toil and sweat
Here in the dim workshop of dust,
In order that it might shine through heaven
And sound through eternity.[9]

Here again we see how naturally the preacher modulates into a form of prose poetry and takes up elements of the patristic exposition of Scripture and makes them his own. Here too we can see how naturally a passage based on biblical imagery can move into the use of imagery taken from the Danish countryside, so that the cross becomes the tree of life surrounded by 'the May-green crown of beech leaves whose precious stones are singing birds'. Here, through Grundtvig's art, the Spirit makes a new and living pattern of imagery through the fusion of these varied elements. But again Grundtvig returns to the theme of the cross and to the disuse of its sign.

We have considered it popery that in old time people continually signed themselves with the cross and had it always before their eyes in their private rooms and placed it beside all their roads. We are right to do so in so far as people usually imagined what is foolish, that the God whom we worship can be served by human hands or that the visible in itself can be more than a shadow of the invisible. But he who depends on actions and worships shadows is an idolater. But surely, when we also considered the cross itself and its constant use and appreciation as fanaticism, then we made a still greater error, and that has, alas, only too much been the case as we can rightly conclude from the oblivion and the contempt into which the sign of the cross has fallen.

Yes my friends, this is already enough to teach us how dead and powerless the word of the cross has become among us, for if the word could not even preserve its sign, what then would it be able to effect? If even the shadow was disgusting to us, how much more would the reality be? Or, is it really any more possible to love, revere and continually remember the word of the cross while despising and abolishing the sign, than it would be to despise and set aside the letters of the Bible when one loves what it signifies, the word of the living God on the tongues of prophets and apostles? Certainly I think not. And if in baptism we have received the sign of the holy cross on our face and on our breast, as a testimony that we shall believe on the crucified Lord Christ, and if the same sign was united to the blessing which was given to us when first we came as guests to the Lord's table, how then should we be steadfast in our baptismal covenant and living in the Lord's communion, if we did not have this sign of the Son of Man constantly before our eyes, and if we did not have a heartfelt love for it, as a remembrance both of the fellowship of his sufferings and the power of his resurrection?

Although then a sign can never profit us unless we, in spirit and in truth, have and seek what it signifies, and although there has been an un-Christian, nay, an anti-Christian misuse of the sign of the cross as of the letter of the Scriptures and of all that visibly and concretely signifies the great mystery of godliness, God as revealed in the flesh, justified in the Spirit, seen of angels, preached among nations, believed on in the world, taken up into glory, nevertheless it is just as sure that we cannot possibly have the Spirit of Christ, who is the Spirit both of the prophets and the apostles, who both creates the signs of life and makes them living, unless the signs which he has created are both important and dear to us. We cannot have the Spirit, unless the life which he works in us creates a deep reverence for the visible signs, which are the work of his hands i.e. his instruments, and creates a living use of them; for remembrance, for warning, for confirmation.[10]

This is indeed to give a positive evaluation not only to this particular traditional gesture but to the whole world of Christian signs and symbols. We get here a glimpse into one of the areas where Grundtvig would have found much that was congenial in the thought and practice of the Oxford movement if he had only been able to enter into a less controversial relationship with its leaders.

Just so little, therefore, as someone without deep reverence for the Scriptures and a frequent study of them could become an instructed Christian, let alone a Christian wise man, just so little could anyone hope to find, I dare to say, a happy bearer of the cross, let alone a Pauline preacher of the word of the cross, or a martyr like Stephen, who did not gladly consider, love and use the sign of the cross. Certainly, it does not itself work miracles but it is inseparably connected with the word which has worked them from the Church's foundation, and which works them till the end of time. Amongst us, had things gone so far that even the priests seldom, or only reluctantly, placed the cross in baptism over the Lord's crib, or raised it up at the altar, for those who would have fellowship in the body and blood with the crucified but risen and ascended Lord? Had they gone so far that scarcely at the grave side could we bear the holy sign which we all should have embraced in our cradle and borne triumphantly, as our King's victorious banner, all our life long? Then indeed, it need scarcely amaze us that there was so little understanding of the deep mystery of the cross, and still less love of it, so little vision of the crown of life and still less joy and strength to fight for it. For if even the image of the cross was a burden to us, what would the reality be? If we struggled to avoid the sign, which yet faithfully reminded us of the victories gained under the banner of the word, how should we have courage to meet tribulation? If we had no eye for the wreath of glory which on earth sprang from the cross and was placed upon the martyrs' heads, holding it in blessed remembrance, how should we have a thought of the heavenly crown which precisely here has its only present image?[11]

A quarter of a century after this sermon was composed Grundtvig wrote a hymn on the same theme. Here he is still more insistent on the danger of giving too much importance to the sign in itself, without the word which goes with it, for in themselves signs are of no avail. But at the same time, Grundtvig is no less insistent on the power of the cross to protect us from the evil one, when the outward sign and the inward intention are united. Indeed he stresses this particular point even more strongly. He declares that the word of the cross is the Christian's shield and the sign of the cross the device upon that shield. Certainly, here he must have in mind the white cross on the red ground which makes up Denmark's national flag. He ends with the remarkable statement that 'making the sign of the cross is still the terror of the powers of the air'. Once again we recall his idea that the sign hovers between the visible and the invisible, linking and distinguishing inner and outer realities in human life.

But in the end, even more interesting than his evaluation of the sign is his understanding of the meaning of the cross itself. The cross leads into life. It is the tree of life. It not only wipes away sin but brings healing in place of death. It is the life-giving, healing character of the cross which is underlined here as in so many other places. We move from the crib by the way of the cross to the gift of eternal life; the crown which God places on his creation's story.

> 1. The word of the cross, foolishness for the world,
>   Is yet the truth of God and in it
>   There is with the power of God
>   The blood of Jesus as the sap of life
>   Which wipes away the traces of sin,
>   Wherever it is sowed around the world
>   The healing herb for death grows up.

2. The sign of the cross and the word of the cross
   Only fools on earth will separate.
   Only as the servant of the word can our hand
   Be used by the Spirit of Life
   So that at the bath in the stream of life
   It can make the sign of the cross
   As a protection for God's little ones.

3. The word of the cross in the sign of the cross
   Gives strength to the Church's bulwark
   Only when with hand and mouth
   It is built upon the foundation of faith
   As a sign that we are bound to him
   Who for us bore the shame of the cross
   And is both the lion and the lamb of God

4. Vain is the cross in the earth,
   The cross of wood or silver or gold
   The cross made with three fingers or five
   Without the word which has life in it
   Without the name of Jesus Christ,
   A shield against all power and cunning
   The word of victory here and beyond.

5. Only in the strength of the Lord's voice,
   On our forehead and our breast
   Is the cross, the sign of heaven,
   Sign and proclamation of that peace of God
   Which in the Church of God
   Rejoices soul and heart alike
   Under all the quarters of heaven.

6. The word of the cross, that is our shield
   Against all the assaults of the fiend.
   The sign of the cross made strong by the word
   Is the proud device on our shield.
   When it is recalled with faith
   Signing with the cross
   Is still the terror of the powers of the air.[12]

CHAPTER 18

The Ministry of Angels

I

We can see the seriousness with which Grundtvig took the Church's traditional patterns of belief, especially as they are expressed in its hymns and
liturgical forms, in a sermon preached on the feast of the Annunciation in
1842.[1] A reading of this sermon shows that the many references to angels in
his hymns are not merely figures of speech, or sentimental decoration. Rather
they express a deeply felt and coherent view of the nature and activity of
angelic spirits.

From the outset it becomes clear that Grundtvig regards the denial of belief
in angels as only a part of the whole nineteenth century tendency to deny the
reality of the bond uniting earth and heaven which has been established both
in creation and in the incarnation. Grundtvig's understanding of the angels
is strongly christological, centred on the person of Christ. Both in the old and
the new covenant angelic visitations have prepared the way for God's mighty
acts and for the coming of God's messages. The references to angels of God
ascending and descending upon the Son of Man, to the vision of Jacob's
ladder, to the angels with Abraham beneath the oak at Mamre, all point to
this function of the angels in helping to bring together the two parts of God's
creation, heaven and earth, created first in harmony, separated then by sin,
and now restored to a more perfect unity in Christ. It is in Christ that the
reconciliation is brought about; the part of the angels is altogether in relation
to him.

Here, as in other places, Grundtvig asserts that redemption in Christ
involves the restoration of what was in the beginning. This is true both at the
personal and the universal level. It would seem that for him personally, a
sense of the presence and protection of angels had been a vivid experience of
childhood. This was not a thing to be despised or ignored. Memories of the
reality of angels, whether from the childhood of humanity, or from the
childhood of the individual, are for him indications of that dim memory of
original innocence which persists within us, of that vision of a world at
harmony in itself and transfigured by God's glory. At the personal level, this
sense is a part of the recovery of contact with our own childhood perception
of things which Grundtvig constantly advocates.

Grundtvig knew only too well the force with which both the rationalism of the eighteenth century and the critical spirit of the nineteenth denied this belief,

... The memory of the festive days of God's mighty acts, and of the great visions and revelations of them, has grown cold and weak in the course of time ... Self-opinionated cleverness has established a yawning gulf between heaven and earth, which is not supposed to be crossed either from above or from below ... It has become the fashion to think, either that there are no angels, or that if there really are, and that in days of old they visited the earth, as we read, in the service of the Most High, all this could not possibly happen now, and it would be the wildest enthusiasm, and gross superstition to expect it.

To recover and revive that childlike faith in the nearness of heaven and earth can never be an easy thing. For Grundtvig, as we have already suggested, it is intimately bound up with the whole possibility of belief in the incarnation. The rejection of angels is only one aspect of the rejection, by human reason, of the great paradox of the divine-human exchange which he sums up, more than once, in the words, 'the Son of God in the crib, the Son of Man at God's right hand.' Grundtvig draws comfort from the thought that the Blessed Virgin herself lived in a comparable age of blindness and unbelief, and he does not hesitate to ponder on the significance of her as an historical example. In his sermon, which we shall quote, we seem to see her as a young Danish girl in the late eighteenth century, sitting under a rationalist preacher, puzzled as to whether she really understands him, still more as to whether she should believe him, for this eternal problem posed for human reason seemed to Grundtvig to have taken on a particular urgency in his lifetime. In the force of his rejection of the spirit of the age, touched by the icy hand of unbelief, and in the strength of his affirmation of the real restoration of the paradisal harmony between heaven and earth brought about by the child-bearing of the blessed Mary, we can again see a power of conviction similar to that expressed by his English contemporary, John Keble, when he wrote,

> Yearly since then with bitterer cry
> Man hath assailed the Throne on high,
> And sin and hate more fiercely striven
> To mar the league 'twixt earth and heaven.
> But the dread tie, that pardoning hour
> Made fast in Mary's awful bower,
> Hath mightier proved to bind than we to break,
> None may that work undo, that Flesh unmake.[2]

If in much of his writing Grundtvig stresses the earthly, human element in Christian faith and life to an extent which is unusual among theologians, here he constantly stresses its heavenly and eternal side. It is true that as he comes to the story of the incarnation he emphasises that all this is not *un*natural or *un*-reasonable. God works through nature and grace alike. The birth of the Lord is prepared for by the birth of John the Baptist. But though it is not un-natural, he knows that to talk of angels as creating links between earth and heaven has a supernatural quality which seemed strange to the nineteenth century mind which tended more and more to think of the physical universe as a self-contained, self-sufficient organisation. And it is therefore the more significant that throughout this sermon on the Annunciation Grundtvig stresses the importance of this element of Christian belief, which for many reasons, not least on account of the realism of its other-worldliness, has been so little appreciated among nineteenth and twentieth century Western Christians. In stressing the reality of the angelic world, however, Grundtvig is not only pointing to the reality of a world beyond this one, he is also affirming the heavenly nature of the Church's life and worship already now, its direct connection with the eternal world of God's immediate presence, the share which even in this world we have in that divine activity.

In this sense there is a strongly eschatological flavour in Grundtvig's re-ferences to angels. His sermons are full of an understanding of the way in which the whole life and worship of the Church on earth is to be united with the praise and service of the Church in heaven. In itself this is a theme common to all pre-Enlightenment Christianity, and remembered by Grundt-vig from his childhood knowledge of the old Lutheran hymns. But it may be that there is also here a sign of the influence of his later knowledge of the hymnody of the Latin West and of the liturgical books of the Eastern Church. In the monastic offices of the Byzantine rites this note is struck again and again, as 'the Church upon earth, together with the powers above, offers to the triune God, the thrice-holy hymn of praise and adoration'. Through his hymn writing Grundtvig himself did much to strengthen the note of praise and thanksgiving in the worship of the Danish Church; here we can discern some of the motives for his action. It is only out of a life of praise and thanks-giving that we can be prepared and worthy to receive the Lord when he comes to us in his word and sacrament. This involves a new awareness of the many dimensions of human existence, of the unrealised potential for what is eternal to be found in creatures who are living in time. In this work of preparation the angels have their part, in visiting us, and lifting up our feeble prayer and uniting it with theirs, so that the Church's liturgy becomes a real participation in the celestial liturgy, a foretaste of the life of heaven. Thus, like the mother of the Lord herself, we are made ready by the visitation of angels.

All this indeed is seen in the context of christology. All centres on Christ. Grundtvig was too good a son of the Reformation to wish to give to the angels any function or status in our life, independent of their relationship with Christ. But he knew only too well, from his own experience, that to use the Reformation principle of 'Jesus only', in a negative or exclusive sense, ends in destroying the very thing that it intends to safeguard. 'Those who speak of the presence of our Lord Jesus, without the holy angels, talk at random and do not know what they say.' For where the Lord of heaven and earth is, there the whole creation must necessarily come together to worship, and both the heavenly and earthly orders of beings must be united in the adoration of their common Lord.[3]

II

So the 1842 sermon begins,

Christian friends, it is written, the Sadducees say that there is no resurrection, and that there is neither spirit nor angel; and when we see from the gospels that a great many of the foremost priests and scribes were Sadducees, and continued to be so, while the Spirit of God evidently rested upon the Son of Man, and God's angels ascended and descended upon him, and he not only powerfully witnessed to the resurrection by raising up the dead, but showed on the great Easter morning that he was himself the resurrection and the life, then it cannot but be that the Virgin Mary had also heard in the synagogue at Nazareth that it was only childish credulity and irrationality which took literally what we read in the book of Moses about the angels who visited Abraham in the grove at Mamre, and refreshed themselves with him under the oak, and brought Lot out of Sodom, and that all that had been said about revelations of angels in more recent times, was mere fairy-tale, either made up by impostors, or circulated by superstitious enthusiasts, who imagined that they themselves had visions and revelations.

But the gospel for today, which has put the Sadducees of all time to shame and turned their wisdom into foolishness, teaches us, that either unbelief had found absolutely no entrance into the blessed among women, or that it must have given way before the powerful witness which the angel Gabriel had given to himself six months earlier, when he had revealed himself to old Zacharias in the temple, and said to the doubting priest who asked for a sign, 'I am Gabriel, who stand before God's face, and am sent to speak to you and bring you joyful tidings; but since you have not believed my word, you shall be dumb, and shall not speak until the day that it comes to pass.

Yes, my friends, it was not for nothing that Gabriel reminded Mary about her cousin Elizabeth, who should be the mother of the Baptist. And it must not be in vain, that today's gospel reminds us of this same connection, which casts light on God's wonderful governance of things, which always makes use of the natural as far as it reaches, and here makes use of the relationship and friendship between Mary and Elizabeth in order to prepare the great announcement, to prepare the Lord's mother. And we can well understand, that in the midst of an age, to a large extent openly unbelieving, and on the whole horribly self assured and unspiritual, in which our Lord was pleased to be born — that in such an age the woman who was to be his mother, needed greatly to be strengthened in her faith in the living interchange between heaven and earth, and in the almighty effects of God's Word and Spirit. There was enough to be read of this in Holy Scripture, and there were innumerable traces of it from the days of old; but many of those who seemed both learned and virtuous were scornful of it, and against it they raised the most daring objections.

We who have lived in only too similar days, know that even for believers, even for the devoutest of women, in such evil days, there goes as it were a devastating whirlwind over their heart's paradise, which as an icy hand touches their faith and hope, and all their dear memories. But we can also well understand that the amazing thing which happened to the devout old Zacharias, and the incredible thing which happened to her cousin Elizabeth who, according to the angel's word, became with child in her old age, was for Mary's heart like dew on parched meadows, yes, like the breath of spring after winter's cold. Her childhood faith with all her childhood dreams was woken from sleep. All God's angels who, according to the Scriptures, had visited the people of Israel and the land of Judah in days of old, became living for her. Yes, she in spirit saw again the ancient ladder of heaven set up, on which the patriarch Jacob saw the angels ascending and descending, and the Lord himself standing at the top. And though she, like him, found it awesome to be so near the house of God and the gate of heaven, yet she could not have suppressed the secret wish, that she also might be worthy to see a vision of angels, and to hear a voice from them who stand before God's presence and sing out his praise both day and night in his temple. And thus she was prepared for the revelation of which we read in today's gospel, though the news that she should bear the Son of the Highest was something which had never arisen in her heart, and of which she had never dreamt, since it went far beyond what she could either pray for or understand.[4]

We have here an interesting example of the way in which Grundtvig will take a New Testament passage and bring it directly into his own historical context. At first sight he may seem excessively naive in drawing so close a parallel between two such different periods of history. But his method is rooted not only in his view of the divine way of action but also in his understanding of human nature. From the beginning, being made in God's image and likeness, human beings have an inherent capacity for relationship with the divine, and in this relationship with the divine there are constant features which seem only slightly affected by more superficial social and cultural changes.

In this way, my friends, we shall strive to free ourselves from the prevailing misunderstanding of the supernatural and the extraordinary as something un-natural and unreasonable, when it is in reality only the sublime, which from the day of creation has a natural connection with us, as heaven has with earth. Since it is the same God who created both parts, both heaven and earth, both angels and men to his glory, to the eternal song of praise which shall be sung by all his angels and his servants, by all his creation in all his dominions. It is he who created man in his own image and likeness to wonderful glory, as David sang, 'When I consider the heavens, the works of thy hands, the moon and the stars which thou hast ordained, then I must say, Lord what is man that thou art mindful of him, and a son of man that thou visitest him. Thou madest him a little lower than the angels, but thou crownest him with honour and glory, thou placest him over the works of thy hands, and hast put all things under his feet.

Yes, just as sun and moon and stars, the visible lights of heaven, are set to shine by day and night for the children of men, to serve their growth and their joy, to guide their ways and divide their times, so are the holy angels, the spiritual lights of heaven, whose clothing is like lightning, set to serve the little ones on earth, those who shall inherit the kingdom of God, watching and escorting them, enlightening and gladdening them, so that we ought much more to be surprised that they now no longer let themselves appear to the faithful, than that of old they revealed themselves as God's appointed messengers to Abraham, God's friend on earth, and to the woman who found grace in his eyes. And indeed, my friends, we all need to be prepared by such thoughts, if we are again to have real confidence in the marvellous holy history, and come to a living acknowledgement of the fact that the God of heaven, who did not leave himself without witness even in the darkest days of heathendom, does so still less now in the days of the new covenant, among the children of light.

Yes, we greatly need it, for things have gone no better in Christendom than they did formerly in the land of Israel. Here as there the memory of the festival days of the mighty acts of God, and of the great visions and revelations of them, has grown cold and weak in the course of time. Here as there, self-opinionated cleverness has established a yawning gulf between heaven and earth, which is not supposed to be crossed either from above or from below. Here as there it has become the fashion to think, either that there are no angels, or that if there really are, and that in days of old they visited the earth, as we read, in the service of the Most High, all this could not possibly happen now, and it would be the wildest enthusiasm, and gross superstition to expect it. But it is not so long since our forefathers still sang,

> God grant his holy angels bright,
> His heavenly armies to watch around us and protect us.
> May they go with us on the way,
> And bring us all home along the right path.
> May they further what we undertake,
> And at night stand about our beds,
> And finally at our days' end,
> May they bring our souls into thy hands,
> And bring them from this vale of tears
> Into the glad house of heaven.[5]

But on the one hand these verses are now so little heard, that it is mostly only from our childhood days that even the older among us remember them, and even then as a dying fall, and on the other hand not even then did they sound as a thanksgiving and glad expectation from the Spirit's paradise, but as a sigh from the vale of tears, that is from the abyss. For only there is the vale of tears; the earth is the Lord's, and the fullness thereof, and the redeemed community is God's house, the dwelling place of the Most High, where the river of life waters his garden. And yet, Christian friends, if this conception of the invisible, but yet real garden of Eden, which God planted in flesh, when he let his Son rest under a woman's mother heart, and play on her knees, if this conception is to be more than a glimmering shadow, if it is to become a living and joyful truth for us, then the distance between heaven and earth must in the Spirit disappear for us, much more than the world boasts about, with its new discoveries which have physically made even the longest distances on land and sea virtually to disappear. For a paradise without angels, is like a wood without birds, or a beautiful song which no one sings or hears.

The new discoveries to which Grundtvig refers must refer primarily to the use of steam engines both on land and sea. It is an interesting example of how much he is alive to the most recent industrial developments. It suggests to us how fascinated he would have been by all the more recent developments of technology which have strikingly reduced the distance between one part of our planet and another. But this reduction of the divisiveness of distance within the human world of space and time is for him not to be compared with the transformation brought about by God's initiative in the incarnation which bridges a gulf of an altogether different kind.

Here Grundtvig points to a new understanding and experience of the world as created by God, a world in which the earth is in open communion with paradise, in which the angels move freely from one part of God's kingdom to another, in which it is possible to see the spirit messengers guiding the children of men, just as the sun and the moon and the stars guide them on their earthly journeys. This creation is restored in its wholeness and can be perceived in its beauty precisely because the whole of what God has made, heaven and paradise and earth, has been drawn into a new unity with God himself in the incarnation of the Word, and in this unity open relationship and communication has been restored between the different levels of the created order.

It is certainly true that when we have the saviour, our Lord Jesus Christ and he is all to us, the ground of our heart and our portion for ever, then we need no other light, no other guide or teacher. But it is also true that whoever speaks of the presence of our Lord Jesus without the holy angels speaks at random, and does not himself know what he says. For the Lord will never be without his heavenly servants and companions, who perform his word when they hear the sound of his voice. They ascended and descended upon him, even when he went about in the form of a servant, and they follow him now gladly as Lord in heaven, wherever he comes and takes shelter and establishes his dwelling. And he never comes without first being announced and foretold by a heavenly forerunner like Gabriel in today's gospel; he does not come before all is prepared so that he may be received with worthy joy and praise, as in Mary's song of praise, 'My soul doth magnify the Lord, and my spirit hath rejoiced in God my Saviour, who has regarded his humble handmaiden, for behold from henceforth, all generations shall call me blessed.' And the hearts of men learn such worthy, joyful and heavenly notes of the song of praise only from the heavenly singers, the holy angels, who announce the Lord, accompany and follow him, and comfort those who long for him with the great word, 'He will soon come again.'

Therefore, my friends, it is not at all, as many think, simply that when we just industriously repeat the hymns of praise which we find written either in the Bible, or in our fathers' hymn-book, then we are ready to receive the Lord worthily, and then we lure down God's angels to sing with us. No, it is first from the angels that we learn how the true hymns of praise sound, and it is only by learning from them, as children, that we come to meet together with psalms and hymns and spiritual songs, and sing and play gracefully in our hearts before the Lord. So soon, therefore, as the faithful become unbelieving in this matter, and will do without the angels, or do not dare to acknowledge them as their heavenly guides and teachers, then with the angels, the heavenly song of praise also dies away from their hearts and their lips; they find it flat, tasteless and old-fashioned, and change it for their own high sounding words, which taste too much of earth to be considered in heaven, and are much too narrow to contain its joy.

On the other hand, when we again miss the angels and sigh after them in Jesus' blessed name, which the angel Gabriel first named on earth, and when they simply come near, as they do at once, as soon as a heartfelt sigh in Jesus' name is heard, then our eyes are enlightened, so that we can see what before we blindly threw away with Mary's song of praise and with our fathers' Christmas hymn, 'It is right that we should always honour him by singing with the angels, Glory and praise to God in the highest.' Then the tone of the song of praise sounds darkly in our ears, the tone we had forgotten, and thus we are prepared to learn it again from the angel hosts who first brought it to earth in the great night of Christmas. When we have learnt it not from without, but from within in angelic wise, then the Lord comes, so that we can sense it by the light which shines around us, by the peace which fills us, and by the fullness of joy which visits our hearts. Amen.[6]

III

Reading such a sermon we can hardly fail to reflect on the relation of faith to imagination which it implies. On the first sight it seems to be a simple expression of Grundtvig's description of himself as an old-fashioned believer, an almost naive affirmation of a literal and uncritical acceptance of traditional points of view. But we know that Grundtvig, as a scholar and a thinker, was by no means naive, and even though he was highly critical of the typical critical attitudes of his time, he was not at all unaware of them or of their force.

But even a first reading of the sermon shows us again that Grundtvig does not cease to be a poet when he writes in prose, 'For a paradise without angels is like a wood without birds, or a beautiful song which no-one sings or hears.' This paradise of which he speaks is no other-worldly place, it is a paradise made known here in this world,

the invisible, but yet real garden of Eden, which God planted in flesh, when he let his Son rest under a woman's mother heart and play on her knees.

It is the life of the Christian community, and of the Christian within it, a life lived in conscious awareness of the nearness of God to our daily living.

That paradise is perceived by faith, but by a faith which involves a wholeness of human perception and certainly includes the imagination and the senses. To speak about angels here, is to speak about the activities of the imagination when it begins to become sensitive to the hidden quality of things as created by God. Thus faith in the incarnation is intimately connected with an awareness of the activity of angels in Christian worship, with a sense of the heavenly character of the corporate prayer of the Church, which prepares us to realise the other-worldly potentials which are inherent in human nature. It is also linked with the less massive, more personal and fleeting perceptions of the many dimensions of reality, those 'epiphanies' which many writers and artists have celebrated in the twentieth century. In a time when structured systems of belief have been more and more questioned, the sense that works of art, visual, musical, literary, give us access to non-temporal dimensions of existence has grown stronger. So we see again Grundtvig's insistence that while faith goes beyond nature it does not go against nature. His vision of an interpenetration of earth and heaven is prepared by a rebirth of the Christian imagination, a rebirth which not only his hymns, but his poetry in general, are aimed to bring about.

These epiphanies are often occasions when we perceive the inadequacy of our usual perception of time as a simple line which moves through the past from the present to the future. We become aware of the intersection of the timeless with time, and begin to sense the meaning of older conceptions of the relation of the temporal with the eternal in which time itself is conceived of as containing an angelic dimension, a created reflection of eternity, which while it does not involve a direct entrance into the eternity of God yet makes us vividly aware of it. Is not this above all, our experience both of poetry and music in their finest manifestations? As George Steiner says, quoting Claude Levi-Strauss, 'the invention of melody is the supreme mystery of man', and Steiner continues, 'it may well be that man is man, and that man 'borders on' limitations of a peculiar and open otherness because he can produce and be possessed by music.'[7] This open otherness is something which Grundtvig seems constantly to express both in his poetry and his prose, both of which at times border on the world of music.

We see also, as we have seen in many other places, that Grundtvig was a man very strongly in touch with his roots, both in the personal sense that the childhood experiences of a transfigured world were still real within him, and also in the more historical sense that through his wide reading of Greek and Norse mythology on the one side, and the literature of Christian prayer and worship on the other, he was well aware of the large part angelic beings had played in the past of human society both in the Christian tradition and in the pre-Christian religions which had prepared it. In such a sermon we are able to see how it is, that in appearing to be pre-modern Grundtvig is in fact beginning to be post-modern. He can speak to a world which in the last twenty years has become again strangely aware of the presence of angels both good and evil, to such a degree that even theologians have not been able to remain wholly unaware of the fact. He can speak to a western world which is more willing, at least at times, to take note of the experience and even of the wisdom, of societies which in the past have been considered primitive and undeveloped. Grundtvig writes as a man who is conscious of the role angelic spirits have played, not in one culture, but in many, and who knows in his own experience that there are moments of artistic and poetic inspiration and activity which seem to call out for explanation in terms of the intervention of angels, of angelic calls and annunciations. These are things 'learned from within, in angelic-wise'. In this context he tells us we know the presence of the Lord, 'by the light which shines around us, by the peace which fills us, and by the fullness of the joy which visits our hearts'. Would we be wrong to think that here he is speaking from experience?

Above all, as we have already noted, Grundtvig makes these affirmations, not by repudiating the christological principle on which Reformation theology is based, but by reinterpreting it in a radical and creative way. The reformers encountered a Christian world where, especially in the realm of popular practice and belief, everything seemed to be in confusion. The prayers of the saints, the intervention of angels, the veneration of holy objects and holy places, all these things were flourishing in the early sixteenth century. There was an immense multiplicity of ways and means by which God's presence might be made known to believers. But somehow, in the midst of all this exuberance something essential had been lost, a sense of proportion, a sense of the one thing necessary, a realisation of the absolute centrality of Christ in the whole of Christian faith and prayer and life. That centrality must at all costs be reasserted and reaffirmed, both in theory and practice. The multiplicity of images had ceased to be means which opened the way between earth and heaven and instead had become solid screens which separated the two worlds, one from another.

In reasserting the priority of the one thing necessary there was an increasing tendency on the part of the reformers to adopt a reductionist tactic; all that is not strictly *necessary* is to be laid aside. The celebration of the angels, the prayers of the saints, the love of holy places, are these things strictly necessary? Are they useful even? Do they not become distractions from what all acknowledge to be the heart of the matter? Better then to cut them out altogether. So, in the Genevan Reformation, at its most radical, the whole wealth of visual sign and symbol disappeared from the church buildings. So, more generally, the reformers were so anxious about an unbalanced cult of the saints that it seemed better to say nothing about them at all. Over the centuries, in both the main traditions of the Protestant world, one was left with a kind of Christo-monism, the figure of a solitary Jesus and a heaven empty of saints, a heaven empty of angels. The reductionist tactic had in the end undermined the very thing it was meant to safeguard.

In the face of this tendency, indeed in the face of its underlying principle, Grundtvig proposes a totally different way, based on a principle of fullness and inclusivity. The centrality of Christ, the priority of the doctrine of our justification by grace through faith, is not in any way questioned. But now it is interpreted inclusively and not exclusively, and all the secondary matters of faith and belief come back in their true place and proportion, and are seen to be, if not in the end strictly *necessary* in the sense that where they are absent the central affirmation can no longer be made, yet still an *integral* part of that affirmation in its fullness, so that where they are denied, the central affirmation becomes diminished, pulled out of shape and ultimately inaccessible.

The world in its plenitude, is created for the increase of joy. God's action is not to be reduced or confined by any purely human criteria of what is necessary and strictly useful. There is, in the work of grace and nature alike, an exuberant multiplicity which may in the end be neither necessary or useful in our ordinary understanding of those words. The world both physical and spiritual is prodigal in its extravagance. It is something which goes quite beyond all our calculations of necessity and utility.

Just as sun and moon and stars, the visible lights of heaven, are set to shine by day and night for the children of men, to serve their growth and their joy, to guide their ways and divide their times, so do the holy angels, the spiritual lights of heaven, whose clothing is like lightning, serve the little ones on earth, those who shall inherit the kingdom of heaven.

There is an immense and incalculable exuberance in the divine activity both in creation and redemption, both in heaven and on earth. God is not to be measured and confined by our thoughts and expectations. This is a theology in which themes such as amazement, growth and joy have taken a central place and given to terms such as necessity and usefulness their own strictly secondary and ancillary position.

Epilogue

I

Looking back over the many years in which, from time to time, I have been involved in the study of Grundtvig, there are a number of tentative conclusions which stand out;

1. Grundtvig is a man who speaks to the situation of our post-Communist era. One of the most perceptive bishops of the Church of England has recently written 'Our society, indeed our world, is increasingly dominated by a fragmented individualism, as harsh in many aspects as the collectivism it has replaced. But unless we can find a 'third way' collaborative and inter-dependent, a 'relationship society' in which we can learn how to live for each other and especially for the weakest and the poorest, we shall never begin to discover a more satisfying way of life.'[1]

Grundtvig's view of humanity is radically collaborative and inter-dependent. His view of society embodies a third way which is neither in-dividualistic nor collectivist. It is not just that he thinks that people ought to work together and depend on one another. He sees the relationship society as the only truly human society, for human beings find themselves only when they find that their life is rooted in the life of God, three in one.

2. He is a man who speaks to the situation of a world which is deeply per-plexed by the strength and persistence of feelings of national identity. We thought we had left these things behind, but they now come back to us in frighteningly irrational and destructive ways. Grundtvig is a man who takes these questions of national awareness with the utmost seriousness. He knows how important these questions are, and how much human beings need the sense of belonging and identity which active participation in a national community can give. But he sees that nations, no less than individuals, only function properly when they function in a collaborative and interdependent way. The nations have need to work with one another and to respect one another's differences; they too discover themselves in discovering their neighbours.

3. Inseparably connected with this sense of national identity is Grundtvig's understanding of the importance of languages and the differences of languages. The languages of our planet, especially those spoken by relatively small numbers of people, are under great threat; statistically speaking it

seems likely that the great majority of them will have died out in the next century. Grundtvig believes passionately that languages are among the greatest of God's gifts to humanity, and that each one has its own specific beauty and excellence. Knowing how difficult, yet how rewarding, it is to translate from one language to another, even when they are as closely related as English is to Danish, it is saddening and perplexing to see how little time, energy and thought our society is willing to spend on learning to appreciate the languages of others, and to understanding the full meaning of their diversity and difference.

4. But if Grundtvig is a man who values and cherishes the differences between peoples and languages, he is a man who still more values and affirms the possibilities of communion and unity within the human family. As a priest, a preacher and a pastor in the Church of Christ he is passionately concerned for the unity and integrity of the Church through time and through space. He is, I believe, though this has not been widely recognised, one of the major ecumenical prophets of the nineteenth century. His insights could be of direct use in our problems today.

His wonderful sense of the poetic, many-layered nature of language, his feeling for the living presence of the past, in and through the vicissitudes of history, point towards a church which is one in its freely accepted diversity. This 'poetic-historic' view of things provides a sovereign antidote to temptations towards authoritarian and literalist systems of whatever kind, which seek to reduce all to unity by decreeing uniformity.

5. The strongly poetic nature of Grundtvig's theology is also to be seen in his awareness that the whole living world, and not humanity alone, is involved in the drama of God's self disclosure. For him the earth too is made in God's image. In opening themselves to the divine realm men and women find that their sense of bodily solidarity with the natural world is strengthened and not weakened. It is not only a solidarity in death; more deeply it is a solidarity in transfiguration and resurrection.

6. This all-inclusive sense of the way in which humans belong together with other living beings speaks powerfully to people outside the North American, Western European world. In surprising ways Grundtvig's vision of Christianity takes up themes characteristic of the primal religions, insights whose importance has been realised afresh as people have sought to struggle with the problems raised by our environmental dilemmas. Even more powerfully, Grundtvig's conviction that the *almue*, the ordinary man and woman, have latent inner resources, which when released can lead to the transformation of society, has called out a deeply committed response in developing countries both in Africa and Asia. There is clearly unfinished business here.

7. When we return to that Christian world to which Grundtvig so entirely belonged, we have had reason to see in these pages that Grundtvig's view of
the Christian faith is constantly crossing the barriers between Catholic and
Protestant, and between East and West in the Christian world. It is highly
unitive. His vision of God's purpose is not restricted to the drama of sin and
redemption, however vital that may be. Rather, he thinks in terms of a
purpose of love which begins in creation, grows through the transfiguration
of the things that are made, and comes to the fulfilment of that purpose in the
revelation of God's kingdom, or, as he loves to say, the union of human and
divine through the marriage of heaven and earth.

As a distinguished Danish novelist, critic and historian of culture, Martin
A. Hansen, wrote in the years after the second world war, there is something
in Grundtvig which looks towards the future. Surveying the history of the
west since the Reformation, he stresses the importance of the distinction
between individual and person.

The path of personality is just as strictly defined in Grundtvig as in Kierkegaard.
But in Grundtvig one has a stronger feeling that this path is quite different to that
of individualism — it is in fact its opposite. In Grundtvig the personal cannot
develop without immediately being transmitted and united with the personal in
others. Grundtvig has the effect of an originator after the three others, Luther, Kant
and Kierkegaard. The last is the Protestant consummator. Grundtvig belongs to the
future, he transcends Protestantism and in him a culture seems in embryo.[2]

II

Throughout the writing of this book I have been tantalised and at times tor-
mented by the problems of translation, and in particular by the problems of
translating poetry. Of course the example of Grundtvig himself, the arch-
translator, has stood as a permanent rebuke to moods of defeatism, but not
everyone has his particular combination of abilities. I have however been sustained by two recurring thoughts; first that if the work is honestly, however
inadequately, done then at least something of the original must shine
through, second, that this book is only a provisional one. It is my greatest
hope that before long it will be superseded, that enough of the splendour of
the original will appear to entice other scholars in the English-speaking world
to take up the task. To translate Grundtvig in any adequate way would be the
work of not one person but of many, not of one effort but of many. I hope
that this preliminary study may set in train a process of Grundtvig
assimilation and affirmation.

Meanwhile, to conclude, I intend to present three hymns which may each
in their own way sum up different aspects of Grundtvig's understanding and
presentation of the Christian faith. Each one in its own specificity expresses
something of the heart of what Grundtvig was and did. I shall present them

with a minimum of commentary since by now they are able to speak for themselves.

The first hymn has its roots in an Old Testament psalm, Psalm 87. This is a psalm which speaks about Jerusalem, Sion, the city which is beloved both by God and man.

> On the holy mountain stands the city God has founded,
> The Lord loves the gates of Sion
> More than all the dwellings of Jacob.
> Glorious things are spoken of you,
> O city of God.

An old and standard commentary on the psalms speaks of this psalm as expressing the highest point of the universalism of the psalter. In it the psalmist declares that in a mysterious way Sion is not only the mother of all the tribes of Israel, but of all the nations in the world. Of all, it shall be said, that they also were born there. Then at the end there comes the image which has most of all caught Grundtvig's attention,

> The singers and the dancers will say,
> 'All my fresh springs are in you.'

> 1. All my springs shall be in you,
>   That was God's word in the ancient days
>   To the people who had no equal
>   Who bore our Lord's mother within them.

> 2. All my springs shall be in you,
>   That was God's word in the fullness of time,
>   When he was born, whom angels praise
>   When the virgin Mary bore him within her.

> 3. All my springs shall be in you,
>   So resounds the voice from open heaven,
>   The voice of the Father at Jesus' baptism,
>   My Son, I am well pleased in you.

> 4. All my springs shall be in you,
>   That is God's word in the days of grace
>   To the bath, which has no equal,
>   The Spirit bath, our Lord bore within him.

> 5. All my springs shall be in you,
>   That is the high speech of God the Father
>   To the baptism, which in the earth's valley
>   Our Lord bears hidden in himself.

6. All my springs shall be in you,
   From you, earth and heaven shall be reborn,
   The multitude of nations, tongues and stars
   With all that I have eternally borne in me.[3]

The shape of the hymn is perfect. It begins with Israel, it centres down on Mary and Jesus, it opens out again, not only to Israel but to the whole human family and in the end to all creation. From you earth and heaven are reborn, the whole of God's creation nations, languages and stars, with all that God, from all eternity, has borne within himself.

This is one of Grundtvig's feminine hymns, delicate as well as strong.

The second hymn begins from a text of the gospels. It shows us Jesus as the fulfilment of the longing and expectation of many generations. It begins with the past to which Jesus and his contemporaries look back, but not only that, it begins with the past of Jesus and his contemporaries to which we look back. It begins with the expression of a widespread nostalgia. If only we had been alive then ... But at verse three the mood and the rhythms change. It is we who are lucky now. Verse four expresses, as only Grundtvig can, that the days of the gospel message are now and not any other. Very simply Grundtvig says that not only do we hear God's Word now but that we may also see him in our midst. In large parts of his writing, as indeed in large parts of the biblical tradition, the ear seems to be privileged over the eye. We hear God's Word even when we do not see him. Here, though the world does not see him, we are given that privilege. Jesus stands before us in the midst of his people as he did in the midst of his frightened disciples on the first Easter day. In his presence heaven and earth are reunited. Paradise is planted again in the desert of the heart.

1. Eyes you were blessed indeed
   You who saw God's Son on earth,
   Ears you indeed were rich
   When you listened to his word,
   On whose tongue alone prevail
   The truth of God and God's grace.

2. Many kings and prophets
   Had longed to see your day.
   The sighing of hearts and the singing of angels
   Prophesied the golden year
   When God's light and life would triumph
   In its strength over death and darkness.

3. How lucky are we Christians now
   The time of grace is not past;
   But enlightened by the gathering of the Church
   We too are the favoured children of grace.
   Eyes see and ears hear
   The one who brings us God's word.

4. He who grants us light and life
   With his Spirit and his Word,
   He who binds up all the broken
   At his font and altar board
   Jesus Christ, bringing our gladness
   Living comes, is present with us.

5. He, though the world does not see him
   Yet stands before the eyes of faith,
   And at every instant his word
   Penetrates to the heart,
   Kindles light in the dark of the grave,
   Plants paradise in the desert.

6. The poor heart was born blind
   But now it sees the rays of his godhead,
   The soul was dead and we were pained,
   But now it lives in his Spirit,
   Born again to God's kingdom,
   We even see it in his light.

7. Eyes you are blessed indeed
   You who see God's Son on earth,
   Ears you indeed became rich,
   When you heard the word of life.
   Heart, when you believed the word,
   The tree of life sprang up from its root.[4]

This I think we may say is one of Grundtvig's masculine hymns. In its fourth verse it seems to echo the formula from the Byzantine rite for ordination which speaks of the divine grace, 'Which always heals what is wounded and makes up what is lacking'. Certainly that healing, all supplying grace is celebrated in these lines.

This third hymn also begins from verses in a psalm, in this case Psalm 89, 'Blessed are the people who hear the festal shout. They shall walk in the light of his countenance'. This is a fuller and more elaborate statement than the two preceding ones, which works by a constant reiteration of the images of the interchange, the *vekselvirkning* of heaven and earth, the *admirabile commercium*, what Luther calls the *fröhliche Wechsel*. In the first verse it is the exchange of Spirit and dust, in the third verse it is the heart with its depths and its heights, in the fourth verse it is the tongue with its light and its power and its healing, in the fifth it is the divine human exchange itself which takes the centre of the stage and in the sixth again the divine grace which heals what is wounded and makes up what is lacking. Again we find in the end that paradise is here and now.

1. How blest are that people who have an ear for the sound
   Which comes from above,
   Who already here echo the eternal song,
   Hallelujah;
   So all God's angels are astonished to hear
   How heavenly the earthly bells sound
   When the Spirit with the tongues of the heart of dust
   Sings out the depths of its longing.

2. How blest is the dust, which in the creator's hand
   Came so close to God,
   Enlivened by him with a royal spirit
   To heroic deeds,
   Gifted in grace, with hand and mouth
   To gain and to gladness at all times
   To become like his God, at the best
   And speak with him as with a neighbour.

3. How blest is the heart in the human breast,
   With fear and hope,
   Which is moved with delight by the voice of heaven
   And the call of the Spirit,
   Which has room in its lowly hut
   For longings as deep as the sea is wide,
   For hope which rises up higher
   Than eagles or angels on wing.

4. How blest is the tongue in the human mouth,
   With life and speech,
   Which puts down its roots in the depths of the heart
   To eternal solace
   Which shines with the light in the word of life,
   Which glows with the fire on the table of grace
   And grants to the hearts that weep
   God's peace and the gladness of heaven.

5. How blest are that people who have Jesus for king,
   Mary's son,
   As his brothers and sisters they all have things well,
   Open and hidden,
   God's peace in their heart, God's word in their mouth,
   With the hope of glory at all times
   For they, as the chosen of God the Father,
   Share kinship with his only begotten.

6. How blest is each soul which in the Saviour's name
   From the hand of grace,
   Received healing for its hurt, and for all its loss
   With life and Spirit,
   With the Spirit of the Father and the life of the Son
   With the strength of the martyrs in a trembling reed
   With the power as the proof of glory
   With the keys to paradise.[5]

Afterword

by
Nicholas Vladimir Lossky, Professor in the University of Paris X,
and in the Orthodox Theological Institute of St. Sergius.

We must be grateful to Canon Allchin for acquainting us with a major figure of the Christian world, hitherto known to only a few. N.F.S. Grundtvig was a fellow-countryman and a contemporary of Kierkegaard whom everybody knows and regards as a great thinker and theologian. Thanks to Canon Allchin's thorough study of Grundtvig and very attractive presentation of his life and extraordinarily rich work, the barrier of language (for those of us who do not read Danish) has been broken down and an outstanding theologian, poet and liturgist, author of many hymns, has been revealed to us.

Perhaps the most striking thing about the theology of Grundtvig, as presented in this book, the fruit of many years of study and reflexion on the part of the author, is the discovery in Denmark in the nineteenth century, of a truly patristic approach to the Christian mystery. This should in no way be understood as a mere knowledge of the thinking of the Fathers whom Grundtvig knew very well indeed. In other words, it is not simply an interest in the past which characterizes this theology. Grundtvig, as we learn, was indeed profoundly attached to the past: not only the Fathers or the early medieval history of the Church, but also the Anglo-Saxon past, and more generally the past of the peoples of the North. However, as Canon Allchin shows, he was as passionately interested in the present. And it is in this sense that his theology is comparable to that of the Fathers of both East and West.

The Fathers of the Church witnessed to the fundamental truth of Christianity, 'Jesus Christ, the same yesterday, and today and for ever' (Heb. 13,8), Jesus Christ whose Incarnation and redemptive work manifested the love of God the Trinity. But they witnessed to that eternal truth *in their time* and *to their time*. They had a profound sense of the present, in communion with past events. Past and present unite in what T.S. Eliot, another patristic Christian, called 'the point of intersection of the timeless with time'. There is no doubt that Grundtvig would have highly appreciated the *Four Quartets*.

This marriage of past and present in an encounter between time and eternity results in the fact that those who truly witness to their time, take their own time seriously, generally transcend their time: their witness becomes a witness for all times. This is the case with the Fathers of the Church; this is the case for Grundtvig.

Another aspect of Grundtvig's theology should be emphasized as something he has in common with the Fathers. It is the very important fact that his theology is not only an exercise in intellectual speculation. His theology is concentrated on the nature of salvation offered to human beings and through them to the whole of creation. It is therefore what might be termed a 'utilitarian' theology. At the same time, it is doxological. There is no divorce or watertight separation between Grundtvig as preacher, Grundtvig as poet and above all, Grundtvig as hymn-writer, liturgist in other words.

In several ways, all this makes him comparable to several specific Fathers of the Church. Only two will be considered here: one 'Eastern' and one 'Western', although the terms are not altogether satisfactory, for the two are very close to one another in many ways. The 'Easterner' is St Basil the Great. The 'Westerner' is his friend St Ambrose of Milan.

Everyone knows St Basil as the author of the Treatise on the Holy Spirit, of other works, of canons and many letters. But we have to remind ourselves of the fact that in his preaching he revealed a deep concern for the life of the city, (comparable to Grundtvig's concern for contemporary history). St Basil's sermons in defence of the poor, addressed to the rich are among the strongest expressions of the radicalism of the Gospel. We also have to remind ourselves of his building hostels and hospitals for the poor, the needy and the sick.

In this care for the poor and the appeal to the rich, he is of course very close to St Ambrose whose sermons on the same subject are very similar to St Basil's. What is more, St Ambrose's interest and concern for the political life of his time is too well known to be even mentioned. He had begun his life in politics and on becoming a bishop he did not lose his care for political affairs and the defence of justice. We all remember that he was also a hymn-writer.

St Basil's interest in politics appears in his famous Eucharistic Liturgy in which we find most beautiful prayers for the powers that be and for the peace of the world. This Liturgy is also probably the most explicit among all about the cosmic character of the Eucharistic prayer: the prayer encompasses not only all imaginable human situations but also all aspects of natural life, the whole of creation. This, Canon Allchin has shown, is one of the characteristics of Grundtvig's theology.

Thus, as theologian, hymn-writer, liturgist and poet, Grundtvig deserves to be compared with these two prestigious predecessors.

Canon Allchin insists on the deep connexion between Grundtvig and his country, Denmark. And it is probably precisely because he was profoundly Danish, that is local, profoundly attached to his culture but certainly not in any way exclusive of other places and cultures, that he deserves to be recognized as universal, catholic. Catholicity is by definition unity in diversity or diversity in unity after the model of the Holy Trinity.

Through revealing Grundtvig to us, Canon Allchin has done more: he has revealed Denmark to the English speaking world, and beyond, to the whole world through translations of his book which would be most welcome.

Nicholas Lossky

Notes

Prologue

1. Quoted in A.M. Allchin, 'Grundtvig and England', *Heritage and Prophecy*, 18.
2. Jakob Balling, *Kristendommen* (Copenhagen, 1986), 277.
3. A.M. Allchin, 'N.F.S Grundtvig and Nationalism in Wales', *Grundtvig-Studier* (1992), 33-45. D.J. Davies first came to Denmark in 1924 when he attended the International Folk High-School at Elsinore. Here he met a young Irish student, Noëlle French and they decided to get married. Davies was to become the leading economist in the early years of the Welsh National Party. His wife became an authority on Grundtvig, publishing a brief but well rounded study in 1931, *Education for Life: A Danish Pioneer*, and in 1944 a second book published for Plaid Cymru, *Grundtvig of Denmark: A Guide to Small Nations*, a study of Grundtvig's thought about national identity. They were an interesting couple since he came from a Welsh working class mining family, while she came from an aristocratic Anglo-Irish background. Noëlle Davies became an active member of the Grundtvig Society and contributed the English summaries published in *Grundtvig-Studier* until 1964.
4. Povl Eller, *Salvingerne på Frederiksborg* (Copenhagen, 1976), 53.
5. The church bells are rung on week-days even though there is usually no service.
6. *Den Danske Salmebog*, no. 372.
7. *Værker i Udvalg*, vol. VII, 470.
8. Johannes Knudsen, *Danish Rebel: A Study of N.F.S. Grundtvig* (Philadelphia, 1955), x & xi. Johannes Knudsen, one of the outstanding scholars of the Danish-American community was president of Grandview College, Des Moines, Iowa, from 1942-1952 and later Dean of Graduate Studies in the Lutheran School of Theology in Chicago. He was one of the leading interpreters of Grundtvig's work in the U.S.A.
9. Christian Thodberg, *Syn og Sang: Poesi og Teologi hos Grundtvig* (Copenhagen, 1989), 140.
10. N.F.S. Grundtvig, *Vartovs-Prædikener 1839-1860*, ed. Holger Begtrup (Copenhagen, 1924), 244-47.

Chapter 1: Childhood to Ordination

1. Quoted in A.M. Allchin, 'Grundtvig and England', *Heritage and Prophecy*, 18.
2. Jakob Balling, *Kristendommen* (Copenhagen, 1986), 277.
3. A.M. Allchin, 'N.F.S. Grundtvig and Nationalism in Wales', *Grundtvig-Studier* (1992), 33-45. D.J. Davies first came to Denmark in 1924 when he attended the International Folk High-School at Elsinore. Here he met a young Irish student, Noëlle French and they decided to get married. Davies was to become the

leading economist in the early years of the Welsh National Party. His wife became an authority on Grundtvig, publishing a brief but well rounded study in 1931, *Education for Life: A Danish Pioneer,* and in 1944 a second book published for Plaid Cymru, *Grundtvig of Denmark: A Guide to Small Nations,* a study of Grundtvig's thought about national identity. They were an interesting couple since he came from a Welsh working class mining family, while she came from an aristocratic Anglo-Irish background. Noëlle Davies became an active member of the Grundtvig Society and contributed the English summaries published in *Grundtvig-Studier* until 1964.

4. Povl Eller, *Salvingerne på Frederiksborg* (Copenhagen, 1976), 53.
5. The church bells are rung on week-days even though there is usually no service.
6. *Den Danske Salmebog,* no. 372.
7. *Værker i Udvalg,* vol. VII, 470.
8. Johannes Knudsen, *Danish Rebel: A Study of N.F.S. Grundtvig* (Philadelphia, 1955), x & xi. Johannes Knudsen, one of the outstanding scholars of the Danish-American community, was president of Grandview College, Des Moines, Iowa, from 1942-52 and later Dean of Graduate Studies in the Lutheran School of Theology in Chicago. He was one of the leading interpreters of Grundtvig's work in the U.S.A.
9. Christian Thodberg, *Syn og Sang: Poesi og Teologi hos Grundtvig* (Copenhagen, 1989), 140.
10. N.F.S. Grundtvig, *Vartovs-Prædikener 1839-60,* ed. Holger Begtrup (Copenhagen, 1924), 244-47.

Chapter 2: Conflict and Vision

1. Whitsun Monday 1814 (Frederiksberg Church, Copenhagen). Quoted in F. Rønning, *N.F.S. Grundtvig: Et Bidrag til Skildring af Dansk Åndsliv i det 19. Århundrede,* vol. II,2. (Copenhagen, 1909), 7-8.
2. *Ibid.,* 2-6.
3. William Michelsen, 'Grundtvig's Christian Breakthrough 1810-12', *Tradition and Renewal,* 50.
4. Sigurd Aage Aarnes, 'Grundtvig the Historian', *Ibid.,* 54.
5. *Ibid.,* 59.
6. *Ibid.,* 57.
7. The name of an early medieval earth-work defending southern Denmark, comparable to Offa's Dyke.
8. Andreas Haarder, 'Grundtvig and the Old Norse Cultural Heritage', *Ibid.,* 80.
9. M. Wynn Thomas (ed.), *Diffinio Dwy Llenyddiaeth Cymru* (Cardiff, 1995), 184.
10. *Værker i Udvalg,* vol. VII, 345-46.
11. The words *folk* and *folkelig* correspond in dictionary terms both to nation and national, and to people and popular. But in Danish, and particularly in Grundtvig, they convey a more positive meaning than in English, suggesting moral obligation as well as simple identity, responsibility for, as well as solidarity with a particular historic community. See the article by Vagn Wåhlin, 'Denmark, Schleswig-Holstein and Grundtvig in the 19th Century', *Heritage and Prophecy,* 255-69.

12. Jakob L. Balling, 'Grundtvig, Dante, Milton, and the Problem of European Continuity', *Heritage and Prophecy*, 78.

13. *Ibid.*

14. Quoted in an essay on this poem by Christian Thodberg in *Syn og Sang: Poesi og Teologi hos Grundtvig* (Copenhagen, 1989), 174.

15. See Jørgen I. Jensen's valuable article in Hans Boll-Johansen and Flemming Lundgreen-Nielsen (eds.), *Kaos og Kosmos: Studier i Europæisk Romantik* (Copenhagen, 1989), 31-33.

16. Christian Thodberg, *op. cit.*, 204. I use the version given by Thodberg in this essay, to which I am greatly indebted.

17. J.P. Bang, *Grundtvig og England: Studier over Grundtvig* (Copenhagen, 1932), 41.

Chapter 3: New Directions, Inner and Outer

1. Hans Henningsen, 'The Danish Folk High School', *Heritage and Prophecy*, 286.

2. Niels Lyhne Jensen (ed.), *A Grundtvig Anthology: Selections From The Writings of N.F.S. Grundtvig, 1783-1872* (Cambridge, 1984), 106.

3. For Grundtvig's first three visits to England see Helge Grell, *England og Grundtvig* (Århus, 1992).

4. S.A.J. Bradley, ''Stridige Stykker snild jeg forbandt': Grundtvig's creative synthesis of Anglo-Saxon sources', *Grundtvig-Studier* (1996), 101.

5. *Ibid.*, 103-4.

6. *Ibid.*, 104-5.

7. *Ibid.*, 105.

8. *Ibid.*, 106.

9. *Ibid.*, 108.

10. For Noack's account of Grundtvig's meeting with the poetry of the Anglo-Saxons see 'Grundtvig and Anglo-Saxon Poetry', *Heritage and Prophecy*, 33-45.

11. These two essays are to be found in Jørgen Pedersen, *Fra Augustin til Johs V. Jensen: Essays og Afhandlinger* (Copenhagen, 1991), 92-165 & 165-204.

12. Jørgen Elbek, 'Grundtvig og de latinske salmer', *Grundtvig-Studier* (1959), 57.

13. Grundtvigs *Sang-Værk*, vol. 3, no. 233, 471-72.

14 Jørgen Elbek, *op. cit.*, 58.

15. Jørgen Pedersen, *op. cit.*, 195-6.

16. In a remarkable passage in his one-volume study of Grundtvig, still after seventy years one of the most valuable books of its kind, Edvard Lehmann makes the point that Grundtvig's turning to the Middle Ages was not based on a purely individual or aesthetic attraction to the medieval Catholic world. Rather he saw there a life which was 'not only more devout and more Christian but also stronger and more human' than that of his own time. He believed that there were resources there which would speak directly to the peasants and the urban poor who were nearer to that medieval world than the educated classes. So he grasped the idea of the renewal of the parish 'not just as a historian but as an organiser'. He saw the church gathered around the sacraments as a source of new life, both spiritual and material for the whole community. 'This is what the English would call 'high church' and 'low church' united in one; the sanctuary of the church borne on the people's

shoulders, borne by the people, made up of the people — that is Grundtvig's democratic church'. Edvard Lehmann, *Grundtvig* (Copenhagen, 1929), 176-79.

17. Hans Henningsen, 'The Danish Folk High School', *Heritage and Prophecy*, 285.
18. *Den Danske Salmebog*, no. 167, verse 7.
19. Sigurd Aarnes, 'Grundtvig the Historian', *Tradition and Renewal*, 62-66.
20. William Michelsen, *Tilblivelsen af Grundtvigs historiesyn* (Copenhagen, 1954), 42.
21. *Grundtvigs Erindringer og Erindringer om Grundtvig*, 180-81.
22. *Ibid.*, 181.
23. *Ibid.*, 182.
24. *Ibid.*, 184.
25. Helge Toldberg, 'Nugent Wade i Helsingør', *Grundtvig-Studier* (1948), 48.
26. *Ibid.*, 49.
27. *Ibid.*, 50-51.
28. *Ibid.*, 53.

Chapter 4: Unexpected Fullfilment

1. *Grundtvig-Studier* (1949), 103. The translation made by Dr. Noëlle Davies is taken from the English summaries of an article by Kaj Thaning, *'Grundtvig og den Grundlovgivende Rigsforsamling'*, 35-74.
2. F. Rønning, *N.F.S. Grundtvig: Et Bidrag til Skildring af Dansk Åndsliv i det 19. Århundrede*, vol. IV,1. (Copenhagen, 1913), 47-48.
3. *Ibid.*, 68.
4. *N.F.S. Grundtvigs Poetiske Skrifter*, ed. Svend Grundtvig, vol. VII (Copenhagen, 1889), 474-76. The first two verses are part of a poem signed 'Frederik Skjald', 'Frederik the Poet'. The second three verses are part of a separate poem written at the same period.
5. *Ibid.*, 476.
6. *Værker i Udvalg*, vol. VIII, 368 ff.
7. *Ibid.*, 370-71.
8. *Ibid.*, 371.
9. Leon Litvack, *J.M. Neale And The Quest For Sobornost* (Oxford, 1994), 95-100.
10. *Letters of John Mason Neale D.D., selected and edited by his Daughter* (London, 1910), 189-90.
11. *Ibid.*, 190-91.
12. *Ibid.*, 191.
13. Steven M. Borish, *The Land of the Living: The Danish folk high schools and Denmark's non-violent path to modernization* (Nevada City, California, 1991), 149.
14. *Grundtvig Archive*, 448.25.p.
15. *Ibid.*, 448.25.q.
16. John Mason Neale, *op. cit.*, 191.
17. *Ibid.*
18. *Ibid.*, 191-92.
19. Jakob Knudsen, *Idé og Erindring* (Copenhagen, 1949), 187-88.
20. Jakob Knudsen, *Livsfilosofi: Spredte Betragtninger* (Copenhagen, 1948), 172.
21. *Ibid.*, 178.

A.M. Allchin: N.F.S. Grundtvig (Darton, Longman and Todd 1997) — Erratum
to a regrettable error, the endnotes for the Prologue have deen duplicated, while the
notes for ch. 1 have been omitted. Below you will find the correct endnotes for chapter 1.

Chapter 1: Childhood to Ordination

Værker i Udvalg, vol. VII, 470.

Ibid., 216.

Ibid., 143-53.

Grundtvigs Erindringer og Erindringer om Grundtvig, 18-9.

This account of the land reforms of the eighteenth century owes much to the
discussion of the subject in Steven M. Borish, *The Land of the Living: The Danish
folk high schools and Denmark's non-violent path to modernization* (Nevada City,
California, 1991), 113-47.

Ibid., 145-46.

F. Rønning, *Den Grundtvigske Slægt: Bidrag til dens Historie* (Copenhagen, 1904),
the two chapters on the Grundtvig brothers in West Africa come at the end of
the book, 112-28 and 129-43 respectively.

N.F.S. Grundtvig, *Poetiske Skrifter,* ed. Svend Grundtvig (Copenhagen, 1880),
vol. I, 341.

The episode is described at length in F. Rønning, *N.F.S. Grundtvig: Et Bidrag
til Skildring af Dansk Åndsliv i det 19. Århundrede,* vol. II. 1. (Copenhagen, 1908),
166-72.

Ibid., 197-98.

Twenty-fifth Sunday after Trinity 1823, *Grundtvigs Prædikener,* vol. 1, 437.

N.F.S. Grundtvig, *Poetiske Skrifter,* vol. I, 326. As often happens Grundtvig's
reference to the liturgy is very precise. At the end of the ordination prayer,
said by the bishop, during which he and the assistant clergy lay on hands, the
bishop first says 'Amen' alone, and adds 'Say all from your heart Amen'. The
clergy respond 'Amen' and the bishop concludes the whole by saying 'Amen
in Jesus' name, Amen'. The same formula is still in use today at ordinations.
This solemn, triple Amen is a formula which Grundtvig himself sometimes
uses at the end of a sermon. (see *Danmarks og Norgis Kirke-Ritual: 1685-1985*
(Haderslev, 1985). A new edition of the original work, published by Udvalget
for Konvent for Kirke og Theologi, with ample notes by Urban Schrøder).

Ibid., 324.

Ibid., 331.

Chapter 5: Last Impressions

1. *Grundtvigs Erindringer og Erindringer om Grundtvig*, 236. (Otto Arvesen's account).
2. *Ibid.*, 237.
3. *Ibid.*, 231. (Ernst Trier's account).
4. *Ibid.*, 162-63. (Frederik Barfod's account).
5. *Ibid.*, 166.
6. I am grateful to Dr. Kim Arne Pedersen for having access to these letters which are deposited at the Centre for Grundtvig Studies in Århus by Pastor Emeritus Tage Brummer.
7. The text of Grundtvig's daily prayer has survived in different versions. This translation is made from that of Louise Skrike. See her memoirs published in *Vrå Højskoles Årsskrift 1931-32*, 'Et Tilbageblik'.
8. *Grundtvigs Erindringer og Erindringer om Grundtvig*, 243-44. (H.P.B. Barfod's account). Grundtvig's fears of a German invasion reflect confused memories of the Danish defeat in 1864.
9. *Ibid.*, 245.
10. Frederik Helveg, *Indberetning til Kultusministeriet ang. Grundtvigs Gudstjeneste Palmesøndag 1867*. Royal Library, Copenhagen, 43-168-68. I am indebted to my friend Søren Jensen for this document, and for much assistance about the life of Helveg. See also his article on Helveg in *Kirken af levende Stene: Den grundtvigske tradition i dansk kirkehistorieskrivning* (Copenhagen, 1994), 79-108.
11. Helveg, *op. cit.*
12. *Grundtvigs Erindringer og Erindringer om Grundtvig*, 239-40. (Fr. Hammerich's account).
13. *Ibid.*, 240.
14. Helveg, *op. cit.*
15. Edmund Gosse, *Two Visits to Denmark: 1872, 1874.* (London, 1911), 78.
16. *Ibid.*, 84.
17. *Ibid.*, 83.
18. *Ibid.*, 85-87. In regard to the accuracy of Gosse's memory, the comment of his biographer Ann Thwaite is instructive. 'Not only did his memory betray him. He very often changed things deliberately to make a better story'. Henry James said that he had 'a genius for inaccuracy'. Ann Thwaite, *Edmund Gosse: A Literary Landscape* (Oxford, 1985), 2-3.
19. *Grundtvigs Erindringer og Erindringer om Grundtvig*, 262-63. (Fr. Hammerich's account). The book by George Hickes referred to is *Linguarum Veterum Septentrionalium Thesaurus*, 1705.
20. *Ibid.*, 263. The translation of the lines from the poem is by Kevin Crossley-Holland in *The Anglo-Saxon World — An Anthology* (Oxford, 1984), 59.

Chapter 6: Discovering the Church

1. P.G. Lindhardt, *Grundtvig: An Introduction* (London, 1951), 37.
2. N.F.S. Grundtvig, 'Kirkens Gienmæle', ('The Church's Rejoinder') (Copenhagen, 1825), *Værker i Udvalg*, vol. II,319.
3. *Ibid.*, 321.

4. Alasdair MacIntyre, *Whose Justice? Which Rationality?* (London, 1988), 355.

5. Sigurd Aage Aarnes, 'Grundtvig the Historian', in *Tradition and Renewal*, 61 (Translation emended).

6. N.F.S. Grundtvig, 'Kirkens Gienmæle, ('The Church's Rejoinder'), *Værker i Udvalg*, vol. II, 335-37.

7. *Ibid.*, 337-38.

8. *Ibid.*, 338.

9. N.F.S. Grundtvig, 'Kirkelige Oplysninger især for Lutherske Christne', ('Churchly Instructions especially for Lutheran Christians') (Copenhagen, 1840-42), *Værker i Udvalg*, vol. III,365.

10. N.F.S. Grundtvig, 'Kirkens Gienmæle', ('The Church's Rejoinder'), *Værker i Udvalg*, vol. II,339-40.

11. *Grundtvig og Ingemann: Brevvexling 1821-1859*, ed. Svend Grundtvig (Copenhagen, 1882), 198.

Chapter 7: The historic Ministry

1. N.F.S. Grundtvig, *'Om den sande Christendom'* og *'Om Christendommens Sandhed'*, (*'On the true Christianity'* and *'On the Truth of Christianity'*) (2nd ed., Copenhagen, 1865), 254.

2. N.F.S. Grundtvig, 'Skal den Lutherske Reformation virkelig fortsættes?', ('Shall the Lutheran Reformation really be advanced?') (1830), *Værker i Udvalg*, vol. III, 291.

3. *Ibid.*, 291-92.

4. *Ibid.*, 292.

5. This sentence refers to the Danish custom of hanging a wreath over a newly built building once the roof framework is completed.

6. *Ibid.*

7. A. Gratieux, *A.S. Khomiakov* (Paris, 1939), vol. 2,134-35.

8. N.F.S. Grundtvig, 'Den christelige Børnelærdom', ('Elementary Christian Doctrine') (1868), *Værker i Udvalg*, vol. VI, 74-75.

9. *Grundtvig-Archive*, 448.18.b. For a fuller account of Palmer's heated, but not altogether unfriendly exchange with Grundtvig, see *Heritage and Prophecy*, 30-31.

10. *Grundtvig-Archive*, 446.6.a.

11. *Ibid.*, 446.6.b.

12. *Nordisk Tidskrift For Christelig Theologi*, ed. P.Chr. Kierkegaard, vol. 4 (Copenhagen, 1842), 119-47.

13. *Ibid.*, 144-45.

14. *Ibid.* For a fuller account of Grundtvig's visit to Oxford in 1843 and a discussion of his remarkably erenic reaction to Newman's conversion at the end of 1845, see A.M. Allchin and A. Pontoppidan Thyssen, 'Grundtvig's Relationship to England', *Heritage and Prophecy*, 19-32. There are many places in which Grundtvig's thoughts at this time may be seen as foreshadowing elements in the current Anglican-Lutheran dialogue, both in Europe and in North America.

Chapter 8: Trinity in Unity

1. Hal Koch, *Grundtvig*, (Copenhagen, 1940), 200-1.
2. Alasdair Heron (ed.), *The Forgotten Trinity: A Selection Of Papers Presented To The BCC Study Commission On Trinitarian Doctrine Today* (London, 1991), xi.
3. Nicholas Lossky, *Lancelot Andrewes The Preacher* (Oxford, 1991), e.g. 334-36. 'Taking everything together, one can say that if Lancelot Andrewes's theology is at once Christological and Pneumatological, it is above all Trinitarian. And just like his Christology and his Pneumatology, the Trinitarian theology of Lancelot Andrewes is essentially orientated towards the salvation of man', 335.
4. Melvin Dieter in *John Wesley: Contemporary Perspectives*, ed. John Stacey (London, 1988), 171. 'A Christ-centred trinitarian pneumatology became the heart-beat of Wesley's understanding of a believer's relationship with God'.
5. Morten Mortensen, 'Helligånden, Guds røst på jord', in *For Sammenhængens Skyld*, ed. Christian Thodberg (Århus, 1977), 44-45.
6. Regin Prenter, 'Grundtvig's treenighedslære', in *N.F.S. Grundtvig: Theolog og Kirkelærer*, ed. Udvalget for Konvent for Kirke og Theologi (Borum, 1983), 62.
7. Erik Krebs Jensen, 'Hjertets gudbilledlighed', in *For Sammenhængens Skyld*, 82.
8. N.F.S. Grundtvig, 'Den christelige Børnelærdom', ('Elementary Christian Doctrine') (1868), *Værker i Udvalg*, vol. VI,115-16.
9. *Ibid.*, 125.
10. Regin Prenter, *op. cit.*, 63-64.
11. N.F.S. Grundtvig, 'Den christelige Børnelærdom', ('Elementary Christian Doctrine) (1868), *Værker i Udvalg*, vol. VI,152-53.
12. It will be important in the future to look further into Grundtvig's teaching about our participation in the divine life and nature, particularly in the light of the current rediscovery of the importance of the doctrine of deification in Martin Luther himself, a development which owes much to the quality of the dialogue between the Lutheran and the Orthodox Churches. In this connection the writings of two Finnish Lutheran theologians, Tuomo Mannemaa and Simo Peura are of particular importance.
13. Prenter, *op. cit.*, 71.
14. *Ibid.*, 71-72.
15. *Ibid.*, 72.
16. *Ibid.*, 72.
17. Jakob Balling, *Kristendommen*, 44.
18. *Ibid.*, 107.

Chapter 9: The Earth made in God's Image

1. N.F.S. Grundtvig, 'Nordens Mythologi' (1832), in *Udvalgte Skrifter*, vol. V, 408.
2. For this subject, especially in its Old Testament development see Robert Murray, *The Cosmic Covenant: Biblical Themes of Justice, Peace and the Integrity of Creation* (London, 1992).
3. Fourth Sunday after Trinity 1866, *Grundtvigs Sidste Prædikener*, vol. 1,588-89.
4. Fourth Sunday after Trinity 1838, *Grundtvigs Prædikener*, vol. 11,254.
5. *Ibid.*, 255.
6. *Ibid.*, 255-56.

7. *Ibid.*, 256-57.
8. See for instance *The Right to Hope: Global Problems, Global Visions. Creative Responses To Our World In Need.* (Earthscan Publications, London, 1995). This work contains a collection of the work of artists and writers from many different cultures and backgrounds which seeks to show ways in which the human heart and imagination may be openend to the plight of our world and to the inner resources latent within people which can promote healing and new life. In a characteristic opening contribution to the volume, Archbishop Desmond Tutu writes, 'Africans have a thing called *umbuntu*; it is about the essence of being human, ... it embraces hospitality, caring about others ... We believe that a person is a person through other persons; that my humanity is inextricably caught up, bound up, in yours ... We are made for interdependence. The law of our being is the law of complementarity' (p. 1). It is interesting to note that *Danida* (The Danish International Development Agency) is a primary supporter of this book.
9. Septuagesima Sunday 1834, *Grundtvigs Prædikener*, vol. 7,103.
10. *Ibid.*, 104. In particular, Grundtvig refers here to the theology of Irenaeus.
11. Charles Gore (ed.), *Lux Mundi* (Oxford, 1889), 429. It is interesting that in this essay Paget quotes Martensen's *Dogmatics*.
12. Septuagesima Sunday 1834, *Grundtvigs Prædikener*, vol. 7,104-5.
13. *Grundtvigs Sang-Værk*, vol. 1, no. 145,325-26.
14. Annunciation 1832, *Grundtvigs Prædikener*, vol. 5,121-22.
15. Nineteenth Sunday after Trinity 1862, *Grundtvigs Sidste Prædikener*, vol. 1, 207-8.
16. *Ibid.*, 208. I am much indebted to Harry Arronson's fine work *Mänskligt och kristet: En studie i grundtvigs teologi* (Stockholm, 1960) here and in other places.
17. Fifth Sunday after Trinity 1841, *Grundtvigs Vartovs-Prædikener*, 61.
18. *Ibid.*, 61-62.
19. Annunciation 1865, *Grundtvigs Sidste Prædikener*, vol. 1,431.
20. Annunciation 1868, *Grundtvigs Sidste Prædikener*, vol. 2,85-86.
21. Edwin Muir, *Collected Poems* (London, 1960), 104.
22. Lucas Van Rompay, 'Memories of paradise, the Greek 'Life of Adam and Eve' and early Syriac tradition', in *Aram: A Festschrift for Sebastian P. Brock* (Oxford, 1993), 560- 61.
23. *Ibid.*, 562.
24. William Wordsworth, *Selected Poems*, ed. D. Walford Davies (London, 1994), 115, from 'Lines written a few miles above Tintern Abbey'.

Chapter 10: A cheerful, simple, active Life om Earth

1. Hans Henningsen, 'The Danish Folk High School', *Heritage and Prophecy*, 285.
2. K.E. Bugge, 'Grundtvig's Educational Thinking', *Ibid.*, 277.
3. Daniel W. Hardy, *God's Ways With The World: Thinking and Practicing Christian Faith* (Edinburgh, 1996), 202.
4. For Nigeria see the article 'Education for Life', by Kachi E. Ozumba, *Grundtvig-Studier* (1993), 105-118, and for the Philippines, 'Grundtvigs skoletanker i Filippinerne', by Lilian Zøllner, *Grundtvig-Studier* (1994), 199-228.
5. See Holger Bernt Hansen, 'Grundtvig, Europe and the Third World: Dilemmas

and Challenges', *Grundtvig-Studier* (1993), 119-40, and Holger Bernt Hansen, 'Grundtvig and the Third World: The Transfer of Grundtvig's Ideas to other Peoples and Cultures', *Heritage and Prophecy*, 299-322.

6. The case of Liang Shuming is particularly interesting. Here is a thinker and social activist of some stature in pre-Communist China, whose life and ideas have been attracting new attention both in the West and in China in the last few years. Liang understood Grundtvig in terms of his own key concept *lixing*, a term of Confucian origin which 'referred both to reason (which is the dictionary meaning of the word) and to the ability to enter into interpersonal relationships on the basis of high ethical principles'. Such a term suggests the interaction and fusion of thought and action, of love and knowledge which we have seen was so important for Grundtvig. See the chapter by Stig Thøgersen, 'Liang Shuming and the Danish Model', in *Cultural Encounters: China, Japan and the West*, eds. S. Clausen et al. (Århus, 1995), 277.

7. *Rodfæstet Universalisme: N.F.S. Grundtvigs poesi, menneskesyn, kultursyn, skolesyn*, ed. Lilian Zøllner (Vejle, 1996), 178.

8. Hans Henningsen, 'The Danish Folk High School', *Heritage and Prophecy*, 285.

9. *Ibid.*, 285.

10. Daniel W. Hardy, *op. cit.*, 173-74.

11. *Værker i Udvalg*, vol. VIII,146.

12. Steven M. Borish, *The Land of The Living: The Danish folk high schools and Denmark's non-violent path to modernization* (California, 1991), 187.

13. Roar Skovmand, 'Grundtvig and the Folk High School Movement', *Tradition and Renewal*, 327-28.

14. Steven M. Borish, *op. cit.*, 189.

15. *Ibid.*, 191-92.

16. *Dansk Udsyn*, 1949, *Hæfte 1*, 1-10. For a very interesting account of the life of Ingeborg Appel written by her daughter, see Margrethe Christensen, *Ingeborg Appel og Askov* (Copenhagen, 1967).

Chapter 11: Eternity in Time

1. In fact the number of holy days was not at first so drastically reduced as it is now. In the service book of 1685, among the feasts of Christ there are the Circumcision, January 1st, the Epiphany, January 6th, the Presentation of Christ in the temple, February 2nd; among Marian feasts, the Visitation, July 2nd, is there as well as the Annunciation, March 25th; of the saints' days, St. John the Baptist, June 24th and All Saints' Day, November 1st, remain, as also Michaelmas Day, September 29th. These feasts were either abolished or transferred to the nearest Sunday by royal decree in 1770. It is important to remember that at this time the three great feasts were each celebrated for three whole days. *Danmarks og Norgis Kirke-Ritual: 1685-1985*, ed. Udvalget for Konvent for Kirke og Theologi (Haderslev, 1985), 142-43.

2. Christian Thodberg, 'At tale en sang — Grundtvigs poetiske raptus på prædikestolen', in Poul Lindegård Hjorth, Erik Dal og David Favrholdt (eds.), *Fra Egtvedpigen til Folketinget: Et festskrift til Hendes Majestæt Dronning Margrethe II ved regeringsjubilæet 1997* (Copenhagen, 1997), 245-71.

3. In his introduction to Thorvald Hansen's valuable study of the Danish com-

munities in America *Church Divided: Lutheranism Among the Danish Immigrants* (Des Moines, 1992), vii, Martin E. Marty writes, 'Grundtvig, sorting his and his followers' way through the tumults of early modernity in Denmark did what so many of his kind did elsewhere. They looked for the identity of the church in its natural expressions of landscape, nation, heritage, peoplehood — and then drew, of course on the Bible and of course, on Lutheran teachings — to set forth their distinctives'. Precisely the reverse is the case.

4. *Den Danske Salmebog*, no. 204.
5. Genesis 8:22.
6. Cf. *Danish Painting, The Golden Age: Catalogue for the Loan Exhibition at the National Gallery 1984*, for an introduction to this period. The case of P.C. Skovgaard (1817-75) a friend and disciple of Grundtvig is particularly interesting. As a colleague remarked of him 'Plant life is what Skovgaard prefers to paint and what he has highly identified himself with, from the greatest of the trees down to the finest little grassy plant. He *belongs* in woodland nature.' The editor of the catalogue remarks that his 'immersion in detail is reminiscent of several of John Constable's detailed sketches from the early 1820s'. But he seems to have had no direct knowledge of Constable's work. See also Bente Scavenius & Poul Borum (eds.), *Malernes og Forfatternes Danmark* (Copenhagen, 1986).
7. Giuseppe Gatt, *Constable* (London, 1968), 12. For a preliminary theological assessment of Constable's work see Reginald Askew's article 'The Church in Constable's Landscape', *Theology* (vol. xcix, no. 787, Jan. 1995, 6-15). In his lectures on 'The History of Landscape Painting' (1836), Constable says, 'We are no doubt placed in a paradise here if we choose to make it such. All of us must have felt ourselves in the same place and situation as that of our first parents.' (10) There are parallels between the developments of English and Danish romanticism, in painting as well as in poetry, which deserve further attention.
8. William Blake, *Poems and Prophecies*, ed. Max Plowman (London, 1927), 335, from 'Auguries of Innocence'.
9. Third Sunday after Easter 1838, *Grundtvigs Prædikener*, vol. 11,195.
10. *Ibid.*, 196-97. The two lines of verse come from an old night-watchman's song.
11. *Ibid.*, 197.
12. Twenty-fifth Sunday after Trinity 1823, *Grundtvigs Prædikener*, vol. 1,437.
13. Third Sunday after Easter 1838, *Grundtvigs Prædikener*, vol. 11,197.
14. *Ibid.*, 198.
15. Poul Borum, *Digteren Grundtvig* (Copenhagen, 1983), 123.
16. For the feeling for celebration in contemporary Danish society see Chapter 8, 'Hygge and the Art of Celebration' in Steven M. Borish's book *The Land of the Living: The Danish folk high schools and Denmark's non-violent path to modernization* (Nevada City, California 1991), 264-80.
17. *Værker i Udvalg*, vol. VIII,254-55. The poem is in the current edition of the folk high-school song book. I have known it sung more than once on social occasions.
18. See A.M. Allchin, *Praise Above All: Discovering the Welsh Tradition* (Cardiff, 1991), 94-102.

19. See Andreas Haarder's admirable article 'Grundtvig and the Old Norse cultural heritage' in *Tradition and Renewal*, 84-85.

Chapter 12: Advent

1. The three sermons are found in *Grundtvigs Prædikener*, vol. 10,77-81, 82-86 & 86-91.
2. First Sunday in Advent 1836, *Ibid.*, 77.
3. *Ibid.*, 77-78.
4. *Ibid.*, 78.
5. *Ibid.*, 79.
6. *Anglican-Orthodox Dialogue: The Moscow Agreed Statement* (London, 1977), 91.
7. First Sunday in Advent 1836, *Grundtvigs Prædikener*, vol. 10,79-80.
8. *Ibid.*, 80.
9. *Ibid.*, 81.
10. Second Sunday in Advent 1836, *Ibid.*, 82.
11. *Ibid.*, 83.
12. *Ibid.*, 83-84.
13. *Ibid.*, 84-85.
14. *Ibid.*, 85.
15. Third Sunday in Advent 1836, *Ibid.*, 88-89.
16. *Ibid.*, 91.
17. *Den Danske Salmebog*, no. 66.
18. Psalm 118:19-29.
19. These words literally translated *your bath and your board* are frequently used by Grundtvig to refer to the two Gospel sacraments.
20. *Den Danske Salmebog*, no. 368.

Chapter 13: Christmas

1. Christmas Day 1821, *Grundtvigs Præstø Prædikener*, vol. 2,114.
2. *Ibid.*, 115.
3. Christmas Day 1822, *Grundtvigs Prædikener*, vol. 1,82.
4. John Keble, *On the Mysticism Attributed to the Early Fathers of the Church.* Tract 89 (Oxford 1840), 177.
5. Percy Dearmer, Ralph Vaughn Williams & Martin Shaw (eds.), *Oxford Book of Carols* (Oxford 1928), no. 24.
6. Christmas Day 1822, *Grundtvigs Prædikener*, vol. 1,82-83.
7. *Den Danske Salmebog*, no. 85.
8. *Den Danske Salmebog*, no. 81. The writings of Hans Christian Andersen have, one supposes, had much to do with the continuing vitality of such popular lore in the imagination of Danish people, certainly in the earlier part of this century, to some extent still today.
9. Christmas Day 1832, *Grundtvigs Prædikener*, vol. 6, 72-73.
10. Saunders Lewis, *Selected Poems*, trans. Joseph P.Clancy (Cardiff, 1993), 40.
11. Christmas Day 1832, *Grundtvigs Prædikener*, vol. 6,73.
12. *Ibid.*, 74.
13. Christmas Day 1845, *Grundtvigs Vartovs-Prædikener*, 133 & 134. The four lines of verse come from one of the best known of Thomas Kingo's Easter hymns.

Chapter 14: Annunciation

1. Annunciation 1836, *Grundtvigs Prædikener*, vol. 9,156.
2. *Ibid.*, 156.
3. Jean Vanier, *Community and Growth* (London, 1979).
4. Annunciation 1836, *Grundtvigs Prædikener*, vol. 9, 156-57.
5. *Grundtvigs Sang-Værk*, vol. 5, no. 193,337-40.
6. Second Sunday in Lent 1837, *Grundtvigs Prædikener*, vol. 10,137-38.
7. *Ibid.*, 137.
8. *Ibid.*, 140.
9. An interest in the role of Mary in Christian life is to be found in nineteenth century Germany, in the distinguished Bavarian Lutheran churchman, Wilhelm Löhe.
10. Annunciation 1837, *Grundtvigs Prædikener*, vol. 10,151-52.
11. *Ibid.*, 152.
12. *Ibid.*, 152-53.
13. *Ibid.*, 153-54.
14. *Ibid.*, 154.
15. *Ibid.*, 155.
16. *Den Danske Salmebog*, no. 63.
17. Annunciation 1837, *Grundtvigs Prædikener*, vol. 10,155-56.
18. Lancelot Andrewes, *Ninety-Six Sermons* (Library of Anglo-Catholic theology, Oxford 1841), vol. 1,151. Quoted in A.M. Allchin *The Joy of All Creation: An Anglican Meditation on the Place of Mary* (London, 1993), 47.
19. Isaiah 66:7-14.
20. *Grundtvigs Sang-Værk*, vol. 1, no. 204, 418-21.
21. It is interesting in this connection to note the remarks of Jaroslav Pelikan in his recently published book, *Mary through the Centuries: Her Place in the History of Culture* (London, 1996), about the crucial role of the typological and allegorical approach to Scripture in the development of Marian thought and devotion. Having spoken of the positive part played by such methods of interpretation he continues, 'Conversely, the rejection of both the Marian celebration and the allegory came together, first in the Reformation and then in the Enlightenment and its aftermath. Looking back at both developments, in the Middle Ages and in the Reformation and Enlightenment, it is difficult to avoid the tough questions of loss and gain ... Vastly different though they seemed to be in their approach to the Bible, therefore, a fundamentalist literalism and a modernist historicism both yielded a two-dimensional perspective in the reading of the Bible. At the same time they also led to an impoverishment in the attitude toward Mary' (35-6). It is this impoverishment of which Grundtvig was aware and which he combatted so strongly. It is sad that Grundtvig finds no place in Pelikan's impressive and widely ranging study.
22. It is interesting that in the rather full discussions of the place of Mary and the saints in Christian doctrine which have taken place in the official Lutheran-Catholic conversations in the USA, the theology of Grundtvig seems never to have been mentioned. *The One Mediator, the Saints and Mary: Lutherans and*

Catholics in Dialogue, VIII. eds. H.G. Anderson, J.F. Stafford and J.A. Burgess (Minneapolis, 1992).

23. Charles Moeller, *Mentalité Moderne et Evangélisation, Dieu Jésus-Christ, Marie, L'Eglise* (Brussels, 1962), 272. This book is the second, revised and enlarged edition of a book originally published in 1954. I have not been able to check whether the passage quoted formed part of the original edition or not. In either case, the work as a whole represents an impressive and balanced attempt at a re-statement of traditional Roman Catholic positions. It is a work prophetic of the spirit of Vatican II.

Chapter 15: Easter

1. 'Easter Dawn', *Grundtvigs Christelige Prædikener eller Søndags-Bog*, vol. 3,294-315. In adapting his sermons for publication Grundtvig seems to have adopted varying procedures. Some sermons become almost theological essays, others, as in this case, show the poetic quality of his preaching in a highly developed form.
2. *Ibid.*, 295-96.
3. *Ibid.*, 296-99.
4. *Ibid.*, 299-300.
5. *Ibid.*, 304-5.
6. *Ibid.*, 305-7.
7. *Ibid.*, 307-9.
8. Ibid, 313-15.
9. For a helpful discussion of Grundtvig's prejudices against the Greek Church, and particularly against the Nicene Creed which he thought had usurped the place of the Apostles' Creed in the East, see Flemming Fleinert-Jensen, 'N.F.S. Grundtvig et la tradition byzantine', in *Irenikon*, tome lx, no. 2, 1987, 163-76.
10. Easter Sunday 1837, *Grundtvigs Prædikener*, vol. 10,171-76.
11. *Ibid.*, 172.
12. Grundtvigs *Sang-Værk*, vol. 1, no. 220, 444-45.
13. *Den Danske Salmebog*, no. 212.
14. Grundtvigs *Sang-Værk*, vol. 1, no. 210, 332-33.
15. Edvard Lehmann, *Grundtvig* (Copenhagen, 1929), 199-200.
16. Grundtvigs *Sang-Værk*, vol. 1, no. 338, 604.
17. Easter Monday 1837, *Grundtvigs Prædikener*, vol. 10,176-80.
18. *Ibid.*, 177.
19. *Ibid.*, 178.
20. Archimandrite Sophrony (Sakharov), *Saint Silouan The Athonite* (Essex, 1991), 448-56.
21. Grundtvigs *Sang-Værk*, vol. 1, no. 221, 445.
22. Grundtvigs *Sang-Værk*, vol. 1, no. 223, 446-47.
23. *Den Danske Salmebog*, no. 372.

Chapter 16: Whitsun

1. See Derec Llwyd Morgan, *The Great Awakening in Wales* (London, 1988), 70.
2. Jakob Knudsen, *Idé og Erindring* (Copenhagen, 1949), 185.

3. *Ibid.*, 185-86.

4. *Ibid.*, 24.

5. Whitsun Day 1837, *Grundtvigs Prædikener*, vol. 10, 224-26.

6. N.F.S. Grundtvig, *Kort Begreb af Verdens Krønike*, vol. 1, Copenhagen 1814, xx-xxi. (1814 World Chronicle). I am grateful to my friend Dr. Johannes B. Glenthøj for this reference.

7. Whitsun Day 1837, *Grundtvigs Prædikener*, vol. 10,225.

8. This perception has been important in the work of Dr. Kachi Ozumba in Nigeria, as Holger Bernt Hansen points out. Nigerians have known their own kind of Latin school, a school for death, which has acted as an alienating force and raised up an educational elite out of touch with the common people. In this context Grundtvig's idea of education for life can speak powerfully, and takes a new form 'aiming at awakening the popular dynamics and the people's own potentials, by introducing what is called the awareness curriculum, based on the living word and drawing on material from history, folklore and traditional arts'. *Grundtvig-Studier* (1993), 130-31.

9. John D. Davies, *The Faith Abroad* (Oxford, 1983), 22-23.

10. *Rodfæstet Universalisme: N.F.S. Grundtvigs poesi, menneskesyn, kultursyn, skolesyn*, ed. Lilian Zøllner (Vejle, 1996), 173.

11. Whitsun Monday 1838, *Grundtvigs Prædikener*, vol. 11,225.

12. *Ibid.*, 226-27.

13. Vladimir Lossky, *The Mystical Theology of the Eastern Church* (London, 1957), 85.

14. Whitsun Monday 1838, *Grundtvigs Prædikener*, vol. 11,227.

15. *Ibid.*, 227-28.

16. Whitsun Monday 1832, *Grundtvigs Prædikener*, vol. 5,226-27.

17. *Ibid.*, 227-28.

18. Martin Schwartz Lausten, *Danmarks Kirkehistorie* (Copenhagen, 1987), 22.

19. See *Morsø Frimenighed, 1871-1971*, ed. Per Fisker, 35-36. See also *Kirken af levende Stene* (Copenhagen, 1994), 135. An interesting parallel to this picture is to be found in a painting by the Swedish artist Johan Blackstadius (1816-98) in Nordiska Museet, Stockholm, 'Sankt Sigfrid døber folket i Småland' (1866). This is a far more elaborate composition full of allegorical detail, but at the centre there is a young mother with a child being baptised; on this occasion, however, the central figure is a bishop resplendent in vestments and mitre, rather than two monks robed with suitable monastic (and Lutheran?) simplicity. *The Waking of Angantyr: The Scandinavian past in European Culture*, ed. Else Roesdahl and Preben Meulengracht Sørensen (Acta Jutlandica LXXI:1, Aarhus, 1996), 106.

20. *Den Danske Salmebog*, no. 243.

21. *Den Danske Salmebog*, no. 247.

22. On the use of imagery in Brorson's hymns see the essays in *Brorson: en bog i 300 året for salmedigterens fødsel*, ed. Jan Ulrik Dyrkjøb (Copenhagen, 1994).

23. *Grundtvigs Præstø Prædikener*, vol. 2,317. A communion service held on Friday August 30th 1822.

24. *Ibid.*, 318.

Chapter 17: The Sign of the Cross

1. Good Friday 1846, *Grundtvigs Kors-Prædikener*, ed. N. Clausen-Bagge, 51-52.
2. Good Friday 1855, *Ibid.*, 94.
3. *Ibid.*, 95-96.
4. T.S. Eliot, *The Complete Poems and Plays* (London, 1969), 260-62.
5. St. Stephen's Day, *Grundtvigs Christelige Prædikener eller Søndags-Bog*, vol. 2, 65-81.
6. See eg. Christian Thodberg's article, 'The Importance of Baptism in Grundtvig's view of Christianity' in *Heritage and Prophecy*, 133-52.
7. St. Stephen's Day, *Grundtvigs Christelige Prædikener eller Søndags-Bog*, vol. 2, 65-67. These verses both by Kingo come from Den Danske Salmebog, no. 104 and 41, respectively.
8. *Ibid.*, 67-68.
9. *Ibid.*, 69-70.
10. *Ibid.*, 73-75.
11. *Ibid.*, 75-76.
12. *Grundtvigs Sang-Værk*, vol. 5, no. 149 A & B, 253-55. The hymn exists in two slightly varying versions, the first of five verses, the second of six. I have translated the second version, but have taken the liberty of transferring verse 4 from the first version to the second.

Chapter 18: The Ministry of Angels

1. Annunciation 1842, *Grundtvigs Vartovs-Prædikener*, 72-76. The Danish church, as we have seen, maintained the feast of St. Michael and All Angels until towards the end of the eighteenth century. In the Service Book of 1685 the preacher was instructed to preach for that day 'about the angels, and the great benefit and protection which we have from them, for which reason we should duly praise and thank God', *Danmarks og Norgis Kirke-Ritual: 1685-1985*, ed. Udvalget for Konvent for Kirke og Theologi (Haderslev, 1985), 18.
2. John Keble, as quoted in A.M. Allchin, *The Joy of All Creation: An Anglican Meditation on the Place of Mary* (London, 1993), 154-55.
3. For a brief discussion of a Christocentric way of understanding the mission of the angels, see Regin Prenter, *Skabelse og Genløsning* (2nd ed., Copenhagen, 1955), 250-55.
4. Annunciation 1842, *Grundtvigs Vartovs-Prædikener*, 72-74.
5. *Ibid.*, 74-75.
6. *Ibid.*, 75-76.
7. George Steiner, *Real Presences* (London, 1989), 19. The general thesis of the book, that supremely great works of art have always been and must necessarily be sustained by a sense of transcendent presence which impinges on the world of space and time, is interestingly relevant to Grundtvig's theology in which faith, praise and worship stand so close to one another.

Epilogue

1. Simon Barrington Ward, Bishop of Coventry, writing in the London *Guardian*, 1/1/97.
2. Martin A. Hansen, quoted in *Heritage and Prophecy*, 14.
3. *Den Danske Salmebog*, no. 396.
4. *Den Danske Salmebog*, no. 142.
5. *Den Danske Salmebog*, no. 335.

Select Bibliography

This bibliography lists only a selection of the more important works in English. For a comprehensive listing of works on Grundtvig, the reader is referred to the annual bibliographies in *Grundtvig-Studier.*

a. Anthologies

N.F.S. Grundtvig: Selected Writings. Edited and with an introduction by Johannes Knudsen, Philadelphia 1976.

A Grundtvig Anthology: Selections from the Writings of N.F.S. Grundtvig (1783-1872). Translated by Edward Broadbridge and Niels Lyhne Jensen. Edited, annotated and introduced by Niels Lyhne Jensen, William Michelsen, Gustav Albeck, Hellmut Toftdahl, Chr. Thodberg. General editor: Niels Lyhne Jensen, Cambridge 1984.

b. Studies

Noëlle Davies, *Education for life: A Danish pioneer*, London 1931.

Hal Koch, *Grundtvig.* Translated from the Danish with introduction and notes by Llewellyn Jones, Yellow Springs, Ohio, 1952.

P.G. Lindhardt, *Grundtvig: An Introduction*, London 1951.

Ernest D. Nielsen, *N.F.S. Grundtvig: An American Study*, Rock Island, Illinois, 1955.

Donald Juel Sneen, 'The Hermeneutics of N.F.S. Grundtvig'. Unpublished dissertation. Princeton, New Jersey, 1968.

Kaj Thaning, *N.F.S. Grundtvig.* Translated by David Hohnen, Copenhagen 1972.

c. Collective Works

N.F.S. Grundtvig, Tradition and Renewal: Grundtvig's Vision of Man and People, Education and the Church, in Relation to World Issues Today. Translated by Edward Broadbridge. Edited by Christian Thodberg and Anders Pontoppidan Thyssen, Copenhagen 1983.

Heritage and Prophecy: Grundtvig and the English-speaking World. Edited by A.M. Allchin, D. Jasper, J.H. Schjørring, and K. Stevenson, Aarhus 1993.

Index